Free DVD  **Free DVD**

Essential Test Tips Video from Trivium Test Prep

Dear Customer,

Thank you for purchasing from Trivium Test Prep! Whether you're looking to join the military, get into college, or advance your career, we're honored to be a part of your journey.

To show our appreciation (and to help you relieve a little of that test-prep stress), we're offering a **FREE *TExES Core Subjects Essential Test Tips* Video** by Trivium Test Prep. Our video includes 35 test preparation strategies that will help keep you calm and collected before and during your big exam. All we ask is that you email us your feedback and describe your experience with our product. Amazing, awful, or just so-so: we want to hear what you have to say!

To receive your **FREE *TExES Core Subjects Essential Test Tips* Video**, please email us at 5star@ triviumtestprep.com. Include "Free 5 Star" in the subject line and the following information in your email:

1. The title of the product you purchased.
2. Your rating from 1 – 5 (with 5 being the best).
3. Your feedback about the product, including how our materials helped you meet your goals and ways in which we can improve our products.
4. Your full name and shipping address so we can send your **FREE *TExES Core Subjects Essential Test Tips* Video**.

If you have any questions or concerns please feel free to contact us directly at 5star@triviumtestprep.com.

Thank you, and good luck with your studies!

TExES Core Subjects EC-6 391 Study Guide

2 Practice Tests and Exam Prep

J.G. Cox

ISBN-13: 9781637985069

Table of Contents

Online Resources

rivium includes online resources with the purchase of this study guide to help you fully prepare for the exam.

Practice Test

In addition to the practice test included in this book, we also offer an online exam. Since many exams today are computer based, practicing your test-taking skills on the computer is a great way to prepare.

Review Questions

Need more practice? Our review questions use a variety of formats to help you memorize key terms and concepts.

Flash Cards

Trivium's flash cards allow you to review important terms easily on your computer or smartphone.

Cheat Sheets

Review the core skills you need to master the exam with easy-to-read Cheat Sheets.

From Stress to Success

Watch "From Stress to Success," a brief but insightful YouTube video that offers the tips, tricks, and secrets experts use to score higher on the exam.

Reviews

Leave a review, send us helpful feedback, or sign up for Trivium promotions—including free books!

Access these materials at: www.cirrustestprep.com/texes-core-subjects

Introduction

Congratulations on choosing to take the TExES Core Subjects exam! By purchasing this book, you've taken the first step toward becoming a teacher in Texas.

This guide will provide you with a detailed overview of the TExES Core Subjects exam, so you will know exactly what to expect on test day. We'll take you through all of the concepts covered on the exam and give you the opportunity to test your knowledge with Practice Questions. Even if it's been a while since you last took a major exam, don't worry; we'll make sure you're more than ready!

What is the TExES?

The Texas Examinations of Educator Standards: Core Subjects exam is a criterion-referenced test used to assess the subject-matter expertise of prospective EC – 6 teachers.

What's on the TExES Core Subjects exam?

The exam contains selected-response questions only. Most of the answer options will be multiple-choice, but some questions may have more than one answer or will require the examinee to use a technology feature. The exam is broken into five subject exams, as described in the table below.

TExES Core Subjects Exams
English Language Arts and Reading & Science of Teaching Reading
45 selected-response questions *12 Standards:* ▪ Oral Language ▪ Phonological and Phonemic Awareness ▪ Alphabetic Principle ▪ Literacy Development and Practice ▪ Word Analysis and Decoding ▪ Reading Fluency ▪ Reading Comprehension ▪ Development of Written Communication ▪ Writing Conventions ▪ Assessment and Instruction of Developing Literacy ▪ Research and Inquiry Skills ▪ Viewing and Representing
Mathematics
40 selected-response questions *9 Standards:*

- Number Concepts
- Patterns and Algebra
- Geometry and Measurement
- Probability and Statistics
- Mathematical Processes
- Mathematical Perspectives
- Mathematical Learning and Instruction
- Mathematical Assessment
- Professional Development

Social Studies

40 selected-response questions

10 Standards:

- a comprehensive knowledge of the social sciences and recognition of the value of the social sciences
- can effectively integrate the various social science disciplines
- can use knowledge and skills of social studies, as defined by the TEKS, to plan and implement effective curriculum, instruction, assessment and evaluation
- History
- Geography
- Economics
- Government
- Citizenship
- Culture
- Science, Technology and Society

Science

45 selected-response questions

11 Standards:

- manages classroom, field, and laboratory activities to ensure the safety of all students and the ethical care and treatment of organisms and specimens
- understands the correct use of tools, materials, equipment, and technologies
- understands the process of scientific inquiry and its role in science instruction
- has theoretical and practical knowledge about teaching science and how students learn science
- knows the varied and appropriate assessments and assessment practices to monitor science learning
- understands the history and nature of science
- understands how science affects the daily lives of students and how it interacts with and influences personal and societal decisions
- knows and understands the science content appropriate to teach the statewide curriculum in physical science
- knows and understands the science content appropriate to teach the statewide curriculum in life science
- knows and understands the science content appropriate to teach the statewide curriculum in Earth and Space science

- knows unifying concepts and processes that are common to all sciences

Fine Arts, Health, and Physical Education

40 selected-response questions

5 Art Standards:

- understands how ideas for creating art are developed and organized from the perception of self, others, and natural and human-made environments
- understands the skills and techniques needed for personal and creative expression through the creation of original works of art in a wide variety of media; can help students develop those skills and techniques
- understands and promotes students' appreciation of art histories and diverse cultures
- understands and conveys the skills necessary for analyzing, interpreting, and evaluating works of art; is able to help students make informed judgments about artworks
- understands how children develop cognitively and artistically; knows how to implement effective, age-appropriate art instruction and assessment

10 Music Standards

- a comprehensive visual and aural knowledge of musical perception and performance
- can sing and play a musical instrument
- a comprehensive knowledge of music notation
- can create and arrange music
- a comprehensive knowledge of music history and the relationship of music to history, society, and culture
- can apply comprehensive knowledge of music to evaluate musical compositions, performances, and experiences
- can plan and implement effective music instruction and provide students with learning experiences that enhance their musical knowledge, skills, and appreciation
- understands and applies appropriate management and discipline strategies for the music class
- understands student assessment and uses assessment results to design instruction and facilitate student progress
- understands professional responsibilities and interactions relevant to music instruction and the school music program

4 Health Standards:

- applies knowledge of the relationship between health and behavior and the factors that influence these
- can communicate concepts and purposes of health education
- can plan and implement effective school health instruction and integrate it with other content areas
- evaluates the effects of school health instruction

10 Physical Education Standards:

- demonstrates competency in a variety of movement skills; helps students develop these skills
- understands principles and benefits of a healthy, physically active lifestyle; motivates students to participate in activities that promote this lifestyle

TExES Core Subjects Exams

- uses knowledge of individual and group motivation and behavior to create and manage a safe, productive learning environment; promotes students' self-management, self-motivation, and social skills through participation in physical activities
- uses knowledge of how students learn and develop to provide opportunities that support students' physical, cognitive, social, and emotional development
- provides equitable and appropriate instruction for all students in a diverse society
- uses effective, developmentally appropriate instructional strategies and communication techniques
- understands and uses formal and informal assessment to promote students' physical, cognitive, social, and emotional development in physical education contexts
- evaluates the effects of personal actions on others and seeks opportunities to grow professionally
- collaborates with colleagues, parents/caregivers, and community agencies to support students' growth and well-being
- understands the legal issues and responsibilities of physical education teachers in relation to supervision, planning and instruction, matching participants, safety, first aid, and risk management

6 Theatre Standards

- plans and implements effective theatre instruction and assessment; provides students with learning experiences that enhance their knowledge, skills, and appreciation of theatre
- understands and applies skills for creating, utilizing, and/or performing dramatic material
- understands and applies skills for producing and directing theatrical productions
- understands and applies knowledge of design and technical theatre
- understands and applies knowledge of theatre from different cultures and historical periods
- understands and applies skills for responding to, analyzing, and evaluating theatre; understands the interrelationship between theatre and other disciplines.

How is the TExES Core Subjects exam scored?

The 210 selected-response questions are scored on a computer.

Raw scores are first calculated, and then scores are transformed to scaled scores from 100 – 300.An overall score of 240 is the passing score for each subject exam. Scores do not expire. Examinees who pass a subject exam do not need to take that subtest again if the exam must be retaken because all parts were not passed; however, examinees must wait 30 days and are limited to five attempts to take a certification exam. Scores are reported within 7 days of testing. They will be emailed to you if you chose this option when registering, or you can view them in your account.

How is the TExES Core Subjects exam administered?

The TExES Core Subjects exam is a computer-based exam available at testing centers in Texas and throughout the United States. The testing appointment is 5 hours in duration and includes 15 minutes of tutorials; 70 minutes for the English Language Arts and Reading exam, 70 minutes for the Mathematics exam, 50 minutes for the Social Studies exam, 55 minutes for the Science exam, and 35 minutes for the Fine Arts, Health, and Physical Education exams.

About Cirrus Test Prep

Cirrus Test Prep study guides are designed by current and former educators and are tailored to meet your needs as an incoming educator. Our guides offer all of the resources necessary to help you pass teacher certification tests across the nation.

Cirrus clouds are graceful, wispy clouds characterized by their high altitude. Just like cirrus clouds, Cirrus Test Prep's goal is to help educators "aim high" when it comes to obtaining their teacher certification and entering the classroom. We're pleased you've chosen Cirrus to be a part of your professional journey!

1 English Language Arts and Reading

Oral Language

Human Language

Human language varies among cultures throughout the world, but all languages share some similarities. All languages are learned by human babies at roughly the same time, regardless of location. All languages also have basic rules—**grammar**—that specify how words should be put together. Languages from anywhere in the world have a way for people to communicate when an action occurs (in time); however, the way this time is indicated—through verb conjugation, word endings, or separate words that indicate when an action occurs—varies widely. All languages also have a more formal form and a more casual or slang form as well as various dialects and accents. Dialects and accents may be particular to a certain geographic location or group in a society. In contrast to a **dialect** is what is known as an **idiolect**, which is a particular language form or structure used solely by one individual.

Further, all languages are rooted in the context of their use. **Pragmatics** is the study of language within its context or the understanding of the social rules of language use. Language can also be studied in terms of **phonology** (the organization of sounds), **morphology** (the study of words and their parts), **syntax** (how words combine to form groups like phrases, clauses, and sentences) and **semantics** (the study of what words mean or to what they refer).

Human language varies widely in terms of syntax. Some languages, such as English, tend to put the subject of the sentence before the verb. Other languages like Berber and Hebrew put the verb before the subject. This might be referred to as **subject-verb inversion**.

These nuances can be tricky; when speaking in English, the subject must agree with the verb in terms of singularity or plurality. For example, one would not say, "She eat pizza." Rather, one would say "She eats pizza." It is important to note that **subject-verb agreement** may vary based on **dialect** (variations of language based on user) and **register** (variation based on the use of the language). For example, in some dialects and registers, such as African American Vernacular English (AAVE), the plural verb is sometimes used with a singular subject (for example, "She eat pizza"). When instructing students in oral language conventions, it is important to respect dialects and registers and explain that such nuances are not "correct" or "incorrect" but rather more or less-tailored to a particular speaking situation.

Children who are learning two languages may engage in **code switching**, or alternating between two languages or dialects. It occurs most often when children begin a sentence in one language but complete it in another language. This is a somewhat remarkable thing, and it shows that these children are maintaining grammatical rules in both languages. Code switching is natural, normal, and expected, and it is no cause for concern. Rather than chiding students for code switching, teachers should use these opportunities to expand students' vocabulary and knowledge in both languages, depending of course on the teacher's proficiency in the children's native languages. Constantly correcting students for code switching undermines their overall development and does not validate their need to communicate.

Practice Question

1. A prekindergarten teacher reminds students to call her "Mrs. Arnette" instead of "teacher." This educator is helping students understand which concept?
   A. code switching
   B. phonology
   C. pragmatics
   D. semantics

Language Acquisition

Language acquisition is the process through which humans develop the ability to understand and create words and sentences to communicate. Many experts believe that children have an innate ability to acquire **oral language** from their environments. Even before babies can speak, they cry and coo in reaction to environmental stimuli or to communicate their needs. They recognize basic variants in the speech patterns of those around them, such as articulation; they can also identify contrasts when exposed to new languages. This awareness, cooing, and crying quickly turn into **babbling**—the first stage of language acquisition. This stage generally lasts from six months to around twelve months. In this stage, infants make a variety of sounds but may begin to focus on sounds for which they receive positive reinforcement. For example, babbles such as *baba* and *yaya* tend to garner praise and excitement from parents, so these may be repeated until the coveted *mama* or *dada* is produced.

Did You Know?

Ninety-five percent of all babbling by babies throughout the world is composed of only twelve consonants: *p, b, t, d, k, g, m, n, s, h, w, j*.

At around one year old, but varying from child to child, children start using first words, generally nouns. During this single-word stage, or **holophrastic stage**, these solitary words are generally used to express entire ideas. For example, "Toy!" may mean "Give me the toy." After a few months, this shifts to two-word utterances such as "Mommy go" or "David bad." The **two-word stage** may last through early toddlerhood but generally gives rise to the **telegraphic phase** of oral language development at around age two and a half. In this stage, speech patterns become more advanced, though sometimes prepositions, articles, and other short words are missing. Telegraphic speech includes phrases such as "See plane go!" and "There go teacher." This stage persists until children are mostly fluent in the home language, generally at age three or four.

Practice Question

2. A young child utters "go" to ask to go to the playground. What stage of language development is this child in?
   A. babbling
   B. two-word stage
   C. telegraphic phase
   D. holophrastic stage

Listening

Some students may be introverted and others more extroverted; however, all children need help to develop basic skills in speaking and listening to enable them to become effective communicators. There will be times when students must employ **passive listening** where they listen to a speaker or presentation without conversing. These occasions might be at school assemblies, when watching a movie, or when listening to a storyteller. Passive listening, so long as it is done intently, is not necessarily bad; it just implies a lack of two-way communication. In fact, some occasions, such as being a respectful audience member, will require students to employ passive listening skills.

Active listening, on the other hand, should be employed whenever there is two-way communication. Active listening is used in many positive behavioral support programs, so if a school or program employs one of these, active listening may become a skill about which teachers are daily reminding students. The goal of active listening is to ensure that the listener has correctly understood the speaker. This is often extended to include an understanding of and empathy with this speaker. Generally, active listening involves making appropriate **eye contact** with the speaker, waiting for the speaker to finish, and then responding in a way that shows understanding.

Not only should teachers be active listeners to ensure they understand what students are thinking and feeling, but they should also encourage students to employ these techniques whenever they are listening to directions or holding conversations. Active listening can also help students avoid conflict with each other as they refrain from interrupting and practice valuing the thoughts and opinions of others.

Part of listening and responding may involve different **types of questioning** as listeners check for understanding. Speakers generally employ either open-ended questions ("What does your house look like?"), which require a significant response, or closed-ended questions ("Do you like fried chicken?"), which generally require only a simple one-word answer. Speakers may even ask rhetorical questions, which do not require a response but are designed to make the listener think.

An even deeper type of questioning comes from **metacognition**, or an awareness of one's own thinking. Teachers can help students think from a metacognitive perspective by teaching them to ask themselves questions both about their content knowledge ("Have I seen this before?" "Do I know this or need more practice?") and from a socioemotional perspective ("Am I feeling cranky because I am tired or hungry?" "How would I feel if that happened to me?").

During more formal speaking situations, especially those in which the audience is primarily involved in passive listening, several other measures must also be considered. **Audience awareness** involves being aware of those to whom one is speaking and their level of engagement and interest. One way to increase engagement both in formal and informal speaking situations is through appropriate volume and **articulation**, or clarity of speech. It may help teachers to periodically self-assess their own classroom speaking and listening by asking themselves questions such as "Am I keeping an appropriate volume or raising my voice frequently?" and "Am I asking students enough open-ended questions and using active-listening techniques?" Modeling effective communication for students is an important way to help teach these skills.

Practice Question

3. Which of the following is an active listening strategy that can be taught to kindergarten students?
   A. emphasizing proper articulation
   B. maintaining eye contact
   C. using open-ended questioning
   D. practicing oral presentations

Assessment and Instruction of Oral Language

Much of what young children learn about language is from what they hear and say in everyday contexts. Teachers must remember that what students hear at school may be different from their **home language**, or the language they hear and speak at home.

Instructing students in oral language skills has significant overlap with other general language and literacy skills, but it should focus on the following:

- phonological skills: understanding of sounds in oral communication
- morphological skills: understanding word parts and different forms of words
- vocabulary skills: knowing what words mean
- syntax: knowing how to put words together
- pragmatics: knowing the social rules of language

To help students gain oral language skills, teachers should model appropriate speaking and provide multiple opportunities for students to practice speaking and listening. For example, teachers can have students complete projects or assignments in pairs or groups, hold class discussions, or provide opportunities for **think-pair-share** exercises, where students turn and speak about course content with peers.

Subtleties or pragmatics may be more challenging to teach, but instruction in **tone**, or the manner of speaking, is useful and helps avoid judgments associated with any particular dialect or register. For example, the distinction between a formal and informal tone could be introduced and practiced.

> **Think About It**
>
> What are some ways to update parents on second language development when parents are monolingual non-English speakers?

Students should also be given developmentally appropriate activities to help develop listening skills. For example, students could be asked to summarize information they hear or identify the main idea(s) of a recording or speech.

Students of all ages can also be given opportunities to speak to the class, from show-and-tell time for young students to planned oral presentations for older students.

Practice Question

4. A first-grade student says, "She is a smarting lady." The teacher could most likely help develop this student's oral language skills in terms of which domain?
   A. phonology
   B. vocabulary
   C. pragmatics
   D. morphology

Early Literacy

Foundations

Phonological awareness is the general ability to understand that within the structure of oral language, there are subparts. These parts include individual words; **syllables**, or units (typically containing a single vowel sound) within words; **onsets**, or the beginning consonant sounds of words (*sw*-im); and **rimes**, or the letters which follow (sw-*im*). Having phonological awareness is a crucial early stage in learning to read and write, and it can be fostered in the initial levels through singing songs and repeating rhyming words and phrases. Any activities or speech that seeks to break language into component parts or that help establish an understanding of syllables, onsets, and rimes—"Would *Son*-ya come to circle time?" "Do you want a *c*-at or a *h*-at for your birthday?"—are good choices for helping students begin to recognize the parts within language.

The **alphabetic principle**, or **graphophonemic knowledge**, presumes an understanding that words are made up of written letters that represent spoken sounds. In order to procced with more advanced reading concepts, children must first have a firm grasp of letter sounds. There is no firm rule on the pace at which the letter sounds should be mastered in their entirety, although most experts agree that those with the greatest frequency and those that will allow children to begin sounding out short words quickly should generally be introduced first. It is also sometimes easiest for children to master simple sounds—/t/ and /s/, for example—over more challenging or confusing sounds such as /b/, /d/, and /i/. Regardless of the way a curriculum breaks up practice with the alphabetic principle (a letter of the week or a teaching of the letters and sounds in rapid succession, etc.), teachers should recognize that repetition is key and students must be given multiple exposures to each letter and sound.

Phonemes are distinct units of sound and are the basic units of language. There are twenty-six letters in the alphabet, and there is some agreement among researchers that there are at least forty-four phonemes in English—some letters represent different phonemes and some phonemes are made up of more than one letter. There are eighteen consonant phonemes such as /r/ and /t/, fifteen vowel phonemes such as /Ā/ and /oi/, six *r*-controlled vowels such as /Ä/, and five digraphs such as /ch/ and /sh/. **Phonemic awareness** or **phonetic awareness** refers to the knowledge of and ability to use these phonemes. This awareness generally does not come naturally, and students will need explicit instruction to master these skills. It is often best to differentiate instruction and work with students in smaller groups when working on phonemic awareness because proficiency levels may vary substantially.

Did You Know?

The alphabet song was copyrighted in 1835 but is actually an adaptation of a Mozart melody.

Table 1.1. Phoneme Chart

Phoneme	Example	Phoneme	Example	Phoneme	Example
Consonants		***Vowels***		***R-Controlled Vowels***	
/b/	bat	/a/	lap	/ã/	hair
/d/	dog	/ā/	late	/ä/	art
/f/	fish	/e/	bet	/û/	dirt
/g/	goat	/ē/	see	/ô/	draw
/h/	hat	/i/	hit	/ēə/	rear
/j/	jump	/ī/	ride	/üə/	sure
/k/	kick	/o/	hop	***Diagrams/Digraphs***	
/l/	laugh	/ō/	rope	/zh/	measure
/m/	milk	/oo/	look	/ch/	chick
/n/	no	/u/	cut	/sh/	shout
/p/	pot	/ū/	cute	/th/	think
/r/	rat	/y//ü/	you	/ng	bring
/s/	sit	/oi/	oil		
/t/	toss	/ow/	how		
/v/	vote	/ə/ (schwa)	syringe		
/w/	walk				

Table 1.1. Phoneme Chart			
/y/	yak		
/z/	zoo		

Various activities can aid students in developing phonemic awareness. **Phoneme blending** involves students putting given sounds together to make words. To work on phoneme blending, teachers can say sounds and ask students what word is made: "I like /ch/ /ee/ /z/. What do I like? That's right, I like cheese." Teachers can also ask students to simply repeat or chorally repeat the sounds in words during circle time or storybook reading: "The car went vvvvv-rrrrr-oooo-m!"

Phoneme segmentation is generally the inverse of phoneme blending and involves students sounding out a word. Phoneme segmentation is important both for reading and spelling a word. More advanced phonemic awareness activities include **phoneme deletion,** in which a phoneme is removed to make a new word (e.g., ramp – /p/ = ram) and **phoneme substitution,** where one phoneme is changed to make a new word (e.g., fla/t/ to fla/p/).

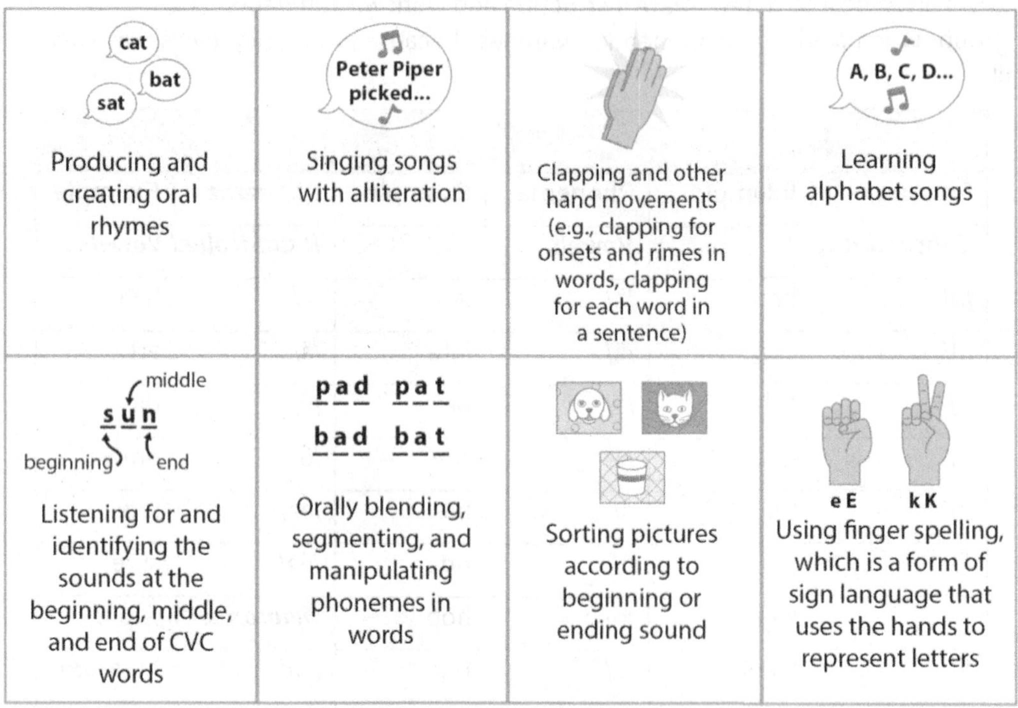

Figure 1.1. Phonological Awareness Strategies

Teachers should work on phonemic awareness with students in a variety of contexts. Having students manipulate language orally—"What word could I make if I took away the first letter of *cow*?"—and encouraging students in high-interest literacy activities in centers with alphabet boards, letter cards, alphabet sorters, and other manipulatives will provide multiple opportunities for students. Educators should also remember students will have varying backgrounds, skill levels, English language proficiencies, and possibly speech and language delays and hearing loss. Some students may need modifications for certain activities; this should be considered in the planning of inclusive activities.

Practice Question

5. A teacher says hat and instructs students to produce the sounds they hear in the word. Which strategy is the teacher using to build phoneme awareness?
   A. phoneme blending
   B. phoneme deletion
   C. phoneme segmentation
   D. phoneme substitution

Word Analysis and Decoding

Phonics is an age-old strategy for helping students read by connecting written language to spoken language or by correlating certain sounds with certain letters or groups of letters. Seminal to phonics instruction is a subset of the alphabetic principle—**letter-sound correspondence**. This correspondence is simply the knowledge of a phoneme associated with a given letter. Letter-sound correspondence is a foundational skill for effective phonics instruction, as most phonics strategies will require students to draw rapidly on this memory bank of letter sounds. As previously mentioned, most strategies for introducing students to the letter sounds draw on **high-frequency letter-sound correspondence,** where the most frequent and useful letter sounds are taught first. This will allow students to begin reading as soon as possible without having to wait for mastery of each letter sound.

Phonics instruction draws on the strategy of **decoding,** or the ability to pronounce the sounds of written words orally and glean meaning. Because of its focus on the specific sound structures of words, phonics instruction tends to involve more explicit, direct instruction and is not without critics, who believe it overemphasizes the mechanics of reading while sacrificing the enjoyment.

Helpful Hint

There are four types of phonics instruction: synthetic phonics instruction (explicit, direct instruction of phonemes and graphemes), analytic phonics instruction (focuses on onset and rime), analogy phonics instruction (focuses on word families), and embedded phonics instruction (teaches phonics via actual books).

However, most classrooms today employ a combination approach that balances inquiry-based student learning, allowing for the open exploration of high-interest literacy games and activities, with more direct instruction when necessary. Teachers may have any number of mandated or suggested organizational structures for teaching decoding, such as centers balanced with a teacher-directed table or a mandatory computer-based phonics drill segment, but it is highly likely that whatever curriculum a program or school uses, it will contain some phonics component. This approach is proven to work for most students and is adaptable to a variety of student skill levels and special learning needs.

Part of helping students become strong decoders is teaching certain patterns in the English language to help them when they encounter unfamiliar words. One of these patterns, described in Table 1.2., involves syllables.

Table 1.2. Syllable Patterns		
Closed Syllables	end in a consonant short vowel sound	hat <u>hip</u>-ster
Open Syllables	end with a vowel long vowel sound	go <u>lo</u>-cate

Table 1.2. Syllable Patterns		
Vowel-Consonant-*e* (VCe)	end with silent –*e* long vowel sound	take ren-o-vate
Vowel Teams	more than one vowel letter makes one sound	sea green-er
R-controlled Syllables	vowel + *r*	stir in-jur-ious
Consonant-*le* (C-le)	consonant + *le*	ta-ble lit-tle

There are some syllable patterns that do not fall into any of these types, such as –*ive*, –*ion*, –*age*, and –*ture*.

Syllable division patterns can also help students decode and spell words:

- VCCV division pattern: Syllable division is between the two consonants, and the accent is on the first or second syllable (in-sect, com-bine, in-sist).
- VCV division pattern: Syllable division is before the consonant, and accent is on the first or second syllable (ro-bin, re-quest, u-nite).
- VCCCV division pattern: Syllable division is after the first consonant, and accent is on the first or second syllable (sand-wich, hun-dred, ex-treme).

Students may also benefit from learning about **vowel combinations**: digraphs (groups of two letters) and trigraphs (groups of three letters).

Table 1.3. Digraph and Trigraph Vowel Combinations			
ai	*ee*	*ign*	*olt*
au	*ea*	*ing*	*oll*
ay	*eu*	*oo*	*ou*
aw	*ew*	*oa*	*ow*
augh	*ei*	*oe*	*ue*
all	*ey*	*oi*	*ui*
ald	*eigh*	*oy*	
alm	*ie*	*old*	
alt	*igh*	*olk*	

As students learn these common patterns, they can categorize words based on family. For example, students can be asked to group words based on vowel sound patterns such as –*aw* words like *claw, draw, jaw, paw, straw* or –*eep* words like *keep, deep, sweep*.

Some words are decodable, meaning they follow basic principles of phonics. These words can typically be sounded out effectively if basic structural deviations, like long vowel sounds with a word ending in *–e*, and various digraphs, where two letters make a single sound such as /th/ and /ay/, are mastered.

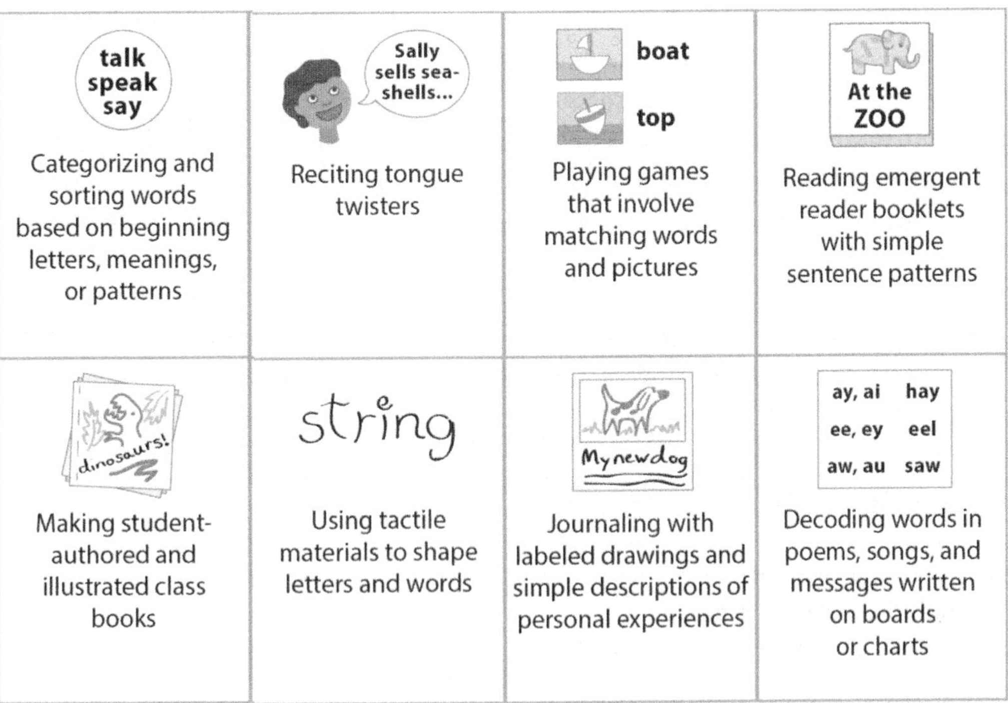

Figure 1.2. Phonics Classroom Strategies

However, there are some words that deviate from basic sound structures and cannot be sounded out. These words must be presented to students with great frequency so they can simply be memorized. These words must become **sight words**, or words that require no decoding because they are instantly recognized and read automatically. It is recommended that some high-frequency decodable words, such as *and* and *get*, also be memorized by sight so as to increase reading rate and fluency. There are many lists of such words. The most popular is the Dolch word list, which contains 315 words that are purported to be the most frequently used in English. Early childhood teachers might post some of these high-frequency words around the classroom for maximum exposure or encourage students to play games with sight word flashcards. Repetition will lead to mastery of these words and will help students read more quickly, fluently, and easily.

Students should also learn to analyze the structure of word parts, known as **morphemes**. Morphemes come in various types. **Free morphemes** are words on their own (e.g., *help*, *go*, *big*), while **bound morphemes** must be added to another morpheme (e.g. *–ly*, *–ing*, *un–)*. Morphemes can also be derivational or inflectional. **Derivational morphemes** are affixes (prefixes and suffixes) that, when added to another word, create a new word. Derivational morphemes include prefixes like *un–*, *re–*, *pre–* and suffixes like *–able*, *–ive*, and *–ion*. In contrast to derivational morphemes, **inflectional morphemes** simply denote a plural or tense but do not make an entirely new word or change the word to a new part of speech. For example, *–s*, *–ed*, and *–ing* are inflectional morphemes.

Because they help form new words, derivational morphemes are essential building blocks of the English language. Derivational morphemes are added to **roots**, or base words, in English. These roots are often derived from Latin or Greek. Related to morphology is **etymology**—the study of the history or origin of words—which often focuses on tracing the root back to its origin and meaning.

With roots and affixes or derivational morphemes, new words are formed. For example, *cent* is a Latin root meaning "one hundred." **Affixes** or derivational morphemes are added to words or roots to change their meanings. For example, the prefix *per–* can be added to *cent* to make the word *percent*, effectively changing the meaning to "one part in a hundred." Likewise, the suffix *–ury* can be added to *cent* to make the word *century*, effectively changing the meaning to "a period of one hundred years."

Did You Know?

Some English words that come from French or German words often originate from Latin words. This means that the great majority of English words have a true Greek or Latin origin.

Similar and related to basic morphological understanding is **morphophonemics**—the intersection of morphology and phonology (sounds). Students with morphophonemic awareness understand that as word parts change, sounds may also change. For example, the word *keep* has a vowel digraph that makes a long /e/ sound, but when the word is converted to past tense *kept*, the sound it makes is now a short /e/.

Practice Question

6. The word *elephant* is
   A. decodable.
   B. a high-frequency word.
   C. not composed of phonemes.
   D. inappropriate for phonics instruction.

Reading Fluency

Fluent Reading

Fluency refers to the rate, accuracy, and expression of a piece when read. Fluency is an important measure of a student's reading development; lack of fluency will hamper overall comprehension as well as enjoyment of reading. Reading **rate** is a measure of reading speed and is generally calculated in words per minute. The Texas Essential Knowledge and Skills (TEKS) specifies that students should aim to read sixty words per minute by the end of first grade and ninety words per minute by the end of second grade. **Accuracy,** or the correct decoding of words, is generally entwined with rate when measuring fluency, as reading quickly but incorrectly is not desirable.

While fluency is not limited to oral reading, it is virtually impossible to assess fluency during silent reading, and most educators rely on frequent oral reading assessments to help determine student progress. While several standard measures exist, one of the most researched is the Hasbrouck-Tindal oral reading fluency chart. This chart is designed to measure progress over the course of the school year and from grade to grade and compares students in percentiles with their peers on a scale of words read correctly per minute. It is important to remember that all students will develop fluency on a different timeline, and assessments of fluency are most accurate when they are developmentally appropriate and when they are not presented as high-stakes testing situations.

In addition to rate and accuracy, **prosody,** or the overall liveliness and expressiveness of reading, is also a skill to nurture in students. Prosody may involve appropriate pauses and various changes in pitch and **intonation** (variation of tone) based on punctuation and the overall meaning of the piece. Developing prosody in students should involve a combination of modeling by teachers—as they read stories, passages, and even directions aloud—and giving students plenty of opportunities for oral reading practice.

Helpful Hint

There are various software applications that allow teachers to record and track students' oral reading progress. While this technology cannot replace frequent live listening to students reading, it can augment it and speaks to the importance of oral reading in gauging students' overall literacy development.

Educators may find it challenging to find time for oral reading assessment in the classroom as they balance multiple priorities; however, teachers must make time to listen to all students, regardless of grade level, read aloud with regularity. While examining written work and performance on independent or group practice activities may give some indication of a student's overall development, to get the fullest picture teachers must gather as much data as possible. Assessing student fluency through oral reading is seminal to an overall understanding of a particular student's learning situation.

Fluency is highly correlated with comprehension because students who struggle to read and decode individual words will have difficulty comprehending entire sentences and paragraphs. Additionally, students who read at a very slow rate may have trouble recalling what they have read. It is well worth the time investment to listen to students read aloud as much as possible.

Practice Question

7. A second-grade teacher notices that his students often read in monotone during oral reading practice. Which strategy would best help his students develop prosody?
   A. setting aside timed oral reading each day
   B. modeling an appropriate reading rate
   C. using ability grouping for silent reading
   D. having students act out a play from a script

Stages of Literacy Development

To achieve full **literacy**, or the ability to read and write, children often go through stages. Before children sound out words, they are in an **emergent literacy** stage, typically lasting from preschool to early kindergarten. During the emergent literacy phase, children are able to recognize **environmental print**, or words in their surroundings, such as "STOP" on a red stop sign. They may also know the letters and even some letter sounds. Children then develop **alphabetic fluency**, where they begin to apply phonics skills, decode basic words, and even read orally word-by-word. This is the learning-to-read stage, which often takes place in late kindergarten and lasts through first grade.

In the third stage of literacy development, often referred to as the **transitional stage**, students are less reliant on adult help for unknown words and begin to apply strategies on their own. In this stage, children begin to comprehend the whole text instead of reading word-by-word. This stage often occurs during second grade.

After the transitional stage, students enter the **intermediate stage**, which marks the movement from learning to read to reading to learn. Many experts believe that students must be reading to learn by the end of third grade to have the best opportunity for learning in the years that follow. In the intermediate stage, students begin to read longer texts, learn vocabulary, and consider perspectives in the texts they encounter.

In the last stage of literacy learning, **advanced reading,** students are fully fluent and read and write a variety of complex texts. The advanced reading stage may vary but often emerges between the ages of eleven and fourteen.

Practice Question

8. When should students ideally begin reading to learn instead of learning to read?
   A. first grade
   B. second grade
   C. third grade
   D. fourth grade

Reading Comprehension

Genres

It is important that students of all ages be exposed to a wide variety of texts. **Informational texts,** or **nonfiction texts,** are texts about the world around us and generally do not use characters to convey information. Science and social studies texts fall into this category. These informational texts are often structured in such a way to organize information in a format that is accessible and meaningful to students.

As part of an introduction to different types of texts, a teacher might ask elementary-aged students to analyze elements of their textbooks or workbooks. Do they have bold headings to help the reader understand when new ideas are being introduced? Do they have **sidebars** to give readers additional information alongside the main body of text?

In contrast, **literary texts,** or **fiction texts,** are usually stories made up by the author. While they may contain true elements or be based on actual events (as in literary nonfiction), they usually include plenty of elements designed to keep and capture the reader's interest. They generally have **characters,** which may be real or imagined people, animals, or creatures, and a **plot,** or sequence of story events. The **setting** of fiction texts may be any time or place past, present, future, real, or imagined. While teachers may put a lot of focus on short stories that are highly accessible for young students, it is also important to expose children to other genres so that students get comprehension practice with texts that are unfamiliar at first.

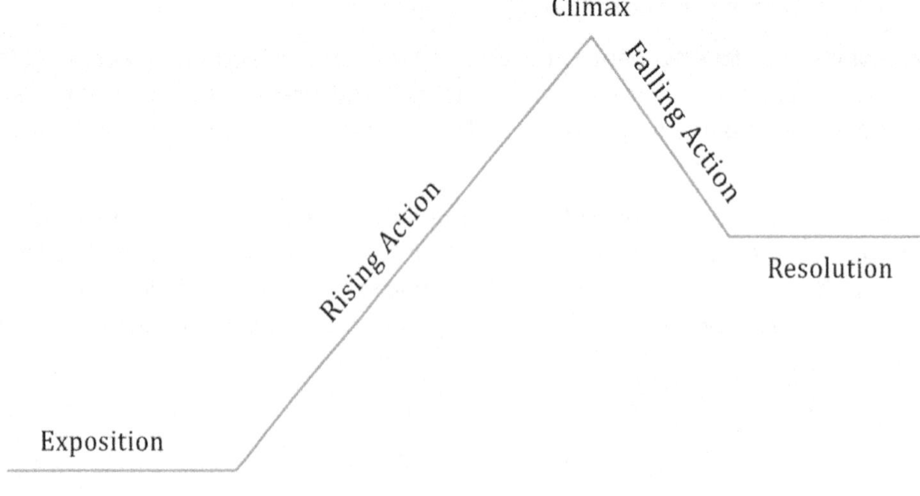

Figure 1.3. Plot Pyramid

In **drama**, most of the story is centered around dialogue between characters. They are usually separated into segments like chapters known as **acts** and smaller subsegments (generally with a consistent setting) known as **scenes**. Using drama in the classroom is a great way to get students interested in different types of texts. Consider setting up a simple **stage** in a kindergarten or elementary classroom as a natural outgrowth of a dramatic play center sometimes found in preschool classrooms. Building on students' innate curiosity and imagination, the possibilities are endless. Acting out dramas not only helps students work on expressive reading (prosody), but it also reinforces social and emotional learning as students analyze the emotions and actions of characters.

While poetry may be associated with older children, even young students can appreciate and recognize **rhyme**. Poetry with rhyme can help reinforce phonological awareness and is a natural outgrowth of many young children's love of song. **Meter**—or the rhythm, or beat, of the poem—can also be used to engage young students with different texts as a beat can be clapped to, stomped to, or even danced to! Many timeless books for children—such as *One Fish, Two Fish, Red Fish, Blue Fish* and *Each Peach Pear Plum*—have both rhyme and meter and give young children exposure to poetry. Young writers may even begin to write simple poems with one or two **stanzas**, or groups of **lines** similar to paragraphs. Students should be encouraged to recognize and create their own rhyming words as an additional outgrowth of phonological awareness. Asking students to name all the words they can think of that rhyme with *dog*, for example, will allow for continued practice with rhymes.

Children's literature is a genre in its own right. It often includes **myths**, **legends**, or **folktales** written for a young audience. It tends to have characters who are children or if animals or mythical creatures are the characters, they tend to behave in the way a child would. The genre also tends to focus on characters who learn an important lesson, often one that is applicable to life as a whole. Other characteristics of children's literature include accessible vocabulary and situations or events that children can relate to and find appealing. Many children's books, even those for intermediate readers, often include vivid illustrations to help bring the plot to life.

> **Think About It:**
>
> In selecting books and passages for curricular integration, what genres are most appropriate for social studies? Music? Art?

Much of today's literature—both for young children and older children—is not entirely new but rather reconceptualizes or reinterprets timeless themes and traditions. For example, "coming of age" is an important milestone in many cultures throughout the world, celebrated and honored in myriad ways. Thus, it is a popular topic for many stories. Additionally, various cultural patterns, traditions, and symbols can be found in books and stories for children. Some, like the Cinderella legend, can be found in some form in literature from multiple places throughout the world.

Literature for children may also be based on mythologies from long ago, such as those from ancient Greece or Rome. These tales have often been reinterpreted in an accessible and contemporary format. Religious traditions from various cultures often underscore popular stories; for example, almost all cultures have some sort of origin or creation myth surrounding the natural world. Christian beliefs also influence some popular children's literature as do positive character traits that exist beyond any religious framework, such as treating others with kindness and respect.

The structural elements of literature such as characters, setting, conflict, plot, resolution, point of view, and theme can be introduced alongside other literacy activities, even with students who are pre-readers. Consider bringing these elements into guided storybook while asking questions such as:

- "Who are the characters on this page?" (characters)
- "Where does this story happen?" (setting)
- "Why was __________mad/happy/worried, etc.?" (conflict/plot)

- "What happened after______?" and "How was (problem) fixed?" (conflict/plot/resolution)

Although **point of view**, or the perspective from which the story is told (first person, *I*, *we*; third person, *he*, *she*, *it*, or *they*; sometimes second person, *you*), may be harder for very young students to grasp, teachers can begin introducing the basic concept of differing points of view by reading the **narrator's** part in one voice and each different character in a different voice and encouraging students to do the same. For older students, second-person point of view can be practiced by reading and writing letters: to other students, the teacher, or administrators or other school personnel.

> **Check Your Understanding:**
>
> What are some classroom activities you might implement to give students practice with the structural elements of literature?

Practice Question

9. A teacher wants to select multicultural literature for her students to read. Which genre should she type into the library's search feature?
   A. poetry
   B. folktale
   C. literary nonfiction
   D. expository nonfiction

Text Complexity

Finding a balance between the complexity of a text and an individual student's current level of literacy development can be challenging. Many programs recognize this challenge and structure goal setting and student assessments in a growth-over-time approach. Regardless of the milestones laid out by a school or district, teachers should always aim for students to tackle ever more sophisticated texts as they develop the foundational skills they need to take on new challenges; however, this does not mean to push students beyond what they can decode. Giving students developmentally inappropriate texts may lead to a denigration of confidence and a lack of interest and enthusiasm for reading.

Many factors contribute to a text's complexity. Before determining appropriateness, texts should be evaluated qualitatively, quantitatively, and per their match to the reader. Quantitative measurements include anything for which a number can be calculated (e.g., **word frequency**, length of words and **sentence length**, and average number of syllables per word). These quantitative calculations may result in a range or score being allotted to a text. The most popular of these is that calculated by MetaMetrics, a company that uses word frequency and sentence length in an equation that yields a score. MetaMetrics assigns scores to both readers and texts. Those assigned to readers typically come from standardized tests and measure a student's current level of reading ability; these are called reader measures.

MetaMetrics also assigns **Lexile ranges** to texts called Lexile test measures. While these ranges do not have a direct correlation to grade level in the strictest sense, charts can be used to glean the typical ranges for a given grade. The company purports that the best results come when the reader measure falls within a "sweet spot" range per the text measure.

> **Helpful Hint**
>
> Qualitative text measures refer to the qualities of a text that cannot be assessed via a formula. Required background knowledge demands, levels of meaning and purpose, language conventions and clarity, and overall structure are all qualitative measures of text complexity.

More than likely, much of what students read (textbooks, passages in software programs, published children's literature) has already been assigned a Lexile text measure. Teachers can raise students' chances of enjoyment and comprehension of texts by ensuring that the Lexile text measure fits within the average range for the grade level and, more importantly, for the individual student's reader measure.

Beyond standardized text levels are individualized text levels. Text that is at a student's **independent level** will be easy for the student to read on his or her own with approximately 95 percent accuracy. Text at the **instructional level** is generally used in instructional situations in which scaffolding is available. These texts are challenging but still manageable, with students reading with approximately 90 percent accuracy. Texts at the **frustration level** are challenging texts that are read at lower than 90 percent accuracy. Typically, such texts are only appropriate when individual support is available.

Practice Question

10. A teacher wants to select a text for the class based on its qualitative measures. Which strategy should the teacher use?

    A. access the Lexile score and see if it falls within the suggested range for the grade level

    B. run the text through a program that provides a score such as ATOS or Flesch-Kincaid

    C. examine the text to determine the complexity of content-area vocabulary

    D. give an assessment to students to identify students' Lexile reading measure

Comprehension Strategies

A student's text comprehension can be influenced by various factors:

- word analysis skills (sometimes called 'word attack skills'), which are various strategies for decoding
- prior knowledge—the student's familiarity with the content and structure of the text
- language background and experience—the level of English language fluency
- previous reading experience—how much exposure to text the student has had
- fluency—the ability to read with appropriate rate, accuracy, and expression
- vocabulary development
- ability to monitor understanding
- text characteristics (such as genre and complexity)

Before students read any texts, they should set a **purpose** for reading, such as to learn about a new person, place, or idea; how to do a task; or to enjoy a fictional story. Also prior to reading, students should engage in other **prereading strategies**, such as **previewing** the text; noting the title, headings, graphics, bolded words, or other features; **making predictions** about what the text will be about; and **connecting**

prior knowledge. For example, if the text is about sailing a boat, students might connect past experiences they have had with boats or what they already know about boats. Another consideration is characteristics of certain text types that **identify the genre**. For example, if the text includes a list of steps, students may predict that it will provide some procedural information.

In developing comprehension, a distinction between **literal comprehension** (what is stated directly in the text) and **inferential comprehension** (what must be inferred) should be made. Typically, literal comprehension is easier for young readers than inferential comprehension.

One part of literal comprehension is identifying the **central**, or main, **idea** of a story or article. This is a prerequisite to **summarizing**, or condensing the main elements of a story or passage. Literal comprehension also involves recalling key details and identifying basic elements such as point of view (usually first or third person), setting, main characters, and order-of-story events.

Students can also practice literal comprehension by identifying **facts** (statements of truth backed by empirical evidence) and **opinions** (statements of authorial beliefs).

Inferential comprehension involves higher-order thinking skills, such as inferring the **theme** or message of a text, **making predictions** about what will happen next, and **inferring** or concluding something based on text evidence.

Helpful Hint

Beginning in third grade, the TEKS requires students to "synthesize information to create new understanding." Synthesis is the process of putting information together, either from multiple parts of texts, multiple texts, or from the text and other sources.

Making inferences is an important skill in developing overall comprehension as it allows students to go deeper than the literal meaning and make conclusions based on previously obtained knowledge and experiences. Whenever teachers ask students to make an inference based on a text, they should be sure to ask them to support their inference with evidence. "How do you know this?" "What made you think this?" "Which part of the story/passage made you think this?" are all good follow-up questions for inferring students. As students advance in their comprehension skills, it is also important to ensure that students know that sometimes we all make faulty inferences and that we must constantly evaluate whether we are projecting our own beliefs and experiences onto a text that lacks support for a conclusion we drew.

Beyond literal and inferential comprehension is **evaluative comprehension**; this is when students begin to consider their own thoughts and beliefs in relationship to the text as they analyze more deeply. This might involve analysis of a character in a literary text or detecting faulty reasoning in an argumentative text. Evaluative comprehension is often best practiced and assessed through open-ended questions for discussion or an extended constructed response.

It is also highly worthwhile that students comprehend images or graphics embedded in texts. This helps students get the most from informational texts like textbooks and informational websites or educational software. Pointing out and helping students understand how visual elements promote a greater understanding of concepts or ideas that the author is trying to convey will help students be cognizant of these important elements that exist alongside text. Images can also aid struggling readers to decode. While students should not be reliant on pictures, most texts for young readers include ample images to aid in students' overall understanding and enjoyment, and these should be pointed out and discussed when appropriate.

Reading comprehension must be constantly monitored. Students need to be explicitly instructed in **self-monitoring,** or **self-evaluation** of their own understanding, as they read. This can be done using these strategies:

- visualizing
- questioning
- drawing conclusions
- making connections
- summarizing
- annotating
- rereading

> **Think About It**
>
> What strategies could help students develop their ability to visualize as they read?

When students become aware that their comprehension has broken down, they should apply what some call "**fix-up**" strategies. These may include (but are not limited to)

- adjusting the reading rate (slowing down),
- rereading confusing parts,
- looking up unknown words,
- reading aloud, and
- asking for peer or teacher support (typically as a last resort).

To aid students in developing a toolbox for comprehending texts, teachers can implement a variety of techniques. **Think-alouds,** where teachers explain their own self-monitoring as they read, are one strategy. Helping students use maps, webs, or outlines to track key information in a text is another. Other types of graphic organizers, such as **KWL charts,** where students identify what they already know about a topic, what they want to learn, and then what they did learn after reading are also useful and appropriate. Using reading logs or reading journals where students track what they've read and write in response to these texts is another useful instructional tool.

Figure 1.4. KWL Charts

Teachers can also put students in small groups or whole class discussions about texts or to debate their beliefs about a character or opinion presented in a text.

Sometimes pre-teaching important background information needed to fully comprehend a text may be necessary. For example, as students read literature from different cultures, they may first need basic information on that culture such as where it is located and what life is like there. Texts that include references to languages other than English may also require pre-teaching and/or reference tools such as a list of commonly used non-English terms in the story and their meaning.

Practice Question

11. In a lesson with fourth-grade students, the teacher wants to provide a sentence frame to help students identify the theme of a folktale. Which sentence frame would be most useful?

A. The message about life in the story is:

B. The parts of nature in the story are:

C. The main character does things like:

D. The setting is a place where people:

Vocabulary Development Strategies

Did You Know?

The average native-English speaking American knows about 42,000 words.

Part of comprehension of any text rests on an understanding of words themselves. Students acquire new vocabulary both through **formal** methods, such as classroom instruction, and **informal** methods, such as hearing new words spoken or used in context. Vocabulary is also developed via **explicit** instruction, such as introducing content-area words to students along with their definitions and examples, and via **implicit** means, such as students learning a content area word by reading a content area text.

Students can be taught new vocabulary explicitly via the Frayer Model (a specific type of graphic organizer), through semantic maps (where students connect the word to other ideas in a web), or through word walls (where students or groups of students look up the word, write a succinct definition, and provide an accompanying image to post in the classroom). Students may also create **analogies**, or relationships among words, to help them remember and understand new vocabulary.

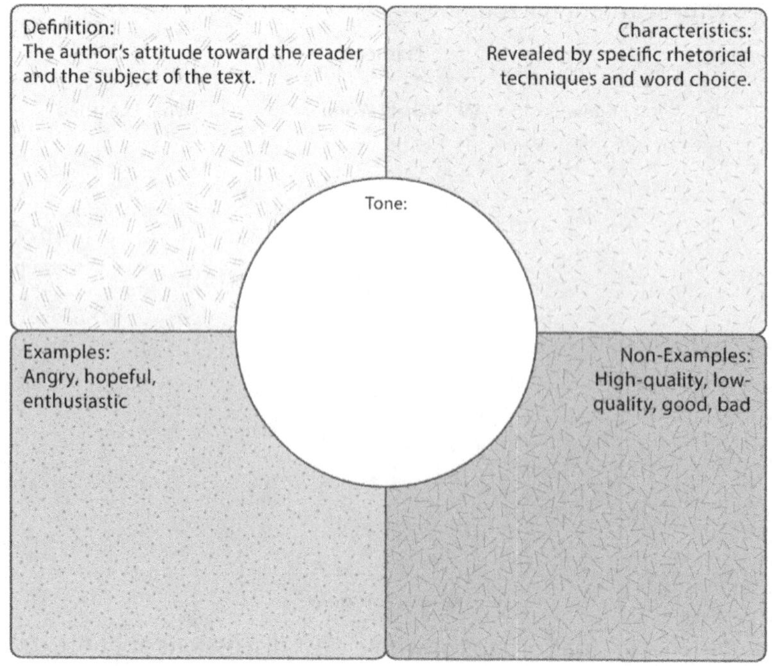

Figure 1.5. Frayer Model

Students should also be taught to learn new words as they encounter them. This may involve

- using context clues, such as definition, restatement, **synonym** (another word in the text with a similar meaning) or **antonym** (another word in the text with the opposite meaning);
- using morphological clues, such as known roots or affixes;
- looking up the word in a dictionary or glossary;
- identifying the category of the word based on its context or structure (for example, noun, verb, adjective);
- understanding nuances in word meanings, such as figurative meanings, multiple meanings, **homographs** (words that are spelled the same but have different meanings), or **homophones** (words that sound the same but have different meanings and spellings); and
- using technology, such as built-in dictionary features in digital texts.

As students read, they should monitor their understanding of vocabulary as part of their overall comprehension. Students learning English as a second language may need additional vocabulary support, such as pre-teaching, picture dictionaries, or digital translators.

Practice Question

Read this sentence a student encounters in a passage:

I like the paintings for their realism. They look just like photographs.

12. Which strategy should the teacher recommend to help the student identify the meaning of the underlined word?

A. think about the possibility the word is being used figuratively
B. find the antonym in the sentence that follows
C. identify the phrase in the next sentence that tells what the word means
D. consider the category of words that end in -ism that this word belongs to

Writing Conventions

Developmental Stages of Writing

In their overall plan for developing literacy in students, teachers should give students plenty of opportunities to practice writing alongside reading and analyzing texts. It is important to ensure conscious writing instruction and practice as research suggests that this is sometimes an overlooked component of literacy curriculum. Some studies even suggest that many prekindergarten and kindergarten students spend less than three minutes a day on writing practice.

Learning to write involves three distinct components: **conceptual knowledge, procedural knowledge,** and **generative knowledge**. In helping young students develop conceptual knowledge of writing, teachers should focus on activities that show students the link between print and its intended purpose. Environmental print is a great resource for helping students develop this knowledge as teachers point out classroom signs and posters or those in the school building and on the playground. They can further build early conceptual knowledge by having students **draw** or **scribble** to communicate their own feelings and ideas.

Table 1.4. Stages of Emergent Writing

Stage	Example
Drawing	
Scribbling	
Letter-like forms	
Transitional writing	
Word and phrase writing	

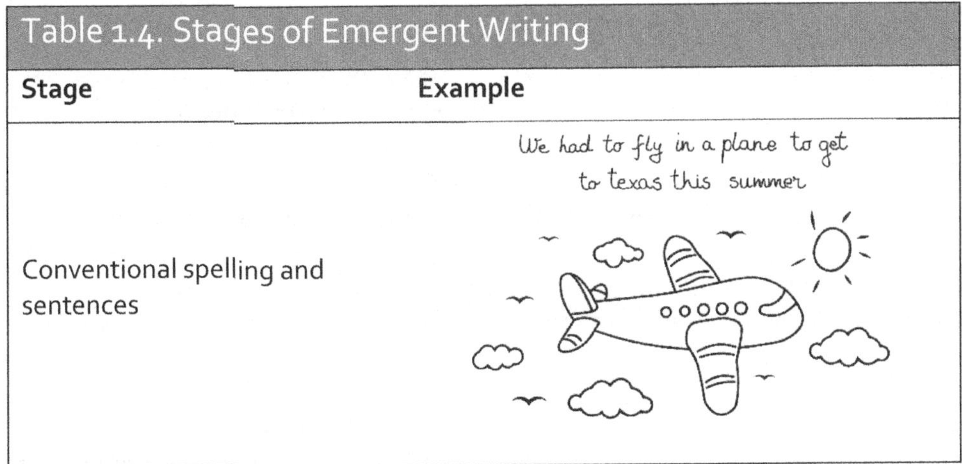

Table 1.4. Stages of Emergent Writing

Stage	Example
Conventional spelling and sentences	We had to fly in a plane to get to texas this summer

Procedural knowledge involves the nuts and bolts of writing. Procedural knowledge–building activities are those that build awareness of basic letter formation, the knowledge that words are made up of letters, the knowledge that words have spaces between them, and the overall mechanics of writing. Procedural knowledge and the alphabetic principle are entwined, and the letter sounds and names should be reinforced when consciously instructing correct letter formation.

Additionally, procedural knowledge of writing will coincide with the development of fine motor skills. Fine motor skills development in the classroom cannot be overemphasized, particularly in a preschool or kindergarten setting. As in any part of emergent literacy, teachers will have students with widely divergent levels of fine motor proficiency. It is essential the classroom provides a variety of opportunities for students to build these skills through the use of manipulatives such as alphabet boards and puzzles and a variety of writing implements such as crayons, markers, and pencils.

> **Did You Know?**
>
> Although computer-generated documents are quickly overtaking hand-written records, fine motor skills are also needed for typing. Typists must be able to isolate individual finger movements in a small space.

Part of fine motor skills proficiency is developing **pencil grip**, or the ability to hold a writing instrument properly. To teach students how to grip the pencil properly, teachers can ask them to make an OK signal with their thumb and pointer finger and then insert the pencil in between.

Another part of fine motor skills proficiency is the development of **graphomotor skills**, or handwriting skills. The TEKS require

- kindergarten students to begin printing upper- and lower-case letters;
- first-grade students to print words and sentences;
- second-grade students to print all cursive letters;
- third-grade students to write words and thoughts in cursive;
- fourth-grade students to write legibly in both print and cursive to complete assignments; and
- fifth-grade students to write legibly in print and cursive.

Practice Question

13. In a kindergarten classroom, a teacher notices that one student becomes quickly fatigued after writing the first few letters of his name. Which strategy should the teacher employ?
    A. direct instruction in graphomotor skills, including tracing letters with the correct stroke
    B. providing opportunities for fine motor skills development, such as cutting and working with clay
    C. grouping the student with a peer who can write his name to offer scaffolding
    D. shifting to embedded writing instruction where the student writes words from stories

Spelling Development

The mechanics of writing will generally involve explicit spelling instruction, and this will likely be part of a program's curriculum. It is important to view spelling as part of a developmental continuum and not overemphasize correct spelling too early when preschool students are still forming mock letters or letter strings. However, a standard **continuum of spelling** can be referenced to tailor spelling instruction appropriate to grade level while always keeping in mind the differing developmental levels within the classroom.

Table 1.5. Continuum of Spelling	
By the end of first grade, most students should be able to correctly spell short words with . . .	▪ short vowel sounds with a consonant-verb-consonant (*cat, dog, pin*) pattern [CVC]; ▪ vowel-consonant pattern (*up, egg*) and [VC]; ▪ simple consonant-vowel pattern (*go, no*) [CV]; and ▪ consonant blends and digraphs in simple and high-frequency words (*chat, that*) [CCVC].
By the end of second grade, most students should be spelling words with . . .	▪ final consonant blends (*rant, fast, bend, link*) [CVCC]; ▪ regular long vowel patterns (*ride, tube*) [CVC]; ▪ double consonant endings (*lick, fuss*); ▪ more complex long vowel patterns (*suit, fail*); and ▪ *r*-controlled vowels (*near, bear, hair, are*).

Table 1.5. Continuum of Spelling	
By the end of third grade, most students should be able to spell words with . . .	▪ non-*r*-controlled but other consonant influences vowels (*stall*, *draw*); ▪ diphthongs (*coil*, *soon*, *enjoy*, *wow*); ▪ soft *g*'s and *c*'s (*dice*, *hedge*); ▪ short vowel patterns (*head*, *sought*); ▪ silent consonants (*tomb*, *known*, *gnaw*, *wrote*); ▪ advanced digraphs and blends (*phase*, *character*, *whose*); ▪ contractions; ▪ two-syllable words; ▪ compound words; ▪ words with suffixes that show number or degree (*fastest*, *foxes*); and ▪ special spelling rules such as doubling the final letter on CVC words when adding certain suffixes (*napping*, *saddest*).

Did You Know?

Diphthongs are sounds created by two vowels together.

Explicit spelling instruction will generally begin with simple consonant-vowel-consonant (CVC) patterns and progress as students learn new phonics structures. Practice with homophones, or words that have the same pronunciation but a different spelling and meaning, should begin in third grade, or sooner for some students. Common homophones include *there/their/they're*, and *to/two/too*. It is important to point out to students that software applications that might detect spelling errors in other words often fail to pick up on spelling errors with homophones, so students should be extra vigilant when editing and revising writing containing these words.

Knowledge of spelling rules or patterns is also important. Some of these are **position-based patterns,** such as

- *i* before *e* (except when a long *a* sound is present);
- when there is a vowel blend (e.g., *ee/ea/ai/oa*), the sound made is typically a long vowel sound based on the first letter; and
- when there is a vowel-consonant-*e* pattern (such as *take* or *rate*), the vowel is usually long.

Other spelling rules are based on suffixes:

- Drop the silent *e* before adding any suffix that begins with a vowel (*give/giving*).
- Keep the *e* when the suffix starts with a consonant (*use/useful*).
- Drop the *y* when adding a suffix (*baby/babies*).

Other common spelling rules can be learned and taught with word families, such as words that end in *–ion* (*vacation*, *station*, *decision*) or words that end in *–ck* (*luck*, *duck*, and *struck*).

It is also important to balance more explicit spelling practice with time to allow students to practice the third part of emergent writing, generative knowledge. In this domain students learn to write for a purpose that goes beyond simply forming a word and other mechanical concerns. While preschool students may not be able to write their own stories, teachers at this level can still give students practice by having them dictate a story that the teacher writes for them and perhaps even reads back to the class.

As students master more of the procedural knowledge of writing, they can begin generating more pieces on their own. Students generally progress from writing letter strings and word-like structures under a picture they have drawn to writing and spelling simple words to constructing sentences to constructing stories.

As students begin to generate more written text, it is also important to emphasize the distinctions between spoken and written text. In speech, meaning can be conveyed in part through tone, pitch, and volume. In writing, punctuation is used to achieve meaning, but it is not always as easy to understand as speech. For example, though an exclamation point is used for emphasis, without context, it might not be clear if the sentence is to be read excitedly or angrily.

Spoken language also tends to be less formal than written language. Slang, for example, is almost always more appropriate in speech than in written communication.

Practice Question

14. Which word has a CVC pattern?
    A. gap
    B. onto
    C. drink
    D. and

Parts of Speech

Understanding the structure of language is an important part of effective oral and written communication. Students may not consistently use parts of speech correctly in their writing and speaking until well into their elementary years. Recall that within oral language development are phases in which children leave out needed articles, prepositions, and other linking words. Once speech becomes fully developed and students are generating their own sentences and paragraphs, basic rules of grammar can be introduced. Many structured language arts curriculum resources begin with a study of the eight parts of speech and their function within a sentence.

Check Your Understanding:

What are the major phases of oral language development?

Nouns are words that indicate a person, place, thing, or idea. They may be either common (*student, teacher, room, school*) or proper (*Blanca, Ms. Robinson, Idaho, Frederick Douglass Elementary School*). **Common nouns** are not capitalized, but **proper nouns** must be capitalized. Nouns may also be singular or plural, and students will need practice in forming the plural form of nouns by adding either *–s* or *–es*.

Pronouns are words that take the place of nouns. They may either serve as subjects (*I, you, he, she, it, we, they*) or as objects (*me, you, her, him, it, us, them*) and are known as **subject pronouns** or **object pronouns**, respectively. Pronouns should always have an **antecedent**, or noun to which they refer. Pronouns must agree in number, person, and gender with their antecedents. Pronoun errors are frequent in developmental writers, and ambiguous pronoun references, lack of pronoun-antecedent agreement, and incorrect use of subject and object pronouns are all common mistakes.

As discussed above, pronouns generally also indicate the perspective or person in which a piece is written. First-person writing generally uses pronouns such as *I*, *me*, *we*, and *our*, and second-person writing uses the pronoun *you*. Third-person texts use a variety of pronoun such as *he*, *she*, *it*, and *them*. Shifts in pronoun person are common in student writing, and teachers need to provide help to students who unnecessarily change point of view in a writing assignment.

Verbs describe an action or state of being or occurrence. They can be action verbs, which like their name implies, describe actions such as *walk, eat,* and *speak*, or linking verbs, which describe states of being or link a subject to additional information (*is, become, seem*). Some verbs may be action verbs or linking verbs depending upon their specific use. If verbs are merely linking a subject to further information, they are considered linking verbs, but if they are expressing an action, they are considered action verbs.

Examples:

This soup tastes bad.

In this sentence, the verb *tastes* links the subject *soup* to its predicate adjective *bad*, so *tastes* is being used as a linking verb.

I taste the soup.

In this sentence, *taste* is describing an action, so it is an action verb.

Helping verbs always appear alongside another main verb and show the tense (*will* be, *had* eaten) or possibility (*may* be, *could* last, *might* enjoy) of another verb. Helping verbs are used to **conjugate**, or change, many verbs to different **tenses**. Unnecessary shifts in tense from present to past or future are prevalent in student writing, and English language learners and native speakers alike will need lots of practice with forming challenging tenses such as the present and past perfect and challenging irregular past tenses with verbs such as *to lie*.

Adjectives modify and describe nouns, and their use is essential to descriptive writing. Student errors with adjectives generally include using an incorrect comparative or superlative form ("He is tallest than me!") or confusing adjectives and adverbs ("She eats hungry/She eats hungrily.").

Adverbs modify adjectives, verbs, or other adverbs and frequently end in *–ly*. Student errors with adverbs are similar to those with adjectives and generally involve incorrect use of comparatives and superlatives or using adjectives and adverbs interchangeably.

A **preposition** is a word that expresses a relationship between words, and it usually comes before a noun or pronoun. Prepositions help form links in speech and writing, and student errors most frequently involve their omission. Additionally, English language learners may find using prepositions challenging, particularly when they are part of colloquial expressions (e.g., driving me *up* the wall, a pig *in* a poke, etc.).

A **conjunction** joins words or sentence parts together. There are both coordinating conjunctions (*and, but, or, nor, for, yet, so*), which join two independent clauses to form compound sentences, and subordinate conjunctions (*before, while, because, as*, etc.), which join dependent clauses to independent clauses to form complex and compound-complex sentences.

Table 1.6. Subordinating Conjunctions	
Time	after, as, as long as, as soon as, before, since, until, when, whenever, while
Manner	as, as if, as though
Cause	because
Condition	although, as long as, even if, even though, if, provided that, though, unless, while
Purpose	in order that, so that, that
Comparison	as, than

An **interjection** expresses a spontaneous feeling and is usually followed by a comma or exclamation point. *Oops, whoa*, and *hmm* are examples of common interjections.

Determiners are not parts of speech in themselves but have a similar function: explaining what a noun refers to. They may be adjectives that are used as articles such as *a*, *an*, and *the*; possessive adjectives and pronouns (*my, his, ours, your*); demonstrative pronouns such as *this*, *that*, *these*, and *those*; or any other words that quantify, distribute, or show a difference (*a little, half, other, such, quite*).

> **Helpful Hint**
>
> Students can use the mnemonic PAPA N VIC to remember the eight parts of speech.

Like prepositions, determiners are challenging for English language learners. In some languages, determiners are used in only some situations and not others, and some languages lack certain types of English determiners entirely. English language learners who struggle with determiners might benefit from being paired with a native speaker for peer review to help insert needed articles into a piece.

Contractions are two words combined with an apostrophe. The following are the most common types of contractions:

1. subject pronoun + verb (*she's = she + is; I've = I + have*)
2. verb + *not* (*can't = can + not; shouldn't = should + not*)
3. interrogative adverbs (*what's = what + is; who's = who + is*)

Students should begin learning common contractions in first grade and should advance to more complex contractions in subsequent grades. After students master the basic construction of contractions, they should also practice **commonly confused words** that involve contractions, such as *its* versus *it's* and *whose* versus *who's*.

Additionally, variations exist across all parts of speech in different languages. American Sign Language, as just one example, does not use what one might think of as conjugated verbs to show tense; rather, a sign indicating now, next, before, and so on is inserted into the beginning of the sentence to show the intended meaning. It is important for teachers to understand that grammatical knowledge will be more challenging for some students, and they should strive to ensure the classroom is a place where all students are being supported in their learning.

Practice Questions

15. Which of the following is a preposition?
   A. our
   B. from
   C. has
   D. so

16. Which of the following skills do students need to master before they can determine whether an adjective or adverb is most appropriate to use in a sentence?
   A. understanding the difference between a noun and a verb
   B. understanding the difference between a noun and a pronoun
   C. understanding the function of prepositions
   D. being able to form compound sentences

Punctuation

Many of the mechanical choices writers must make relate to **punctuation.** While creative writers have liberty to play with punctuation to achieve their desired ends, academic and technical writers must adhere to stricter conventions.

The **period** is the most common **terminal punctuation** mark, used to end declarative (statement) and imperative (command) sentences. Examples include the following:

- *Sarah and I are attending a concert.*
- *Meet me outside the concert hall one hour before the show.*

The **question mark**, another common terminal punctuation mark, is used to end interrogative sentences (questions). Example: *How many people are attending the concert?*

While the difference between the period and the question mark is usually obvious, confusion sometimes occurs when questions are stated indirectly. In that case, the period is usually preferable. Example: *I wonder how many people are attending the concert.*

Exclamation points end exclamatory sentences, in which the writer or speaker is exhibiting intense emotion or energy; thus, writers should carefully consider their use of exclamations. In fact, the exclamation point should be used reservedly or not at all in academic writing unless the exclamation point is within a quotation that a writer incorporates into the text. The emphatic usage of *what* or *how* without asking a question, however, demands the usage of the exclamation point. Example: *What a great show that was!*

> **Helpful Hint**
>
> The exclamation point has impact only in contrast to its frequency of usage. That is, if the exclamation point is used frequently, each exclamation will be less impactful. On the other hand, if the exclamation point is used sparingly, its use will draw the reader's attention and emphasize the information contained in the sentence.

The **colon** and the **semi-colon,** though often confused, each have a unique set of rules surrounding their use. While both punctuation marks are used to join clauses, the construction of the clauses and the relationship between them varies.

The **semi-colon** is used to show a general relationship between two independent clauses (IC; IC). Example: *The disgruntled customer tapped angrily on the counter; she had to wait nearly ten minutes to speak to the manager.*

When using the semi-colon with a conjunctive adverb to join two independent clauses, the pattern is as follows: independent clause, semi-colon, conjunctive adverb, comma, independent clause. Example: *She may not have to take the course this year; however, she eventually will have to sign up for that specific course.*

> **Helpful Hint**
>
> *Let's eat Grandma*, OR *Let's eat, Grandma.* While this well-known example is humorous, it also demonstrates the need for comma accuracy.

The **colon**, somewhat less limited than the semi-colon in its usage, is used to show a relationship between two clauses and, moreover, to highlight the information contained in the second clause—usually a list, definition, or clarification. While the clause preceding the colon must be an independent clause, the clause that follows doesn't have to be. Examples include the following:

- Incorrect. *The buffet offers three choices that include: ham, turkey, or roast beef.*
- Correct. *The buffet offers three choices: ham, turkey, or roast beef.*
- Correct. *The buffet offers three choices that include the following: ham, turkey, or roast beef.*

A writer should also use the colon to separate a title from a subtitle (Title: Subtitle), to separate the hour and the minutes (9:30 a.m.), to follow certain parts of a letter or memo (To:, From:, Date:, RE:), and to follow a formal salutation (To whom it may concern:).

Neither the semi-colon nor the colon should be used to set off an introductory phrase from the rest of the sentence:

- Incorrect. *After the trip to the raceway; we realized that we should have brought ear plugs.*
- Incorrect. *After the trip to the raceway: we realized that we should have brought ear plugs.*
- Correct. *After the trip to the raceway, we realized that we should have brought ear plugs.*

Many people are taught that, when reading, a comma represents a pause for breath. While this trick may be useful as a way of helping young readers build fluency, it is not a helpful guide for comma usage when writing. Rather, proper comma usage is guided by a set of specific rules.

The following list summarizes the most important comma usage rules:

1. Commas are used to separate two independent clauses along with a coordinating conjunction.

George ordered the steak, but Bruce preferred the ham.

2. Commas are used to separate coordinate adjectives.

The shiny, regal horse ran majestically through the wide, open field.

3. Commas are used to separate items in a series.

The list of groceries included cream, coffee, donuts, and tea.

4. Commas are used to separate introductory words and phrases from the rest of the sentence.

Slowly, Nathan became aware of his surroundings after the concussion.

For example, we have thirty students who demand a change.

5. Commas are used to set off non-essential information and appositives.

Estelle, our newly elected chairperson, will be in attendance.

6. Commas are used to set off introductory words from quoted words if the introductory words are not an independent clause.

Elizabeth said sadly, "I want to go home right now for spring break."

7. Commas are used to set off the day and month of a date within a text.

My birthday makes me feel quite old because I was born on February 16, 1958, in Minnesota.

8. Commas are used to set up numbers in a text of more than four digits.

We expect 25,000 visitors to the new museum.

> **Helpful Hint**
>
> To determine if information in a sentence is nonessential and thus should be set off with commas, remove that information from the sentence. If the meaning is changed, it is essential information and needs no commas. If the meaning is NOT changed, commas are needed.

Quotation marks are used for many purposes, the most common of which are related to academic writing and citation. First, quotation marks enclose titles of short, or relatively short, literary works such as short stories, chapters, and poems. (The titles of longer works, like novels and anthologies, are italicized.) Additionally, quotation marks are used to enclose direct quotations within the text of a document where the quotation is integrated into the text. If a quotation is within another quotation, then the inner quotation uses single quotation marks.

Writers also use quotation marks to set off dialogue. Occasionally, quotation marks are used to enclose words used in special sense or for a non-literary purpose. (*The shady dealings of his Ponzi scheme earned him his ironic name "Honest Abe."*)

When considering quotation marks versus italics in notating a title, the question of short versus long is a useful guide. A chapter title is written in quotation marks, while the book title itself is italicized. Short poetry titles are written in quotation marks; long epic poem titles are italicized. An article title is written in quotation marks, while the name of the newspaper is italicized.

Apostrophes, sometimes referred to as single quotation marks, have several different purposes.

1. show possession: *boy's watch, John and Mary's house*
2. replace missing letters, numerals, and signs: *do not = don't,* 1989 = '89
3. form plurals of numerals, signs, and lowercase letters: *a's*

Other marks of punctuation include the **en dash** (to indicate a range of dates, for example), the **em dash** (to indicate an abrupt break in a sentence and emphasize the words within the em dashes), the **parentheses** (to enclose insignificant information), the **brackets** (to enclose added words to a quotation and to add insignificant information within parentheses), the **slash** (to separate lines of poetry within a text or to indicate interchangeable terminology), and the **ellipses** (to indicate information removed from a quotation, to indicate a missing line of poetry, or to create a reflective pause).

Practice Question

17. Which punctuation should be added to the following sentence?
Freds brother wanted the following items for Christmas a red car a condo and a puppy.

A. Fred's / Christmas; / car, /condo,
B. Fred's / Christmas: / car, / condo,
C. Fred's / Christmas: / car,
D. Fred's / items' / Christmas: / car, / condo,

Constructing Sentences

Good writers use a variety of sentence structures to convey their meaning. While young students will generally start with **simple sentences** consisting of a single, independent clause, students should be encouraged to write more advanced sentences as appropriate. **Compound sentences** are made when two independent clauses are joined together using a comma and coordinating conjunction; a semicolon, either alone or with a transitional expression such as *however* or *moreover*; or a colon. Generally, a semicolon alone is only used to join two closely related independent clauses ("My mother likes chocolate; she is a chocoholic."). A colon is generally only used to introduce a second independent clause which is an example or elaboration upon the first ("I have only one thing to say to you: I am very disappointed.").

Complex sentences are formed when a dependent clause is joined to an independent clause with a subordinating conjunction, relative pronoun, or other word. A **dependent clause** is so called because it cannot stand on its own as a sentence, unlike an **independent clause**. The dependent clause may be added anywhere: the beginning, the middle, or the end of the sentence.

My mother, *who is a gardener*, likes to spend most of her time outdoors.

In this sentence, the dependent clause is "who is a gardener," beginning with the relative pronoun *who*.

Because she likes to spend most of her time outdoors, my mother is a gardener.

Here, the dependent clause is "[b]ecause she likes to spend most of her time outdoors," beginning with the subordinating conjunction *because*.

My mother is a gardener *as she likes to spend most of her time outdoors*.

In the sentence above, the dependent clause is "as she likes to spend most of her time outdoors," beginning with the subordinating conjunction *as*.

Compound-complex sentences are merely compound sentences with one or more dependent clauses ("My mother is a gardener, but she does not like to spend time outdoors because she has allergies.").

Practice Question

18. Which of the following is a compound sentence?

A. Jeremy likes to fish by the ocean because he finds it peaceful and relaxing.
B. I wish I could buy a new car, but I do not have enough money right now.
C. Jenny is a writer, and she writes for thirty minutes every day because she has to keep motivated.
D. While the train slowly chugged along the tracks, my little dog stared curiously out the window.

Written Communication

Teaching Writing Conventions

Mechanics are the structural elements of writing and include punctuation, capitalization, spelling, grammar, and general conventions of usage. Like most procedural knowledge of writing, this proficiency may vary significantly from student to student and grade level to grade level. A kindergarten class, in particular, may be focused on a unit about capitalizing the first word in a sentence, whereas a second-grade class may be working on forming the past tense of verbs.

Teachers must also ensure they do not presume knowledge of standard English conventions among students for whom English is not the first language. The correct use of prepositions, irregular verbs, and pronouns may be particularly challenging for these students until they become more experienced in common usage patterns. Teachers should always aim for growth versus perfection when helping students develop skills in editing their writing for errors in mechanics, as these skills continue to build throughout a student's schooling.

Grammar and mechanics drills were once standard practice, but they are no longer viewed as an evidence-based best practice. Using authentic writing tasks is generally preferred over out-of-context drills. For example, when assigning students to write a dialogue between two people, teaching rules for the use of quotation marks is appropriate and authentic. Similarly, when working on identifying point of view in a literary text, a mini-lesson on pronouns would be useful and appropriate.

Additionally, it was once believed that knowledge of the terminology of linguistics was necessary; most educators now believe that application is preferred over knowledge of terms. This does not mean that explicit instruction does not have a place, only that it must be connected to its application. So for example, if the lesson is on the use of a comma and a coordinating conjunction for a compound sentence, students should apply this punctuation in their own writing.

> **Think About It**
>
> How did you learn about the mechanics of writing? Was this method effective?

Beyond the basics of forming sentences and paragraphs, students should be instructed on the finer points of text creation. Each piece of writing has a unique **style**, or approach. Style can describe the author's choice of words. Similar to style is **voice**, which is comprised of diction, detail, imagery, syntax, and tone. Both word choice and structure can make a piece formal, informal, or somewhere in between. One part of selecting a style is the intended **purpose** and **audience**. Teachers should always draw students' attention toward the readers of their pieces. For example, a more formal style would be called for when writing a letter to the principal advocating for a longer recess than would be necessary when writing a note to a friend. Students should also consider the style of pieces they read to determine why the author might have chosen a particular style convention: Did the writer intend to argue a point to a hostile audience? Is the writer trying to inform a group of third graders about the difference between income and expenses? Was the style formal or informal?

When writing expository texts, students should develop an overall **thesis**, or main or controlling idea that guides their writing. Each paragraph should present support for this idea and have its own **topic sentence**, stating the focus of that paragraph. Evidence in each paragraph, such as expert opinions, examples, statistics, and reasons should support the topic sentence.

Practice Question

19. As part of a unit in which students write letters to family members describing what they did in school yesterday, a second grader struggles to begin. What should the teacher recommend?

    A. organizing things the student likes and dislikes about school in a T-chart

B. thinking about the audience and what that person would want to know
C. deciding on a style and voice to convey a degree of formality
D. reviewing the mechanics of forming the greeting and closing of a friendly letter

The Authoring Cycle

Students should understand that writing is a process and that even professional writers go through several phases before their finished product is released. This **authoring cycle** generally includes several phases in which ideas are transformed into written form to effectively communicate meaning. Students first need to **brainstorm** ideas. This can take many forms, and teachers might have the entire class generate ideas for writing topics and record them on the board or screen as an initial step.

Students can then create their own webs or **outlines** to organize their ideas. This initial planning can help students organize their overall point and supporting details. These activities can be based on a book they have read, where they take a stance on the work (e.g., "I liked the book," "I did not like the book," "My favorite/least favorite part was...") and then list the reasons why or why not. Students might also write a simple expository piece in which they introduce an overall topic and then use supporting details to inform the reader. Brainstorming activities can also help students organize the events they wish to recount when writing narratives.

After the brainstorming is complete, students draft their piece and link their ideas together with an introductory statement, support, and concluding section or statement. With scaffolding, students must then go through a **revision** and **editing** process in which they strengthen their piece through the addition of more supporting details and connecting words (*because*, *also*, *then*) and proofread for capitalization, end marks, and spelling.

Students should have practice with both peer revision and self-revision. In **peer revision,** classmates aid in putting a second set of eyes on a text to offer feedback for improvements. Receiving feedback helps reinforce that the overarching purpose of writing is to communicate ideas, so the perceptions and suggestions of multiple readers must be taken into account when revising a piece. In **self-revision,** students revise their own writing. Self-revision can be challenging; one useful strategy is to have students read their pieces aloud to catch potential errors.

Check Your Understanding

What type of rubric or checklist could students use for self and peer revision?

Teachers may aid students in the revision process by providing a simple checklist to help students ensure they have met certain criteria. One simple revision checklist is the **COPS** mnemonic. This stands for **C**apitalization, **O**rganization, **P**unctuation, and **S**pelling and is used with success in many elementary classrooms.

Students should also **publish** their work after the final copy is created, particularly if the writing project was significant in scope. Having students read their work aloud is one simple and immediate way to publish a piece, as is posting it on a classroom or school bulletin board. Teachers may have students organize and bind their work into a simple book with string or brads or collect student work into a class-wide literary sampler.

If a teacher uses student portfolios in the classroom, he or she may have students prepare their piece for inclusion into a digital or physical folder. This may involve transcribing the piece digitally, adding illustrations, or matting it on construction paper. Teachers should also emphasize to students that seminal to the idea of publishing is sharing the work with others. This is a great way to build a home–school connection while encouraging students to share their work with parents. Teachers should also show student work samples or portfolios at parent conferences to further build the home–school connection.

Practice Question

20. Which is a way to publish student writing? Select ALL that apply.
    A. hosting a poetry night where students read their work aloud
    B. holding a parent conference to discuss writing progress
    C. asking students to type their piece on the computer
    D. having students trade a bound book they have created with a friend to read and enjoy

Formal and Informal Assessment

Assessment of English language arts and reading is essential. **Formal assessments** measure student progress using standardized measures. Formal assessments may be oral, written, or computer-based. For example, annual state tests and Wechsler Scales are commonly used formal assessments. Generally, formal assessments are purchased from a publisher who has specified both administration and scoring procedures. An advantage to using a formal test is that a great deal of effort has gone into making sure that it accurately measures what it claims to measure; however, formal assessments are expensive and time-consuming, and therefore are not practical for daily application.

Informal assessments are regularly used to assess classroom performance and drive ELA instruction. Certain teacher-made tests, anecdotal records, portfolio assessments, conferences, and project-based assessments are all examples of informal assessments that may be used in the classroom. Typically, informal assessments are created by teachers or committees of teachers, but have not gone through the rigorous validation processes of formal assessments. Most districts use informal benchmark tests, but provide some degree of standardization in the administration and scoring of the test.

Formal assessments are frequently used to make educational placement decisions and measure the effectiveness of educational programs, while informal tests are used to help districts, schools, and teachers make informed classroom decisions.

Practice Question

21. Which of the following is an example of an informal assessment?
    A. annual state testing
    B. college admissions tests
    C. IQ tests
    D. portfolio assessments

Formative, Summative, and Diagnostic Assessments

Depending on the goal of the assessment instrument, teachers may use formative, summative, or diagnostic assessments. **Diagnostic assessments** are formal or informal assessments given before a learning experience that provide teachers with a baseline of student's skills. Formal diagnostic assessments include Developmental Reading Assessments (DRA), Dynamic Indicator of Basic Early Learning Skills (DIBELS), and Comprehension Attitude Strategies Interests (CASI). Each of these formal diagnostic assessments provide teachers with information about student reading levels; however diagnostic assessments may also be used in other content areas. Informal diagnostic assessments include student self-assessments, anticipation guides, KWL charts, and pre-tests. Anticipation guides ask students questions about the content to spark student interest and activate prior knowledge; they can be used as a diagnostic assessment as they reveal students already know before launching a new unit.

Formative assessments are used throughout the learning experience to help teachers make instructional decisions and to provide feedback to students. Examples of formative assessments include anecdotal records, questioning techniques, and pop quizzes. Generally, formative assessments do not provide quantifiable data, but they are valuable for providing teachers with information to tailor instruction to specific student needs.

Table 1.7. Examples of Formative Assessments	
Assessment Type	**Description**
anecdotal records	notes that teachers keep that indicate student performance according to learning or behavior goals
observation	watching students perform a learning activity to determine strengths and weaknesses so that students may receive targeted remediation
pop quiz	a short, unexpected assessment used to indicate student strengths and weaknesses regarding newly learned material; more useful for giving the teacher and student feedback rather than for grades
ticket out the door (exit ticket)	open-ended questions that students must answer in ending a lesson; provide insight about student strengths and challenges in relation to new learning
think/pair/share	requires students to think about a question related to content and then articulate their answers to a partner, which allows them to practice active listening and learn from one another; serves as a formative assessment when teachers observe discussions and ask partner groups to share their answers
journals/learning logs	allow students to journal their thoughts and questions throughout a learning experience; used by teachers to assess student understanding
discussion	informs the teacher about general understanding of learning topics; requires that care be taken to prevent some students from dominating the conversation as others avoid participation
questioning	helps teachers gain insight into student understanding; requires that care be taken to maintain student engagement by calling on students at random and giving ample think time to the class
signaled responses/choral responses	In a signaled response, a student performs a gesture to answer a question. Gestures could include giving a thumbs up or thumbs down, standing up or sitting down, or walking to a certain corner of the classroom. Signaled responses require everyone to engage on a physical level; however, some students will copy one another rather than thinking independently. In a choral response, everyone in the class gives the answer at the same time. For short answer questions, choral responses can improve student engagement. Students must be explicitly told prior to each learning experience whether the expectation is to raise their hand or call out answers.

Summative assessments may be formal or informal and evaluate student achievement after learning takes place. Standardized state tests are an example of a formal summative assessment. End-of-unit tests and benchmark tests are examples of informal summative assessments. Summative assessments may be used for accountability and grades as they are a measure of student performance in relation to the objectives.

Regardless of type, an assessment will only be accurate if it is aligned with the instructional objectives and learning activities. Therefore, how the teacher will use formative and summative assessments is a crucial part of the planning process that should not be overlooked.

Practice Question

22. A teacher is gathering information about her students at the beginning of the school year to determine their reading levels. She wants to find out what skills they are entering school with. Which assessment tool should she choose?
    A. diagnostic assessment
    B. formative assessment
    C. summative assessment
    D. aptitude test

Norm-Referenced vs. Criterion-Referenced Assessments

Standardized assessments fall into two categories: norm-referenced and criterion-referenced. Norm-referenced assessments measure an individual student against a group of other test takers, typically those of the same age or grade level. Results are reported in a percentile ranking.

Norm-referenced tests are most often used to measure achievement, intelligence, aptitude, and personality. Achievement tests measure what skills a student has mastered. These often fall under categories like reading and mathematics.

Check Your Understanding:

What could a teacher learn about students' developing literacy through observation?

Achievement tests are generally multiple choice and require test takers to answer a standardized set of questions. Popular achievement tests include:

- Iowa Test of Basic Skills (ITBS)
- Peabody Individual Achievement Test
- Wechsler Individual Achievement Test (WIAT-III)
- Stanford Achievement Test

Because norm-referenced tests compare students to one another, the results must be given in a format that makes possible such a comparison. The most common way to do this is the **percentile**. A percentile is a score that shows where a student ranks in comparison to ninety-nine other students. For example, a percentile of 81 would mean that the student in question has performed equal to or outperformed eighty-one out of the other ninety-nine students who took the same test. A percentile of 14 means that the student only performed equal to or outperformed fourteen of the other ninety-nine test takers.

These percentiles are usually determined early in the development of a standardized norm-referenced assessment using an early group of test takers known as a **norming group**. Depending on the assessment instrument, these norming groups may be students in a particular school (school average norms) or district (a local norm group). They may also be students with a particular diagnosed exceptionality or special learning situation (special norm group). More often, they are national norm groups. These groups are carefully selected to be representative of the nation as a whole. One criticism of norm-referenced tests is that national norm groups are not always current and truly representative. Students might be taking a test that has not been recalibrated with a new norming group in some time.

Norm-referenced tests base their percentiles on the bell-shaped curve, also called the normal curve or the normal distribution. Often tests are modified so the results will generate a bell-shaped curve. This distribution of scores has three primary characteristics:

- It is symmetrical from left to right.
- The mean, median, and mode are the same score and are at the center of the symmetrical distribution.
- The percentage within each standard deviation is known.

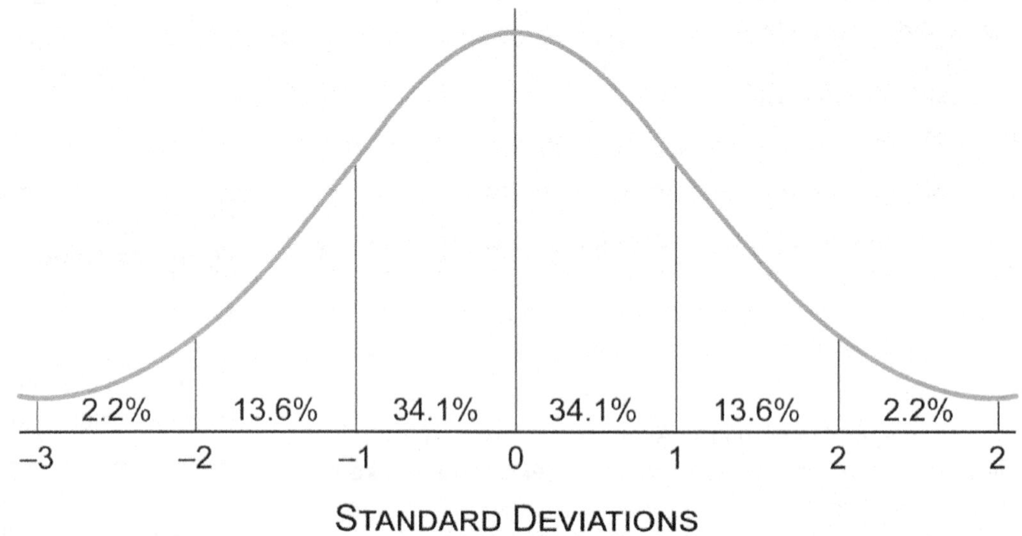

Figure 1.6. Bell-Shaped Curve (normal distribution)

Not all standardized assessment instruments use percentile. There are also **grade-equivalent scores,** which provide a result in a grade level. This means that the student's performance is equal to the median performance corresponding to other students of a certain grade level. For example, if a student scores at a tenth-grade reading level, that would mean their score was the same as the median for all tenth graders who took the test. Some assessment instruments also use an age-equivalent score, which simply compares a student's results to the median score of other students of a certain age.

Criterion-referenced tests measure an individual's performance as it relates to a predetermined benchmark or criteria. These tests are generally used to measure a student's progress toward meeting certain objectives. They do not compare test takers to one another but rather compare student knowledge against the set criteria. Criterion-referenced tests include everything from annual state tests like STAAR to those created by teachers or educational publishers to assess mastery of learning objectives.

One new incarnation of the criterion-referenced test used by many states is **standards-referenced testing** or **standards-based assessment**. These tests measure a student's performance against certain content standards as defined by each grade level and subject. They are typically scored in categories such as basic, proficient, and advanced; or unsatisfactory, satisfactory, and advanced. Most annual state accountability tests such as STAAR, PARCC, and many others are standards-based, criterion-referenced tests.

Practice Question

23. Harvey scores in the 89th percentile on the Stanford Achievement Test, an annual norm-referenced test. What do these results mean?
    A. He got 89 percent of the questions correct.
    B. Eighty-nine percent of students did the same as or better than Harvey did.
    C. Harvey did the same as or better than 89 percent of students.
    D. Harvey did well enough to be part of the norming group.

Emergent Literacy Assessment

Students who are not yet fluent readers will need specific assessment techniques to ensure they are mastering foundational skills that form the building blocks of later reading instruction. Since concepts of print are the first stage of reading development, these skills must be mastered thoroughly. Most of the time, these assessments are informal and might include any of the following:

- asking students to point to the parts of a book (e.g., title, front cover, back)
- presenting students with a book and observing as they interact with it
- asking students to point to a word, sentence, or picture

As students progress to developing phonetic awareness or overall phonemic awareness, assessment is also conducted in a highly interactive manner. Students might be asked to clap out sounds or words, think of rhyming words, repeat words or sounds, and so on.

Once students begin to work on letter recognition and sound-symbol knowledge, a letter chart or letter-sound chart can be used as assessment tools. Students can cross off each letter or letter sound once it is mastered. The same assessment method with a chart or list can be used for sight words (often with a Dolch word list), consonant blends, digraphs, diphthongs, and other challenging sounds.

There is an important distinction between children's ability to sing the alphabet song or point to and say letters or sounds in order (which many master quite early) and the different (though related) skill of letter and letter-sound recognition in isolation. For this reason, it is a good idea to always assess phonics skills in different contexts. For example, students can be asked to point to certain letters or sounds (/b/, /ch/, /i/) in a book or story. This type of **embedded phonics** assessment ensures that students can transfer knowledge and apply it in connected texts.

In addition to more structured assessment methods like charts and lists, phonics skills can be assessed through any number of hands-on activities. Students can play with letter/sound cards or magnets and form or dissect words. Students can match up cards with different rimes and onsets or different target consonant or vowel sounds.

In assessing decoding, or the ability to sound out a word and glean meaning, an oral assessment approach continues to be the gold standard. There are many assessment tools designed specifically to aid in assessing such skills, including the popular **Quick Phonics Screener**, which assesses a student's ability to read a variety of sounds and words.

When assessing decoding skills, it is important to note student strengths and weaknesses. But teachers must also develop a general idea of the student's overall approach and "word-attack skills," or methods of decoding unfamiliar words. Attention to how students approach any oral reading task can provide significant information on strategies they are already using, as well as those they do not use but might find beneficial. Though the age of the student certainly comes into play, sometimes older students still mastering decoding might be able to verbalize the way they approach such challenging words. Questions posed to the student about strategy or method can also yield valuable information.

In addition to these methods, there are also several published assessment instruments for pre-readers and emerging readers:

- Letter knowledge and phonemic awareness can be assessed using the **Dynamic Indicators of Basic Early Literacy Skills (DIBELS)** and the **Early Reading Diagnostic Assessment (ERDA)**.
- The **Comprehensive Test of Phonological Processing (CTOPP)** and **Phonological Awareness Test (PAT)** can also be used as instruments to assess phonemic awareness.
- Other instruments that assess early reading skills include the **Texas Primary Reading Inventory (TPRI), Test of Word Reading Efficiency (TOWRE)**, and even the kindergarten version of the **Iowa Test of Basic Skills (ITSB)**.

Regardless of the assessment instruments used, assessing emerging readers can be challenging since young children often find assessment scenarios intimidating. Any single assessment only provides part of the full picture. The fullest picture of a student's pre-reading development can best be gleaned through observation and input from both parents and teachers. Portfolios, observational records, checklists, and other informal assessment methods can provide much insight into the development of emergent readers.

Practice Question

24. A kindergarten teacher who wants to assess student mastery of phoneme blending would most likely

A. ask students to add affixes to various root words.
B. have students match up cards with onsets and rimes and say each word.
C. ask students to remove a letter from a word, add a new one, and read the new word.
D. have students point to items in the classroom that begin with a certain letter sound.

Literacy Assessment

Assessing each student in an individual oral context is not always possible. This can make assessing reading skills and metacognitive reading strategies a challenge. Further, it is often hard to fully assess any one student's individual thought process. With these caveats, assessing reading skills and strategies with an eye for gaps that might be addressed through intervention is an important task.

Word-attack skills can be assessed through observation and oral reading. Teachers should take note of what happens when students encounter words they do not know. Do they immediately ask for help? Skip over the word? Reread the word? Slow down? Speed up? Assessing word-attack skills relies on observation of students as they read aloud but also on the assessment of underlying skills that lead to a strong word-attack tool kit. Do students make use of all text features and graphic elements? Do they sound out the word or make inferences based on roots and affixes? Do they use context clues?

Helpful Hint

Asking comprehension questions after listening to students read is a simple, effective way to monitor oral comprehension.

Assessment of vocabulary typically happens in the context of breadth (the number of words one knows) or depth (the ability to use the vocabulary in varied and nuanced ways). It also happens in the context of an isolated assessment (a vocabulary test) or as an embedded assessment as an adjunct to another assessment, such as one of reading comprehension or oral fluency.

Such assessments can also be context-independent: "What does *contortion* mean?" or context-dependent: "What does the word *contort* mean in the following sentence?" Educators should consider what "bank" they will draw vocabulary from in order to assess students. Typically, teachers assess vocabulary students will need to comprehend the language of classroom instruction, the textbook, and any literature the class will read. Reference materials such as the *Children's Writer's Word Book* and the *EDL Core Vocabularies* define "target" words per grade level. Published standardized vocabulary instruments such as the classic **Peabody Picture Vocabulary Test (PPT)**, which requires no reading or writing, can also be used to assess individual students.

Assessing oral fluency is generally done by assessing reading accuracy, prosody, and automaticity. This can be tracked in numerous ways. Teachers may keep **running records** that track accuracy, self-correction, and use of fix-up strategies and word attack skills. Running records use forms so teachers can mark errors, self-corrections, and how students use cues to make meaning of texts. These forms are filled out as the student reads the same text the teacher has.

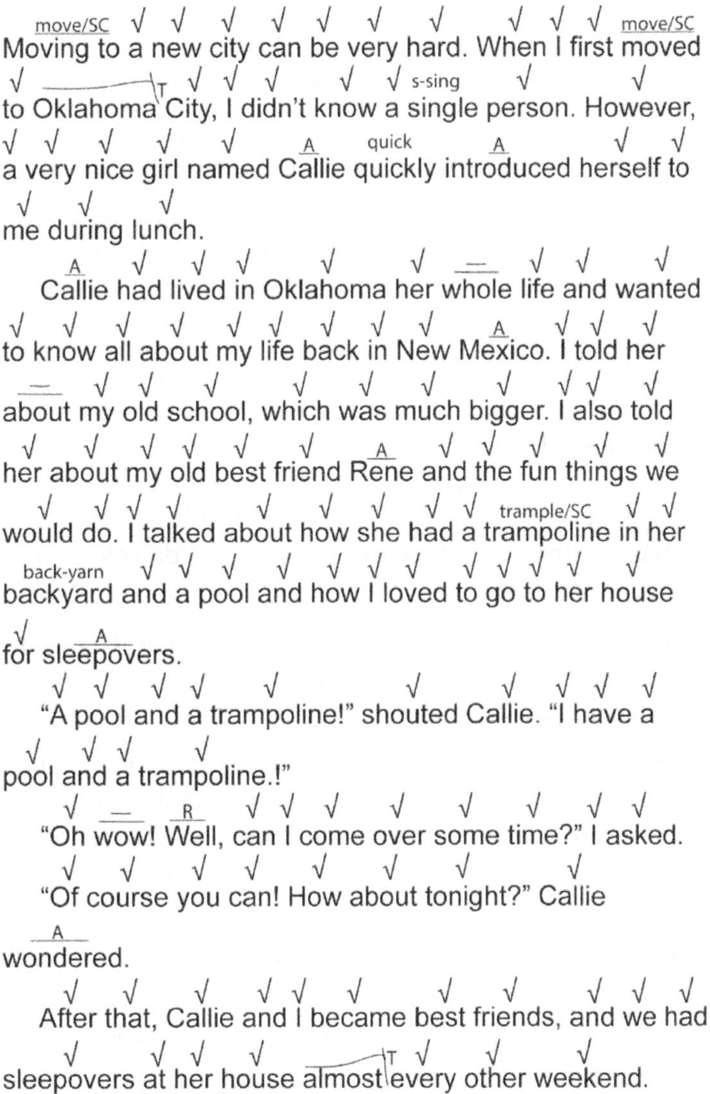

Figure 1.7. Running Record

Students can also be measured for oral reading skills using various fluency norms charts that indicate average words read correctly per minute per grade. While several standard measures exist, one of the most researched is the **Hasbrouck-Tindal oral reading fluency chart**. This chart measures progress over the course of the school year and from grade to grade. It compares students in percentiles with their peers on a scale of words read correctly per minute.

Table 1.8. Hasbrouck-Tindal Oral Reading Fluency Chart			
	Words Correct Per Minute (50th percentile)		
Grade	**Fall**	**Winter**	**Spring**
1	---	29	60
2	50	84	100
3	83	97	112
4	94	120	133
5	121	133	146
6	132	145	146

Comprehension while reading silently can be assessed through **cloze exercises**. In these exercises, words are removed from the text and students must fill them in. There are other written exercises aimed at determining level of comprehension. Some students might struggle to answer written questions. Therefore, a full assessment of silent reading comprehension should include an oral component as well.

As previously mentioned, one of the most common assessments is the Informal Reading Inventory (IRI). There are multiple versions created by various entities. One of the more popular versions is **Pearson's Qualitative Reading Inventory (QRI)**. These assessments include oral reading of word lists that assess accuracy of word identification. The QRI also contains passages and questions that assess both oral and silent reading comprehension. Standardized norm-referenced test batteries such as the Iowa Test of Basic Skills and Stanford Achievement Test, as well as several criterion-referenced tests such as the STAAR, also test reading comprehension.

Aside from standardized, published instruments, teachers often use **curriculum-based assessments** (CBA). These assessments compare what students know versus what has been taught. Any ongoing assessments based on curriculum, such as spelling or vocabulary tests, are forms of CBA.

Comprehension assessment does not require a lengthy formal written test. Simply asking students to recount or retell a story they have read or to recall the most important or interesting parts of a text can provide valuable data. Further, self-assessment should be ongoing and explicitly taught to all readers to monitor comprehension. As students self-assess, they can apply fix-up or fix-it-up strategies as needed when comprehension breaks down.

Both **writing** and **reading** journals are also used in language arts assessment. Writing journals typically give students the opportunity to practice writing without evaluation. Teachers can direct students to utilize a new skill in their journal entry or engage in a timed or untimed **freewrite,** an unstructured writing period designed to increase students' fluency and comfort with writing. Reading journals allow students to respond to a specific book or text by recording their questions and analysis. The teacher may supply specific prompts or allow students to choose their own topics. This can be a very useful tool in helping students prepare for a book talk.

Helpful Hint

Rubrics are usually categorized as either holistic or analytic. Holistic rubrics involve only one category and provide an overall score. Analytic rubrics assess work across multiple categories that are then added together to comprise the total score.

Reflective journal entries can be very helpful when the teacher is trying to assess a student's overall comfort with the content, the student's ability to make connections, or identify multiple areas of misunderstanding. Reflective journal entries should have a guiding question. This can change from lesson to lesson or be a consistent question used each time the students journal, like "What content do you feel confident about?" "What content do you have questions about?" or "How does this relate to one other thing we have studied previously in this unit (or a past unit)?" Changing the question each time allows for more directed assessment based on the specific content of the unit. Furthermore, keeping a consistent question allows the teacher to assess growth in students' reflective abilities.

Grading more formal written work like essays or reports often relies on a rubric. **Rubrics** are fixed scales that measure performance, offering detailed descriptions of criteria that define each level of performance. Rubrics set the expectations of an assignment, thereby clarifying the standards of quality work and improving consistency and reliability in evaluations.

Practice Question

25. A reading teacher asks her sixth-grade students to skim the text and turn the bold paragraph headings into questions. After the students have read the text silently, the teacher asks them to write answers to each of the questions. What skill is the teacher assessing?

A. identifying tone
B. recalling main ideas
C. activating background knowledge
D. making inferences

Using Assessment Data

Data from reading assessments can be used in many ways. In schools using a **Response to Intervention (RTI)** framework, all students should be screened for reading proficiency early and often. Ongoing assessment (progress monitoring) should be implemented as reading interventions occur.

In an RTI framework, **universal screenings** may occur with any number of assessment tools to determine which students would benefit from interventions. The data will then be used to determine goals for students identified as "at risk" of not meeting reading objectives. These students will typically receive early intervening services (Tier 2 intervention) through many possible avenues, though small-group reading instruction is the most common.

As these Tier 2 interventions occur, educators will continue to monitor progress and use assessment data to determine if the student is responding or needs more intensive intervention (Tier 3. This type of intervention is usually in a smaller group and of a greater frequency and longer duration. Assessment data is also used for the following:

- to differentiate instruction for all students (Tier 1 interventions), including but not limited to
  - assessing the independent, instructional, and frustration reading levels for each student and selecting appropriate texts;
  - providing scaffolds and supports for individual students per the principles of the Universal Design for Learning; and
  - using data for flexible grouping strategies that group students by skill level for optimal instruction but constantly reassess and adapt based on student progress
- to plan and conduct small-group interventions (Tier 2 or Tier 3. by
  - assessing skill gaps where students need additional instruction or practice, and

- grouping students for interventions based on similar instructional goals/learning needs (keeping in mind principles of flexible grouping)

> **Think About It**
>
> What are the limits to different types of assessment data? Why should multiple data sources be used?

Assessment data can and should also be used on a macro level to make improvements to instruction and support teachers across the content areas. Administrators and support staff might use reading assessment data in a variety of contexts, such as

- determining individual classrooms/grade levels that might need additional support;
- determining grade-level or school-wide curricular needs;
- determining efficacy of classroom/grade-level or school-wide curricular or intervention approaches;
- designing intervention approaches or teacher support systems on a school-wide level;
- recognizing trends across grade levels (e.g., students are not adequately prepared for instruction on spelling words with *r*-controlled vowels at the beginning of second grade);
- providing planning or instructional recommendations to teachers;
- identifying teachers or classrooms to serve as mentors; and
- planning topics for professional development events.

Assessment data should also be used as a point of communication with parents and families. This builds a home-school connection and keeps parents informed about their child's progress. Some best practices include the following:

- Communicate frequently about student progress. No one likes to be "suddenly" informed of a problem that was ongoing for some time.
- Help parents understand assessment results and what the data will be used for.
- Explain that an assessment is a snapshot in time and only one part of the overall picture of a student's learning situation.
- Provide concrete actions that can be taken for improvement.
- Make data available to parents in different ways. For example, do not merely review score reports at conferences—have work exemplars, portfolios, or other sources as well.
- Recognize that parents are also an informal source of assessment data. They can provide valuable insight into home study habits.
- Meet parental needs, including language needs or time constraints.

Practice Question

26. After reviewing the data from annual standards-based assessments, a teacher sees that results show most third- -grade students are struggling with the meaning of homographs. Which area of instruction would be most helpful?

A. roots and affixes
B. graphophonic cues
C. context clues
D. analogy-based phonics

Research and Media Skills

The Research Process

Research and library skills are an important part of developing overall student literacy. Generally, there are seven steps in the research process:

1. **Focusing on the topic and planning**. This might be as simple as having students pick a topic they want to learn more about or developing a **research question** they wish to answer. For large projects, students should also develop a **research plan** or **research timeline**. Such a document lays out what will be done and when. This helps students stay on track to complete a task that may seem large or overwhelming at first.

2. **Finding background information and conducting a preliminary search**. This involves getting a general overview of a topic and possible subtopics. During this stage students may Google a topic or read the *Wikipedia* page devoted to a particular topic.

3. **Locating materials**. This could involve working at the library and searching online. Teachers should encourage students to explore a wide variety of possible resources. As appropriate per the research topic, students should also be encouraged to seek out **primary sources,** or firsthand accounts. Primary sources may be speeches or diaries, surveys or census data, photographs of an event, and several other media that give eyewitness accounts of an event. Many primary sources are available online, and many sites organize these sources into an accessible format for students. Of course, many materials that students find will also be **secondary sources,** or non-firsthand accounts. These include the majority of books, articles, and web pages devoted to a topic.

4. **Evaluating sources**. Students need to determine if certain sources are useful and accessible to them. For example, a library database may generate results for articles in publications to which the library does not have a subscription. Some resources may be inaccessible to students as they may be overly technical or written for an older audience. Students should also make sure they have **credible sources** written by experts. This stage in the research process might be a good time to introduce the different types of information available on the internet and the qualities that help increase reliability (listed author, .edu or .org domain, publication date, etc.).

5. **Understanding information and note taking**. Students must first comprehend the information they find. Such information may not always be in narrative text. **Graphs and charts** that contain numerical information can be very useful sources for research projects. Students can be instructed in extracting information from these resources by

- looking at the title of the graph or chart;
- identifying what is being measured;
- identifying the units used;
- understanding colors or shading;
- understanding what is shown in different parts of the chart or graph (e.g., column headings, totals, *x*-and *y*-axes);
- identifying trends or major takeaways; and
- drawing conclusions about what the graph or chart shows.

After information is comprehended, students should take notes. Note taking may involve the use of formal note cards or simply jotting down main ideas. As developmentally appropriate per student age, teachers should ensure students understand the idea of **paraphrasing,** or changing the author's words into their own, as they take notes. Paraphrasing can help students prevent **plagiarizing**, or presenting someone else's words as their own work.

6. **Writing**. This includes organizing all the notes into sentences and paragraphs. Students need to be cognizant of the overall organization of their work as they introduce a focused topic, provide support, and write a conclusion. Depending on the age group with which teachers work, they may have students make a poster or use another outlet to present their research instead of a formal paper.

7. **Citing sources**. This may include in-text **citations** and preparing a bibliography. To simplify these elements for young students, teachers might use a simpler works cited/bibliography page where students simply list titles of books and authors. Students in the upper elementary grades may work to develop more sophisticated bibliographies in MLA style, as it is generally regarded as the simplest citation style and the one to which students are first introduced.

Of course, these steps may be greatly simplified for very young students and per the scope of the research project. However, even kindergartners can gather information from sources to answer a simple research question, and first-grade students can contribute to a simple class-wide research project with teacher support. The key is introducing students to the various parts of the research process while providing scaffolding as needed to support students as they explore new outlets for their developing literacy.

Did You Know?

Microsoft Word has tools that help users manage citations and bibliographies. These features are available under the "References" tab.

Practice Question

27. During a unit on flags, a kindergarten class asks many questions about flags from other states and countries. Which research activity would be most appropriate for the teacher to plan for her students to further explore flags?

A. direct them to conduct an online search for three primary sources on flags
B. take them to the library and have them use the database to find flag-related articles
C. have them write a paper on state flags citing two secondary sources
D. help students find pictures of different flags online and talk about the design of each

Digital Tools

Increasingly, schools are incorporating digital learning tools into their curriculum. Many schools have one or more subscriptions to various educational technology platforms that may enhance student learning and **digital literacy**, which is defined as the ability to find, use, and create digital information.

Some students may have extensive experiences with accessing digital information at home through previous use of computers, tablets, or phones. However, a similar level of digital literacy among students cannot be assumed, and students should be given instruction in how to use **digital tools** in the classroom.

Digital tools also provide an excellent way to differentiate literacy instruction through the use of adaptive software programs that target practice for each student's current skill level. Technological tools can also aid students with special needs or limited English proficiency as they navigate the day-to-day activities in the classroom. Devices and applications such as those that allow nonverbal children to communicate and those that help English language learners quickly translate new words may become indispensable learning aids.

Teachers should also incorporate digital tools into the writing process as appropriate. This may include the use of word processing or presentation software to aid in student drafting and revising and even perhaps the use of digital storytelling sites, which help students create and publish visual stories. The classroom or school may even have a website or social media page for publishing student-created content. Before publishing any student work online, however, always check with administration and secure necessary parental consent.

As students use visual tools to find information and create messages to communicate with others, they should be instructed on the different levels of formality associated with different platforms. For example, a news article or an academic website will be more formal than a blog or email to a friend.

Digital tools can also be used to increase the home-school connection. Many textbooks and EdTech programs offer home log-ins. School libraries may offer eBooks to check out to read at home in addition to print texts. Various educational technology publishers offer parent dashboards to help parents stay informed on student progress. The key is making sure parents understand how to interpret this information.

Practice Question

28. A fourth-grade teacher wants students to learn to search for information digitally. Which activity is most appropriate?
    A. ask students to find multiple websites about the same topic
    B. ask students to look up definitions for content-area words in a digital dictionary
    C. give students a list of questions and have them find the answers online
    D. give students the name of a famous person and ask them to find pictures of that individual

Understanding Media

Media has rapidly evolved over the last century. **Radio** was once the primary media outlet for news and entertainment. Although it is still used, its popularity has been supplanted by other types of media as technology has become more advanced. **Movies** became popular with the invention of film in the early twentieth century. **Television** became a mainstream product in the 1950s, bringing broadcast media into people's homes. The **internet**, which became popular in the late 1990s and early 2000s, quickly led to the creation of many new genres of media, including podcasts, social media, and video/music streaming. Today, media is usually categorized into four types:

- **print media** (physical magazines and newspapers)
- **broadcast media** (film, TV, and radio)
- **outdoor media** (billboards and banners)
- **digital media** (websites, social media, and podcasts)

Media—regardless of the type—will always influence society, and some of these influences are negative. For example, media can allow people to easily disseminate false information and spread harmful stereotypes or biases. It can also desensitize people to violence and suffering through repeated exposure.

However, not all of the impacts of media are negative. The internet can spread information much more quickly than other types of media and allows people from all over the world to collaborate. It also gives people access to news that was not traditionally available through radio, newspapers, or television. The internet can be particularly useful to populations who historically have not been able to produce traditional broadcast media.

Media is also the primary way through which businesses advertise their products or services. **Advertisements** are found in all types of media, and are often the main way that media content is funded. For example, ads may be shown before or during streaming videos, and news websites usually sell ad space to raise revenue.

Helpful Hint

Advances in technology have allowed businesses to target very specific groups of customers. As part of a media literacy program, students can study how their online habits shape the types of ads they see.

In many types of media, the line between ads and content can become blurred. This is especially true for digital media, wherein **sponsored content**—ads paid for by businesses—might be integrated into social media accounts or websites. As part of media literacy, students should be taught how to identify ads or sponsored content in all types of media.

Practice Question

29. Which of the following is an example of broadcast media?
    A. a social media account
    B. a newspaper
    C. a radio show
    D. a billboard

Analyzing Media

Media literacy is the ability to find and effectively analyze media content. All types of media—from magazines to movies to podcasts—can be analyzed in much the same way as traditional texts. Students should learn to assess both the content and context of the media they consume. Import aspects of media analysis include

- the message or main idea of the content,
- the intent or purpose of the people who produce the content,
- the effect the media has on the audience, and
- the techniques used to produce this effect.

Teachers often begin the process of analyzing media by explaining to students that no media is completely neutral: every piece has a **message**. Students should be able to identify the key information communicated in a piece of media and understand how it builds the message.

To place media's message in the proper context, students must look for the **intent** of its producers—who made this piece of media and why? Every piece of media has a purpose. Like informational texts, media can inform, persuade, or entertain.

To identify the purpose of a piece of media, students should first identify the person or organization behind it. Knowing this information allows students to assess the producer's **bias** so they can evaluate the strength of the content. Asking the following types of questions can help students determine bias:

Helpful Hint

As part of a media literacy program, students should learn how advertising drives content in digital media. Often, the intent of producers is simply to attract viewers and raise ad revenue.

- Is the producer a person or company with a vested interest in the subject matter?
- Are the producers experts in their fields, or do they have any professional qualifications?
- Is the producer a magazine or news organization with a known political bias?
- How are the producers funded and how might this affect their biases?

Once the creator is identified, the intent of the media can be analyzed. For example, if a notable scientific study is being covered in media, the intent of the media creator will determine how that study is presented:

- The university that did the study may promote it with an upbeat article on its website.
- A news site may drive traffic to its site by focusing on sensationalized aspects of the study.
- A company may use the study to advertise their own products.
- Social media accounts may use the study to promote a specific political agenda.

Media can have many different **effects** on the consumer and can affect an individual's knowledge, attitudes, beliefs, and behaviors. These effects might change the way an individual thinks or behaves or reinforce existing beliefs and behaviors.

To help students develop skills in evaluating various types of media, they should be exposed to multiple sources of information and learn how to compare and contrast them. For example, an informational article or podcast could be compared to a documentary film on the same topic. Similarly, advertisements across various platforms like radio, print, and film—both past and present—could be compared to identify techniques used and how those impact the viewer, reader, or listener.

Along with comparing media representations of various topics, students should be taught to confirm facts from a variety of sources and spot examples of media messages that contain lies or claims that cannot be verified through other sources. Again, the availability of technology can be a help. For example, in the past, the public often had to rely on word of mouth to confirm the claims of advertisers about a product or service; now, online reviews can reveal much and help consumers make informed purchases.

Helpful Hint

Propaganda is communication designed to influence public opinion, often through partial truths—or even total falsehoods. Students should learn to identify propaganda.

Practice Question

30. A fifth-grade teacher wants to design an activity to help students confirm the accuracy of information in a YouTube video about a historical topic. Which activity is most appropriate?

A. having students compare the information in the video to multiple photographs covering the same topic
B. assigning students the task of creating their own videos on the same topic
C. encouraging students to use the information in the video to create a multimedia presentation on the same topic
D. asking students to compare the information in the video with that in multiple print sources

Creating Media

The use of varied media often makes a message clearer and more engaging. Students will likely work on media projects such as presentations, videos, posters, charts, graphs, and audio recordings. Often, these types of projects promote curricular integration as students use media skills to analyze and present information across content areas.

Teachers should help students learn to create high-quality and engaging multimedia projects. Effective presentations should

- contain an appropriate balance of media elements;
- use sound, images, and video aligned with the overall message of the presentation;

- offer opportunities for audience participation, if possible; and
- be aligned with the project purpose and audience.

Students should strive to use media in their work for a specific purpose—often to elaborate on a point or help the audience visualize something. The use of media elements as "decoration" or "fluff" is generally not a best practice. Students should therefore be taught to recognize and evaluate effective presentations, both those they make themselves and those made by others. Rubrics customized for specific types of media can be very helpful for both teacher and student evaluation of media.

With the increased use of media comes more responsibility. Students should use appropriate online etiquette and must learn to navigate fair use issues in the digital space.

Students creating and posting media must follow basic **netiquette** protocols, meaning they should use a communication style appropriate to the online environment. Most schools and districts have netiquette policies, which might include

- keeping the people behind digital communications in mind at all times;
- remembering that nothing posted online is private or temporary;
- using an appropriate tone for the audience;
- maintaining the privacy and confidentiality of others;
- avoiding the use of all caps, emojis, or slang.

When creating media, students must also learn how to correctly use and cite media sources. **Copyright** is the legal ownership of a work of art. Copyrighted works can only be reproduced or repurposed under specific conditions.

Fair use refers to the legal use of **copyrighted** work without the permissions of the rights-holder in certain circumstances. Fair use doctrine follows four main guidelines:

1. Purpose and character of use: Education and nonprofit use of copyrighted works is usually permitted. Works that are transformative—meaning they add something substantially new—are also usually able to use copyrighted materials.

2. Nature of the work: Personal, creative works of art are less likely to be considered for fair use.

3. Amount and substantiality of the work: Using small portions of copyrighted works is often permitted.

4. Effect of the use on the market for copyrighted material: Reproduction of copyrighted materials that substantially affects the ability of the original creators to market their products is not allowed.

Helpful Hint

Types of art that CAN be copyrighted include written works, painting, photographs, musical compositions, movies, and sound recordings. Things that CANNOT be copyrighted include recipes/formulas, ideas, slogans, and common knowledge.

Classroom use of copyrighted content often falls under fair use guidelines because it is for educational purposes; however, the principles of fair use must still be considered. For example, it may be appropriate for students to use properly cited images in a slide presentation given to the class. It would not, however, be appropriate for students to use those copyrighted images on their personal websites without the copyright-holder's permission. In these cases, the material has two different purposes: one is a limited educational setting; the other is the broad online dissemination of someone else's work.

Of course, not all media is copyrighted. Work that is in the **public domain** is free for use because its copyright has expired, was forfeited, or never existed. Students can be directed to sites that offer photos and images in the public domain.

Additionally, some work falls under a **Creative Commons** license. Creative Commons (CC) is a nonprofit that helps content creators designate how their work may be used. All CC content must be attributed to its creator. Further, there are multiple types of CC licenses that dictate how the work may be used. Some require that the content only be used for noncommercial purposes or that it only be reused if the new work will also fall under a Creative Commons license.

Students and teachers should also be aware of liability before using images or videos featuring other students. Schools and districts will typically have a media release policy and associated forms that parents must sign. Without such documentation, photos and videos of students should not be posted on any online platforms, including class websites or social media pages.

Practice Question

31. A teacher assigns an activity wherein student groups create a website highlighting the life and work of a well-known author of the past. What should the teacher advise students before they begin?

    A. They can use any type of media on the site because it is for educational purposes and thus falls under fair use.

    B. They should avoid the use of any images on their website because of the risk of copyright infringement.

    C. They should seek out image sources that are in the public domain or that have certain types of CC licenses.

    D. They can use most types of media on the site but should provide links to the original sources for proper citation.

Answer Key

1. C: Pragmatics refers to the social uses of language. Addressing the teacher by her name is part of the social function of language as it is used in a social interaction.

2. D: In the holophrastic stage, children use one word to denote a broader desire or meaning. This is the stage after babbling.

3. B: This is a core part of active listening and can help kindergarten students focus on a speaker. The other activities are not a part of active listening.

4. D: The student says "smarting" instead of "smart," showing that the forms of words, or their morphology, might need further refinement.

5. C: The strategy of phoneme segmentation requires students to separate the phonemes in a word.

6. A: The word *elephant* can be decoded using phonics strategies.

7. D: This would give students practice reading expressively.

8. C: Experts concur that by the end of third grade, students should make the shift from the transitional to the intermediate stage of literacy development.

9. B: Folktales are often old stories passed down in a specific culture.

10. C: This is a qualitative feature of the text. The others are all quantitative measures.

11. A: The theme refers to the general, overarching message about life that is presented in a text.

12. C: The phrase "look just like photographs" explains what realism means and is thus the best strategy.

13. B: The student is still young and most likely has not yet developed the fine motor skills to hold a pencil and form letters for sustained periods of time.

14. A: The pattern is *g* (consonant) *a* (vowel) *p* (consonant).

15. B: The word *from* is a preposition.

16. A: Because adjectives modify nouns and adverbs modify verbs, adjectives, or other adverbs, this is a foundational understanding that must precede a discussion of when an adjective or adverb is most appropriate. The other choices are not relevant to adjective versus adverb use.

17. B: To be possessive, *Fred's* requires an apostrophe before the *s*. *Christmas* needs a colon to indicate the upcoming list, and *car and condo* should be followed by commas since they are items in a series.

18. B: Two independent clauses are joined with a comma and the coordinating conjunction *but*.

19. B: Determining the audience and purpose is the first phase of any writing assignment.

20. A, D: Publishing involves sharing work with others; hosting a poetry night where students read their work aloud and having students trade a bound book they have created with a friend to read and enjoy both involve sharing work with others.

21. D: Portfolio assessments are informal tests that are used by teachers to make instructional decisions.

22. A: Diagnostic assessments pre-test students before a learning experience.

23. C: Harvey's score was equal to or better than 89 percent of students to whom he is being compared.

24. B: When students say the onset and rime together, they are blending both phonemes together.

25. B: The paragraph headings and the questions generated from them are clues to the main idea of each paragraph. Asking students to answer the questions requires them to recall **main ideas from the text.**

26. C: The context of the sentence in which the homograph is written will clue its meaning. Instruction in looking for context clues will aid students in determining the meaning of these types of multiple-meaning words.

27. D: This activity scaffolds students learning and helps them begin to develop research skills. The other activities are not developmentally appropriate for a kindergarten class.

28. C: This would help students create and use search terms and locate information online.

29. C: A radio show is broadcast in real time to listeners.

30. D: Comparing sources of information is a good way to confirm the accuracy of information.

31. C: Public domain and certain types of Creative Commons (CC) licenses allow use without permissions.

2 Mathematics

Mathematics Foundations

Math Past and Present

Humans have long had an interest in math. Prehistoric people likely understood patterns in nature and began to understand and distinguish between one and many. They then began to count, or tally, as evidenced by marks carved in stone. As early as 3000 BCE, the Sumerians began using counting and measuring for practical purposes; however, the Babylonians who followed them invented a more complex number system and even understood and used fractions and basic algebra, likely for commerce and taxation.

The Egyptians, who discovered the world's first paper, wrote math texts on papyrus, some of which date to around 1800 BCE. The Egyptians used a system akin—and most likely the precursor to—Roman numerals, where symbols stood for base units. By 1200 BCE, the Chinese had developed a true decimal system, including the concept of place value. The Egyptians are also believed to have discovered the quadratic formula.

The Greeks made giant strides in geometry between roughly 600 – 200 BCE, including the work of Pythagoras, Hippocrates, Hippasus, Euclid, and Archimedes. The Salamis Tablet, a counting board made of marble, is one of the first mathematical tools and dates to 300 BCE. By 36 BCE, the Mayans had likely developed the idea of zero.

During the early common era (CE), Indians, Chinese, and Greek scholars continued to make advancements in algebra, calculus, and trigonometry. By 780 – 850 CE, Persians, who used Indian numerals, began to lay the foundation for what we think of as modern algebra, including the concepts of balancing and reduction.

More recent history has brought numerous breakthroughs, including the development of Cartesian math by René Descartes and Newton's discovery of computing functional roots in the seventeenth century. Notable scholars of the twentieth century include German female scientists Emmy Noether, who in 1915 proved the symmetry theorem, and Alan Turing, whose 1936 Turing machine could perform calculations using an input/output device, a memory center, and a central processing unit.

> **Did You Know?**
>
> The median salary of an actuary is over $100,000 per year.

Today, professional mathematicians are still learning and developing new theories and ideas. People with math skills are in high demand in computer-related fields, engineering, finance, and management. In addition, actuaries—those who assess mathematical risk for insurance companies—tend to be people who majored in some type of math field. The government also employs math experts in the armed forces, the National Security Agency (NSA), and National Aeronautics and Space Administration (NASA). In fact, the NSA is the largest employer in the world of individuals with a degree in math.

Practice Question

1. Which of the following statements describes how the Egyptians wrote numbers?
   A. They used the Indian number system.
   B. They used a system similar to Roman numerals.
   C. They wrote numbers in words using Greek.
   D. They wrote numbers as decimals.

Mathematics Instruction

Teaching math requires knowledge of research, or evidence-based math instructional techniques, some of which are described in this section.

Explicit, Systematic Instruction

Systematic math instruction involves a step-by-step process of **modeling**. One such type of modeling is a **think-aloud**, where the teacher describes his thought process while solving an example problem. After the demonstration, the teacher should offer **guided practice**, where the students and teacher work on a problem together. This should be followed by **independent practice**, where students work alone or with other students to solve a problem. The teacher should then assess understanding and offer feedback and clarification as needed.

Visual Representations

These are sometimes called *schematic diagrams* or *representations*; they are visual tools. They include fraction strips, models, or multiplication arrays that help students correctly solve problems. Research suggests that these tools lead to greater accuracy in problem solving, especially for young students still developing procedural knowledge.

Word Problem Instruction

This involves helping students understand math vocabulary and how to translate problems into algorithms or visual representations.

Cognitive Strategies

Students should be taught to plan or **decide** how to approach a problem, and then select an appropriate strategy from their existing knowledge base. As they work, they should **monitor** how things are going and employ estimation or rounding skills to see if their answers make sense. If their approach is not working, they should **modify** it accordingly.

Talking about Math

Another research-based strategy is to discuss multiple ways of solving a problem and comparing different approaches and perhaps even different answers. This helps students further develop their overall math understanding, including recognizing errors made by others.

Using a CRA Methodology

CRA stands for <u>C</u>oncrete-<u>R</u>epresentational-<u>A</u>bstract. In the first phase, students learn a math concept through the **concrete,** meaning that students and teachers first use tangible materials or **manipulatives**. For example, the class might use an abacus, counting chips, or base ten blocks. In the **representational** stage, the concrete is transformed to the pictorial. During this stage, teachers and students might draw pictures or use dots or tallies. During the **abstract**, or symbolic stage, numbers and standard algorithms are used.

Explore before Explain

In this technique, students are first introduced to a concept with a real-life scenario, such as figuring out the number of blocks needed to build a fence around a classroom desk. After students practice with different ideas, the concept of perimeter can be introduced, explained, and practiced.

Technology to Enhance (Not Replace)

Technology can be particularly useful in classrooms with students who are at various points in their math journeys as well as students with varying levels of English language proficiency. In balanced math instruction, tech tools can help students extend understanding and think about problems with greater depth of thought. Technology, however, should not replace computational capabilities.

At times, math teaching will involve both whole-group, small-group, and even individual help or instruction. Using small-group instruction can be particularly useful when some students are in need of reteaching while others may be ready to explore more with an extension activity.

High-quality math teaching involves frequent assessments, including both ongoing formative assessments and summative assessments at the end of units or after teaching concepts. While written assessments are common, other tools can also be used:

- Individual student whiteboards can show each student's answer to a problem.
- One-problem exit tickets at the end of a class can easily determine students who have successfully grasped a concept and those who may need reteaching.
- Short interactive quizzes via Google Forms, Kahoot, or other platforms can also quickly identify a student's level of understanding.
- Reflection journals or notes can be useful in encouraging students to employ metacognitive strategies and monitor their own learning.

English language learners (ELLs) will also benefit from specific and targeted instructional strategies, particularly when working with word problems. To help these students, math vocabulary should be taught explicitly, math banks or glossaries should be provided, and sentence frames should be used as needed to help students break down word problems. Manipulatives can also be very useful with ELLs as can simplified assessment strategies that limit the need for students to provide long oral explanations. For example, instead of asking "How did you solve that problem?" students could be asked, "Did you add or subtract first?"

Effective math teachers are also aware of common student mistakes and misconceptions. Some common misconceptions include the following:

- adding instead of subtracting (after subtraction is first introduced)
- believing that subtraction is commutative
- believing subtraction should always be from the "bigger number," which creates a problem when subtracting two or three-digit numbers with regrouping
- believing that 0.10 is more than 0.4
- believing that multiplication always makes numbers bigger, which is not true of decimals and fractions
- believing that division should aways be dividing the larger number by the smaller number, which creates a problem when working with fractions

- thinking any multiplication by 10 involves simply "adding a 0," which is not true with decimals

Practice Question

2. When teaching students subtraction, which of the following represents the concrete stage?
   A. The teacher draws three circles and crosses one out.
   B. The teacher holds three blocks and takes one away.
   C. The teacher writes "$3 - 1$" on the board
   D. The teacher asks students to write "$3 - 1 = 2$."

Financial Literacy

Mathematics skills can—and should—be applied by students in authentic contexts whenever possible. One highly important authentic context is financial literacy.

> **Helpful Hint**
>
> If students are taught to erase all their work and start again, they may never be able to recognize their own mistakes. Students should instead practice finding the error in their calculations and erasing only the portions that come after the error.

Students should understand that money exists in various forms outside of hard currency and that **financial institutions**, such as banks and credit unions, help people save, borrow, and invest money. Financial institutions are essential because they not only help people keep their money safe (the Federal Deposit Insurance Corporation—FDIC—insures up to $250,000 in deposits), they also help people earn **interest** on their money. Of course, borrowing money also requires individuals to *pay* interest. Students should therefore learn about different types of borrowing, from low-interest loans like mortgages or student loans, to higher-interest loans like credit cards and payday lending.

When considering what to do with money that is not needed immediately, people should be taught to consider various options. Opening a savings account or buying bonds are very safe **investments**, but they generally offer low returns. Much higher returns can come from investments in stocks, but these are also riskier investments. Options like bonds or real estate usually come with a lower risk.

Most investments also come with taxation. Understanding the different types of taxes that must be paid is another part of financial literacy. Taxes come in many forms:

- income taxes, typically taken out of one's payroll check
- payroll taxes, including Social Security and Medicare, also taken out of one's payroll check
- capital gains taxes, assessed if investments make money
- estate tax, assessed on inheritance
- property tax, typically assessed by the local government and based on the value of property owned
- sales tax (currently 6.25% in Texas) levied on most retail sales and services

To prepare for financial security, students should also learn how to make and plan budgets. They should learn about **fixed expenses**, or expenses that are usually the same each month (for example, mortgage or rent, loan payments), and those that are **variable** (for example, medical bills, groceries, entertainment).

Students should also understand that to make money in a business, profits must exceed expenses; when they do not, a business loses money and action must be taken, such as reducing expenses or finding ways to increase sales.

Practice Question

3. Which of the following activities would help students learn to budget?
   A. examining the P & L statement of a Fortune 500 company
   B. creating a daily schedule of activities that includes how much they will spend
   C. researching the differences between cash and accrual accounting procedures
   D. listing projected income and expenses each month, making sure income is higher

Number Concepts and Operations

Number Theory

A basic foundation in numeracy is vital for establishing the groundwork for understanding advanced mathematical concepts. Students begin working with **natural numbers,** which are used when counting (e.g., 1, 2, 3).

Once a basic understanding of natural numbers is achieved, more advanced concepts, such as whole numbers and integers, can be introduced:

- **Whole numbers** are similar to natural numbers, except that whole numbers include zero.
- **Fractions** are parts of whole numbers and can be expressed as such (1/2) or as a **percent** or part out of 100 (50%).
- **Mixed numbers** contain both numbers and fractions (e.g., $3\frac{1}{4}$).
- **Integers** are positive or negative whole numbers (not fractions or decimals).
- **Rational numbers** are numbers that can be made by dividing two integers. Rational numbers must be expressed as a terminating or repeating decimal (e.g., 0.125 or $0.\overline{66}$).
    - Pi (π) is not a rational number because it does not terminate or repeat (π = 3.14159265...); instead, pi goes on forever with no repeating pattern.
    - Integers are rational numbers because they can be written as fractions with a denominator of 1.

Check Your Understanding

What are some examples of concrete objects that could be used to teach numeracy in the classroom?

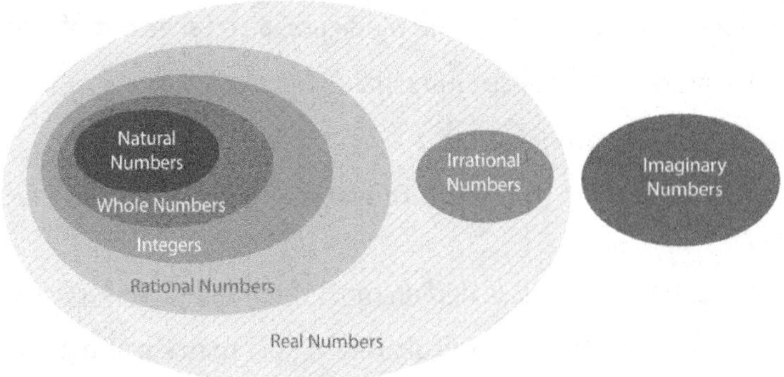

Figure 2.1. Types of Fractions

The set of rational and irrational numbers make up the set of **real numbers**. Real numbers can be represented on a **number line,** where 0 is in the middle, positive numbers are to the right, and negative numbers are to the left. Figure 2.2. shows an example of a number line. (Remember: fractions and decimals are between the integers shown).

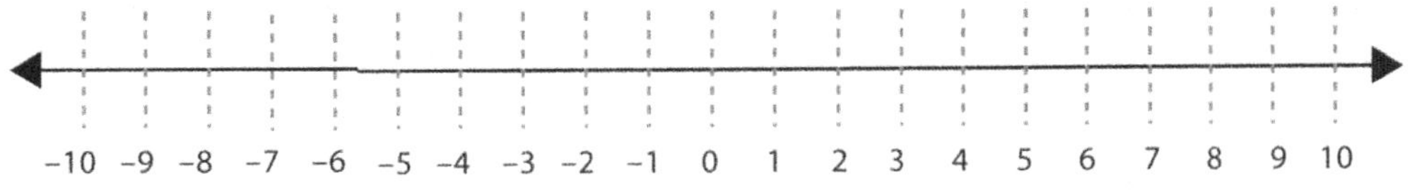

Figure 2.2. Number Line

Every whole number (except 1) is either a prime number or a composite number. A **prime number** is a natural number greater than 1 that can be divided evenly by only 1 and itself. For example, 7 is a prime number because it can only be divided by the numbers 1 and 7.

On the other hand, a **composite number** is a natural number greater than 1 that can be evenly divided by at least one other number besides 1 and itself. For example, 6 is a composite number because it can be evenly divided by 1, 2, 3, and 6.

Practice Question

4. Classify the number $\frac{13}{14}$.
   A. irrational
   B. imaginary
   C. rational
   D. integer

Place Value and Number Sense

A place value chart is a good visual aid to show children how to understand the value of digits. The chart has place values listed right to left in the way numbers are typically formed. The chart also aids in reading and writing multi-digit numbers accurately, as each digit is placed in a column that correlates to its value.

TABLE 3.1. PLACE VALUE CHART

1,000,000	100,000	10,000	1,000	100	10	1		1/10	1/100
10^6	10^5	10^4	10^3	10^2	10^1	10^0	.	10^{-1}	10^{-2}
millions	hundred thousands	ten thousands	thousands	hundreds	tens	ones	decimal	tenths	hundredths

Figure 2.3.

Another way to express a number is by decomposing it. **Decomposing** a number breaks it down into individual parts. For instance, 6,417 can be decomposed to $6{,}000 + 400 + 10 + 7$. Similarly,

composing a number involves adding the individual parts. So, $9{,}000 + 400 + 30 + 1$ can be written as 9,431.

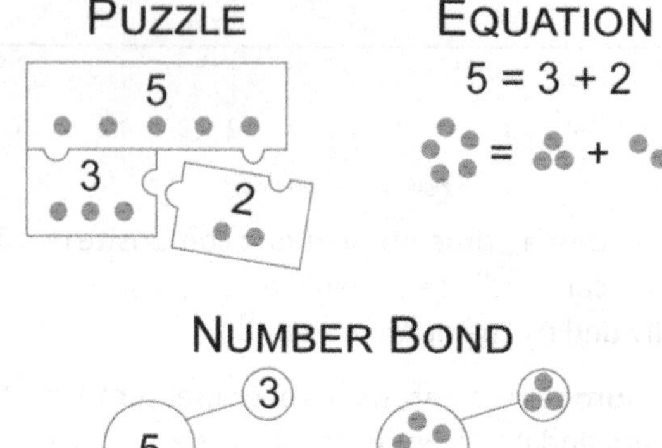

Figure 3.4. Decomposing Numbers

Figure 2.4. Decomposing Numbers

Rounding is another useful skill. When working with large figures, for instance, it is easier to work with values rounded to the nearest ten or hundred—it is not always necessary to work with an exact number. Rounding takes whatever the precise numbers are and makes **compatible numbers,** or numbers that are easier to work with and allow for easier calculations. For example, $492 + 312$ could be converted to $490 + 310 = 800$. Similarly, 31×22 could be converted to compatible numbers to make $30 \times 20 = 600$.

> **Common Student Errors**
>
> - misunderstanding how to expand numbers ($306 = 30 + 6$)
> - decreasing the number in the specified place when rounding down ($163 > 150$)

Rounding can help students **estimate** answers and/or confirm that the answer they come up with to a problem is close to the value it should be.

Like rounding and estimation, **sequencing and patterning** are also part of students' development of number sense. Students should practice finding patterns and extending patterns. For example, the next number in the sequence 12, 8, 4 is 0 (subtract 4). The next number in 10, 25, 40, 55 is 70 (add 15).

Practice Question

5. Which equation correctly decomposes 624?
   A. $600 + 10 + 10 + 4$
   B. $600 + 2 + 4$
   C. $600 + 20 + 4$
   D. $600 + 24$

Operations with Numbers

Young students form the foundations for addition and subtraction by counting forward to add or counting backward to subtract. Children who are proficient with skip counting (i.e., 2, 4, 6, 8, 10, 12...) are adding already, perhaps without even knowing it.

Helping children understand addition written as a standard problem or equation involves familiarizing them with common symbols like the addition and equal signs (+ and =) and words such as *addends*, *plus*, *all together*, *in all*, and *sum*. Once they understand these, they can progress to simple paper-and-pencil exercises with addition sentences or equations (e.g., $3 + 4 = 7$).

Students may also begin exercises with grouping. **Grouping** refers to viewing numbers in a sequence that makes logical sense. For example, there are many ways to group numbers to add up to 10: 1 and 9, 2 and 8, 3 and 7, 4 and 6 all add up to 10. Using **doubles** is a type of grouping where the two numbers used in an addition equation are the same: $2 + 2$, $3 + 3$, $4 + 4$, and so on. Both of these strategies help children strengthen number sense and expand their thinking.

Subtraction can be explained as the inverse or opposite of addition because the two operations cancel each other out. Terms such as *minuend*, *minus*, *take away*, *left*, *remaining*, and *difference* should be introduced.

An extremely useful technique in relating addition and subtraction is a fact family. Just like people, numbers have relationships with each other under certain circumstances. For example, $5 + 2$ is the same as $2 + 5$—they both add up to 7. Having that understanding can help children deduce that $7 - 2 = 5$ and $7 - 5 = 2$. The same three numbers have an addition and subtraction relationship; this relationship is called a **fact family**. A fact family like this one always gives two addition equations and two subtraction equations.

Common Student Errors

- always subtracting the smaller number from the larger number ($953 - 27 = 934$)
- knowing how to perform an operation, but not when
- thinking that subtraction is commutative ($9 - 4 = 4 - 9$)

Multiplication and division are also inverse operations and are typically introduced at a point when a child can comfortably identify numbers up to 20 and is familiar with addition and subtraction. They can begin to understand terms such as *multiplier*, *factor*, *product*, *multiply*, and *times*.

Multiplication is basically repeated addition, so 5×3 is the same as $5 + 5 + 5$. A **multiplication chart** can help students learn the multiples of small whole numbers. In the chart, children can just focus on the diagonals (e.g., $2 \times 2, 3 \times 3, 4 \times 4$) and the section either above or below the diagonal (because of the commutative property of multiplication, which states that 5×3 is equivalent to 3×5).

X	0	1	2	3	4	5	6	7	8	9	10
0	0	0	0	0	0	0	0	0	0	0	0
1	0	1	2	3	4	5	6	7	8	9	10
2	0	2	4	6	8	10	12	14	16	18	20
3	0	3	6	9	12	15	18	21	24	27	30
4	0	4	8	12	16	20	24	28	32	36	40
5	0	5	10	15	20	25	30	35	40	45	50
6	0	6	12	18	24	30	36	42	48	54	60
7	0	7	14	21	28	35	42	49	56	63	70
8	0	8	16	24	32	40	48	56	64	72	80
9	0	9	18	27	36	45	54	63	72	81	90
10	0	10	20	30	40	50	60	70	80	90	100

Figure 2.6. Multiplication Chart

It is no surprise that children develop concrete understanding with the aid of visual representations, such as cookie dough laid out on a baking tray, seats in a movie theatre, or a dozen doughnuts in a box. They are commonly arranged in rows and columns, known as arrays. **Arrays** can help explain multiplication using rows and columns: the number of rows and columns each refer to the factors used in a multiplication equation.

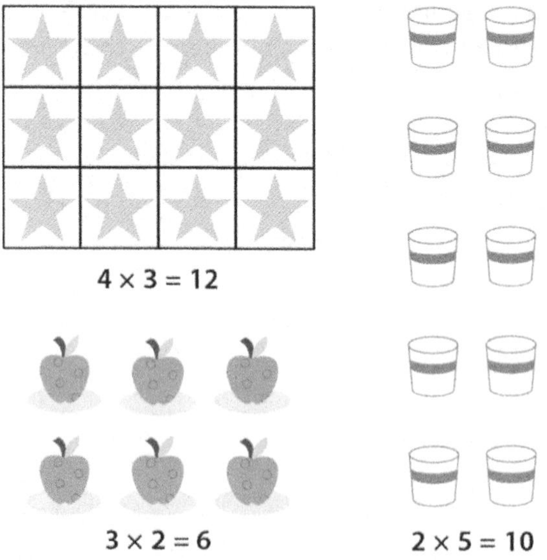

Figure 2.7. Arrays

Just as addition and subtraction are related in fact families, multiplication and division have a relationship too. **Division** is the act of splitting into equal parts or groups. For example, if three friends wish to share a pizza cut into nine slices, how many slices would each friend get? The terms *divisor*, *dividend*, *quotient*, *divided by*, and *remainder* are used in division. In this example, $\frac{9}{3}$ (or $9 \div 3$) equals three wholes. If a

Did You Know?

Multiplication charts have long been a common resource in EC classrooms, but recent research suggests that arrays and other visual representations of multiplication are more effective teaching tools.

number does not completely divide to give a whole number, the division will result in a **remainder**. For example, sharing twelve cupcakes with five friends ($\frac{12}{5}$ or $12 \div 5$) will result in two whole cupcakes per friend with two left over, or a remainder of 2.

Basic divisibility rules, as described in Table 2.1, can also help students when dividing larger numbers.

Table 2.1. Basic Divisibility Rules	
Divisible by 2 if . . .	the last digit is 0 or an even number.
Divisible by 3 if . . .	the sum of all digits is divisible by 3.
Divisible by 4 if . . .	the last two digits are divisible by 4.
Divisible by 5 if . . .	the last digit is 5 or 0.
Divisible by 6 if . . .	the number is divisible by both 2 and 3.
Divisible by 9 if . . .	the sum of all digits is divisible by 9.
Divisible by 10 if . . .	the last digit is 0.

Arrays can also be used with division problems. In Figure 2.8., seven people are to share fourteen pizza slices. How many slices will each person get? The division equation is written as $14 \div 7 = 2$. The fourteen pizza slices are split into seven equal groups, which results in two slices per person.

$$14 \div 7 = 2$$

Figure 2.8. Using Arrays for Division

Multiplication and division are inverse operations and related through fact families. For instance, 3×6 is the same as 6 × 3. They both multiply to give 18. Now, using these same numbers, a child can deduce that $18 \div 3 = 6$ and $18 \div 6 = 3$. The three numbers have a multiplication and division relationship. A fact family such as this one always includes two multiplication equations and two division equations.

Check Your Understanding

How could you use manipulatives to teach students about remainders?

Practice Question

6. A third-grade student is trying to confirm the answer to the problem 244 ÷ 4. The student's answer is 60 R 4. How should the teacher guide this student?
   A. refer the student to the divisibility rules
   B. review use of arrays for division
   C. encourage the student to use compatible numbers
   D. have the student use multiplication to check the answer

Algorithms

An **algorithm** is a set of steps to follow when performing mathematical operations. Even the simplest of computations has an algorithm. Algorithms can be thought of as standard or non-standard. **Standard algorithms** are the most typical ways of solving problems such as "carrying" for addition or "borrowing" for subtraction. **Nonstandard algorithms** or alternative algorithms were popularized in the text *Everyday Mathematics* and include the area or box method of multiplication, the grid or array method, partial products method, and partial sums algorithm. Nonstandard algorithms may be easier for some students to learn or understand.

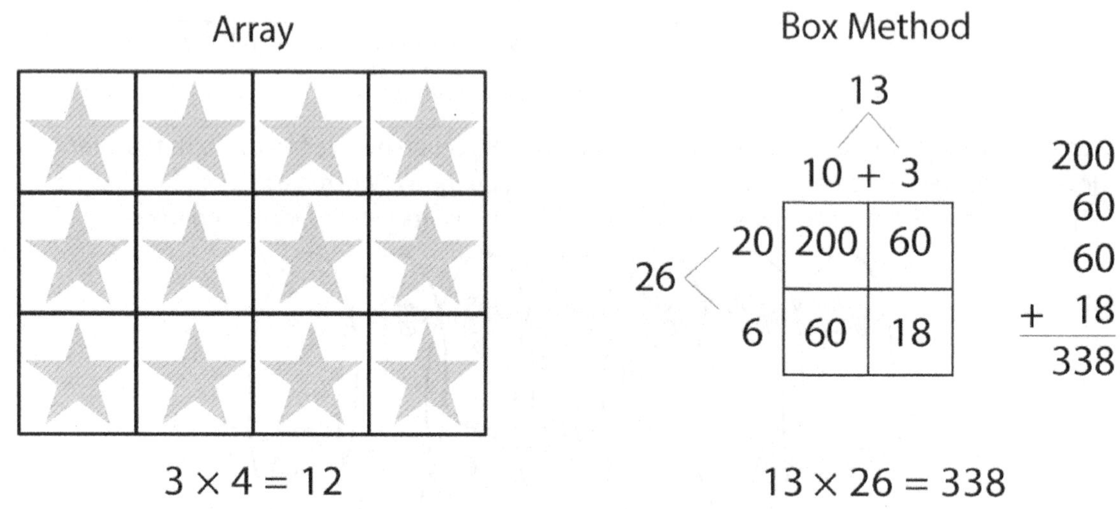

Figure 2.9. Teaching Multiplication

As problems become more complicated, there are rules, or properties, that guide the problem-solver.

Table 2.2. Mathematical Properties

Name	Description	Applies To	Example
Commutative property	The order of the operation does not matter.	addition multiplication	$a + b = b + a$ $ab = ba$
Associative property	Grouping of numbers does not matter.	addition multiplication	$(a + b) + c = a + (b + c)$ $(a \times b) \times c = a \times (b \times c)$
Distributive property	Multiply a value by all the values inside brackets, then add.	multiplication	$a\,(b + c) = ab + ac$

Table 2.2. Mathematical Properties			
Name	**Description**	**Applies To**	**Example**
Identity property	Adding zero or multiplying by one will not change the original value.	addition multiplication	$a + 0 = a$ $a \times 1 = a$
Zero property	Multiplying any value by zero yields a result of zero.	multiplication	$a \times 0 = 0$

Practice Question

7. A third-grade student writes the following: 6 ÷ 3 =2, so 2 ÷ 3 = 6. What could the teacher do to help the student with this misconception?

A. explain that the commutative property only applies to multiplication, not division
B. explain that division can only occur if one number is larger than the other
C. give the student more practice with division fast facts
D. use pictorial representations to show that division is the inverse of multiplication, not the inverse of subtraction

Fractions, Decimals, and Percents

A fraction can be described as part of a whole. The top number of a fraction is called the **numerator**, and the bottom number is the **denominator**. The numerator represents how many of the parts are taken, and the denominator represents how many equal parts the object is split into. A fraction is the division of the top number by the bottom number.

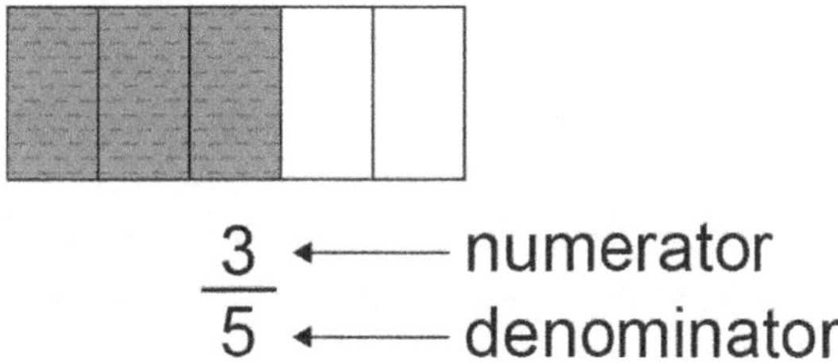

Figure 2.10. Parts of a Fraction

For early learners, a **visual fraction model** is a pictorial way of understanding fractions. It could include objects, shapes, or figures divided into fractions. **Fraction strips** are a good visual representation to allow students to see how parts make up a whole.

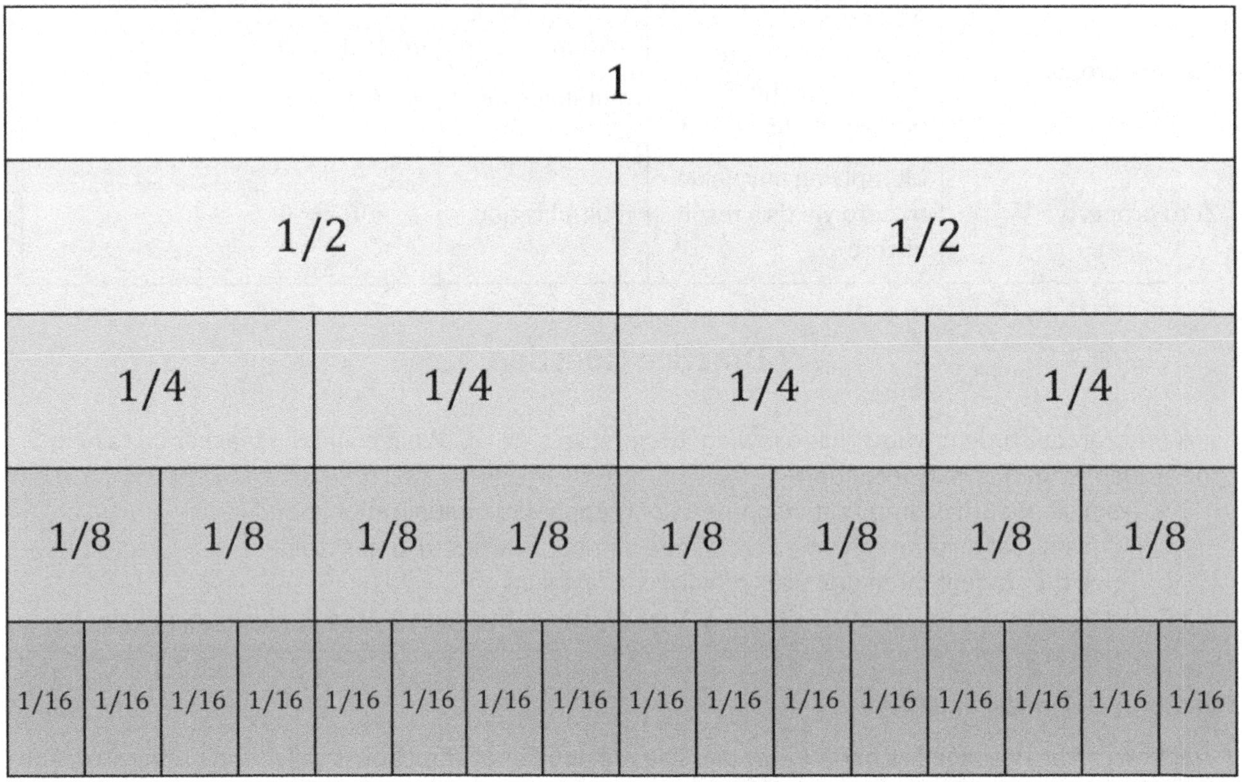

1

1/2 1/2

1/4 1/4 1/4 1/4

1/8 1/8 1/8 1/8 1/8 1/8 1/8 1/8

1/16 1/16 1/16 1/16 1/16 1/16 1/16 1/16 1/16 1/16 1/16 1/16 1/16 1/16 1/16 1/16

Figure 2.11. Fraction Strips

A **unit fraction** is a fraction in which the numerator is 1, such as 1/6 or 1/10. While the numerator stays 1, the denominator is the number that determines whether the value of a unit fraction decreases or increases.

Sometimes fractions must be compared for **relative magnitude**. It is not always apparent which fraction is larger or smaller, but a visual comparison can help. Rectangle A is divided into 4 equal parts, and rectangle B is divided in two parts. The unit fraction in A is 1/4 and the one in B is 1/2. Visually it is clear that 1/4 is smaller than 1/2. Rectangle A has been divided into more equal parts than rectangle B; hence its unit fraction is smaller.

Fractions can be expressed in different ways—ratio, percent, and decimal. These different forms can all represent the same number. A **ratio** is a comparison of two numbers. As its definition indicates, a fraction specifies a part of a whole, but a ratio is an indicator of how much of one thing there is compared to another.

For instance, in a pouch containing eight blue and five red marbles, there are eight blue marbles to five red marbles—or a ratio to 8 to 5, also written *8:5*. In a recipe that calls for six cups of flour and three cups of milk, the ratio of flour to milk is 6:3. Ratios are similar to fractions and illustrate the relationship between part and whole.

Another example is a classroom full of students. There are ten girls, eleven boys, and two instructors in a classroom. The following shows part-to-part and part-to-whole ratios:

Part to Part	Part to Whole
Ratio of boys to girls: $11:10$ or $\frac{11}{10}$	Ratio of boys to all students: $11:21$ or $\frac{11}{21}$
Ratio of instructors to girls: $2:10$ or $\frac{2}{10}$	Ratio of girls to entire class: $10:23$ or $\frac{10}{23}$

A **percent** is a type of fraction where the denominator is always 100, meaning it refers to parts per one hundred. Using 100 makes comparisons simple because the whole is always the same. A percent is easily identifiable by the percent symbol, %, added at the end. Students should first understand that 100% is considered all of everything: 100% of a class with thirty students refers to all thirty students; 50% refers to half—in this case, half of thirty, which is fifteen students ($30 \div 2 = 15$). Graph paper is a very useful tool in teaching percents to students.

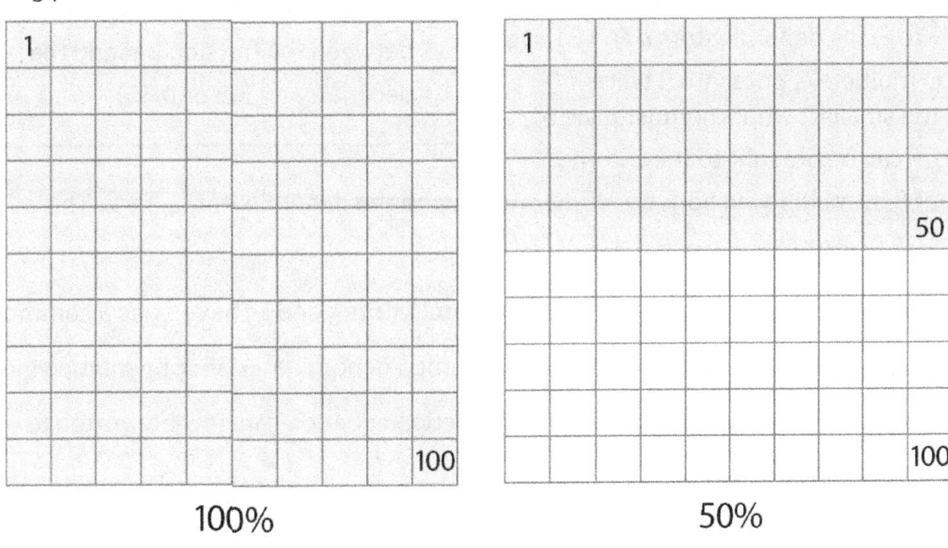

Figure 2.12. Drawing Percents on Graph Paper

A percent can be easily converted into a **decimal** by removing the percent symbol and dividing the number by 100. Also, dividing the numerator of a fraction by its denominator gives a decimal. The following example shows the progression of ratio to fraction to percent to decimal.

Practice Question

8. A teacher is preparing a lesson with the objective of converting fractions to percents. Which of the following skills should students be able to perform before the teacher begins the lesson?
   A. comparing unit fractions
   B. finding the reciprocal of a fraction
   C. decomposing fractions
   D. creating a common denominator

Operations with Fractions

The math operations of addition, subtraction, multiplication, and division can be executed on fractions just as on whole numbers, but with a few modifications. When adding or subtracting two fractions, the denominator is important. For fractions with like (same) denominators, simply add or subtract the numerator and write the final answer over the same denominator. For example:

$$\frac{3}{10} + \frac{5}{10} = \frac{8}{10} \text{ and } \frac{5}{6} - \frac{1}{6} = \frac{4}{6}$$

For fractions with unlike (different) denominators, first find a common denominator. When two or more denominators are the same or brought to the same number, that number is called a **common denominator**. A common denominator can be found by finding the smallest whole number that is divisible by both denominators. Another way is to simply multiply denominators together to result in a common number.

After finding the common denominator, the two fractions can be rewritten with the new denominator and added as usual. For instance, when adding $\frac{3}{4}$ to $\frac{1}{8}$, the denominators 4 and 8 have 8 as a common multiple: 4 goes into 8 twice (4×2); 8 is the smallest whole number divisible by 4 and 8. So, $\frac{3}{4}$ can be brought to the common denominator of 8 by multiplying both the numerator, 3, and the denominator, 4, by 2. This addition equation can now be expressed as $\frac{6}{8} + \frac{1}{8} = \frac{7}{8}$.

> **Helpful Hint:**
>
> **Common Student Errors**
>
> - thinking that the fraction with the larger denominator is larger ($\frac{1}{5} > \frac{1}{3}$)
> - adding the numerators and the denominators ($\frac{1}{3} + \frac{2}{5} = \frac{3}{8}$)
> - misunderstanding the relationship between the fraction bar and the decimal ($\frac{3}{5} = 3.5$ or 0.35)

Similarly, in a subtraction equation like $\frac{3}{5} - \frac{1}{15}$, the denominators 5 and 15 have 15 as a common multiple: 5 goes into 15 three times, so $\frac{3}{5}$ can be brought to a common denominator of 15 by multiplying the numerator, 3, and the denominator, 5, by 3. This subtraction equation can now be written as $\frac{9}{15} - \frac{1}{15} = \frac{8}{15}$.

The following are examples of adding and subtracting fractions with like and unlike denominators.

Addition:

- $\frac{7}{11} + \frac{2}{11} = \frac{9}{11}$ (like denominators)
- $\frac{2}{9} + \frac{1}{3} = \frac{2}{9} + \frac{3}{9} = \frac{5}{9}$ (unlike denominators)

Subtraction:

- $\frac{9}{12} - \frac{2}{12} = \frac{7}{12}$ (like denominators)
- $\frac{5}{6} - \frac{1}{3} = \frac{5}{6} - \frac{2}{6} = \frac{3}{6}$ (unlike denominators)

Multiplying fractions requires the least work. Both numerators are multiplied, and both denominators are multiplied.

Multiplication:

- $\frac{4}{5} \times \frac{3}{7} = \frac{4 \times 3}{5 \times 7} = \frac{12}{35}$

In dividing fractions, first find the reciprocal of the second fraction. A **reciprocal** is found by swapping the numerator and denominator. After taking the reciprocal of the second fraction, simply multiply the two fractions as usual to arrive at the final answer.

Division:

- $\frac{1}{3} \div \frac{2}{5} = \frac{1}{3} \times \frac{5}{2} = \frac{5}{6}$

Multiplication and division can result in large numerators and/or denominators. Fractions should be **simplified**—or **reduced**—for ease of understanding by dividing both the numerator and denominator by their greatest common factor. The greatest common factor—or GCF—is the highest number that can divide exactly into two or more numbers. A **common factor** is a number that can be divided into two or more numbers. The factors of 6 are 1, 2, 3, 6, and the factors of 15 are 1, 3, 5, 15. Both 6 and 15 have common factors of 1 and 3. The largest of those common factors is called the greatest common factor.

In the fraction $\frac{8}{12}$, the numerator 8 and the denominator 12 have 4 as their greatest common factor (i.e., 4 is the highest factor common to both numbers). After dividing both numbers, the reduced fraction is now $\frac{2}{3}$; $\frac{8}{12}$ and $\frac{2}{3}$ are called **equivalent** fractions because even though they are expressed differently, they represent the same quantity.

Fractions are not always less than 1. There are fractions where the numerator is larger than the denominator. These are called **improper fractions**. In such cases, decomposing a fraction can be useful. **Decomposing** fractions involves splitting them into smaller pieces. Consider the improper fraction $\frac{7}{5}$. This can be decomposed into a part equal to 1 and a part smaller than 1: $\frac{7}{5} = \frac{5}{5} + \frac{2}{5}$.

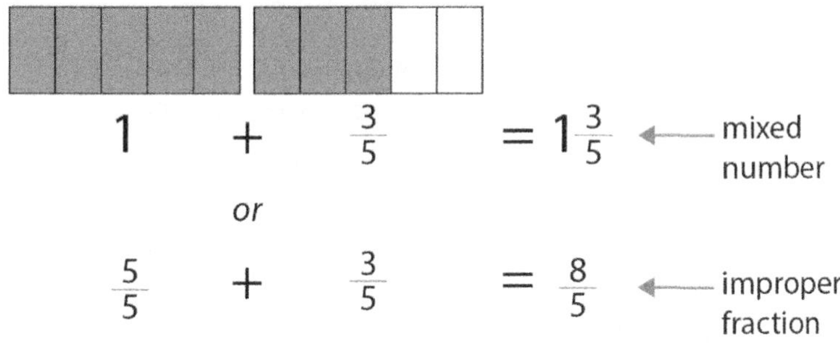

Figure 2.14. Types of Fractions

There are also fractions that contain whole numbers with a fractional part. These are called **mixed numbers**. For instance, $4\frac{2}{3}$ is a mixed number. This number can be decomposed as:

$$= 1 + 1 + 1 + 1 + \frac{2}{3}$$

$$= \frac{3}{3} + \frac{3}{3} + \frac{3}{3} + \frac{3}{3} + \frac{1}{3} + \frac{1}{3}$$

This results in six fractions with a common denominator of 3. Decomposing fractions can make addition and subtraction of some fractions more straightforward.

Many real-life circumstances involve fractions. For instance:

Mom bought $\frac{5}{12}$ of a pound of chicken. Dad bought $\frac{1}{3}$ of a pound of chicken. Who purchased the larger amount?

First, bring both fractions to a common denominator (12 in this case). So, for Dad's chicken weighing $\frac{1}{3}$ pound (multiply both the numerator and denominator by 4), $\frac{1}{3} = \frac{4}{12}$. Upon comparison, $\frac{5}{12}$ is greater than $\frac{4}{12}$ since the numerator 5 is larger than 4. So, Mom purchased the larger amount.

Comparing fractions can also be done by using **grid** or **area models**.

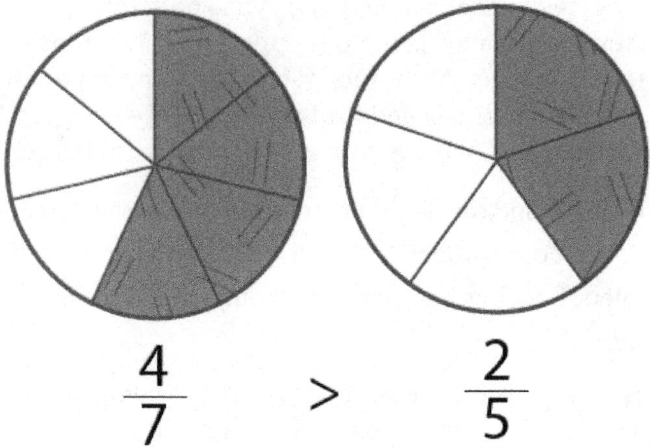

Figure 2.15. Comparing Fractions

Practice Questions

9. Carla divides her pizza into eight equal slices and takes one slice. If the amount of pizza remaining is written as a fraction, the numerator will be which of the following values?
   A. 1
   B. 7
   C. 8
   D. 9

10. Which of the following is the best definition of decomposing fractions?
   A. separating the numerator and denominator into individual numbers
   B. finding the reciprocal of a fraction
   C. splitting a fraction into smaller pieces
   D. creating equivalent fractions

Algebraic Thinking

Algebra Expressions and Operations

Algebraic expressions contain numbers, variables, and at least one mathematical operation. Each group of numbers and variables in an expression is called a **term** (e.g., $3x$ or $16y$). A **binomial** is an algebraic expression with two terms (e.g., $3x + 16y$); a **trinomial** has three terms; and a **polynomial** has more than three terms. Algebraic expressions can be evaluated for a specific value by plugging that value into the expression and simplifying.

To add or subtract linear algebraic expressions, add the variables and numbers (constants) separately. For example:

$$(5x - 3) + (3x - 2) = (5x + 3x) + (-3 - 2) = 8x - 5$$

Now subtract, making sure that the minus sign is distributed through the parentheses:

$$(13x - 5y + 2) - (8x - y - 3) = (13x - 8x) + (-5y - -y) + (2 - -3)$$

$$(13x - 8x) + (-5y + y) + (2 + 3) = 5x - 4y + 5$$

Remember that two negatives in a row is the same as a positive.

When solving multi-step problems, the **order of operations** must be used to get the correct answer. Generally speaking, the problem should be worked in the following order: (1) parentheses and brackets, (2) exponents and square roots, (3) multiplication and division, and (4) addition and subtraction. The acronym *PEMDAS* can be used to remember the order of operations:

Please Excuse My Dear Aunt Sally

P – Parentheses

E – Exponents

M – Multiplication

D – Division

A – Addition

S – Subtraction

The steps "Multiplication–Division" and "Addition–Subtraction" go in order from left to right. In other words, divide before multiplying if the division problem is on the left. For example, the expression $(3^2 - 2)^2 + (4)5^3$ is simplified using the following steps:

1. Parentheses: Because the parentheses in this problem contain two operations (exponents and subtraction) use the order of operations within the parentheses. Exponents come before subtraction:

$$(3^2 - 2)^2 + (4)5^3 = (9 - 2)^2 + (4)5^3 = (7)^2 + (4)5^3$$

2. Exponents:

$$(7)^2 + (4)5^3 = 49 + (4)125$$

3. Multiplication and division:

$$49 + (4)125 = 49 + 500$$

4. Addition and subtraction:

$$49 + 500 = 549$$

Practice Question

11. If $x = 5$, what is the value of the algebraic expression $2x - x$?
    A. 5
    B. 10
    C. 15
    D. 20

Algebraic Equations

In an **equation,** two expressions are joined by an equal sign, which indicates that the two expressions are equal to each other. The two sides of an equation act like a balanced scale: operations can be performed on equations as long as the same operation is performed on both sides to maintain the balance.

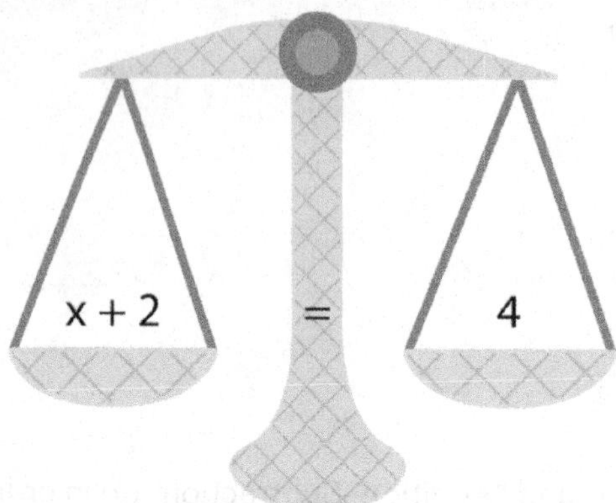

Figure 2.16. Equation Scale

This property can be used to solve the equation by performing operations that isolate the variable on one side. For example, the equation $4x + 12 = 2x + 48$ can be solved for *x* using the following steps:

1. Subtract 12 from both sides of the equation:

$$(4x + 12) - 12 = (2x + 48) - 12 \rightarrow 4x = 2x + 36$$

2. Subtract 2*x* from both sides of the equation:

$$(4x) - 2x = (2x + 36) - 2x \rightarrow 2x = 36$$

3. Divide both sides by 2:

$$\frac{2x}{2} = \frac{36}{2} \rightarrow x = 18$$

Linear equations follow a specific pattern that results in a straight line when graphed. These lines are graphed on a **coordinate plane,** a plane containing the *x*- and *y*-axes. The ***x*-axis** is the horizontal line on a graph where $y = 0$. The ***y*-axis** is the vertical line on a graph where $x = 0$.

The *x*-axis and *y*-axis intersect to create four **quadrants**. The first quadrant is in the upper right, and other quadrants are labeled counterclockwise using the Roman numerals I, II, III, and IV. **Points,** or locations, on the graph are written as **ordered pairs,** (*x*, *y*), with the point (0, 0) called the **origin**. Points are plotted by counting over *x* places from the origin horizontally and *y* places from the origin vertically.

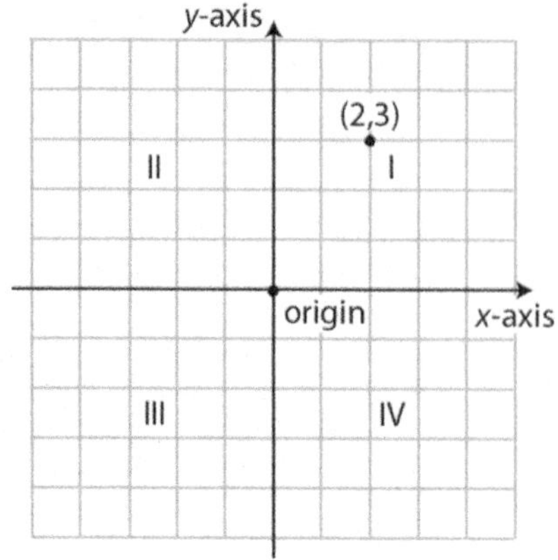

Figure 2.17. The Coordinate System

The most common way to write a linear equation is **slope-intercept form**, $y = mx + b$. In this equation, *b* is the **y-intercept**, which is the point where the line crosses the *y*-axis, or where *x* equals zero. **Slope** is represented by the letter *m* and describes how steep the line is. Slope is often described as "rise over run" because it is calculated as the difference in *y*-values (rise) over the difference in *x*-values (run):

$$m = \frac{y_2 - y_1}{x_2 - x_1}$$

Another way to express a linear equation is in **standard form**: $Ax + By = C$. To graph such an equation, it can be converted to slope-intercept form, or the slope and intercepts can be found from the standard form:

- $m = -\frac{A}{B}$
- x-intercept $= \frac{C}{A}$
- y-intercept $= \frac{C}{B}$

It is easy to find the *x*- and *y*-intercepts from this form. To find the *x*-intercept, simply set $y = 0$ and solve for *x*. Similarly, to find the *y*-intercept, set $x = 0$ and solve for *y*. Once these two points are known, a line can be drawn through them.

Helpful Hint

Linear equations with the same slope are parallel. When two slopes are reciprocal negatives (such as 2 and $-\frac{1}{2}$), the lines are perpendicular.

To graph a linear equation, identify the *y*-intercept and place that point on the *y*-axis. Then, starting at the *y*-intercept, use the slope to go "up and over" and place the next point. The numerator of the slope is the number of units to go up (or down if the slope is negative). The denominator of the slope is the number of units to go right. Repeat the process to plot additional points. These points can then be connected to draw the line.

Helpful Hint

The point-slope equation can be used to find the equation of a line using the slope and one point (x_1, y_1): $y - y_1 = m(x - x_1)$.

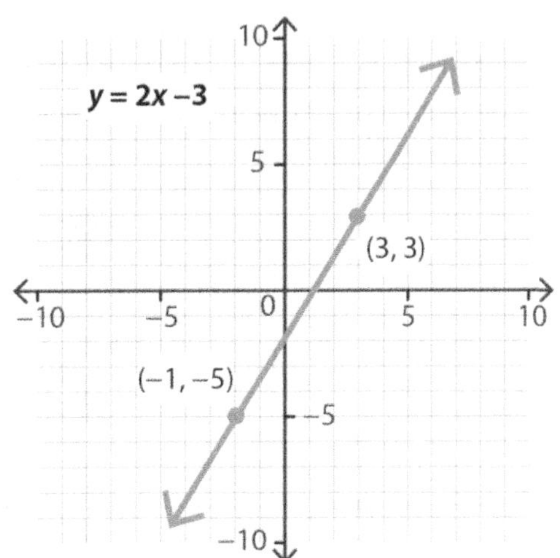

Figure 2.18. Linear Equation

You can also plot the equation by making a table of values and plugging in values for *x* and then plotting the points and making a line. For example, for the equation $y = -2x + 3$:

$x = -1$	$y = 2 + 3; y = 5$	$(-1, 5)$
$x = 0$	$y = 0 + 3; y = 3$	$(0, 3)$
$x = 1$	$y = -2 + 3; y = 1$	$(1, 1)$

To find the equation of a line, identify the *y*-intercept, if possible, on the graph and use two easily identifiable points to find the slope.

Practice Question

12. Which of the following is an equation of the line that passes through the points (4, −3) and (−2, 9) in the *xy*-plane?
   A. $y = -2x + 5$
   B. $y = -\frac{1}{2}x - 1$
   C. $y = \frac{1}{2}x - 5$
   D. $y = 2x - 11$

Functions

Functions demonstrate a relationship between sets of values, called the inputs and outputs. Functions are distinct from **relations** because relations have more than one output for one input, while functions have only one output for every input. All ordered pairs are relations, but only certain relations are functions. The **vertical line test** can be used to identify functions. Because each x value has only one y value, a function will cross a vertical line only once.

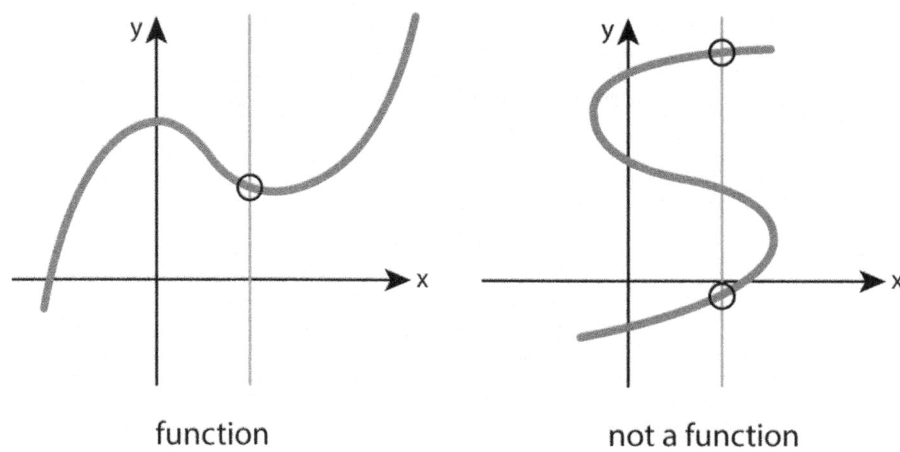

Figure 2.19. Vertical Line Test

To test whether a relation is a function, plug in values to see if outputs are the same.

Relation (more than one output per the same input)

X	Y
-4	$-2, 16$
0	4
2	$12, -6$
6	18

Function (only one output per each input)

X	Y
-4	-2
0	4
2	12
6	18

The input is the **independent variable**, and the output is called the **dependent variable** because it depends on the input. Usually (but not always) *x* is the independent variable, and *y* is the dependent variable. The coordinates found in the function table can then be plotted on a set of axes to find the corresponding graph.

$3x + y = 12$		
x	y	
1	9	$3(1) + y = 12$ $3 + y = 12$ $y = 9$
2	6	$3(2) + y = 12$ $6 + y = 12$ $y = 6$
3	3	$3(3) + y = 12$ $9 + y = 12$ $y = 3$

Tables may be used to connect the *y*-value (dependent variable) to the *x*-value (independent variable) in an equation. The values may be plotted to see whether the relationship is linear, and if it is, to identify a slope and *y*-intercept. The following is the table of values to be evaluated:

x	2	3	4	5
y	8	11	14	17

Plotting the points shows that the relationship is linear with a slope of 3. Another way to determine the relationship is to notice a pattern where the difference between each *x*-value is 1, and the difference between each *y*-value is 3. Since these differences are the same for all *x*- and *y*-values, the data can be modeled as a linear equation. The slope is: $\frac{\text{change in } y}{\text{change in } x} = \frac{3}{1} = 3$. To get the *y*-intercept, when $x = 2$, add 2 more to $3x$ to get 8, the *y*-value. Thus, the equation is $y = 3x + 2$.

The following is an example of a table with **non-linear** values:

Helpful Hint

If the difference between x values and the difference between y values are constant, then the function is linear.

x	1	2	3	4
$f(x)$	2	5	10	17

Note that each value for *f*(*x*) (equivalent of the *y*-value above) is the *x*-value squared, plus 1. This quadratic pattern can be modeled by $f(x) = x^2 + 1$.

Practice Question

13. Which equation describes the relationship between *x* and *y* shown in the table?

x	y
3	11
5	15
7	19

A. $y = -2x - 5$
B. $y = 2x + 5$
C. $y = 4x + 2$
D. $y = x^2 + 2$

Forming and Solving Equations

A key part of math problem solving is forming equations. In forming equations, students must first understand what the question is asking and then determine what is known and unknown (variables).

For example, if a farmer wants to plant 100 corn plants and has 20 rows, how many plants should he put in each row?

In this case, what is known is the number of corn plants and rows; what is unknown is the number of corn plants in each row. So, a simple equation might be set up: 20 = 100 ÷ x. In this way, the word problem is **translated** into a mathematical representation.

Some problems might involve functions. Consider the following example:

Time	4:00	5:00	6:30	8:00	10:00
Miles from ranch house	30	25	17.5	10	0

A group of riders were riding back to a ranch house and covered the distances as recorded in the table shown. If *x* represents the number of hours since the riders left at 4:00, what equation would best represent the distance traveled as a function of time?

To solve, use the equation $y = mx + b$

Set x = hours traveled

Set y = distance from ranch

$$If\ x = 0, y = 30;\ so\ b = 30$$

$$25 - 30 = -5;\ 5 - 4 = 1;\ so\ \frac{change\ in\ y}{change\ in\ x} = -5$$

$$y = -5x + 30$$

The following are additional examples of forming equations from words and their solutions.

Multi-variable Problem:

If b books cost d dollars each and each student must buy 2 books, how much will each student pay for his or her books?

Solution:

Make it into an easier problem. If 100 books cost $2,000, each student would have to pay $\frac{2{,}000}{100} \times 2$, or $40. This is the same as $\frac{d}{b} \times 2$, or $\frac{2d}{b}$.

Percentage Problem:

In a clothing store, the manager earns $\frac{1}{4}$ more than her salesperson. What percentage of the manager's salary is the salesperson's salary?

Solution:

Translate: $m = s + 0.25s;\ m = 1.25s;\ s = \frac{m}{1.25} = \frac{1}{1.25} \times m = 0.8m = 80\%$. The salesperson's salary is 80% of the manager's salary.

To help students solve word problems, the words and their mathematical translations described in Table 2.3. will likely be helpful.

Table 2.3. Translating Word Problems

English Word(s)	Math Translation
is, will be, yields	$=$
what number, how much	"x" (or any variable)
in addition to, increased by, added to	$+$
sum of x and y	$x + y$
difference of x and y	$x - y$
product of x and y	$x \times y$
quotient of x and y	$x \div y$ or $\frac{x}{y}$
opposite of x	$-x$
ratio of x to y	$x \div y$ or $\frac{x}{y}$
a number n less 2	$n - 2$

Table 2.3. Translating Word Problems	
English Word(s)	**Math Translation**
a number *n* less than 2	$2 - n$
a number *n* reduced by 2	$n - 2$
of	times
p percent	$\frac{p}{100}$, or move decimal left two places
half, twice	$\frac{x}{2}, 2x$

Practice Question

14. Valerie receives a base salary of $740 a week for working 40 hours. For every extra hour she works, she is paid at a rate of $27.75 per hour. If Valerie works *t* hours in a week, which of the following equations represents the amount of money, *A*, she will receive?

A. $A = 740 + 27.75(t - 40)$
B. $A = 740 + 27.75(40 - t)$
C. $A = 27.75t - 740$
D. $A = 27.75t + 740$

Geometry and Measurement

Units and Measurement

A **standard unit of measurement** is a defined, universal convention used to quantify the characteristic being measured. Examples include inches, miles, and meters (for distance) or ounces, pounds, and kilograms (for mass). A **nonstandard** unit of measurement refers to items not commonly used for measuring, such as paper clips, popsicle sticks, or an arm length.

Standard units of measurement can be classified into a number of systems. Most countries use the **metric** system, which uses units such as centimeters, kilometers, grams, and kilograms. In the United States, **US customary units** are used, including inches, feet, ounces, and pounds.

TABLE 2.4. Units		
DIMENSION	**US CUSTOMARY**	**METRIC/SI**
Length	inch/foot/yard/mile	meter
Mass	ounce/pound/ton	gram
Volume	cup/pint/quart/gallon	liter
Temperature	Fahrenheit	kelvin, Celsius

The metric system uses prefixes to simplify large and small numbers. These prefixes are added to the base units shown in the table. For example, the measurement "1,000 meters" can be written using the prefix kilo– as "1 kilometer." The most commonly used SI prefixes are given in Table 2.5.

Helpful Hint

A mnemonic device to help remember the metric system is *King Henry Drinks Under Dark Chocolate Moon (KHDUDCM).*

Table 2.5 Metric Prefixes

PREFIX	SYMBOL	MULTIPLICATION
Kilo	k	1,000
Hecto	h	100
Deca	da	10
Base unit	--	--
Deci	d	0.1
Centi	c	0.01
Milli	m	0.001

Units can be converted within a single system or between systems. When converting from one unit to another unit, a **conversion factor** (a numeric multiplier used to convert a value with a unit to another unit) is used:

- $1\ in\ =\ 2.54\ cm$
- $1\ lb\ =\ 0.454\ kg$
- $1\ yd\ =\ 0.914\ m$
- $1\ cal\ =\ 4.19\ J$
- $1\ mi\ =\ 1.61\ km$
- $C\ =\ \frac{5}{9}\ (ºF\ -\ 32)$
- $1\ gal\ =\ 3.785\ L$
- $1\ cm3\ =\ 1\ mL$
- $1\ oz\ =\ 28.35\ g$
- $1\ hr\ =\ 3{,}600\ s$

The process of converting between units using a conversion factor is sometimes known as **dimensional analysis**.

Children often love measuring with rulers or measuring tapes, especially **length** or **height**. They gain a degree of satisfaction in knowing the longest or tallest object in a group. They can also use a nonstandard unit of measurement like a pencil or a stick to measure various things around the house or classroom. They can use a ruler to measure small items. They can now understand terms such as *length, how long, how short, width, tall, height,* and *inches*.

Common Student Errors

- starting at the wrong end of the ruler or at 1 instead of at 0
- counting the lines instead of the spaces on a ruler

People generally use the word *weight* to express how heavy or light something is. Weight is actually the measure of gravity pulling on an object, and **mass** is how much matter is packed into an object. Weight can vary depending on gravitational pull. For instance, the weight of an object on the moon is less than that on Earth because the gravitational pull is weaker on the moon; however, the object's mass remains the same. The standard unit of measurement for mass is kilogram. Mass is typically measured with a **balance** in scientific study. Often, a **scale,** which actually measures weight, is used in the classroom. Scales may report weight in pounds, ounces, or grams and kilograms.

Volume refers to the amount of three-dimensional space an object occupies. Volume is usually measured by multiplying the length, width, and depth of the object. In math, **capacity** is another common measurement, defined as the quantity a container can hold. In the metric system, capacity is measured in liters and milliliters; in customary units, capacity is measured in fluid ounces, cups, pints, quarts, and gallons. Common customary unit conversions are as follows:

- $1\ cup = 8\ fluid\ ounces$
- $1\ pint = 2\ cups$
- $1\ quart = 2\ pints$
- $1\ gallon = 4\ quarts$

Temperature is another measurement students may use during math classes. The most common temperature scales are Celsius and Fahrenheit (though Kelvin is also used in scientific research). The best way to convert Celsius to Fahrenheit is to use the following equation $C = \frac{5}{9} \times (F - 32)$. For example, if the Fahrenheit temperature is 80 degrees, the students would first subtract 32 from 80 to get 48. They would then multiply $48 \times \frac{5}{9} = 26.7$.

Speed, which is distance divided by time, can be measured in meters per second (m/s), but it is more commonly measured in kilometers per hour (km/h) or miles per hour (mph).

As students practice measurement, they should recognize that human **error** can change measurements drastically, and this can create problems with further calculations. Basics of measurement, such as getting down at eye level, correctly filling and leveling containers, and starting at the correct spot on the ruler or measuring tape are all important skills.

To cut down on measurement error, **estimation** or **approximation** of a measurement ahead of time may be helpful. For example, if a student knows she is around 5 feet tall but is measured by a classmate at 70 inches, then the measurement is likely off.

Older children should be familiar with **money,** the denominations of US currency, skip counting, and converting currency. The four most-used coins and their values (penny = 1 cent, nickel = 5 cents, dime = 10 cents, quarter = 25 cents) can be used to show conversions between values, such as the relationships between nickels and dimes, pennies and nickels, and nickels and quarters. Common paper bills ($100, $50, $20, $10, $5, and $1) should also be introduced. Using play money is a great way to practice these types of calculations, particularly when asking students to make change for an amount or use the least number of bills and coins to create a sum.

The comfort of knowing what comes next in their day-to-day schedules has been shown to help children understand and manage **time**; however, teaching the concept of time to children can be a challenging undertaking.

Which type of clock is best to start with—analog or digital? The analog clock has moveable parts and can show elapsed time. It is also visually appealing. It can cover most of the concepts a child is expected to know with regard to time. A digital clock may seem easier, but it is less useful for showing elapsed time or future time (e.g., how many hours until dinner or when to wake up in the morning).

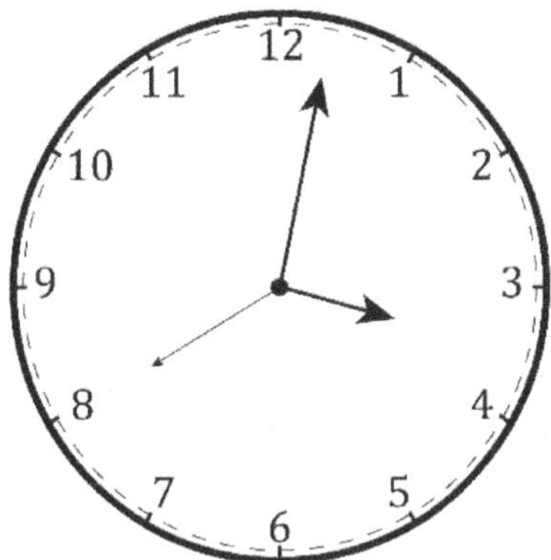

Figure 2.21. Analog Clock Made

An analog clock can introduce students to hours and minutes. The ability to count to sixty will benefit students in this exercise. Teachers can slowly introduce skip counting by fives (for the minute hand). Terms such as *hour*, *minute*, *o'clock*, *half past*, *quarter past*, and *quarter till* can be introduced concurrently. Once children are comfortable with the ins and outs of an analog clock, they can experiment with a digital clock. A fun activity involves matching time on a digital clock to an analog clock. For more precise time measurements, like seconds, a **stopwatch** is another useful measurement tool.

Practice Question

15. A kindergarten teacher asks her students to choose a nonstandard unit to measure the length of the classroom. Which of the following is the most appropriate nonstandard unit for the students to use?

    A. a carpet square
    B. paper clips
    C. a yardstick
    D. popsicle sticks

Classifying Geometric Figures

Geometric figures are shapes comprised of points, lines, or planes. A **point** is simply a location in space; it does not have any dimensional properties such as length, area, or volume. A collection of points that extends infinitely in both directions is a **line**, and one that extends infinitely in only one direction is a **ray**. A section of a line with a beginning and end is a **line segment**. A **straightedge** is a helpful tool for creating geometric figures because it allows for straight line segments to be drawn.

Lines, rays, and line segments are examples of **one-dimensional** objects because they can only be measured in one dimensional (length).

Lines, rays, and line segments can intersect to create **angles,** which are measured in degrees or radians. Angles can be measured with **protractors** or calculated based on other known angles. Angles inside a shape are interior angles; those outside the shape are exterior angles.

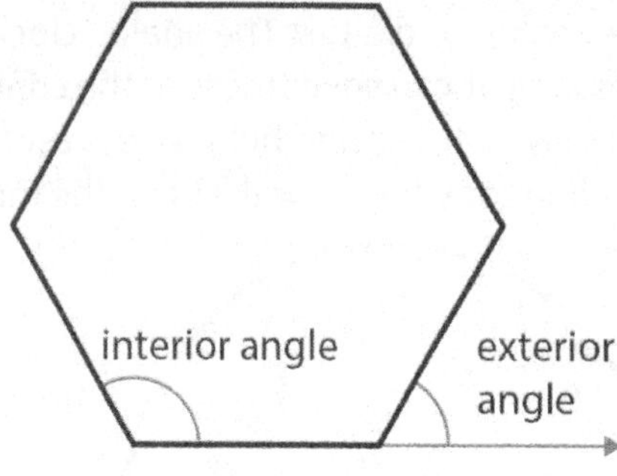

Figure 2.22. Interior and Exterior Angles

Angles less than 90 degrees are **acute,** and angles greater than 90 degrees but less than 180 degrees are **obtuse**. An angle of exactly 90 degrees is a **right angle,** and two lines that form right angles are **perpendicular**. Lines that do not intersect are described as **parallel**. Parallel lines have many properties:

- They have an equal distance between them.
- They never intersect.
- If a **transversal,** or intersecting line, cuts through two parallel lines, it will form eight angles.
- Pairs of internal and external angles made by a transversal are equal.
- Vertically opposite angles made by a transversal are equal.

Two angles with measurements that add up to 90 degrees are **complementary,** and two angles with measurements that add up to 180 degrees are **supplementary**. Adjacent angles (those that touch) have a common vertex and arm, but they do not overlap. The **sum of angles in a triangle** is 180 degrees. When the sum of two adjacent angles equals 180 degrees, they are considered a linear pair.

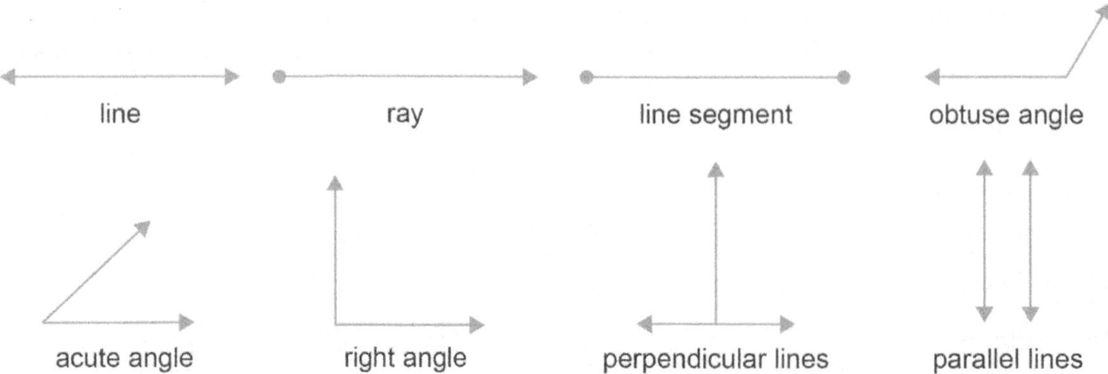

Figure 2.23. Lines and Angles

Two-dimensional objects can be measured in two dimensions (length and width). A **plane** is a two-dimensional object that extends infinitely in both dimensions. **Polygons** are two-dimensional shapes, such as triangles and squares, that have three or more straight sides. **Regular polygons** are polygons with sides that are all the same length. The sum of all the interior angle measurements in a polygon with *n* sides is $(n - 2) \times 180$ degrees, and the sum of all the exterior angles is 360 degrees for any polygon.

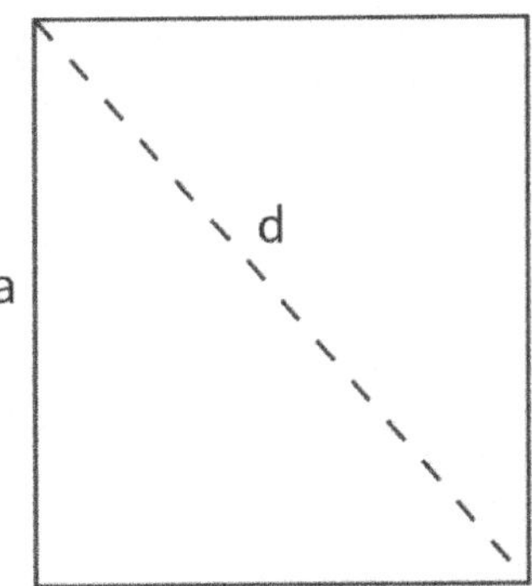

Polygons may also be irregular. **Irregular polygons** have an unequal length of sides and unequal measurements of interior and exterior angles. Unlike regular polygons, which can be partitioned or decomposed to show fractions, irregular polygons cannot be divided into equal parts.

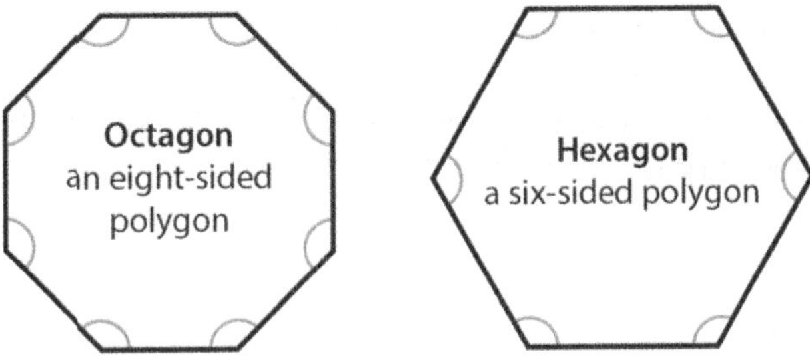

Figure 2.24. Polygons

Three-dimensional objects, such as cubes, can be measured in three dimensions (length, width, and height). Three-dimensional objects are also called **solids,** and the shape of a flattened solid is called a **net**.

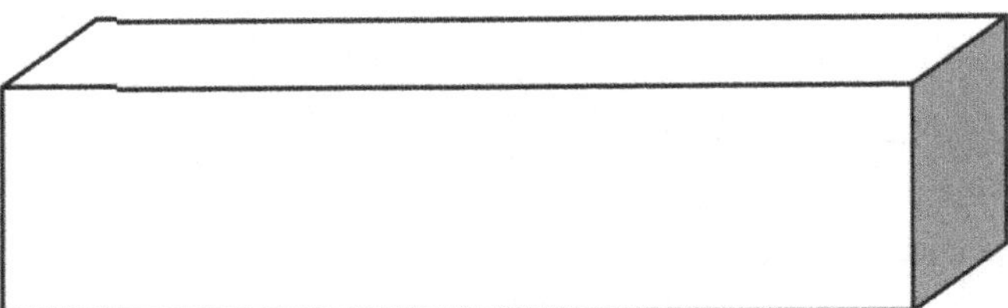

Figure 2.25. Three-Dimensional Object

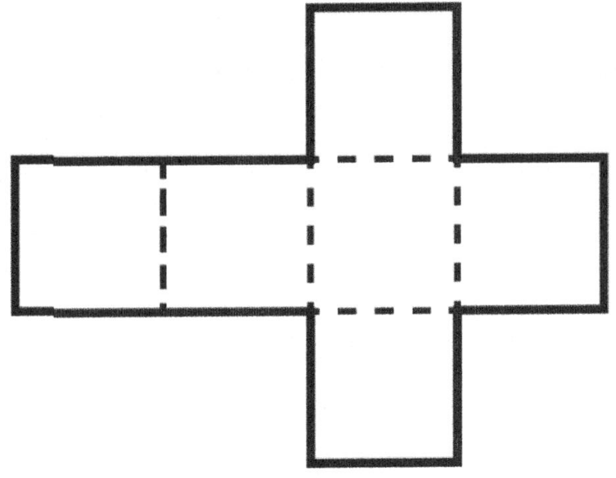

Figure 2.26. Net

Practice Question

16. A second-grade teacher has completed a lesson on categorizing types of two-dimensional shapes. She draws the figure below on the board and asks her students to give a possible name for the shape.

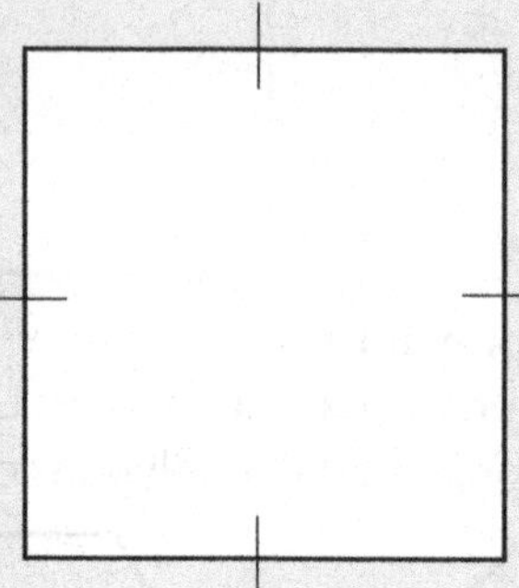

Ari says it is a rectangle, Edmundo says it is a square, and Donny says it is a quadrilateral. Which student(s) correctly named the figure?

A. Ari and Donny
B. Edmundo only
C. Edmundo and Donny
D. all three students

Area, Perimeter, and Volume of Shapes

The **length**, or distance from one point to another on an object, can be determined using a tape measure or a ruler. The size of the surface of a two-dimensional object is its **area**. The area of an object is its length times its width and is measured in square units. For example, if a wall is 3 feet long and 2 feet wide, its area would be 6 square feet. The distance around a two-dimensional figure is its **perimeter**, which can be found by adding the lengths of all the sides.

Table 2.6. Area and Perimeter of Basic Shapes

Shape	Areas	Perimeter
Triangle	$A = \frac{1}{2}bh$	$P = s_1 + s_2 + s_3$
Square	$A = s^2$	$P = 4s$
Rectangle	$A = l \times w$	$P = 2l + 2w$
Circle	$A = \pi r^2$	$C = 2\pi r$ (circumference)

For the rectangle shown in Figure 2.27, the area would be 8 m^2 because 2 m × 4 m = 8 m^2. The perimeter of the rectangle would be 12 meters because the sum of the length of all sides is 2 m + 4 m + 2 m + 4 m = 12 m.

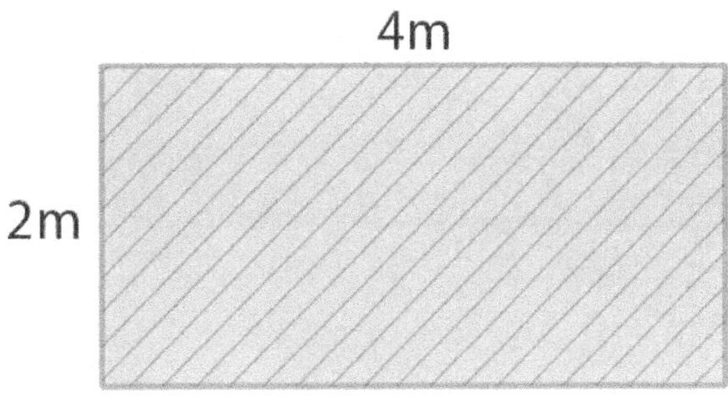

Figure 2.27. Fencing

The **surface area** of a three-dimensional object can be figured by adding the areas of all the sides. For example, the box shown in Figure 2.28. is 4 feet long, 3 feet wide, and 1 foot tall. The surface area is found by adding the areas of each face:

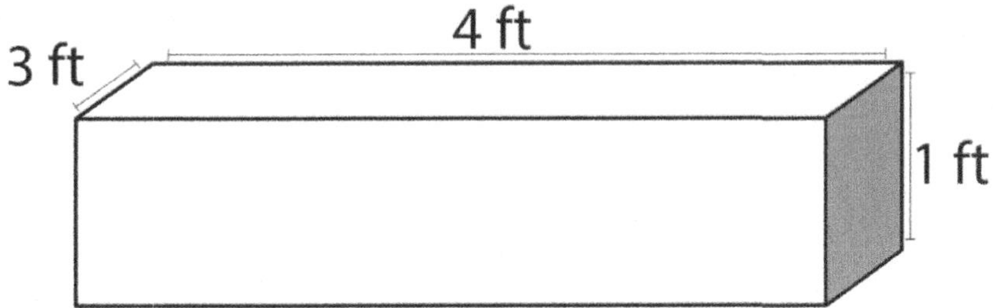

Figure 2.28. Surface Area

- top: $4\ ft. \times\ 3\ ft. =\ 12\ ft^2$
- bottom: $4\ ft. \times\ 3\ ft. =\ 12\ ft^2$
- front: $4\ ft. \times\ 1\ ft. =\ 4\ ft^2$
- back: $4\ ft. \times\ 1\ ft. =\ 4\ ft^2$
- right: $1\ ft. \times\ 1\ ft. =\ 1\ ft^2$
- left: $1\ ft. \times\ 1\ ft. =\ 1\ ft^2$

The surface area is $34\ ft^2$.

A **net** (flattened out three-dimensional solid) can also be used to find the surface area of solids. For example, for a square pyramid with a base with side 6 m and slant height (height in the middle of the triangular faces) of 8 m, the surface area can be calculated with a square and four triangles:

Surface Area = Area of Square Base + Area of 4 Triangles = $6^2 + 4\left[\frac{1}{2}(6 \times 8)\right] = 36 + 96 = 132$ m.

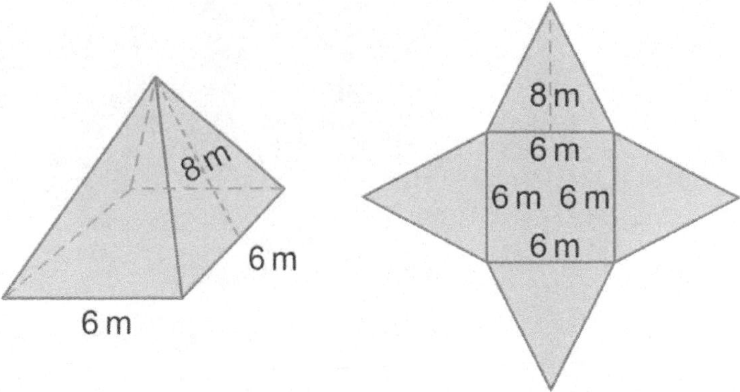

Figure 2.29. Surface Area of a Pyramid

Volume is the amount of space that a three-dimensional object takes up. Volume is measured in cubic units (e.g., ft^3or mm^3). The volume of a solid can be determined by multiplying length times width times height. In the rectangular prism below, the volume is $3\ in. \times\ 1\ in.\ \times\ 1\ in. =\ 3\ in^3$.

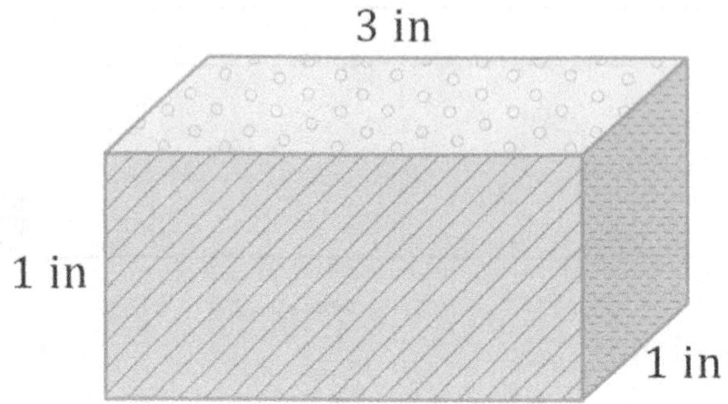

Figure 2.30. Volume

Table 2.7. shows formulas for the surface area and volume of basic solids. Note that the lateral area (LA) is the surface area of the solids without the bases, which are the two parallel faces between the height.

Table 2.7. Area and Volume of Basic Solids		
Solid	**Volume**	**Surface Area**
Sphere (*r* is radius)	$V = \frac{4}{3}\pi r^3$	$SA = 4\pi r^2$
Cube (*s* is side)	$V = s^3$	$SA = 6s^2$
Cylinder (*r* is radius of base; *B* is area of base)	$V = \pi r^2 h$	$SA = LA + 2B = 2\pi rh + 2\pi r^2$
Right Rectangular Prism (*LA*, or lateral area, is the perimeter of base times height; *B* is area of base)	$V = Bh$	$SA = LA + 2B$

Table 2.7. Area and Volume of Basic Solids		
Solid	**Volume**	**Surface Area**
Cone (*h* is height [distance from center to tip]; *r* is radius [distance from center of circle to tip of cone], *s* is slant [length of the edge of the circle to the tip of the cone])	$V = \frac{1}{3}\pi r^2 h$	$SA = \pi rs + \pi r^2$

Figure 2.31. shows an example of finding the volume and surface area of a **right rectangular prism** with a height of 8 cm and square bases with sides of 2 cm. Remember that the bases are the two squares that are on either side of the height.

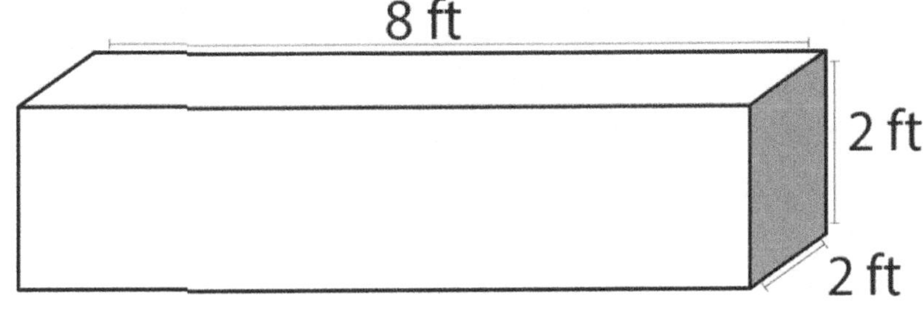

Figure 2.31. Surface Area of a Right Rectangular Prism

$$SA = LA + 2B = [(2 + 2 + 2 + 2) \times 8] + [2 \times (2 \times 2)] = 64 + 8 = 72 \text{ cm}$$

Note that the SA can also be found by adding the areas of all the sides:

$$SA = (2 \times 8) + (2 \times 8) + (2 \times 8) + (2 \times 8) + (2 \times 2) + (2 \times 2) = 64 + 8 = 72 \text{ cm}$$

To find the **area of irregular polygons,** the shape can first be decomposed into regular polygons. Standard area formulas can then be used to find the areas of those regular polygons. These areas would then be added together to get the total area. To find the perimeter of irregular shapes, simply add the length of all sides.

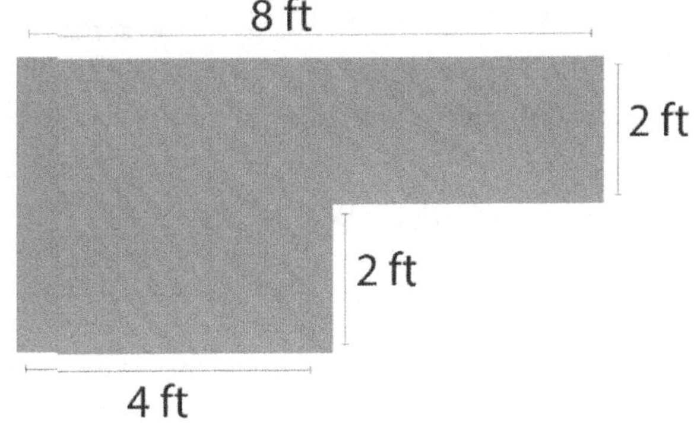

Figure 2.32. Irregular Polygons

Practice Question

17. What is the perimeter of the regular polygon?

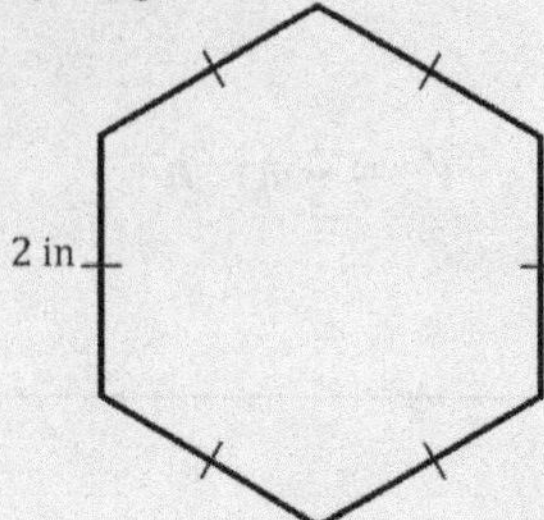

A. 4 in.
B. 8 in.
C. 12 in.
D. 32 in.

Circles

Circles are a fundamental shape in geometry. A **compass** is a tool with a needle, hinge, and pencil that can be used to draw circles or arcs.

A **circle** is the set of all the points in a plane that are the same distance from a fixed point (called the center). The distance from the center to any point on the circle is the **radius** of the circle. The distance around the circle (the perimeter) is called the **circumference**.

> **Did You Know?**
>
> Although traditional compasses have sharp points that may cause concerns for young students, newer types of "safety" compasses can be used by students of all ages.

The ratio of a circle's circumference to its diameter is a constant value called pi (π), an irrational number which is commonly rounded to 3.14. The formula to find a circle's circumference is $C = 2\pi r$. The formula to find the enclosed area of a circle is $A = \pi r^2$.

Circles have a number of unique parts:

The **diameter** is the largest measurement across a circle. It passes through the circle's center, extending from one side of the circle to the other. The measure of the diameter is twice the measure of the radius:

> **Helpful Hint**
>
> "Trying to square a circle" means attempting to create a square that has the same area as a circle. Because the area of a circle depends on π, which is an irrational number, this task is impossible. The phrase is often used to describe trying to do something that can't be done.

- A line that cuts across a circle and touches it twice is called a **secant** line.
- The part of a secant line that lies within a circle is called a **chord**.
- A line that touches a circle or any curve at one point is **tangent** to the circle or the curve. A line tangent to a circle and a radius drawn to the point of tangency meet at a right angle (90°).
- An **arc** is any portion of a circle between two points on the circle. The measure of an arc is in degrees, whereas the length of the arc will be in linear measurement (such as centimeters or inches).
- An angle with its vertex at the center of a circle is called a **central angle**.

- A **sector** is the part of a circle that is inside the rays of a central angle (its shape is like a slice of pie).

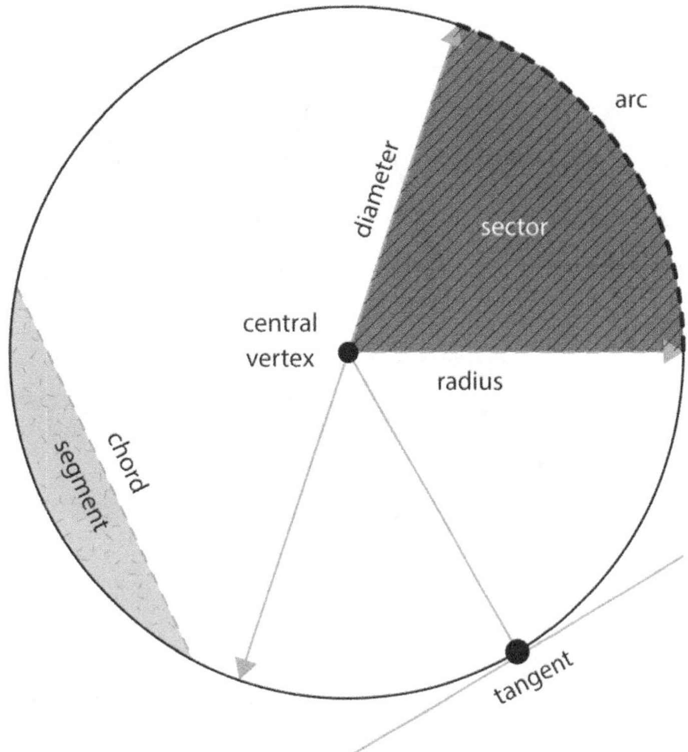

Figure 2.33. Parts of a Circle

Practice Question

18. W, X, Y, and Z lie on a circle with center A. If the diameter of the circle is 75, what is the sum of $\overline{AW}$, $\overline{AX}$, $\overline{AY}$, and $\overline{AZ}$?
    A. 75
    B. 300
    C. 150
    D. 106.5

Triangles

Triangles have three sides, and the three interior angles always sum to $180°$. The formula for the area of a triangle is $A = \frac{1}{2}bh$ or one-half the product of the base and height (or altitude) of the triangle.

Triangles can be classified in two ways: by sides and by angles. A **scalene triangle** has no equal sides or angles. An **isosceles triangle** has two equal sides and two equal angles (often called base angles). In an **equilateral triangle,** all three sides are equal as are all three angles; moreover, because the sum of the angles of a triangle is always $180°$, each angle of an equilateral triangle must be 60°.

A **right triangle** has one right angle (90°) and two acute angles. An **acute triangle** has three acute angles (all angles are less than 90°). An **obtuse triangle** has one obtuse angle (more than 90°) and two acute angles.

Triangles Based on Sides

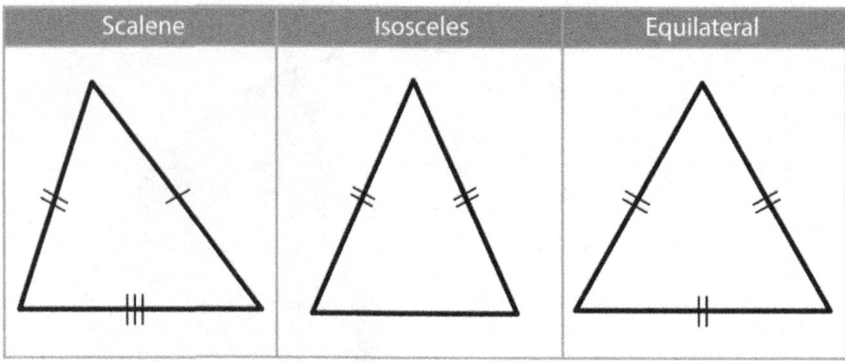

Triangles Based on Angles

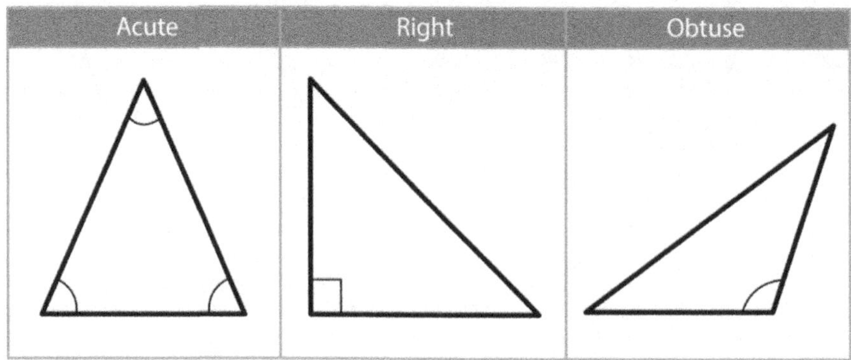

Figure 2.34. Types of Triangles

For any triangle, the side opposite the largest angle will have the longest length, while the side opposite the smallest angle will have the shortest length. The **triangle inequality theorem** states that the sum of any two sides of a triangle must be greater than the third side. This leads to the **third-side rule:** if b and c are two sides of a triangle, then the measure of the third side a must be between the sum of the other two sides and the difference of the other two sides: $c - b < a < c + b$.

Solving for missing angles or sides of a triangle is a common type of triangle problem. Often a right triangle will come up on its own or within another triangle. The relationship among a right triangle's sides is known as the **Pythagorean theorem**: $a^2 + b^2 = c^2$, where *c* is the hypotenuse and is across from the $90°$ angle.

Did You Know?

The Pythagorean theorem is usually credited to Greek philosopher and mathematician Pythagoras; however, many scholars believe it was actually developed after his death by one of his followers.

Practice Question

19. Which of the following could be the perimeter of a triangle with two sides that measure 13 and 5?
    - A. 24.5
    - B. 26.5
    - C. 36
    - D. 37

Working with Shapes

Sides or parts of a shape can be compared to determine **symmetry**, or whether the shape is exactly the same on both sides when a dividing or mirror line is drawn through it. Lines that divide shapes into equal parts are known as **lines of symmetry**. Lines of symmetry (or any other lines) can be used to dissect shapes or change them into new figures. For example, a square can be cut in half to create two rectangles or a parallelogram can be cut in half to make two triangles. Based on how the shapes are dissected, their component pieces may or may not be equivalent.

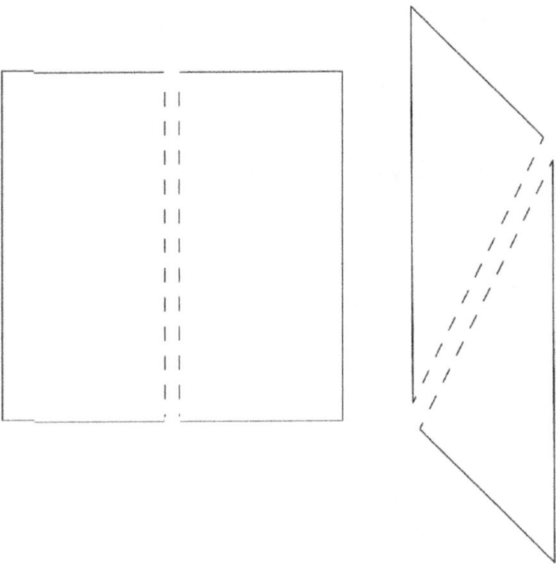

Figure 2.35. Lines of Symmetry

Shapes can also be manipulated or transformed. **Transformation** refers to moving a shape within a coordinate plane. **Reflection** flips the shape but does not change its size or shape; it creates a mirror image. **Rotation**, as its name implies, is the rotation of a shape by a certain degree. A **translation** is distinct from a reflection or rotation because the shape is not turned, flipped, or changed; it is only slid or moved across the plane.

Similar shapes have the same angle measurements and sides that are proportional. The **scale factor** is the ratio of corresponding sides of the figures. If the dimensions of a figure are **dilated** (made smaller or larger with proportional dimensions) by a scale factor of $\frac{a}{b}$, then the surface area of the new dilated solid is multiplied by $\frac{a^2}{b^2}$, and the volume of the new dilated solid is multiplied by $\frac{a^3}{b^3}$.

For example, in the solids shown in Figure 2.36, the scale factor is $\frac{16}{8} = 2$. Therefore, the surface area of the second solid is equal to the surface area of the first solid multiplied by $2^2 = 4$, and the volume of the second solid is equal to the volume of the first solid's volume multiplied by $2^3 = 8$.

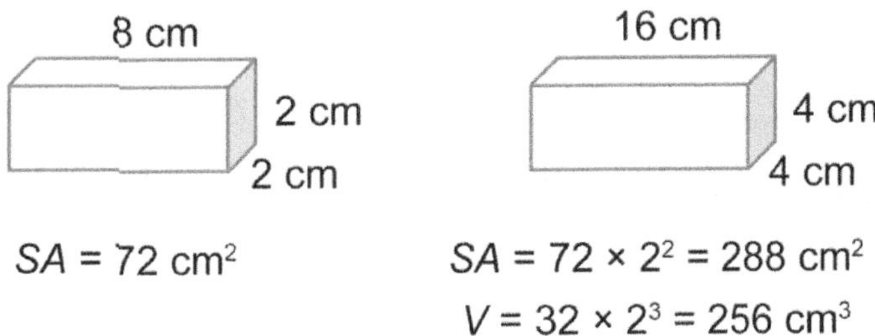

Figure 2.36. Dilated Solids

Relationships between geometric shapes are proven in logical arguments called **proofs**. For example, a problem may ask students to prove that line segments are equal, sides of a shape are equal, or that all angles are **congruent** (have the same degree measurement regardless of their direction).

There are many accepted theorems that can be used in geometric proofs. The following are some of the most commonly used ones:

- All right angles are congruent.
- If two angles are supplementary to the same angle or to congruent angles, they are congruent.
- If two angles are complementary to the same angle or to congruent angles, they are congruent.
- If two angles form a linear pair, they are supplementary.
- **Vertical angles** (angles opposite each other, formed by two crossing lines) are congruent.

Examples

Given that angles A and B are supplementary and angles B and C are supplementary, prove that angle A is congruent to angle C.

1. Given:
$\angle A$ and $\angle B$ are supplementary

$\angle B$ and $\angle C$ are supplementary

2. Definition of supplementary angles:
$m\angle A + m\angle B = 180°$

$m\angle B + m\angle C = 180°$

3. Transitive property:
$\angle A + m\angle B = \angle B + m\angle C$

$m\angle A = m\angle C$

4. Angles A and C are congruent.

Shapes can be used to create patterns or **tessellations**. Tessellations are shapes that completely cover a surface with no gaps or overlaps. Regular tessellations are made of a repeated triangle, square, or hexagon pattern. Semi-regular tessellations contain more than one type of regular polygon (such as triangles and squares).

Tessellations have a pattern that can be determined by finding the vertex or corner of the pattern and counting up the sides of the shapes around it in order.

Figure 2.37. Tessellation

The above semi-regular tessellation has a 4.8.8 pattern because the pattern is one square (4) and two octagons (8).

Practice Question

20. Cone *A* is similar to cone *B* with a scale factor of 3:4. If the volume of cone *A* is 54π, what is the volume of cone *B*?

A. 72π

B. 128π

C. 162π

D. 216π

Probability and Statistics

Data Collection

In quantitative research, data is often collected in surveys, or questionnaires, which often employ a Likert scale to understand people's habits or agreement with statements. Likert scales translate opinions into numerical values (i.e., very likely = 5, somewhat likely = 4, maybe = 3, somewhat unlikely = 2, very unlikely = 1, never = 0).

To be effective, surveys must be given to a representative **sample** within the total **population**. For example, to understand political leanings, a sample of people of various backgrounds, ages, and genders from various locations would be used. This would allow results to be **generalized** or applied to the broader population from the representative sample. If a representative sample is not used (e.g., if the survey is only given to White men in a suburb of Georgia), the results will be skewed and could not be generalized to the entire American population.

Before generalizing data (which can only be done with higher-order statistical tests), researchers often run a preliminary test, called a **goodness of fit** test. Common goodness of fit tests are the Chi-square test and the Shapiro-Wilk test. These tests identify whether the data that one has obtained comes from a sample with a **normal distribution** (see next section). If the data is from a normal distribution, then higher-level **parametric** statistical procedures can be used. If the data is not from a normal distribution, then **nonparametric** statistical tests, which are less powerful, must be used.

Did You Know?

The most commonly used statistical procedures are t-tests and ANOVA, both parametric tests.

Practice Question

21. As part of a class project, a student surveys seven of her peers to determine their favorite ice cream flavors. Because six out of ten of her classmates prefer chocolate ice cream, she concludes that "Americans like chocolate ice cream best." What feedback might her teacher provide?
   A. Her sample did not have a normal distribution, so generalization to all Americans should be questioned.
   B. Her sample was not representative of the entire American population, so generalization is not possible.
   C. Her survey did not include Likert scale items, so it is not reflective of the total population.
   D. Her survey sought to answer only one research question, so a larger sample was needed.

Data Analysis

Statistics is the study of data. Analyzing data requires using **measures of central tendency** (mean, median, and mode) to identify trends or patterns.

The **mean** is the average; it is determined by adding all outcomes and then dividing by the total number of outcomes. For example, the average of the data set {16, 19, 19, 25, 27, 29, 75} is equal to $\frac{16+19+19+25+27+29+75}{7} = \frac{210}{7} = 30.$

The **median** is the number in the middle when the data set is arranged in order from least to greatest. For example, in the data set {16, 19, 19, **25**, 27, 29, 75}, the median is 25. When a data set contains an even number of values, finding the median requires averaging the two middle values. In the data set {75, 80, 82, 100}, the two numbers in the middle are 80 and 82. Consequently, the median will be the average of these two values: $\frac{80+82}{2} = 81.$

Finally, the **mode** is the most frequent outcome in a data set. In the set {16, 19, 19, 25, 27, 29, 75}, the mode is 19 because it occurs twice, which is more than any of the other numbers. If several values appear, an equal and most frequent number of times, both values are considered the mode.

Helpful Hint

Mode is most common. Median is in the middle (like a median in the road). Mean is average.

Other useful indicators include range and outliers. The **range** is the difference between the highest and the lowest numbers in a data set. For example, the range of the set {16, 19, 19, 25, 27, 29, 75} is 75 – 16 = 59. **Outliers,** or data points that are much different from other data points, should be noted as they can skew the central tendency. In the data set {16, 19, 19, 25, 27, 29, 75}, the value 75 is far outside the other values and raises the value of the mean. Without the outlier, the mean is much closer to the other data points.

- $\frac{16+19+19+25+27+29+75}{7} = \frac{210}{7} = 30$
- $\frac{16+19+19+25+27+29}{6} = 22.5$

When a data distribution is symmetrical, the mean, median, and mode are the same; this is called a **normal distribution**. Generally, the median is a better indicator of a central tendency if outliers are present to skew the mean. If a distribution is **skewed left** (outliers tend to be smaller numbers), typically the mean is less than the median, and the median is the best indicator. If the distribution is **skewed right** (outliers tend to be larger numbers), typically the mean is greater than the median, and again, the median is the best indicator. So, the mean tends to be pulled toward the longer "tails" of the data.

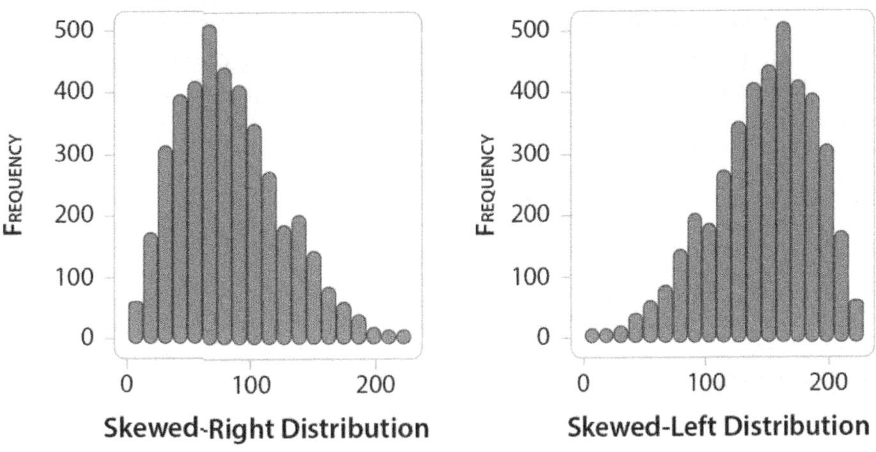

Figure 2.38. Skew

Beyond measures of central tendency and correlations, data may also be analyzed in terms of ratios, proportions, and percent change.

As mentioned earlier, **ratio** is a comparison of two quantities. For example, if a class consists of 15 women and 10 men, the ratio of women to men is 15 to 10. This ratio can also be written as 15:10 or $\frac{15}{10}$. Ratios, like fractions, can be reduced by dividing by common factors.

A **proportion** is a statement that two ratios are equal. For example, the proportion $\frac{5}{10} = \frac{7}{14}$ is true because both ratios are equal to $\frac{1}{2}$.

The **cross product** is found by multiplying the numerator of one fraction by the denominator of the other (*across* the equal sign).

$$\frac{a}{b} = \frac{c}{d} \rightarrow ad = bc$$

The fact that the cross products of proportions are equal can be used to solve proportions in which one of the values is missing. Use *x* to represent the missing value, and then cross multiply and solve.

$$\frac{5}{x} = \frac{7}{14}$$

$$5(14) = x(7)$$

$$70 = 7x$$

$$x = 10$$

A **percent** (or percentage) means *per hundred* and is expressed with the percent symbol (%). For example, 54% means 54 out of 100. Percentages are converted to decimals by moving the decimal point two places to the left.

$$54\% = 0.54$$

Percentages can be solved by setting up a proportion.

$$\frac{part}{whole} = \frac{\%}{100}$$

Percent change involves a change from an original amount. Often percent change problems appear as word problems that include discounts, growth, or markups.

In order to solve percent change problems, it is necessary to identify the percent change (as a decimal), the amount of change, and the original amount. (Keep in mind that one of these will be the value being solved for.) These values can then be substituted into the following equations:

- amount of change = original amount × percent change
- percent change = amount of change ÷ original amount
- original amount = amount of change ÷ percent change

Practice Questions

22. Ken has 6 grades in English class. Each grade is worth 100 points. Ken has a 92% average in English. If Ken's first five grades are 90, 100, 95, 83, and 87, what did Ken earn for the sixth grade?
    A. 80
    B. 92
    C. 97
    D. 100

23. What is the relationship between the mean and the median in a data set that is skewed right?
    A. The mean is greater than the median.
    B. The mean is less than the median.
    C. The mean and median are equal.
    D. The mean may be greater than, less than, or equal to the median.

Data Presentation

Data can be presented in a variety of ways. The most appropriate depends on the data being displayed. **Box plots** (also called box-and-whisker plots) show data using the median, range, and outliers of a data set. They provide a helpful visual guide, showing how data is distributed around the median. In Figure 2.39., 81 is the median and the range is 100 – 0, or 100.

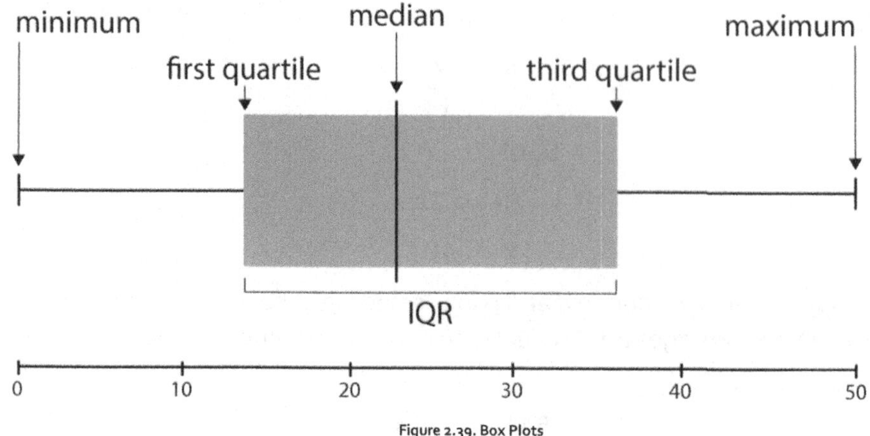

Figure 2.39. Box Plots

Bar graphs use bars of different lengths to compare data. The independent variable on a bar graph is grouped into categories such as months, flavors, or locations, and the dependent variable will be a quantity. Thus, comparing the length of bars provides a visual guide to the relative amounts in each category. **Double bar graphs** show more than one data set on the same set of axes.

Bar graph:

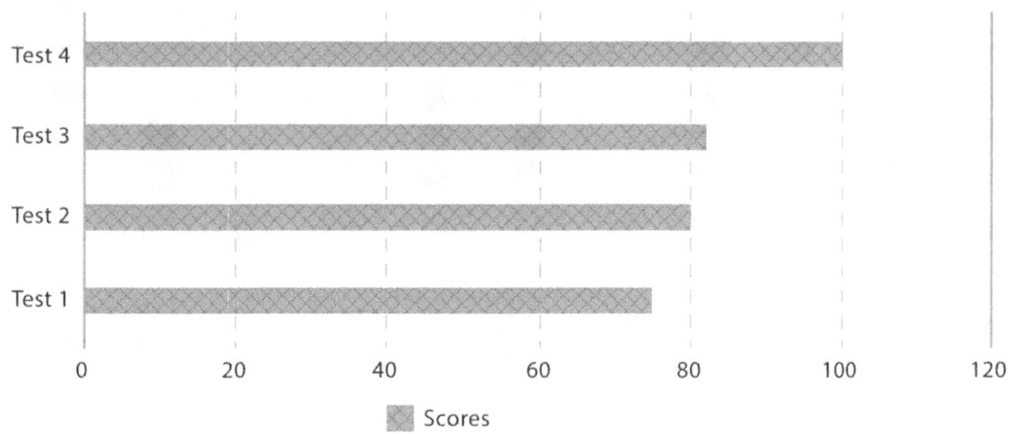

Figure 2.40. Bar Graph

Double bar graph:

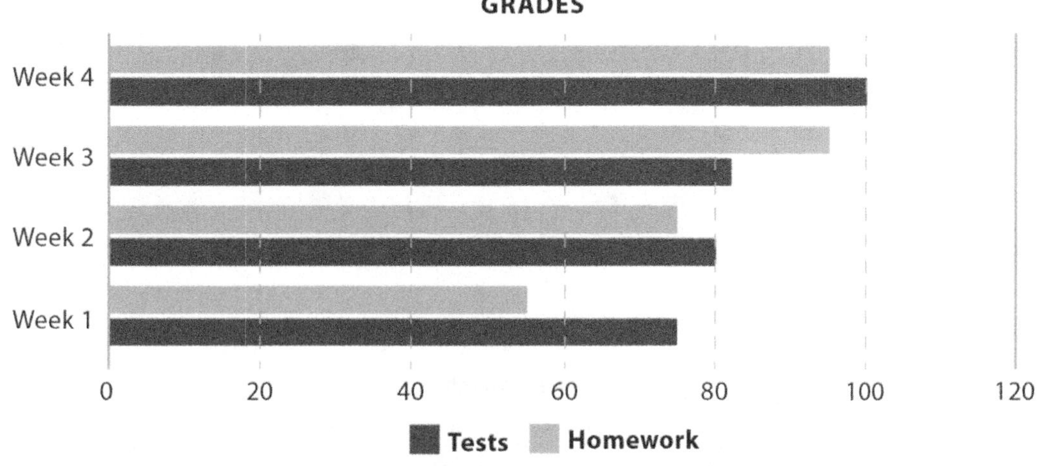

Figure 2.41. Double Bar Graph

Histograms similarly use bars to compare data, but the independent variable is a continuous variable that has been "binned" or divided into categories. For example, the time of day can be broken down into 8:00 a.m. to 12:00 p.m., 12:00 p.m. to 4:00 p.m., and so on. Usually (but not always) a gap is included between the bars of a bar graph but not a histogram.

Dot plots display the frequency of a value or event data graphically using dots, and thus can be used to observe the distribution of a data set. Typically, a value or category is listed on the *x*-axis, and the number of times that value appears in the data set is represented by a line of vertical dots. Dot plots make it easy to see which values occur most often.

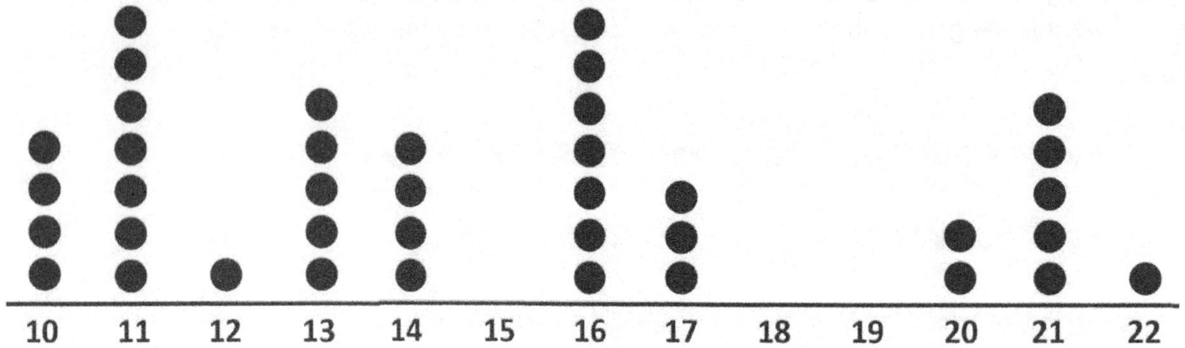

Figure 2.42. Dot Plot

Scatterplots use points to show relationships between two variables which can be plotted as coordinate points. One variable describes a position on the *x*-axis, and the other a point on the *y*-axis. Scatterplots can suggest relationships between variables. For example, both variables might increase, or one may increase when the other decreases.

> **Check your understanding**
>
> What computer programs or digital tools can students use to create charts and graphs?

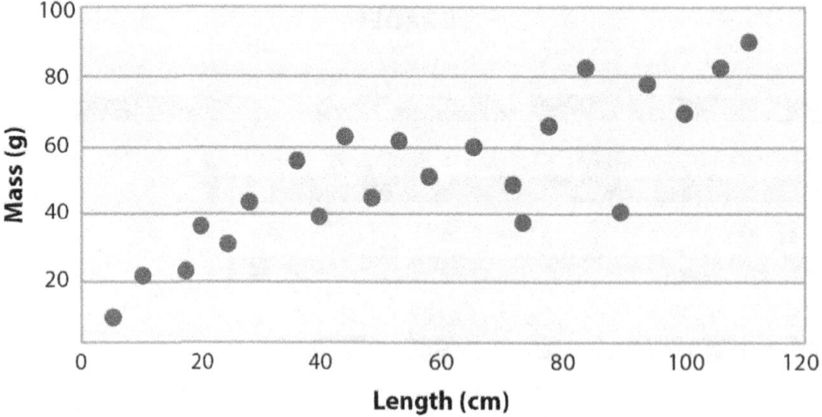

Figure 2.43. Scatterplot

Line graphs show changes in data by connecting points on a scatterplot using a line. These graphs will often measure time on the *x*-axis and are used to show trends in the data, such as temperature changes over a day or school attendance throughout the year. **Double line graphs** present two sets of data on the same set of axes.

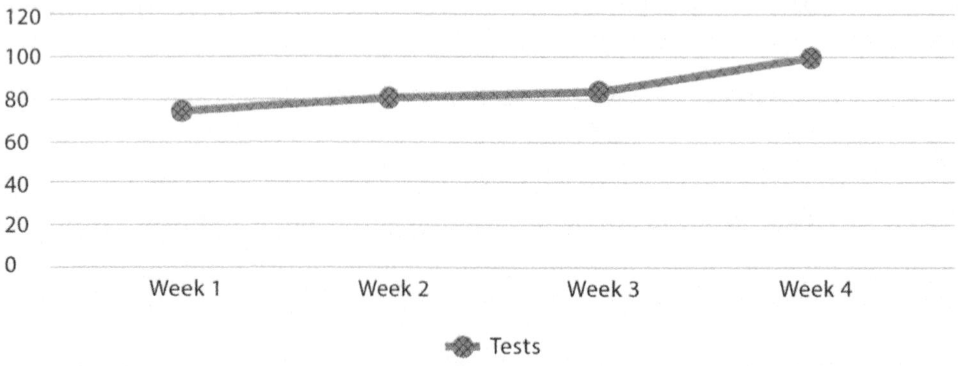

Figure 2.44. Line Graph

Circle graphs (also called pie charts) are used to show parts of a whole: the "pie" is the whole, and each "slice" represents a percentage or part of the whole.

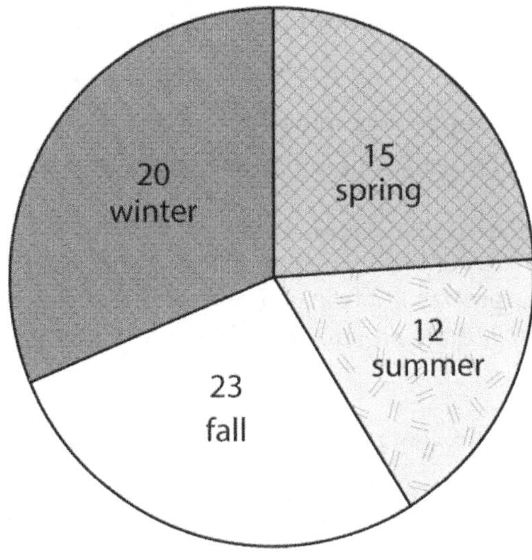

Figure 2.45. Pie Chart

Practice Question

24. The pie graph below shows how a state's government plans to spend its annual budget of $3 billion. How much more money does the state plan to spend on infrastructure than education?

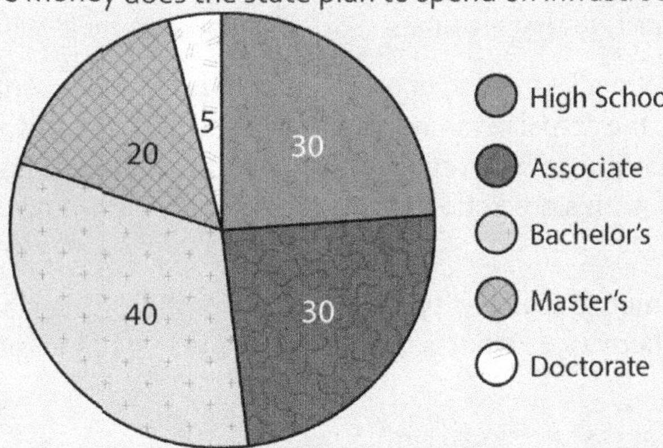

A. $60,000,000
B. $120,000,000
C. $300,000,000
D. $600,000,000

Probability

Sometimes the goal of quantitative research and data analysis is to determine the chance of something occurring or to make a prediction.

Probability is the likelihood, or chance, that something will happen. Probability is expressed as a fraction with the numerator being the number of successful outcomes and the denominator being the total number of outcomes or as a decimal. For example, if there are 25 marbles in a bag and 4 marbles are red, the probability of randomly pulling a red marble out of the bag is or $\frac{4}{25}$ (also written as 0.16 or 16%).

Another example involves a spinner with 8 sections, with 3 that are choice A, 2 that are choice B, and 3 that are choice C. The probability of landing on choice A would be $\frac{3}{8}$ (also written as 0.375 or 37.5%).

Probabilities are always numbers between 0 and 1, inclusive. If there is no chance of something occurring, its probability is 0; if there's a 100% chance of something occurring, its probability is 1.

Replacement means putting something back the way it was before an event occurred. For example, the probability of drawing 4 red marbles out of 25 marbles twice, with replacement, would be $\frac{4}{25} \times \frac{4}{25} = \frac{16}{625}$. The same probability without replacement would be $\frac{4}{25} \times \frac{3}{24} = \frac{12}{600} = \frac{1}{50}$ since there would be one less red marble and one less of the total marbles. Note that probabilities are multiplied when the events are independent from each other.

For the probability of something happening at least one time, take the probably of the event not happening at all, and subtract this probability from 1. For example, the probability of rolling a two on at least one of two dice would be *1 minus the probability of not rolling a two on either die*, which would be $1 - \left(\frac{5}{6} \times \frac{5}{6}\right) = 1 - \frac{25}{36} = \frac{11}{36}$, or 0.31.

Probability can also be **predicted** through a **probability model**. For example, if someone has 3 green socks, 2 blue socks, 4 yellow socks, 6 red socks, and 5 purple socks in a drawer and pulls out 1 sock ten times (putting it back each time), how many times should a sock that is NOT green or blue be expected?

Calculate *P* (not green or blue sock). The answer would be the total number of favorable outcomes (not green or blue socks = 15) divided by the total number of outcomes (20), or 15/20 (or ¾). After converting this to a decimal, the probability of NOT drawing a green or blue sock is 0.75. This is the probability model.

The probability model can then be used to make a **prediction**. If there are 10 draws, you would need to multiply 0.75 × 10 to make a prediction that 7.5 times, a green or blue sock will NOT be drawn.

The prediction can be tested by actually drawing one sock ten times to see how many non-blue or non-green socks are selected. Likely, the actual result will not match the prediction of 7.5 times because the sample size is so small. If the experiment were repeated with a total of 2,000 socks (300 green, 200 blue, 400 yellow, 600 red, 500 purple), with a prediction of 750, the actual result would probably be far closer to the prediction.

Probability can also involve **geometric probability**. For example, probability can also be expressed as a ratio of two areas. Looking at Figure 2.46., what is the likelihood that a point in the white area will be selected?

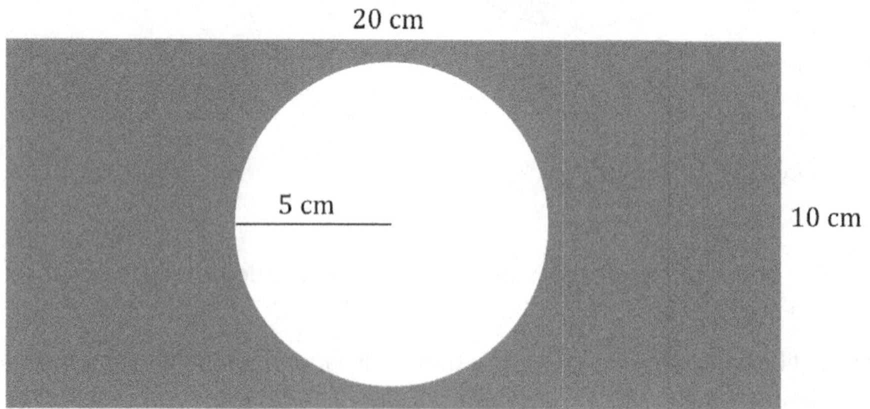

Figure 2.46. Geometric Probability

To find the probability, compare the area of the circle with the area of the rectangle. The area of the circle is $200 - 5r^2$.

$$= 200 - 78.53982 = 121.46018$$

We then need to divide that number by the area of the rectangle, or $20 \times 10 = 200$.

$$\text{So}, 121.46018 \div 200 = 0.61$$

The probability of picking a point in the white circle is about 0.61 or a 61% chance.

Practice Question

25. Some of a hotel's 400 rooms have an ocean view and the rest of the rooms do not. If the probability of getting a room with an ocean view is 35%, how many rooms do NOT have an ocean view?

    A. 140
    B. 200
    C. 260
    D. 300

Answer Key

1. B: The Egyptians used a system that was likely the precursor to Roman numerals.

2. B: In the concrete stage, student understanding is built by using concrete objects or manipulatives.

3. D: Listing projected income and expenses each month would help students see that income must exceed expenses; otherwise, money will be lost, and they will be in debt.

4. C: The number $\frac{13}{14}$ is a rational number because it can be written as a fraction but not as a whole number (without the fraction).

5. C: This equation correctly simplifies and decomposes the number into hundreds, tens, and ones.

6. A: The last two digits of this number are divisible by 4, so this number is divisible by 4 and should therefore not have a remainder.

7. A: Although the commutative property applies to addition and multiplication, it does not apply to division.

8. D: To convert a fraction to a percent, the student will need to convert fractions so they have a denominator of 100.

9. B: Seven of eight pizza slices are left after Carla takes one, so $\frac{7}{8}$ of the pizza remains; 7 is the numerator of this fraction.

10. C: Decomposing fractions is the process of splitting them into smaller pieces.

11. A: Substitute 5 for *x*.

$$2(5) - 5 = 10 - 5 = 5$$

12. A: Use the points to find the slope.

$$m = \frac{y_2 - y_1}{x_2 - x_1} = \frac{-3 - 9}{4 - (-2)} = -2$$

Use the point-slope equation to find the equation of the line.

$$(y - y_1) = m(x - x_1)$$

$$y - (-3) = -2(x - 4)$$

$$\mathbf{y = -2x + 5}$$

13. B: The difference between the *x* value (2) and the difference between the *y* values (4) are both constant, so the function is linear. Find the slope to identify the right equation:

$$m = \frac{y_2 - y_1}{x_2 - x_1} = \frac{15 - 11}{5 - 3} = 2$$

$y = 2x + 5$ is a linear relationship because $11 = 2(3) + 5$. The slope is 2, since there is a constant difference of 2 for the *x*-values and a difference of 4 for the *y*-values. Substitute the *x*- and *y*-values into the equation.

14. D: The amount she makes per hour (*t*) is 27.75, so the amount 27.75*t* will be added to her base salary of $740:

$$\mathbf{A = 27.75t + 740}$$

15. A: Students can lay carpet squares end-to-end to measure the length of the room.

16. D: The figure is a quadrilateral, a square, and a rectangle: it has four equal, parallel sides and four right angles.

17. C: Add the length of each side to find the perimeter:

$2 \text{ in.} + 2 \text{ in.} + 2 \text{ in.} + 2 \text{ in.} + 2 \text{ in.} + 2 \text{ in.} = 12 \text{ in.}$

18. C: All the points lie on the circle, so each line segment is a radius. The sum of the 4 lines will be 4 times the radius.

$r = \frac{75}{2} = 37.5$

$4r = \mathbf{150}$

19. B: Use the third side rule to find the possible values for the third side, and then calculate the possible perimeters.

$$13 - 5 < s < 13 + 5$$

$$8 < s < 18$$

$$13 + 5 + 8 < P < 13 + 5 + 18$$

$$26 < P < 36$$

20. B: Set up a proportion. Cube the scale factor when calculating volume.

$$\frac{54\pi}{x} = \frac{3^3}{4^3}$$

$$x = 128\pi$$

21. B: Generalization is only possible with an adequate sample. Minimum sample size varies based on statistical procedure to be used.

22. C: If Ken has six scores that average 92%, his total number of points earned is found by multiplying the average by the number of scores:

$$92 \times 6 = 552$$

To find how many points he earned on the sixth test, subtract the sum of the other scores from 552:

$$90 + 100 + 95 + 83 + 87 = 455$$

$$552 - 455 = 97$$

23. A: If the data is skewed right, the set includes extreme values that are to the right, or high. The median is unaffected by these high values, but the mean includes these high values and would therefore be greater.

24. A: Find the amount the state will spend on infrastructure and education, and then find the difference.

$$infrastructure = 0.2(3{,}000{,}000{,}000) = 600{,}000{,}000$$

$$education = 0.18(3{,}000{,}000{,}000) = 540{,}000{,}000$$

$$600{,}000{,}000 - 540{,}000{,}000 = \mathbf{\$60{,}000{,}000}$$

25. C: The probability of getting a room without an ocean view is equal to 1 minus the probability of getting a room with an ocean view.

$$P_{view} = 1 - P_{no\ ocean\ view}$$

$$P_{view} = 1 - 0.35 = 0.65$$

Use the equation for percentages to find the number of rooms without a view.

$$part = percentage \times whole = (0.65)400 = \mathbf{260\ rooms}$$

3 Social Studies

Social Studies Skills

Social studies encourages students to investigate questions about people, their values, and the choices they make. In other words, students engage in **inquiry**: they seek information, knowledge, or the truth. Inquiry-based learning in social studies is a process in which students gather information by identifying relevant questions and uncovering sources in order to interpret information and report their findings.

Teachers can help students develop critical thinking skills by encouraging **questioning**. The more questions students ask, the more carefully they evaluate sources and actively research information that helps them to draw conclusions.

Using research and resource materials is a critical component in social studies processes. There are two main types of sources: primary and secondary. **Primary sources** are original records that have information from a person who experienced the event firsthand. Primary sources include original documents like the US Constitution and Declaration of Independence, journals, speeches, physical artifacts, and some first-person accounts in places such as newspapers or historical documents.

Figure 3.1. Primary Source: Photograph Taken During the Great Depression

Secondary sources are texts created by people who did not personally experience or witness the event. They are based on primary sources. Examples of secondary sources include books, research papers and analyses, and some reports or features in newspapers and magazines written by journalists and other writers.

Using a variety of sources is essential when conducting social studies research. Analyzing the relationship between primary and secondary sources relating to the same subject matter gives students a deeper understanding of the topic being studied. Understanding the advantages and disadvantages of each source also helps students understand and actively engage in **data interpretation**: assessing whether their sources are valid or appropriate.

Using primary sources permits students to draw **conclusions** based on their own interpretations of those sources, rather than relying on secondary interpretations. Primary sources also allow students to address the topic more directly and usually provide information found nowhere else; however, certain primary sources may not have any objective information or accurate facts. Moreover, these types of sources can be difficult to find and analyze.

Secondary sources enrich study by providing different perspectives and expert conclusions. Furthermore, using reputable sources may be more efficient; they may be more accessible or easier to understand. However, secondary sources may focus on issues beyond the topic under study, be outdated, or tainted by the author's bias.

Students should consider the **point of view**, or perspective, of the person or group who created the source. For example, a primary source describing a treaty may be very different depending on whether it comes from a Native American or American government source. While virtually all sources contain some **bias**, or slant, informed by the opinion of the author, students should look for and consider signs of this bias, such as harsh or emotional language or even historical inaccuracies.

Some resources are not objective sources at all but simply **propaganda**, or communication designed to promote an agenda. While such posters, advertisements, cartoons, or other media may be useful to understand the goals of certain interest groups, they do not always reveal the prevailing opinion of the time.

Students must think critically when reading or using any source. They should understand how to distinguish between **fact** and **opinion**. Facts are statements that can be proven, and opinions are statements that reflect someone's view; they cannot be proven. Understanding these differences helps students evaluate sources. If students can distinguish between fact and opinion, they can determine the validity of the source in question.

As students work to master the TEKS for their grade levels, they will be required to apply many broad skills:

- categorizing or sorting into categories (e.g., identifying whether bodies of water are lakes, rivers, or streams)
- comparing and contrasting or determining similarities and differences (e.g., noting that the Comal and Rio Grande are both rivers, but only the Rio Grande forms a border with another nation)
- making generalizations or broad conclusions (e.g., determining that, though there are some exceptions, Texas River Authorities are generally the groups responsible for managing Texas rivers)
- understanding chronology or sequence of events (e.g., creating a timeline of events surrounding Texas independence)

- using problem-solving strategies (e.g., finding that, despite having great interest in a certain historical topic for a project, there is a dearth of information available and they will have to problem solve)

Students will also employ decision-making skills as they participate in various guided and independent activities. To make sound decisions, students should use the following checklist:

1. gather information
2. identify options
3. predict potential consequences of these options
4. take action based on these predictions

Practice Question

1. Which of the following are examples of primary sources?
   A. original photographs, first-hand newspaper reports, textbooks, and interviews
   B. memoirs, original photographs, first-hand newspaper reports, and diary entries
   C. speeches, newspaper reports, essays, and reviews
   D. essays, reviews, textbooks, and analytical papers

Teaching the Social Studies TEKS

The social studies TEKS were designed with the intention of providing students with a clear and sequenced learning experience. The Social Studies TEKS employs **vertical alignment**, or linking concepts progressively across grade levels. In this way, students are able to build on their previous learning. Table 3.1. provides an example of the vertical alignment in geography.

Table 3.1. Vertical Alignment in Geography	
Prekindergarten - VII.C.1	The student identifies and creates common features in the natural environment.
Kindergarten - K.4A	The student identifies the physical characteristics of a place, such as landforms, bodies of water, Earth's resources, and weather.
First Grade - 1.5A	The student identifies and describes the physical characteristics of a place, such as landforms, bodies of water, Earth's resources, and weather.
Second Grade	The student identifies major landforms and bodies of water, including each of the seven continents and each of the oceans, on maps and globes.
Third Grade	The student can describe similarities and differences in the physical environment, including climate, landforms, natural resources, and natural hazards.

Table 3.1. Vertical Alignment in Geography	
Fourth Grade	The student identifies, locates, and describes the physical regions of Texas (Mountains and Basins, Great Plains, North Central Plains, Coastal Plains), including their characteristics such as landforms, climate, vegetation, and economic activities.
Fifth Grade	The student describes regions in the United States based on physical characteristics such as landform, climate, and vegetation.

As part of this vertical alignment, the social studies TEKS for grades K – 8 contain the following strands:

- History
- Geography
- Economics
- Government
- Citizenship
- Culture
- Science, Technology, and Society
- Social Studies Skills

This ensures that students gain a deep understanding of each of these topics as they proceed in their social studies education.

As students progress in the TEKS, the cognitive rigor of the objectives also increases. Students in the lower grades may primarily be asked to identify, describe, or explain, while students in higher grades will more often be asked to summarize, interpret, or analyze.

When conducting research, the **research questions** (points of inquiry) and **methodologies** (manners of conducting research) will also gradually become more complex. For example, a kindergartner may simply ask "What does the Texas flag look like?" while a fourth grader may ask "What does the Texas flag symbolize?" Similarly, a young student may conduct research by reading a leveled nonfiction text, while a sixth grader may read and analyze primary sources.

Students of all ages will be exposed to **technology** through social studies lessons. This may include anything from digital mapping or graphic tools to video historical reenactments to presentation software for presenting original research.

Because social studies is so easily **integrated with other content areas,** social studies instruction may often address TEKS from other domains. For example, lessons on entrepreneurship and economics could easily integrate with math concepts; similarly, instruction on analyzing the perspectives in primary source material could integrate with English language arts and reading TEKS.

Check Your Understanding

What are the advantages of curriculum integration?

As part of instruction in the social studies TEKS, teachers should also consider the need for individualized instruction. Some students may need extension and enrichment activities, while others may need additional support. English language learners (ELL) in particular will generally need more vocabulary scaffolds as they encounter new content area words. Pre-teaching vocabulary, use of sentence frames or sentence starters, oral language practice, and resources in the native language are all useful strategies to aid in ELL students' social studies learning.

As in other content areas, parent communication is important. Some social studies topics may be perceived as controversial or concerning by parents. Transparency and openness are key, as is adherence to the TEKS, which reflect the state requirements of what students should learn.

Practice Question

2. Which statement best describes vertical alignment?
   A. Students start with basics, like history, and then add new topics, like economics, as they progress in school.
   B. Students continually review the same content they have already been exposed to in each grade level.
   C. Students progress gradually to more advanced concepts in the same domains they have already been introduced to.
   D. Students must master one content area, like citizenship, before they move to another content area, like geography.

HISTORY

Texas History

Texans before European Contact

Before the arrival of European explorers and colonists, Texas was populated by a number of Indigenous tribes. The migratory **Karankawa** lived along the Gulf Coast; fishers and hunter/gatherers, they moved via canoe and were among the first to encounter Europeans.

Farther inland, the **Caddo** dominated East Texas, living in settled communities and practicing agriculture throughout the region and in the area around the Red River. Organized in the **Hasinai** alliance, the Caddo engaged in brisk trade, and Europeans took part in this economy. Many Caddo died from diseases introduced by European settlers.

Farther west, tribes like the **Comanche**, **Apache**, and **Kiowa** dominated the Great Plains and moved into northern and western Texas. These migratory tribes adopted horses after the introduction of these animals by Europeans. Violent encounters between these tribes and European, Mexican, Texan, and American settlers were common until the late nineteenth century.

Did You Know?

Over 1,200 years ago, a group of Caddo build large mounds about 26 miles west of Nacogdoches, which were likely used for burial and ritual purposes. Today the mounds are part of Caddo Mounds State Historic Site.

Practice Question

3. Which tribe would explorers in the Gulf Coast region of Texas have most likely encountered?
   A. Kiowa
   B. Comanche
   C. Caddo
   D. Karankawa

Spain in Texas

Spain's search for gold in the Americas spurred its exploration throughout the region north to Texas. In 1519 the Spanish explorer who discovered Texas, **Alonso Álvarez de Piñeda**, recommended colonization (though he never actually set foot on the land, only viewing it from his ship as he explored the Gulf Coast). An expedition to Florida led by **Pánfilo Naváez** became stranded on the Texas coast after attempting to return to Mexico; seven years later, the survivors, led by **Cabeza de Vaca**, were rescued. Returning to Mexico, they passed on rumors of gold farther inland in Texas, inspiring exploratory expeditions by **Francisco Vasquez de Coronado** and **Hernando de Soto** in 1540, and **Juan de Oñate** in 1598. None were successful in the search for gold, but they did confirm that the land was suitable for raising cattle.

Ultimately, Texas was less valuable than Mexico and other territories because it proved devoid of gold and silver; however Spain was wary of French incursions southwestward. As France became entrenched north in Québec and the Great Lakes region, French explorers headed south through the Mississippi region. In the seventeenth century, René Robert Cavalier, Sieur de La Salle, led an expedition for France down the Mississippi River, claiming land from the Great Lakes to the Gulf of Mexico and as far west as the Rocky Mountains for France in 1682. **La Salle** called the territory **Louisiana** in honor of King Louis XIV.

La Salle continued farther south, establishing **Fort St. Louis** at Matagorda Bay. While the settlement was eventually destroyed by the local Karankawa, and while La Salle himself was killed by his own men shortly afterward, Spain saw the settlement as a threat. Consequently, the Spanish established missions and presidios to create a buffer zone in Texas to repel French interests in North America.

Following the French and Indian War and the decline of French power in North America, after 1754 the **Marquis de Rubi** issued the ***New Regulation of the Presidios*** moving them to San Antonio. San Antonio thus became the frontier and the presence of presidios to the north was reduced. This reorganization would improve consolidation of efforts against the Apache and Comanche, who attacked Spanish outposts from the north and west. However, Spanish control over its territories north of Mexico was tenuous.

Consequently, in order to strengthen control over Texas, **Governor Francisco Bouligny** of Upper Louisiana and **Governor Bernardo de Galvez** of Lower Louisiana secretly agreed to permit White Anglo settlers in Texas as long as they converted to Catholicism and became Spanish subjects. The **Spanish Conspiracy** was in violation of policy that only encouraged Spanish immigration to New Spain, but it began to strengthen Texas economically.

Whites from the United States began immigrating west in search of opportunities in the region. **Moses Austin** left Connecticut with other settlers for the colony of **New Madrid**, now in Missouri; he prospered mining lead for ammunition in Mine à Breton.

The **Adams-Onís Treaty** of 1819, which delineated the border between the United States and Spain, left New Madrid in United States territory. Moses Austin asked the governor in San Antonio for permission to immigrate to Texas and introduce settlers, duplicating the New Madrid model. Spain eventually granted him land and permitted settlement in Texas. However he died in 1821 and his son Stephen Austin would carry out this project.

Meanwhile, other Anglo (White) settlers had been flowing into Texas without explicit permission from Spain. Also known as ***filibuster settlers***, they immigrated for personal gain but at the same time furthered a US national policy: westward expansion, or the ideal of Manifest Destiny, regardless of borders.

Immigrants to Texas were drawn by the promise of cheap land, which would likely grow in value if Texas became part of the United States. Others settled in Texas as a way to escape crippling debt in the United States.

Practice Question

4. What was Spain's initial motivation in the colonization of Texas?
   - A. exploiting rich natural resources
   - B. mining for gold and silver
   - C. stopping Native American raids
   - D. fear of French intrusion

Mexican Texas

Following Mexican independence from Spain, Mexico established the ***empresario*** system, in which *empresarios*, or land brokers were granted cheap land and given six years to bring families to settle it as long as they enforced Mexican law. Anglos were permitted to colonize the land in order to better secure it for Mexico under the **Colonization Law of 1825**.

Did You Know?

Stephen F. Austin, for whom the city of Austin is named, is often referred to as "the father of Texas."

His family's previous agreements with Spain voided following the revolution, **Stephen F. Austin,** Moses Austin's son and an able diplomat, negotiated the first *empresario* arrangement with the new Mexican government and attracted 300 Anglo families to Texas. Settlers could receive, for a low rate, either 4,000 acres of land for ranching or approximately 177 acres for farming—consequently, many became ranchers. In return, they had to demonstrate evidence of "good reputations" (for example, prove they had no criminal background), convert to Catholicism, and become Mexican citizens. However they would not have to pay taxes for seven years.

Mexico wanted foreign settlers to purchase Texas land at only a thirty-dollar down payment with ten years tax-free to encourage settlement. Yet Anglo settlers did not always consider themselves Mexican and also wanted to bring enslaved persons of African origin, a dilemma because Mexico prohibited slavery. As a result, Mexico began encouraging Mexican settlement in Texas to counter this movement.

Still, by the late 1820s, Anglo settlers outnumbered Mexican settlers and others of Spanish and Spanish-speaking origin (called ***Tejanos*** and ***Tejanas***). Anglo-Tejano relations were active: arguably the strongest example was between Stephen F. Austin and **Martin DeLeon,** the first Mexican *empresario*, from Nuevo Santander. DeLeon and his settlers colonized the land near what is today Victoria, Texas. Austin and DeLeon established active relations, including a postal service, between their colonies.

Tensions were developing between the Mexican government and Anglo-dominated Texas. In 1825, US **President John Quincy Adams** proposed the US purchase of Texas. Mexico rebuffed the offer, increasingly suspicious of Anglo Texan and United States intent in the region. In 1826, following disputes over land rights, the *empresario* Haden Edwards formed an alliance with the Cherokee and led the **Fredonia Rebellion** in northeast Texas, declaring independence from Mexico in protest of revocation of land grants. While unsuccessful, these actions contributed to consolidation of political power over the region.

Following growing tensions and violence in northeast Texas, Mexico passed the **Law of April 6, 1830,** which:

- placed severe restrictions on Texas
- closed immigration from the United States, severing commercial and family ties with the country
- encouraged Mexican and European settlement in Texas to counter Anglo settlement
- provided for customs collections in Texas
- augmented military presence in the region
- further restricted slavery

Some Tejanos were also against the Law of 1830; it threatened their economic interests by interfering with business ties to the United States. They also wanted to separate Texas from the rest of its province (Coahuila) and desired better protection from Native American raids. Furthermore, like many other Mexican citizens, they were resentful of the centralized military dictatorships that had replaced the brief Mexican republic.

The law also settled convicts in Texas. Because *empresarios* and colonists had originally needed to demonstrate evidence of good reputations, this caused resentment; so did the fact that colonists now needed to pay taxes (although the seven-year exemption was to end anyway). Finally, instability in the Mexican government alarmed Mexicans, Tejanos, and Anglo Texans alike; Anglo Texans, many of whom maintained strong ties to the United States, were concerned about violent changes of government in Mexico City in contrast with ongoing democratic elections in the United States.

With the introduction of a strong military presence in Texas, violent clashes began throughout the region reflecting tensions between the centralist, military government and federalists. In 1832, the federalist governor of Texas and Coahuila, **José Maria de Letona** reopened the region to Anglo settlement in violation of the Law of 1830; in response, **Captain Juan (John) Davis Bradburn** arrested his representatives near the border with Louisiana and closed Texas ports. Bradburn and his 150 soldiers had been sent by the Mexican government to occupy Anahuac, near Galveston, Although he reopened the ports, he later arrested the Anglo attorney **Willian Barret Travis** and his partner Patrick Jack.

Texans demanded Bradburn release Travis and Jack during the first disturbance of 1832 in the **Turtle Bayou Resolution**, in which they also protested the Law of 1830 and reaffirmed their allegiance to the original **Constitution of 1824**. In response, Colonel Jose de las Piedras left Nacogdoches, where he had been stationed with a force of 350, and relieved Bradburn of command, releasing Travis and Jack. However, Austin had already approached Velasco to take a cannon to use at Anahuac, clashing with Colonel Domingo de Ugartechea, stationed there with a force of 150. This clash marked the second disturbance of 1832 and the first real violence of the Texas Revolution.

Upon returning to Nacogdoches, de las Piedras ordered Texans to turn in their firearms; instead, they attacked him and on August 2, 1832, he surrendered and was taken to San Antonio.

Despite the violence of the **Disturbances of 1832**, Austin presented them as efforts in support of the 1824 constitution to protest government centralization and the Law of 1830. On October 1, 1832, Anglo Texans and some Tejanos held the **Convention of 1832**. Electing Austin as head of the governing council of San Felipe, where they met, they drafted a resolution calling for the establishment of Texas as a separate state of Mexico, for self-rule, and for the repeal of the Law of 1830.

Though the resolution was rejected, Texans tried again at the **Convention of 1833**; in April of that year, fifty-six representatives drafted a resolution asking the Mexican government to end restrictions on slavery in Texas, allow increased Anglo immigration from the United States, provide Texans more protection from the Apaches and Comanche, improve mail service, and separate Texas from Coahuila.

Meanwhile, the Mexican military leader **Antonio López de Santa Anna**, upon becoming president of Mexico, nullified the 1824 constitution (and its similarities to the US constitution) in favor of a more restrictive one that centralized federal power. Santa Anna dissolved the Mexican Congress and state legislatures; he also violently put down rebellions in several Mexican states. Finally, Santa Anna dismissed self-rule in Texas.

Stephen F. Austin traveled to Mexico City to present Texas's proposals to the government directly, and was imprisoned. Even after Mexico repealed the Law of 1830, Texas was still not granted its own statehood.

At the same time, filibuster settlers continued moving from the United States to Texas and tensions continued to rise. General Martin Perfecto de Cos was appointed military commander of the northern Mexican provinces, including Texas and Coahuila. He sent troops to collect customs at Anahuac, spurring more violence when William Travis led volunteers against Mexican military there. In response, de Cos increased military presence in Texas.

By Austin's release and return to Texas in 1835, tensions were building toward rebellion.

Practice Question

5. Which of the following was a provision of the law of 1830?
   A. Outlawed further U.S. immigration.
   B. Slavery became illegal in Texas.
   C. The modern-day border of Texas were established.
   D. The U.S. gave up all claims to Texas.

The Texas Revolution

The refusal of Colonel John H. Moore and his company to return a cannon to the Mexican military at the **Battle of Gonzales** on October 2, 1835 (wheeling it out with the flag *Come and Take It*) is generally considered the beginning of the Texas Revolution. More volunteers assembled and continued to San Antonio, intending to take the city and de Cos.

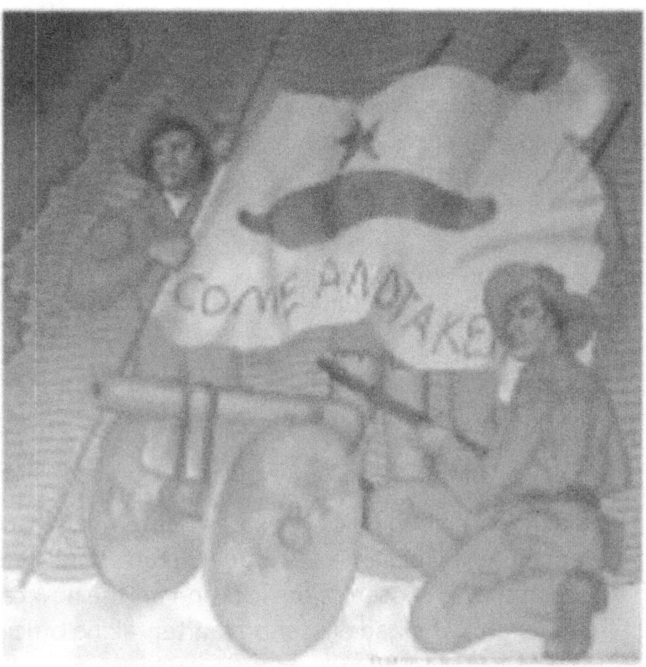

Figure 3.2. Detail of a Mural Depicting the "Come and Take It" Flag at Gonzales, Texas

The volunteers besieged the city; **Ben Milam** led the assault that began the **Battle of San Antonio** (December 5 – 10, 1835) after which de Cos surrendered.

During the siege, delegates met to determine the way forward. They chose **Sam Houston**, the former governor of Tennessee, to lead an army; however other armed groups of volunteers had already sprung up under **James Bowie** in San Antonio, **James Fannin** in Goliad, and elsewhere. As a result, Houston had difficulty organizing and imposing authority beyond the northeast.

By February 1836, Santa Anna himself entered Texas with six thousand troops in an attempt to subdue the uprising. On February 23, San Antonio was besieged again. Meanwhile, during the chaos fifty-nine delegates, among them two Tejanos, signed the **Texas Declaration of Independence** on March 1, 1836, at Washington-on-the-Brazos. Adopting it the next day, they also wrote the first **Texas Constitution**. The delegates confirmed Sam Houston's command of the army and appointed **David Burnet** as interim president of the Republic of Texas.

A few days later, on March 6 Santa Anna attacked the Alamo. **David Crockett**, a former Tennessee congressman and volunteer colonel and William B. Travis led the defense against Santa Anna (James Bowie was either dead or dying at the time within the Alamo), but ultimately Mexico prevailed in the **Battle of the Alamo**; those not killed in the attack were executed, aside from a few whom Santa Anna freed to warn other Texans.

> **Did You Know?**
>
> Santa Anna entered Texas shortly after subduing another uprising in Zacatecas; resistance to his rule was not isolated to Anglo Texans.

Upon hearing the news in Gonzales and facing the Mexican advance, Sam Houston evacuated the city in the ***Runaway Scrape***.

Meanwhile, James Fannin remained at Goliad despite orders to join Houston; defeated by Santa Anna, Fannin's army was executed, too.

Santa Anna pursued Houston, who moved north. On April 20, Houston's and Santa Anna's forces briefly met on the battlefield at the San Jacinto River and White Oak Bayou.

The next day, during the **Battle of San Jacinto,** Houston surprised the Mexicans by attacking in the afternoon rather than the morning. Lasting only eighteen minutes, the battle was won by the Texans. Houston's army captured Santa Anna and while nine Texans died, an estimated 630 Mexicans were killed.

A few weeks later, on May 14, Santa Anna agreed to the **Treaty of Velasco,** which granted Texas independence. Texas thus became an independent republic.

Practice Question

6. Which battle of the Texas Revolution occurred first?
   A. Goliad
   B. Gonzalez
   C. Alamo
   D. San Jacinto

The Republic of Texas

Sam Houston was elected President of the Republic of Texas in September 1836; **Mirabeau Lamar** became vice president; and Stephen Austin became secretary of state. Land near the village of Waterloo (more centrally located than Houston) was chosen as the location for the new capital, which was named Austin in honor of the secretary of state, who had died shortly after taking office.

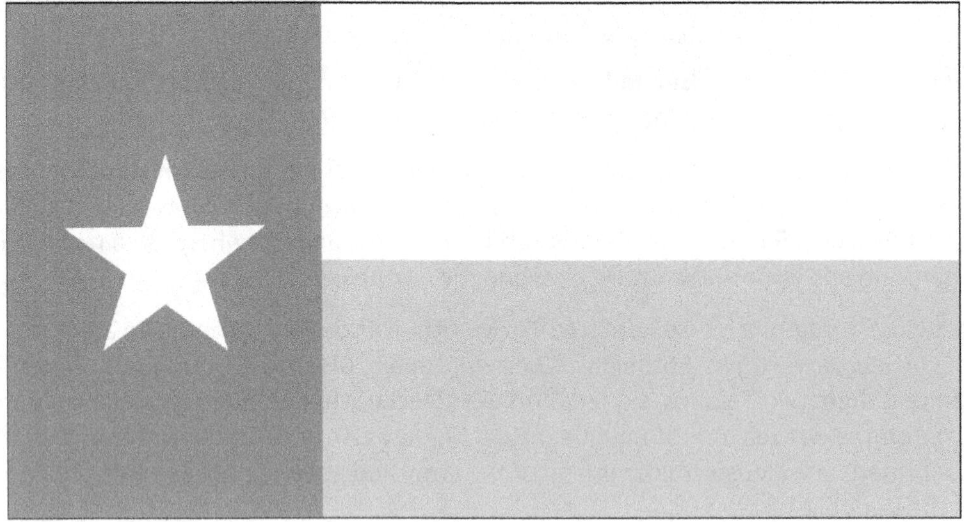

Figure 3.3 Flag of the Republic of Texas

Houston had been elected in a landslide, despite running against Austin; many voters were recent immigrants from the United States who were familiar with him from his military and political service there, and were not familiar with Austin's deep history in Texas.

The Republic faced major challenges. Texas was bankrupt and in enormous debt—over one million dollars—with only five hundred dollars in the treasury at one point. Houston established rangers and militia in place of a costly army and enforced customs collections at Galveston. He also sold the Texan naval fleet. His successor, Mirabeau Lamar, printed three million dollars in currency, causing its value to plummet and making his planned investments in infrastructure impossible.

To raise income, Texas continued to exploit its greatest resource: land. The Houston administration gave land away and even issued ***land scrip***, a currency redeemable in land, in order to attract settlers. The goal was to raise national income by taxing landowners. Lamar reintroduced the *empresario* system, and attracted more immigrants from the north, including recent arrivals to the United States from Europe. Texans of German and Czech heritage live in east-central Texas to this day, around New Braunfels and LaGrange.

As new settlers of European descent arrived in Texas, relationships between people of different ethnicities changed. In the new republic, only male Anglos and Tejanos were considered citizens. Black people (whether enslaved or free), native North Americans, and women of any ethnicity were not. According to the Constitution, free Black men and women could not even live in the country.

Rapidly rising numbers of White immigrants saw Tejanos as a threat or as Mexican agents. At the same time, Texas's relationship with Mexico remained unstable.

> **Did You Know?**
>
> Samuel McCulloch Jr. had fought in the Texas Revolution and was wounded at Goliad; however, he was deprived of Texas citizenship because he was a free Black man.

Tense relations also persisted between Texas and Native American tribes. Although Houston had maintained a stable relationship with the Cherokee in the east, Lamar forcibly removed the Cherokee from their land. He also sent military into Comanche land to protect Anglo settlements.

Texas's foreign relations and borders were also complex. In an attempt to extend its sovereignty to the Rio Grande in New Mexico, Texas troops were halted by the US Army in 1843. However, Texas had a strong relationship with the United States. Sam Houston had fought with the current President Andrew Jackson in the War of 1812; under Jackson, the United States had recognized the Republic of Texas in 1837. Jackson, a proponent of Manifest Destiny, was strongly in favor of Texas joining the Union. But abolitionists were not, given that slavery was an entrenched institution in Texas.

> **Did You Know?**
>
> Sam Houston had lived with the Cherokee in his youth and even been married to a Cherokee woman; he supported diplomacy in relations with Native Americans, not violence or removal.

Houston supported joining the United States; Lamar did not, envisioning Texas as a North American power rivalling the US and Mexico alike. Texas did establish relations with Great Britain, the Netherlands, and France. But Houston and others recognized that the United States, its policy of westward expansion, and its ideal of Manifest Destiny would be threatened by any strong relationships between Texas and European powers, particularly Great Britain.

Fearful of a Texan alliance with Great Britain, the Tyler administration was open to annexation, and President Houston encouraged President John Tyler in this venture. Tyler first proposed annexation in the form of a treaty; however, treaties must be ratified by the US Senate, which rejected it.

Before leaving office, Tyler again proposed annexation to Congress as a joint resolution. This time, the resolution passed. On the Texan side, Congress approved annexation on July 4, 1845; the people confirmed their approval in October. On February 19, 1846, Texas joined the United States as the twenty-eighth state.

Practice Question

7. Why did Sam Houston likely win the first Texas presidential election?
   A. Many voters were familiar with him as a war hero.
   B. Stephen F. Austin dropped out of the race.
   C. He had a policy of tolerance toward Native Americans.
   D. Many voters wanted to preserve slavery.

Annexation and the US-Mexican War

Texas became a state during the administration of President James Polk. For the United States, annexation was part of its policy of westward expansion. Texas's population grew exponentially, with settlers coming mainly from the South—including enslaved people.

Viewing annexation as a provocation, Mexico recalled its ambassador from the United States. Mexico sent troops to the Rio Grande under the command of General Mario Arista; President Polk sent troops under the command of General Zachary Taylor to the Nueces River 200 miles north. Finally, clashes on April 24, 1846, triggered the **Mexican-American War**.

After two years of conflict, the United States and Mexico negotiated the **Treaty of Guadalupe Hidalgo** in 1848 in which the United States gained territory in exchange for fifteen million dollars. Mexico would also abandon any claims to Texas. That same year, Zachary Taylor became president. Territories gained by the US under the treaty include the following:

- New Mexico
- Arizona
- Colorado
- Utah
- Nevada
- California

Under the Treaty of Velasco, the Rio Grande had formed the boundary between Texas and Mexico. With US gains following the war with Mexico, Texas saw fit to claim land as far west as parts of New Mexico and Colorado, in keeping with that treaty. However New Mexicans, with a more entrenched regional history and cultural identity, resisted. At the same time, westward expansion continued to drive debate over slavery in the United States. The American people and government were fiercely divided over whether or not to permit slavery in the enormous new territory obtained following the war.

> **Helpful Hint**
>
> While most new Texans were southerners, many were new immigrants from Europe, including Czechs, Poles, French, Swiss, and numerous Germans. Their cultural heritage persists to this day in central Texas, where some locals spoke German as a first language even into the 1970s.

According to the **Compromise of 1850**

- Congress agreed to admit California as a free state;
- the legality of slavery would be decided by popular sovereignty in the Utah and New Mexico Territories;
- the Fugitive Slave Act was strengthened;
- trade in enslaved persons was abolished in Washington, D.C.; and

- the borders of Texas were established as they stand today.
    - In exchange, Texas received ten million dollars.
    - Given that the US government had not taken on Texas's public debt at annexation, Texas benefitted from the arrangement.

Practice Question

8. What issue remained even after the end of the Mexican-American War?
   A. who had claim to Texas
   B. whether slavery should be permitted in new territories
   C. what nation should govern the newly acquired territories
   D. how much the United States would pay Mexico

The State of Texas

James Pickney Henderson was elected the first governor of Texas following annexation. The state was organized in accordance with a constitution written during the last year of the Republic under the guidance of **Thomas Jefferson Rusk**, with many similarities to the US Constitution. It maintained protections for slavery and also retained the **Homestead Law**, which prohibited the seizure of indebted owners' property and protected women's property rights. Rusk and Sam Houston were elected to represent Texas in the US Senate. Henderson appointed **John Hemphill** as the first chief justice of the Texas Supreme Court. Meanwhile, Texas's population continued to grow, primarily via the migration of White southerners and the Black Americans they enslaved.

Galveston became the largest city in Texas (with approximately 6,000 inhabitants) and an important American port—some claimed it would rival New Orleans and New York City. As the largest port in Texas, Galveston was the gateway for Texas goods, which were in demand elsewhere in North America and in Europe.

Table 3.2. Products Traded at the Port of Galveston

Texas Exports	Texas Imports
▪ cotton ▪ sugar ▪ molasses ▪ cattle ▪ cattle products	▪ manufactured goods ▪ luxury imports (like clothing) ▪ furniture ▪ tools ▪ early industrial implements

Enslaved Black people were also traded at the Port of Galveston.

Texas used the funding from the Compromise of 1850 to settle debts and invest in infrastructure and education. Under the administration of **Governor Elisha M. Pease** (1853 – 1859), the state invested in roads, improvement in river navigability and management, and education. Texas also sought ways to lower taxes for its residents, a tradition that continues. Pease requested a US military presence in the state to protect settlers on the frontier from attacks by the Kiowa, Comanche, and other Native Americans; migration into Texas, mainly from the South, had tripled during the 1850s, and the institution of slavery became more entrenched as a result.

Meanwhile, the entire nation continued to become more divided over slavery. In Washington, Senator Houston voted against the controversial **Kansas-Nebraska Act** of 1854, which opened that territory up to settlement with the legality of slavery to be decided by popular sovereignty. This essentially nullified the Missouri Compromise of 1820, which had forbidden slavery north of the thirty-sixth parallel.

At the time, US senators were chosen by state legislatures (direct election of senators would not take effect until the ratification of the Seventeenth Amendment in 1913). Disapproving of Houston's vote, the Texas State Legislature indicated it would not return him to office, so he returned to Texas to run for governor.

Despite his anti-slavery position, which clashed with supporters of states' rights who believed in the rights of states to determine the legality of slavery, Houston was elected as governor of Texas in 1859.

Practice Question

9. Which offices did Sam Houston hold?
   A. vice-president and president of Texas
   B. president and governor of Texas
   C. attorney general and president of Texas
   D. mayor of Houston and president of Texas

Division and Secession

Most White Texans, whether or not they themselves enslaved other people, supported the practice of slavery. Many believed in notions of White supremacy, aspired to enslave people themselves, or refused federal oversight of state laws at all costs. Therefore in the elections of 1860, opposition to Abraham Lincoln and the Republicans was widespread among those able to vote—White males. Lincoln was not even listed on the ballot in Texas and an alternative, vehemently pro-slavery candidate, Vice President John Cabell Breckinridge, beat Lincoln's opponent Stephen Douglas in a landslide in the state.

Following Lincoln's victory in the presidential election of 1860, South Carolina quickly seceded, followed by Georgia, Alabama, Mississippi, Louisiana, and Florida. Texas followed shortly thereafter. (After Texas joined, the remainder of the Confederate states—Arkansas, Virginia, North Carolina, and Tennessee—followed once war broke out.)

Governor Houston opposed secession, but secessionist leaders like John M. Ford called for special elections for delegates to a convention to consider it. Elections were held on January 8, 1861. Most delegates enslaved people and many were already state representatives. The convention was scheduled for January 28, 1861.

Despite calling an extraordinary meeting of the legislature on January 21 in order to prevent a convention, Houston was essentially without recourse; the legislature failed to act, and the **Secession Convention**, led by **Oran M. Roberts**, later voted overwhelmingly for an **Ordinance of Secession** (with a vote of 166 to eight) on February 1. Texans ratified the ordinance in a special vote on February 23; it passed by 44,317 to 13,020, with only a few counties near the Red River and German-dominated Central Texas voting against. The Secession Convention also wrote a new constitution, specifically stipulating the legality of slavery. A few weeks later, Texas troops forced the Union General David E. Twiggs to surrender at the Alamo; military supplies were taken for Texas.

Texas had not yet joined the Confederacy, and at the time was temporarily once again an independent country. On March 2, Texas Independence Day, secessionists met in Austin to officially declare secession from the United States and allegiance to the Confederate States of America. Despite his decades of service, Governor Sam Houston refused to pledge allegiance to the Confederacy and was replaced by **Lieutenant Governor Edward Clark**. Finally, Texas sent observers to attend the meeting of Confederate delegates in Montgomery, Alabama, determining the organization of the Confederacy.

Practice Question

10. Which of the following had the greatest impact on Texas's secession from the United States?
    A. the election of 1860
    B. the compromise of 1850
    C. the beliefs of Sam Houston
    D. the surrender of David E. Twiggs

Texas at War

While no major fighting took place in Texas, many Texans participated in the Confederate army: 60,000 to 70,000 served, and most were volunteers.

The **Anaconda plan,** the Union plan to blockade and isolate the Confederacy, and its naval blockade did affect Texas. In October 1862, during the **Battle of Galveston,** the Union army occupied the city, at that time the largest city in mostly rural Texas. However the Confederates recaptured Galveston on January 1, 1863; the Union relinquished control and maintained the blockade successfully from New Orleans. The Confederacy continued to export cotton surreptitiously through Mexico and Cuba. But ongoing shortages of medicine, mechanical and farming tools, coffee, clothing, shoes, and other necessities strained the people of Texas and the state's economy.

The Confederacy surrendered at Appomattox on April 9, 1865. Even though the South had surrendered, the final battle of the Civil War took place a month later near Brownsville—the **Battle of Palmito Ranch,** in which Confederate troops fought arriving Union troops.

On June 19, slavery ended in Texas when US General Gordon Granger enforced the Emancipation Proclamation. Despite Lincoln's announcement in 1863, news of emancipation had not reached enslaved Black Texas—slave owners who knew of the decree kept silent. **Juneteenth** is celebrated today in honor of the end of slavery in the state.

Practice Question

11. Which TWO of the following statements describe how Texas was impacted by the American Civil War?
    A. Many early battles of the war were fought in West Texas.
    B. The Union blockade impacted the economy of Texas.
    C. Military training facilities were established in Texas.
    D. Texas soldiers fought for the Confederacy.
    E. The Confederacy surrendered at a site in Texas.

Reconstruction

After the war, Texas suffered economically like much of the South. Given the wartime disruption of production and markets, the devaluation of investments, real estate, stocks, bonds, and currency following the collapse of the Confederacy, and economic uncertainty as Reconstruction loomed, the state faced a depression.

Like most former Confederate states, Texas refused to ratify the **Fourteenth Amendment,** which provided equal protection under the law to American males regardless of race, recognizing Black Americans as US citizens. Consequently, Congress implemented the **Reconstruction Acts** of 1867, which placed the South, including Texas, under military control. Texas was part of **Military District Number Five,** as were Arkansas and Louisiana. At the same time, migration continued into Texas.

Did You Know?

Republicans from the North were scornfully called "carpetbaggers" by supporters of the Confederacy. Southerners who worked with them were derisively referred to as "scalawags."

Because many White supporters of the Confederacy refused to participate, Radical Republicans, including ten Black men, gathered to write a new state constitution in 1868. They ratified the Fourteenth Amendment (as well as the **Thirteenth Amendment**, which abolished slavery). Texas was readmitted into the Union on March 30, 1870.

Meanwhile, the federally supported **Freedmen's Bureau** was established to assist formerly enslaved Black American men and women. Despite the end of slavery, Black men and women faced discrimination and violence, especially from White supremacist groups that formed throughout the South like the **Ku Klux Klan.** Furthermore, many had little or no possessions, skills, or education. The Freedmen's Bureau offered supplies, schooling, and support in finding homes and paid jobs.

Social and agricultural systems were slow to change. Many of those Black Americans who remained in Texas became **sharecroppers,** frequently on the land they had previously worked and for the same landowners. The landowner lent land and equipment; the sharecropper provided labor and kept about one-quarter of the harvest—part of which had to be repaid in order to cover the debt for renting the equipment and land. Given the inadequacy of their final yield for consumption and profit, sharecroppers became bound to the system in a cycle of debt and dependency.

Practice Question

12. Where did many Texas sharecroppers work?
   A. on the lands of those who had previously enslaved them
   B. on lands they were granted via the Fourteenth Amendment
   C. on cooperative farms owned by groups of Black Americans
   D. on cooperative farms owned by the government

Century Reform Movements of the Nineteenth and Early Twentieth Centuries

Throughout much of the nineteenth century, Texas was home to few reform movements, the notable exceptions being the agrarian and labor movements. As early as 1838, a group of Texas printers formed a union. The **Texas Farmers' Alliance** first met in 1877 to organize and plan collective action on behalf of Texas agriculture.

In the 1890s, a **Populist** movement in Texas also took hold; its goals were to increase money in circulation, keep land from foreign landowners, and regulate transportation. Members of the Farmers' Alliance were the party's primary constituency. The party lasted only a short while, however, and much of its agenda became part of the platform of Texas Democrats.

The dawn of the twentieth century saw the growth of more reform movements in Texas, most notably **Progressivism**. Part of this change was due to the rapid move of Texans to cities in the early twentieth century. This progressivism, which sought to improve life through better public health, education, and new public policies to bring more Americans into the civic life of the nation, was countered by the continued prevalence of White supremacist groups and legislation. Poll taxes, voter suppression, and intimidation continued to disenfranchise Black Texans. Furthermore, Texas remained segregated under **Jim Crow** laws.

Nevertheless, fights against White supremacy continued. In 1924, **Miriam "Ma" Ferguson** became Texas governor. Ferguson took steps to fight the Klan, including supporting anti-mask legislation, which curtailed its activities since it depended on anonymity and secrecy to practice its criminal and racist violence. Governor Ferguson also pardoned an estimated 2,000 convicts.

Women's suffrage was often also part of the Progressive agenda. Activists including Rebecca Henry Hayes, Annette Finnegan, Eleanor Brackenridge, and Minnie Fisher Cunningham worked to get women the right to vote in Texas. Women could not vote in state primaries until 1918, and then they voted a woman into public office: Annie Webb Blanton became state superintendent of public instruction.

Texas activists were also influential in the ratification of the Nineteenth Amendment, giving women the right to vote nationally. **Jane Y. McCallum** was president of the Austin Woman Suffrage Association, actively working for women's right to vote. Texas was the first state in the South to ratify the Nineteenth Amendment, on June 26, 1919.

In 1929, the **League of United Latin American Citizens (LULAC)** was founded in Corpus Christi to support Mexican American civil rights. Originally composed of small business owners and skilled workers, LULAC addressed civil rights legislation and still works today.

Practice Question

13. What happened to the Texas Populist movement of the late nineteenth century?
    A. Some of its goals were merged into the Democratic platform.
    B. Some of its members formed the Texas Farm Alliance.
    C. Its members became Progressive supporters of Ma Ferguson.
    D. Its goals became part of the platform of Governor Ma Ferguson.

The Great Depression and the New Deal

Texas, like the rest of the country, suffered from the Great Depression. Despite its diversified economy, the state exhibited severe income inequality. Oil, cattle, and cotton "barons" enjoyed great wealth, but most Texans lived paycheck to paycheck, unable to save or invest.

Following the First World War, national demand for consumer goods dropped; factories began laying people off. Furthermore, demand for agricultural goods dropped as wartime demand for food and fibrous substances declined. The collapsing price of cotton devastated that industry; over-farming in the Great Plains, combined with a major drought in the 1930s, resulted in the **dust bowl**, crop failures throughout the region, including northern Texas. Farmers were forced to leave their land. As the largest migration in American history, 2.5 million left the Great Plains, including parts of the Texas panhandle. Many of these migrants, sometimes called "Okies" because many came from Oklahoma, migrated to California. There they often found conditions not much better than those they had left. Low wages for agricultural labor, deplorable living conditions, and discrimination by local Californians made the experience hard for many.

In 1932, Miriam Ferguson was reelected governor of Texas. At the same time, **Franklin Delano Roosevelt** became president of the United States. His **New Deal** legislation was eagerly adopted in Texas and supported by the Ferguson administration.

During FDR's administration, the United States emerged from the Great Depression and entered the **Second World War**. Texas played an important part in the war as home to several military and training bases, as a producer of military ships and aircraft, and as an essential source of petroleum, petroleum products, and synthetic rubber, all necessary for military activity. Texan war leaders included **Col. Oveta Culp Hobby**, who commanded the Women's Army Corps.

Practice Question

14. Where did many Dust Bowl migrants immigrate?
    A. Oklahoma
    B. Texas
    C. California
    D. Arkansas

Civil Rights Leaders

In 1956, **Henry B. Gonzalez** became the first Mexican American elected to the Texas Senate. A community leader, Gonzalez organized the Hispanic community and became known as a crusader against segregation on the San Antonio City Council, supporting legislation to desegregate public parks and other areas. During his time in the state legislature, Gonzalez continued to focus on civil rights and fighting segregation, filibustering state efforts to bypass civil rights legislation and reinstitute segregation in schools. Despite considerable opposition, in 1961 Gonzalez, with the support of President Kennedy and Vice President Johnson, was elected to the House of Representatives—the first Texan Hispanic American in Congress. Gonzalez served until 1997.

In Washington, Gonzalez supported landmark civil rights legislation and LBJ's Great Society programs. Notably, he opposed the Bracero program, which had provided jobs to migrant Mexican workers beginning in WWII, due to the poor conditions faced by workers under the program. Texas was also a battlefield in the fight for civil rights in the courts:

- In 1950, Heman Sweatt, a Black man, sued the University of Texas when he was denied admission to its law school based on his race.
- Eventually reaching the US Supreme Court, the case ***Sweatt v. Painter*** forced the desegregation of UT.
- *Sweatt v. Painter* became precedent for *Brown v. Board of Education*.
- Thurgood Marshall argued the case.
- Sweatt was backed by the National Association for the Advancement of Colored People (NAACP), led in Texas at the time by **Lulu Belle Madison White**, one of the first female leaders of the organization in the South.

In 1965, **Barbara Jordan** was elected to the Texas State Senate—the first African American woman in the legislature. Jordan focused on civil rights and equality in employment, lobbying for a minimum wage and the creation of the Fair Employment Practices Commission. Jordan also advocated for anti-discrimination wording in business contracts.

Did You Know?

Barbara Jordan attended Texas Southern University in Houston and was a member of its inaugural class and its famous debate team that tied the team from Harvard university in 1954.

In 1972, for the first time Texans sent a woman and a Black Texan to the House of Representatives when they elected her as a representative. As a member of the House Judiciary Committee, Representative Jordan played an important role during the hearings debating the impeachment of President Richard Nixon due to the Watergate scandal. She also advocated for broader civil rights provisions on the national level. Jordan was only able to serve three terms due to illness; she later took a position at the University of Texas.

Practice Question

15. What was MOST significant about the *Sweatt v. Painter* decision?
    A. It focused on law school admissions policies.
    B. It set a precedent for school desegregation.
    C. It involved a public university.
    D. It was argued in a Southern state.

From Blue to Red

At the end of the 1960s, conservatives became more powerful in the United States, and Texas was no exception. Despite giving the country one of its foremost Democrats—LBJ—Texas began to turn from a blue state to a red one.

Conservative working- and middle-class White Texans who had traditionally supported the Democratic Party in the South became disillusioned after the Johnson administration's support of the Civil Rights movement. Democratic strongholds in the South and in Texas began to turn red; Democrats switched parties and became Republicans.

Meanwhile, Texas continued to grow. More conservative Republicans migrated to Texas suburbs, bringing more Republicans to the state. Conservative Democrats declined in Texas, as they did elsewhere in the United States, so Republicans were more likely to defeat liberal Democrats in moderate-to-conservative districts, putting more Republicans in office throughout the state. While many Democrats remained in power throughout the end of the twentieth century, the trend toward a Republican Texas was rooted in the beginning of the conservative movement in the 1970s.

Also during the 1970s and 1980s, fluctuations in the oil market led to economic change in Texas. The **1973 oil crisis** was triggered by oil-producing Arab countries, which imposed an **oil embargo** on the West in retaliation for its support of Israel during the Yom Kippur War that year. OPEC states inflated oil prices. Consequently, oil-producing areas like Texas experienced huge economic growth as the price of oil skyrocketed. Later, in 1979 the Iranian Revolution deposed the Shah of Iran, a major US ally in the Middle East. As Iran was an important source of world petroleum, instability from the revolution increased prices further, causing the **energy crisis**. Finally, the beginning of the Iran-Iraq War in 1980—a conflict between two major oil producers—further destabilized the market and raised prices.

Dizzying growth in the oil industry brought revenue to Texas, especially Houston. However, during the 1980s, slowed manufacturing and conservation measures taken in response to the 1970s crises resulted in an **oil glut**, and oil prices began to fall. The petroleum industry suffered. Eventually, the energy sector would diversify and invest in natural gas resources throughout Texas and Louisiana.

Texas remained central on the political stage throughout the 1980s as well. **Senator Lloyd Bentsen**, a Democrat, was the vice presidential nominee in 1988. Bentsen was an influential senator and served on the Joint Economic Committee, Finance Committee, and Campaign Committee; he eventually became Secretary of the Treasury under President Clinton. Bentsen was succeeded by **Senator Kay Bailey Hutchison**, Texas's first female senator. Hutchison served on the Commerce, Science, and Transportation Committee throughout her tenure from 1993 – 2013; she focused on deregulating Amtrak, improving security after the attacks of September 11, 2001, and nurturing NASA and research in STEM (science, technology, engineering, and math).

In 1990, **George W. Bush**, son of the Republican national leader and contemporaneous president George H.W. Bush, ran for governor against the popular Democratic incumbent **Ann Richards**. He would serve as governor until his controversial election to the national presidency in 2000. Bush's governorship emphasized criminal justice, capital punishment, tax cuts, and faith-based social service models. Bush also instituted educational reforms. Some of his state policies influenced later change at the national level, another example of Texas's influence on the country.

Following Bush's election as president, Lieutenant Governor **Rick Perry** took over. Perry was elected as governor in 2002 and became the state's longest-serving governor, remaining in office until 2015. State government became solidly Republican under Perry's watch; at the same time, urban and suburban populations increased while rural populations decreased.

Governor **Greg Abbott**, formerly Perry's lieutenant governor, was elected in 2015 and continues the conservative Republican agenda of state government in Texas.

Practice Question

16. Which TWO women served as governor of Texas?
    A. Ma Ferguson
    B. Kay Bailey Hutchison
    C. Barbara Jordan
    D. Ann Richards
    E. Jane McCallum

Texas Today

Texas, with its long border with Mexico, remains a flashpoint in the debates over **immigration reform** in the United States. It is estimated that Texas is home to the second-highest population of undocumented immigrants in the country. Many are from Mexico and Central America, but others come from Asia, South America, Africa, and elsewhere. The state and the country continue to struggle to find a long-term solution for the millions of people who reside in the United States without documentation. Whatever the outcome, Texas will remain at the forefront of the debate.

Texas is a global leader in **medical research**, with several world class hospitals and research facilities throughout the state, notably in Houston at the Texas Medical Center. People from around the country and the world travel to the state for cutting edge treatment, especially in cancer, children's care, and to access the newest medical technology and medical trials at hospitals like M.D. Anderson Cancer Center, Texas Children's Hospital, and other leading institutions.

Texas is also a national leader and major international player in **technological manufacturing and export**. The state surpasses California in technological manufacturing and generates hard currency by exporting to Mexico. Texas Instruments, Verizon, and other companies in Dallas and San Antonio provide manufacturing jobs for thousands of Texans. The business-friendly climate of the state has encouraged tech startups in the fast growing cities of Austin, San Antonio, and Houston, where more tech development is under way.

With five of the fastest-growing cities in the country (Houston, Austin, Dallas, Fort Worth, and San Antonio) Texas continues not only to grow in population size, but to experience rapid **urbanization** and its accompanying problems. Urbanization challenges include the following:

- overwhelming traffic on freeways built to accommodate far smaller populations
- the immediate environmental impact of an influx of people and automobiles
- long-term concerns about affordable housing and sustainable development

Rapid **suburbanization** as city dwellers and the middle class aspire to homeownership or larger homes beyond urban areas has a negative environmental impact. Suburban sprawl is a feature of the Texas landscape, placing a heavy burden on roads, reservoirs, drainage systems, and other existing infrastructure. The state must find ways to keep up with growth.

Texas remains one of the most economically and politically influential states of the Union; the history of Texas will no doubt continue to have an impact on the history of the United States as a whole in the twenty-first century.

Practice Question

17. Which Texas city would a person seeking cutting-edge medical treatment most likely visit?
    A. Houston
    B. Dallas
    C. San Antonio
    D. El Paso

American History

Native Americans

Prior to European colonization, diverse Native American societies controlled the continent; they would later come into economic and diplomatic contact, and military conflict, with European colonizers and United States forces and settlers.

Major civilizations that would play an important and ongoing role in North American history included the **Iroquois** in the Northeast, known for longhouses and farming in the Three Sisters tradition; they consisted of a confederation of six tribes. The **Algonquin** were another important northeastern civilization; rivals of the Iroquois, the Algonquin were important in the fur trade. Algonquin languages were spoken throughout the Great Lakes region.

Farther west, the **Shawnee** were an Algonquin-speaking people based in the Ohio Valley; however their presence extended as far south and east as the present-day Carolinas and Georgia. While socially organized under a matrilineal system, the Shawnee had male kings and only men could inherit property. Also matrilineal and Algonquin-speaking, the **Lenape** were considered by the Shawnee to be their "grandfathers" and thus accorded respect. Another Algonquin-speaking tribe, the **Kickapoo** were originally from the Great Lakes region and moved west. The Algonquin-speaking **Miami** moved from Wisconsin to the Ohio Valley region, forming settled societies and farming maize. They too took part in the fur trade as it developed during European colonial times. These tribes later formed the Northwest Confederacy to fight US westward expansion.

In the South, major tribes included the **Creek**, **Chickasaw**, and **Choctaw**, the descendants of the **Mississippi Mound Builders** or Mississippian cultures, societies which built mounds from around 2100 to 1800 years ago as burial tombs or the bases for temples. Sharing similar languages, all the tribes would later participate in an alliance—the Muscogee Confederacy—to engage the United States. The Chickasaw and Choctaw were matrilineal; the former also engaged in Three Sisters agriculture like the Iroquois.

Figure 3.4. Mississippi Mounds

Another major southern tribe, the **Cherokee** spoke (and speak) a language of the Iroquoian family. It is thought that they migrated south to their homeland in present-day Georgia sometime long before European contact, where they remained until they were forcibly removed in 1832. Organized into seven clans, the Cherokee were also hunters and farmers like other tribes in the region and would later come into contact—and conflict—with European colonizers and the United States of America.

The nomadic tribes of the Great Plains like the **Sioux, Cheyanne, Apache, Comanche,** and **Arapaho** lived farther west. These tribes depended on the **buffalo** for food and materials to create clothing, tools, and domestic items; therefore they followed the herds. While widely known for their equestrian skill, horses were introduced by Europeans and so Native American tribes living on the Great Plains did not access them until after European contact. Horseback riding facilitated the hunt; previously, hunters surrounded buffalo or frightened them off of cliffs.

In the Southwest, the **Navajo** controlled territory in present-day Arizona, New Mexico, and Utah. Pastoralists, they had a less hierarchical structure than other Native American societies. The Navajo were descendants of the **Ancestral Pueblo** or **Anasazi**, who practiced Three Sisters agriculture and stone construction, building cliff dwellings.

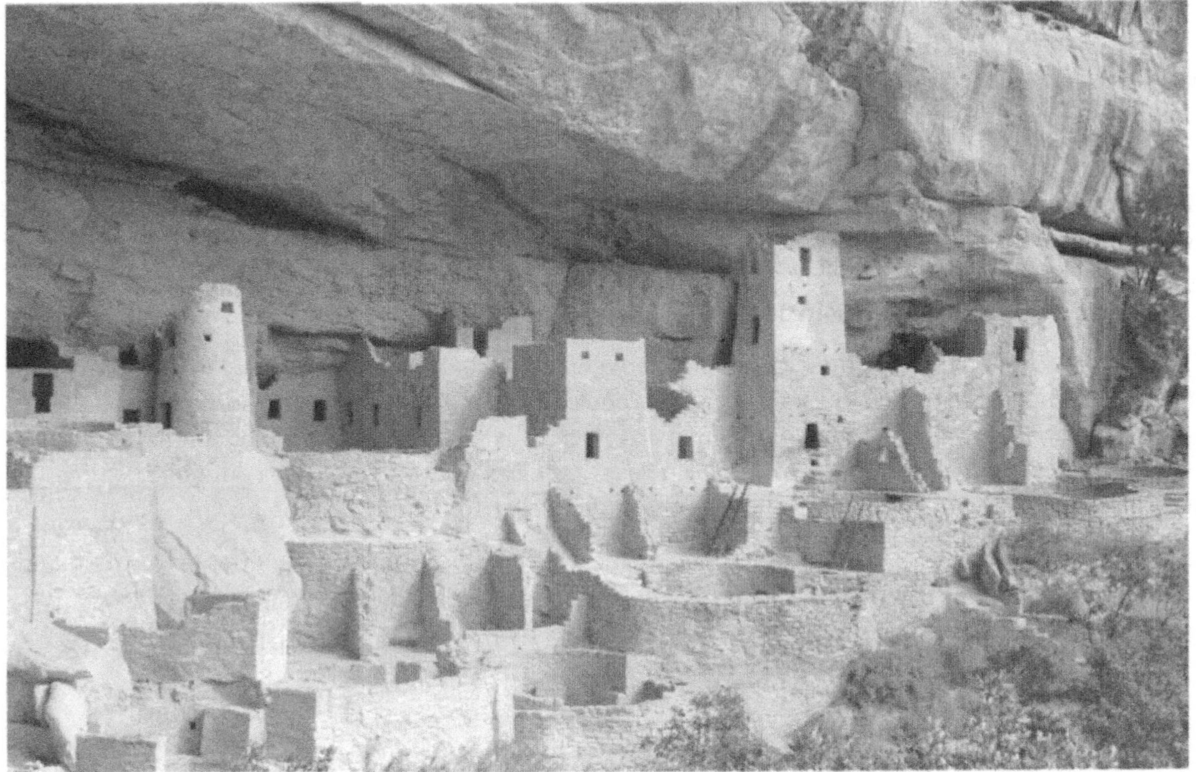

Figure 3.5. Ancestral Pueblo Cliff Palace at Mesa Verde

In the Pacific Northwest, Native American Peoples depended on fishing, using canoes. Totem poles depicted histories. The **Coast Salish**, whose language was widely spoken throughout the region, dominated the Puget Sound and Olympic Peninsula area. Farther south, the **Chinook** controlled the coast at the Columbia River.

Ultimately, through both violent conflict and political means, Native American civilizations lost control of most of their territories and were forced onto reservations by the United States. Negotiations continue today over rights to land and opportunities and reparations for past injustices.

Practice Question

18. Which TWO events contributed to the destruction of Native American populations in North America?

   A. colonists' overuse of natural resources such as bison and timber
   B. European-brought diseases
   C. geographical displacement due to European colonization
   D. conflict over land between France and Spain
   E. the destruction of traditional trade networks by railroads

Early Colonization

When European settlers came to North America in the 1600s, they found an already populated continent. An estimated 60,000 Native Americans lived in the area that would become the first New England colonies. Early relationships between Native Peoples and European colonists, however, were not always centered around conflict. For example, the famous Plymouth Colony, established in 1621, shared a meal with members of the Wampanoag tribe in what would become known as the first Thanksgiving.

Reciprocal relationships were often established in these early years of European encroachment. Colonists needed trading partners to lay the infrastructure of their settlements, and Native Americans sought potential military alliances.

However, conflict-free relationships did not last. European-brought microbes such as measles and smallpox began to ravage Native communities. Tensions over the religious zeal of many colonists and the Native American way of life, along with ongoing encroachment on the land of Native Peoples, led to what is sometimes referred to as **The First Indian War**. The conflict lasted over a year (1675 – 1676) and led to a large loss of lives on both sides—Plymouth Colony in Massachusetts and the Native American alliance that included the Wampanoag, Mohegans, and Mohawk.

Though a treaty ended the war, the relationship between early European colonists and Native Americans remained a complicated one, with vacillations between conflict and cooperation. In some ways, the colonists had a military advantage during military conflicts, having both firearms and a single, shared language allowing for easier alliance-making. However, as time went on and trade continued, Native American groups adopted modern weaponry and formed powerful alliances of their own.

The impacts of early colonization on Native Americans varied by location. Communities in New England had to face land seizure or "purchase" as well as more direct contact via war, trade, and nearby settlements. However, even Native Peoples living in areas somewhat remote from early settlements were impacted by the diffusion of goods, ideas, and disease.

Practice Question

19. Which statement best describes the relationship between Native Americans and early European colonists?
    A. near constant warfare
    B. near constant peace
    C. vacillation between conflict and cooperation
    D. vacillation between armed and diplomatic conflict

The War for Independence

European powers had begun colonizing North America in the sixteenth century to access fur and agricultural resources; by the eighteenth century, Britain controlled most of the east coast of the continent, including the Thirteen Colonies, which became the original United States. France and Britain battled for control of northeastern North America, and following the **French and Indian War**, Great Britain consolidated its control over much of the continent.

Despite British victory in the French and Indian War, it had gone greatly into debt. Furthermore, there were concerns that the colonies required a stronger military presence following Native American attacks and uprisings like **Pontiac's Rebellion** in 1763. Consequently, **King George III** signed the **Proclamation of 1763**, an agreement not to settle land west of the Appalachians, in an effort to make peace; however much settlement continued in practice.

King George III enforced heavy taxes and restrictive acts in the colonies to generate income for the Crown and eventually to punish disobedience. England expanded the **Molasses Act** of 1733, passing the **Sugar Act** in 1764 to raise revenue by taxing sugar and molasses, which were widely consumed in the colonies. In 1765, Britain enforced the **Quartering Act**, forcing colonists to provide shelter to British troops stationed in the region.

The 1765 **Stamp Act**, the first direct tax on the colonists, triggered more tensions. Any document required a costly stamp, the revenue reverting to the British government. Colonists felt the tax violated their rights, given that they did not have direct representation in British Parliament. As a result, they began boycotting British goods and engaging in violent protest. **Samuel Adams** led the **Sons and Daughters of Liberty** in violent acts against tax collectors and stirred up rebellion with his **Committees of Correspondence**, which distributed anti-British propaganda.

Protests against the Quartering Act in Boston led to the **Boston Massacre** in 1770, when British troops fired on a crowd of protestors. By 1773, in a climate of continued unrest driven by the Committees of Correspondence, colonists protested the latest taxes on tea levied by the **Tea Act** in the famous **Boston Tea Party** by dressing as Native Americans and tossing tea off a ship in Boston Harbor. In response, the government passed the **Intolerable Acts**, closing Boston Harbor and bringing Massachusetts back under direct royal control.

In response to the Intolerable Acts, colonial leaders met in Philadelphia at the **First Continental Congress** in 1774 and presented colonial concerns to the king, who ignored them. However, violent conflict began in 1775 at **Lexington and Concord**, when American militiamen (**minutemen**) gathered to resist British efforts to seize weapons and arrest rebels in Concord. On June 17, 1775, the Americans fought the British at the **Battle of Bunker Hill**; despite American losses, the number of casualties the rebels inflicted caused the king to declare that the colonies were in rebellion. Troops were deployed to the colonies; the Siege of Boston began.

In May 1775, the **Second Continental Congress** met at Philadelphia to debate the way forward. Debate among leaders like Benjamin Franklin, John Adams, Thomas Jefferson, and James Madison centered between the wisdom of continued efforts at compromise and negotiations, and declaring independence. Again, the king ignored them. By the summer of 1776, the Continental Congress agreed on the need to break from Britain; on July 4, 1776, it declared the independence of the United States of America and issued the **Declaration of Independence**.

Americans were still divided over independence; **Patriots** favored independence while those still loyal to Britain were known as **Tories**. **George Washington** had been appointed head of the Continental Army and led a largely unpaid and unprofessional army; despite early losses, Washington gained ground due to strong leadership, superior knowledge of the land, and support from France.

Check Your Understanding

What instructional strategies could be used to help students understand the language of the preamble to The Declaration of Independence?

Initially, the British seemed to have many advantages in the war, including more resources and troops. Britain won the **Battle of Brooklyn** (Battle of Long Island) in August 1776 and captured New York City. The tide turned in 1777 at **Valley Forge**, when Washington and his army survived the bitterly cold winter and managed to overcome British military forces.

A victory at **Saratoga** led the French to help the rebels in 1778. France was an important player in the Revolutionary War, sending supplies and troops to aid the Continental Army from 1778-1782. Its assistance is viewed by some scholars as crucial to the ultimate success of Patriot forces.

After Saratoga, fighting shifted south. Britain captured Georgia and Charleston, South Carolina; however, British forces could not adequately control the country as they proceeded to Yorktown, Virginia in 1781. At the **Battle of Yorktown**, British forces were defeated by the Continental Army with support from France and were forced to surrender.

Meanwhile, the British people did not favor the war and voted the Tories out of Parliament; the incoming Whig party sought to end the war. After troops fought for two more years, the **Treaty of Paris** ended the revolution in September 1783. In 1787, the first draft of the Constitution was written, and George

Washington became the first president of the United States two years later. The American Revolution would go on to inspire revolutions around the world.

The Revolutionary War also had impacts on the new nation. In the spirit of freedom and liberty sparked by popular rhetoric, movements for the abolition of slavery began to grow. Other groups began to argue for expanded rights for women. The Anglican Church, or the Church of England in the colonies, largely ceased to exist as its head was the British monarch. Other traditions of the mother country, such as laws dictating land inheritance were abolished. New markets beyond England were also opened for the goods of American farmers and merchants. Additionally, new land in the western territories became "open" for conquest and settlement by Americans.

Practice Question

20. What advantage did the colonists have over the British in the American Revolution?
    A. vast financial wealth
    B. superior weaponry
    C. strong leadership and knowledge of the terrain
    D. a professional military and access to mercenaries

The Government of the Early Republic

Dominating American political thought since the American Revolution, **republicanism** stresses liberties and rights as central values, opposes corruption, rejects inherited political power, and encourages citizens to be civic minded and independent. It is based on **popular sovereignty**, that is, the concept that the people are the source of political power. These ideas helped to form not only the Declaration of Independence but also the Constitution.

The colonies had broken away from Britain because of what they viewed as an oppressive, overbearing central government. As a result, the first government they created, whose framework was called the **Articles of Confederation**, was an intentionally weak, democratic government. Called a "firm league of friendship," it was designed to create a loose confederation between the colonies (now states) while allowing them to retain much of their individual sovereignty.

As a result, the Articles established a weak government with extremely limited authority: it did not have the power to levy taxes or raise an army. The legislature was intentionally and clearly subordinate to the states. Representatives were selected and paid by state legislatures.

It quickly became clear that this government was too weak to be effective, and by 1787, the new government of the United States was already in crisis. Without the power to levy taxes, the federal government had no way to alleviate its debt burden from the war. In addition, without an organizing authority, states began issuing their own currencies and crafting their own, competing trade agreements with foreign nations, halting trade and sending inflation through the roof. Without a national judicial system, there was no mechanism to solve the inevitable economic disputes. Furthermore, there were uprisings in the country.

A convention of the states was called to address problems in the young United States. At the **Constitutional Convention** in 1787, a decision was made to completely throw out the old Articles and write a new governing document from scratch.

The states did not want a central government that was so strong that it would oppress the states or the people, so they decided to prevent the concentration of power by dividing it. **Separation of powers** limited the powers within the federal government, dividing power among three branches: the executive, the legislative, and the judicial. In addition, each branch was given powers that would limit the power of the other branches in a system called **checks and balances**.

The executive branch—via the role of president—has the power to veto (reject) laws passed by the legislature. The legislative branch, consisting of Congress, can override the president's veto (with a two-thirds vote) and pass the law anyway. Finally, the judicial branch, consisting of the Supreme Court and other courts, can determine the constitutionality of laws (**judicial review**).

At the writing of the Constitution, the branch of the federal government endowed with the most power was the legislative branch, which makes laws. Simply called **Congress**, this branch is composed of a bicameral legislature (two houses). While this structure was not originally adopted under the Articles of Confederation, the framers chose it when reorganizing the government, mainly due to a dispute at the convention over the structure of the legislative body—specifically the voting power of each state.

Small states advocated equal representation, with each state having the same number of representatives, each with one vote. However, the more populous states argued for a plan based on **proportional representation**. Each state would be assigned a number of representatives based on its population (enslaved people deprived of their rights would even be counted among the population, benefiting those states with large slave populations). In the end, the **Great Compromise** was reached. There would be two houses: the **House of Representatives** (the lower house) would have proportional representation, and the **Senate** (the upper house) would have equal representation.

This system had two other advantages. The House of Representatives would also be directly elected by the people, and the Senate by the state legislatures. This supported the federal structure of the government: one house would serve the needs of the people directly, and the other would serve the needs of the states. Also, it curbed federal power by fragmenting it and slowing down the legislative process. Today, senators are also directly elected by the people.

Check Your Understanding

How many representatives does Texas have in the U.S. Congress?

Under the Constitution, the federal government is charged with matters that concern the population at large, such as managing federal lands, coining money, and maintaining an army and navy. It also handles conflicts between the states via the federal judiciary and by regulating interstate trade. Matters of regional or local concern are handled by state or local governments. This relationship is best codified in the Tenth Amendment, which states that any powers not explicitly given to the federal government are reserved for the states. The written Constitution can only be amended by a super majority.

State governments are generally modeled after these three branches, with the executive branch headed by the governor, the legislative branch headed by elected representatives, and the judicial branch headed by the state supreme court. **Local governments** have elected officials and generally follow charters that state constitutions have adopted. As they do with the federal government, the people vote for their state and local government representatives.

It took three years for all states to ratify the Constitution, with Rhode Island being the last to ratify on May 29, 1790. Much of the debate was over the lack of guarantees of basic civil rights in the Constitution. As a solution, James Madison in 1789 introduced twelve amendments to the Constitution. Ten of these twelve amendments are known as the **Bill of Rights**:

- **The First Amendment** protects **freedom of speech**. Congress may not pass laws that prohibit people from exercising freedom of religion, the press, assembly, or the right to petition against the government.
- **The Second Amendment** allows citizens to bear arms.
- **The Third Amendment** stops the government from quartering troops in private homes.
- **The Fourth Amendment** protects citizens from searches and seizures without a warrant.

- **The Fifth Amendment** ensures that citizens cannot be punished or subject to criminal prosecution without due process. Citizens also have the power of eminent domain, which means that private property cannot be seized for public use without proper compensation.
- **The Sixth Amendment** gives citizens a right to a fair and fast trial by jury, the right to know the crimes for which they are charged, and the right to confront witnesses. Citizens also have the right to legal representation and to gather testimonies from witnesses.
- **The Seventh Amendment** allows civil cases to be tried by jury (in the Articles of Confederation, only criminal trials could be tried by jury).
- **The Eighth Amendment** disallows excessive bail or fines; it also prohibits cruel and unusual punishment.
- **The Ninth Amendment** gives all rights not specifically enumerated in the Constitution to the people; it provides that the list of rights is not exhaustive.
- **The Tenth Amendment** provides that all other powers not provided to the federal government in the Constitution belong to the states.

Practice Question

21. Which of the following is one of the amendments in the Bill of Rights?
    A. The process of judicial review is a check on power.
    B. The Senate must have equal representation.
    C. The legislature is to have two bodies.
    D. The government cannot quarter troops in private homes.

The Early Republic and Sectionalism

The country was increasingly divided over slavery; **sectionalism** grew, strengthening disunity between the North and the South. Reform movements continued to include **abolitionism**, the ending of slavery. The former slave **Frederick Douglass** advocated abolition. An activist leader and writer, Douglass publicized the movement along with the American Anti-Slavery Society and publications like Harriet Beecher Stowe's *Uncle Tom's Cabin*. He and other activists like **Harriet Tubman** helped free slaves using the **Underground Railroad**. An estimated 100,000 slaves escaped the South between 1810 and 1850 through a system of safe houses, even though these actions violated state laws. The radical abolitionist **John Brown** led violent protests against slavery. Abolitionism became a key social and political issue in the mid-nineteenth century; slavery was the main cause of the **Civil War**.

In the northern states where the climate was less hospitable to mass agriculture, industry and manufacturing were prioritized. The need for a labor force led to the growth of cities and more **immigration**, particularly from European nations like Ireland and Germany. In the two decades prior to the Civil War, an estimated 4.5 million Europeans immigrated to the United States, many settling in the northern states or the Midwest. Immigration and urbanization impacted the culture of the northern states, which some say began to embrace more progressive causes, such abolition and improving educational and political institutions.

Upheaval and limited opportunities in Europe, as well as the promise of land or high-paying industrial jobs, drew these immigrants to the United States, as did the democratic ideals upon which the United States was founded. These immigrants faced challenges such as learning a new language and discrimination fueled by fears of "foreignness" and economic competition.

Check Your Understanding

What types of primary sources might help students understand what life was like for women and children in antebellum America?

However, as the nineteenth century marched on, slavery became the central issue in American society. Antislavery factions in Congress had attempted to halt the extension of slavery to the new territories obtained from Mexico, but they were unsuccessful; in the Compromise of 1850, Congress decided that the voters in some new territories would be allowed to decide whether slavery should be legal or determined by popular sovereignty. In 1854, Congress passed the **Kansas-Nebraska Act**, effectively repealing the Missouri Compromise of 1820 by allowing these states to now decide slavery by popular sovereignty as well. In response, the new **Republican Party** emerged. One of its members, **Abraham Lincoln**, was elected president in 1860 on an antislavery platform.

Practice Question

22. Which of the following effectively repealed the Missouri Compromise?
   A. the Dred Scott decision
   B. the Compromise of 1850
   C. the Kansas-Nebraska Act
   D. the Fugitive Slave Act

Civil War

Following Lincoln's election, South Carolina immediately seceded, followed by Mississippi, Alabama, Florida, Louisiana, Georgia, and Texas. They formed the Confederate States of America, or the **Confederacy**, on February 1, 1861, under the leadership of **Jefferson Davis**, a senator from Mississippi.

Shortly after the South's secession, Confederate forces attacked Union troops in Sumter, South Carolina; the **Battle of Fort Sumter** sparked the Civil War. As a result, Virginia, Tennessee, North Carolina, and Arkansas seceded and joined the Confederacy. West Virginia was formed when the western part of Virginia refused to join the Confederacy.

The reasons for the Civil War were both complex and simple. On one hand, slavery was the central issue; however, slavery was part of deeper divisions related to notions of states' rights (see previous information about the nullification crisis). Though states' rights are seemingly a political issue, they reflect the different economic interests of northern and southern states. Slavery was central to the cash-crop economy of the South but much less central to the more industrialized North that relied on non-forced labor. At the outset of conflict, each side had distinct advantages and disadvantages:

- The North had a larger population of 21 million versus the South's 9 million.
- The North had almost ten times as many manufacturing plants as the South.
- The North had 70 percent of all rail lines.
- The South had a "home field" advantage.
- The South had a long coastline that made blockade a challenge.
- Some historians also believe that the states in the South had better military leadership.

Both sides believed the conflict would be short-lived; however, after the **First Battle of Bull Run** when the Union failed to route the Confederacy, it became clear that the war would not end quickly. Realizing how difficult it would be to defeat the Confederacy, the Union developed the **Anaconda plan**, a plan to "squeeze" the Confederacy, including a naval blockade and taking control of the Mississippi River. Since the South depended on international trade in cotton for much of its income, a naval blockade would have serious economic ramifications for the Confederacy.

However, the Second Battle of Bull Run was a tactical Confederate victory led by General Robert E. Lee and Stonewall Jackson. The Union army remained intact, but the loss was a heavy blow to morale. The Battle of Antietam was the first battle to be fought on Union soil. Union General George B. McClellan halted General Lee's invasion of Maryland but failed to defeat Confederate forces. Undaunted, on January 1, 1863, President Lincoln decreed the end of slavery in the rebel states with the **Emancipation Proclamation**. The **Battle of Gettysburg** was a major Union victory. It was the bloodiest battle in American history up to this point; the Confederate army would not recover.

Meanwhile, following the **Siege of Vicksburg**, Mississippi, Union forces led by General Ulysses S. Grant gained control over the Mississippi River, completing the Anaconda plan. The Battle of Atlanta was the final major battle of the Civil War; victorious, the Union proceeded into the South, and the Confederacy fell. In April 1865, General Lee surrendered to General Grant at Appomattox, Virginia, and the war ended.

Practice Questions

23. What assets did the Confederacy have during the Civil War?
    A. The Confederacy had superior weaponry and production resources.
    B. The Confederacy maintained brisk trade with Europe, enabling it to fund the war.
    C. The Confederacy benefitted from strong military leadership and high morale among the population.
    D. The Confederacy's strong infrastructure allowed it to transport supplies and people efficiently throughout the South.

24) In the Emancipation Proclamation, President Lincoln declared an end to slavery
    A. in Kentucky and Missouri.
    B. in the Union only.
    C. in slave states that had not seceded from the Union.
    D. in the rebel states.

Reconstruction and Industrialization

Reconstruction after the war would bring huge changes in the South and redefine how African Americans fit into American society. The South was in economic ruins; many Southerners, especially newly freed slaves and other African Americans, sought better economic opportunities by moving to the North. Congress passed the Civil Rights Act in 1866 recognizing the rights of former slaves as US citizens; it also passed the Reconstruction Acts the next year, enforcing military occupation of the South. These acts laid out the process for readmission to the Union: among other requirements, states had to ratify the Thirteenth, Fourteenth, and Fifteenth Amendments. These made slavery illegal, recognized equal rights, and permitted African American males to vote, respectively.

Still, agriculture and infrastructure were ruined, and many were bitter over Northern occupation and involvement. Even though the South was forced to accept the end of slavery, Southern states created "Black codes" which restricted the rights of Black Americans. African Americans faced ongoing discrimination and violence in the South, including segregation and threats from hate groups like the Ku Klux Klan. Thus, while African Americans could vote by law, most could not in practice as they faced threat of violence or death.

Violence toward African Americans and Reconstruction reforms led by **Radical Republicans** from the North proved almost insurmountable. Tired of war, the troops sent to assist in the effort were inadequate in number, mismanaged, and often instructed to refrain from engagement. The goal of Reconstruction was largely to rebuild the Union, not necessarily to protect or enfranchise free African-American men and women in the South. Thus, conciliation was prioritized and the aims of "Radical Reconstruction" were unrealized.

Instead, the southern states institutionalized racism and segregation via law. **Black Codes** were the first laws passed in 1865 to limit the movements, work, and earnings of African-American southerners. Such laws expanded in the aftermath of Reconstruction, and new **Jim Crow Laws** legalized and laid out the practices of racial segregation. These laws made segregation the way of the South until the civil rights movement of the 1960s.

The end of the Civil War also brought on an increase in **industrialization**. A British phenomenon, industrialization made its way to the United States. Machines replaced hand labor as the main way of manufacturing, exponentially increasing production capacities. Later in the nineteenth century, the US began developing heavy industry.

The **assembly line** developed by Henry Ford enabled **mass production**. Factors that contributed to this boom included the invention of new products (e.g., the automobile, the telephone, and the electric light), improvement of production methods, an abundance of natural resources and infrastructure (railways opened the West further and connected factories and markets to raw materials), and banking (more people wanted to invest in booming businesses, and banks were financing them).

Did You Know?

With mass production, goods become cheaper. The model T was around $260, which is only roughly $4,400 in today's dollars.

New cities and towns became larger as people started to live and work in urban areas, attracted by employment opportunities. Unfortunately, lack of planning for this phenomenon—**urbanization**—led to inadequate sanitation (which contributed to cholera and typhoid epidemics), pollution, and crime. However, overall, the United States's economy was growing, the middle class was becoming larger, and industry and technology were developing.

Practice Question

25. Which of the following occurred as a result of Reconstruction? Select ALL that apply.
    A. Southern states made new laws.
    B. American troops came to the South.
    C. African American Southerners began voting in large numbers.
    D. Segregation became the norm in public places in the South.

Reform and Civil Rights

As industrialization and urbanization increased in the nineteenth century, some Americans worked to reform society. The first reform movement, predating the Civil War, was **abolition**, or advocacy for the end of slavery. The movement drew Americans from many walks of life, but many were women; this gave White American women a taste of activism and advocacy that carried over into other causes.

One such cause was temperance, or the desire to end the sale of alcohol. The largest of these organizations was the national **Woman's Christian Temperance Union (WCTU)**, founded in 1874. Though advocates of women's suffrage had begun far earlier, the WCTU added women's suffrage to its platform in 1881. The women's suffrage movement finally succeeded with the Nineteenth Amendment, passed in 1920, granting women the right to vote.

The next major wave of reform is collectively known as the civil rights movement. Its foundations began far earlier, but many of its most notable figures were active during the 1960s.

Activists like the **Rev. Dr. Martin Luther King Jr.** and **Malcolm X**, fought for African American rights in the South, including the abolition of segregation, and also for better living standards for Black communities in northern cities. In Montgomery, Alabama, **Rosa Parks**, an African American woman, was arrested for refusing to give up her seat to a White man on a bus. Buses were segregated at the time, and leaders including Dr. King organized the Montgomery Bus Boycott to challenge segregation; the effort was ultimately successful. Building on their success, civil rights activists led peaceful protests and boycotts to protest segregation at lunch counters, in stores, at public pools, and in other public places.

The movement grew to include voter registration campaigns supported by students and other activists (both Black and White) from around the country—the **Freedom Riders**, so-called because they rode buses from around the country to join the movement in the Deep South. Civil rights workers organized the March on Washington in 1963, when Dr. King delivered his famous *I Have a Dream* speech. In 1964, Congress passed the Civil Rights Act, which outlawed segregation.

The civil rights movement extended beyond the Deep South. **Cesar Chavez** founded the **United Farm Workers**, which organized Hispanic migrant farm workers in California and the Southwest who faced racial discrimination, poor treatment, and low pay. The UFW used boycotts and nonviolent tactics similar to those used by civil rights activists in the South. The **American Indian Movement (AIM)** brought attention to injustices and discrimination suffered by Native Americans nationwide. **Feminist** activists fought for fairer treatment of women in the workplace and for women's reproductive rights. Finally, activists in New York and San Francisco began openly fighting for the civil rights of gays and lesbians.

Practice Question

26. How did Martin Luther King and other activists achieve civil rights for Black Americans?
    A. through violent uprisings
    B. using nonviolence
    C. with the help of the Soviet Union
    D. by lobbying Congress only

The Twentieth and Twenty-First Centuries

While the United States became increasingly prosperous and stable, Europe was becoming increasingly unstable. Americans were divided over whether the US should intervene in international matters. This debate became more pronounced with the outbreak of **World War I** in Europe.

Inflammatory events like German submarine warfare (*U-boats*) in the Atlantic Ocean, the sinking of the *Lusitania*, which resulted in many American civilian deaths, the embarrassing Zimmerman Telegram (in which Germany promised to help Mexico in an attack on the US), and growing American nationalism, or pride in and identification with one's country, triggered US intervention in the war. On December 7, 1917, the US declared war. With victory in 1918, the US had proven itself a superior military and industrial power. Interventionist President **Woodrow Wilson** played an important role in negotiating the peace; his Fourteen Points laid out an idealistic international vision, including an international security organization.

However, European powers negotiated and won the harsh **Treaty of Versailles**, which placed the blame for the war entirely on Germany and demanded crippling reparations from it.

After the loss in World War I, Adolph Hitler sought to restore Germany's power and expand its reach by annexing and invading various countries while exterminating people he deemed undesirable such as those of Jewish descent. Germany's 1939 invasion of Poland is commonly considered the beginning of the **Second World War**. In 1940, Germany took Paris. The Battle of Britain began in July of that year; however, Germany suffered its first defeat and was unable to take Britain.

When Japan joined the **Axis** powers of Germany and Italy, the war officially spread to Asia, which was already in conflict. The **Chinese Civil War** was interrupted when Japan invaded China past Manchuria. In response, the Chinese factions joined forces against Japan; the communists became powerful. In June of 1941, Japan attacked the United States at **Pearl Harbor**. Consequently, the US joined the war in Europe and in the Pacific.

Did You Know?

Perhaps the most famous proposal in weapons technology during this time was the Strategic Defense Initiative; popularly known as Star Wars, this outer-space based system would have intercepted Soviet intercontinental ballistic missiles.

Strategic battles were fought throughout the Pacific islands. **President Truman**, who had succeeded Franklin Delano Roosevelt, elected to use the nuclear bomb on Japan to force its surrender rather than invade that country. In 1945, the war ended with Japanese surrender after the US bombed the Japanese cities Hiroshima and Nagasaki.

Allied forces took the lead in rebuilding efforts: the US occupied areas in East Asia and Germany, while the Soviet Union remained in Eastern Europe. The Allies had planned to rebuild Europe according to the Marshall Plan; however, the USSR occupied Eastern Europe. The **Cold War** had begun.

The US, Britain, and the USSR had originally agreed to divide Germany and to hold free elections in Eastern Europe, but by 1945, things had changed. The USSR felt betrayed by the US use of the nuclear bomb; likewise, the US and Britain felt betrayed by the Soviet Union, which had occupied Eastern Europe and prevented democratic elections in order to establish a buffer zone following its extraordinarily heavy casualties in WWII—around twenty million. An ***iron curtain*** had come down across Europe, dividing east from west.

The United States adopted a policy of containment, the idea that communism should be *contained*. Therefore, the United States became involved in the **Korean War** in 1950 and later the controversial **Vietnam War** throughout the 1960s and early 1970s.

Toward the end of the 1960s and into the 1970s, the Cold War began to thaw. The US and USSR signed a series of treaties to limit nuclear weapons. In 1972, President Richard Nixon visited China, establishing relations between the communist government and the United States.

However, the climate would change again in the 1970s and 1980s. The **arms race** was underway. President Ronald Reagan pursued a militaristic policy, prioritizing weapons development with the goal of outspending the USSR on weapons technology.

In 1991, the Soviet Union fell thanks in part to reforms like ***glasnost*** and ***perestroika*** (or openness and transparency). After a coup overthrowing Premier Mikhail Gorbachev, the Soviet leader, the USSR was dissolved. A Soviet war in Afghanistan and military overspending in an effort to keep up with the United States had weakened the USSR to the point of collapse, and the Cold War ended.

By the end of the twentieth century, the United States had established itself as the dominant global economic, military, and political power. It had established military bases and a military presence worldwide, in Europe, Asia, the Pacific, and the Middle East. However, its global power did not prevent conflict. After the terrorist attacks on **September 11, 2001**, the United States began a war in Afghanistan, and later one in Iraq.

Practice Question

27. Which event most directly led to the United States entering into WWII?
A. Hitler's invasion of Poland
B. Japan's attack on Pearl Harbor
C. The Treaty of Versailles
D. The Zimmerman Telegram

SOCIETY AND CULTURE

Foundations of Society

All social groups and cultures share **basic needs**, like food, clothing, housing, and security. To meet those needs, people often form **communities** or groups. In a community, people's needs can be met more easily because people working together can produce more food and protect themselves more efficiently than people living alone. Many communities have a shared identity, such as religion, ethnicity, or language; a shared location; and common interests or behaviors.

Everyone in a community has an impact. Sometimes, that impact can be substantial and can shape the entire future of the group. Consider the impact Abraham Lincoln or Martin Luther King had on the community of the United States. On a smaller scale, people in a community can make or enforce new rules or stop following rules if they become surrounded by a group of non-rule followers.

Communities may also spread their beliefs, interests, behaviors, or broader culture to a new area in a process known as **spatial exchange**, or diffusion. American culture has spread all over the world in this manner; however, it has not always been a one-way street—other cultures have also **exchanged** with American culture.

Sometimes, people find themselves in a new culture as the result of travel or permanent relocation. In order to succeed, these people have to go through **cultural adaptation**—the ability to adjust appropriately to the new way of doing things that might be present in the new culture. This does not at all mean that the elements of one's first culture are lost, only that the individual is able to thrive in the new location.

Cultural adaptation is necessary because what food, clothing, housing, and security look like may vary greatly among groups. A teacher might use the example of a Mongolian reindeer herder to illustrate this. While many Americans may find security in a stable home in one place, nomadic peoples, such as those who pick up their yurts to follow their herds of reindeer, may find security in a portable home that can adapt to the herd's migration.

A teacher might want to show various examples of food and clothing that, while different from each other, still meet the physical needs of a community. Differences in a group of people's **physical environment** (part of the human environment that includes purely physical factors such as climate and vegetation) may dictate food, clothing, and housing choices, as people tend to use the resources most readily available. A teacher may point out the differences in clothing between those living in different climates and how housing and food may also vary based on a location's proximity to the equator. These discussions are easily integrated into science themes as well, and appreciation for differences while maintaining an understanding of unity in purpose to meet basic needs is essential.

Think About It

Some people say that because Texas is a large state with many different climates and landforms, a shared Texas identity does not rest on a shared physical environment.

People in a society may also identify with a certain ethnic or racial group or a certain gender identity. These identities often impact life outcomes due to disparate access to health care, education, and employment opportunities. Such disparities also create **socioeconomic status**, or class, which refers to a person's status in a society based on the combination of social and economic factors such as income, ethnicity, education status, job, and location.

While the ideal might be a human culture in which there is no disparity, this is decidedly not the case. All societies have some form of **social stratification**, or categorization of people into a hierarchy based on socioeconomic status. In some societies, social stratification is based on religious affiliation or birth into a certain group. Most scholars believe that social stratification in the United States and in Texas is based largely on race, gender, income, and other implicit power structures. Typically, this stratification is discussed in terms of the upper class, the middle class, the working class, and the lower class; however, these demarcations may not always be completely accurate. Furthermore, people may perceive themselves to be in a different category than how others may see them.

> **Did You Know?**
>
> Mandarin is the most spoken language in the world, with 12 percent of the world's population speaking it. It is followed by Spanish (6 percent), English (5 percent), Arabic (5 percent), and Hindi (3.5 percent).

Social mobility refers to the ability to move up or down in the social hierarchy. Though there are some paths, such as obtaining a scholarship to a prestigious university or marrying into a wealthy family, many people retain the status of their parents.

Practice Question

28. Which of the following would be most useful for a teacher to show students to help them understand that housing is different in different environments?
    A. images of a New York apartment building and an igloo
    B. drawings of a sprawling suburban home and a simple ranch house
    C. pictures of a Native American woman and man
    D. photos of the White House and the Pentagon

Components of Culture

Every culture has elements of expression that make it unique. Certain **cultural norms**, or attitudes or behaviors that are considered normal, may vary significantly from culture to culture. For instance, typical greetings range from the handshake in the United States to kisses in France. Some cultural norms may be even more subtle. In the United States, where people are often focused on health and thinness, refusing a second helping of dinner might be commonplace; whereas in some cultures, refusing food and drink is considered a very rude practice. Even concepts of physical space and what is appropriate social behavior may vary widely. American travelers to some parts of Asia are often surprised at the size of hotel rooms or how closely people sit together on public transport.

Most cultures have a shared **language** as well as shared **customs** and **traditions**. These may include religious beliefs, food, clothing, recreation, holidays, and even values and beliefs. Customs and traditions vary by location. For example, Independence Day, celebrated on July 4th, is unique to the United States. Similarly, San Jacinto Day, celebrated on April 21st in commemoration of the final battle of the Texas Revolution, is likely unknown outside of the Lone Star State.

Art is another part of any culture. Sometimes, art is an important part of what is left behind by a given culture in a certain time and place. For example, Michelangelo's statue of *David* or painting on the ceiling of the Sistine Chapel stand as lasting reminders of the European Renaissance. The paintings of Georgia O'Keeffe reflect the landscapes of New Mexico, and Andy Warhol's pop art reflects the America of the 1960s.

Music is another part of culture. Jazz, country, rap, and rock and roll are important American musical traditions. With the diversity of America and Texas, however, there are also musical styles of all sorts from all over the world.

Cultural perspectives are also conveyed through storytelling and written **literature**. These stories may be passed down from generation to generation and may contain real or mythical heroes. American "tall tales" about Johnny Appleseed or John Henry are good examples.

Art, music, and literature are often a product of the time in which they were produced. John Steinbeck's novel *The Grapes of Wrath*, which chronicles the life of a family migrating from the Dust Bowl, was published in 1939, just after the real-life Dust Bowl disaster. However, many forms of artistic expression contain timeless themes such as religion, justice, and the passage of time.

As another part of culture, **religion** and **philosophy**—which may be interrelated or separate—may have a tremendous influence on a culture. Large, global religions such as Islam, Judaism, Hinduism, Buddhism, and Christianity have had a huge influence on world history. Philosophical movements such as the Enlightenment movement of the seventeenth century which emphasized individualism and reason had a significant impact on Europe and eventually the United States.

In Texas, religion plays a significant role in the lives of many as roughly 56 percent of Texans are religious, compared with the national average of less than 50 percent. About 77 percent of Texans identify as Christian, with the majority being Protestant. Baptists are the largest Protestant denomination.

Religion is most often passed down in **families**. Families play a key role in any culture as the family unit is one way through which people in a culture meet their basic needs. Individual families may have their own customs, traditions, and beliefs. These may align or be distinct from the surrounding culture. For example, in one family, eating meals together may be the custom; in another, family members may eat most meals separately due to scheduling issues or special dietary needs.

The American (and Texan) family has changed with time. Though women have worked in families considered low-income throughout history, it is true that in many upper-class families, women often did not work outside the home until the later part of the twentieth century. In some instances, women of all socioeconomic statuses were expected to be the primary caretakers of children. This has changed in recent years as now both men and women in many families participate in child rearing.

Practices in raising children have also changed with time. While parents of past generations often prioritized adult activities, research shows that today's parents feel compelled to focus on their children, sometimes at the expense of their own interests.

Practice Question

29. Mr. Wyatt wants to suggest an activity to the art teacher to use as a springboard for his second-grade class's study of different cultural heritages within the United States. Which activity might be a good suggestion?

A. students creating a replica of a Civil War cannon
B. students creating a painting in the cubist style
C. students making a simple Native American doll
D. students finger painting a landscape scene

Cultural Relationships and Change

Few individuals or cultures can provide for all of their needs without help. This leads to **interdependence**, whereby groups or individuals are dependent upon others to meet certain needs. Young children can best grasp this concept by understanding their own dependence on farmers and ranchers to produce the food they eat and on manufacturers to make clothing and products they use.

Elementary-aged students may begin to understand broader ideas of one nation's interdependence upon another. For example, some products not available in one country (like grain in some Middle Eastern countries) must be imported from other countries (like the United States). In exchange, the country with the desired resource receives a payment of cash or a necessary product. This example shows how interdependence leads to the import of grain to some Middle Eastern countries and to the export of grain by the United States. In return, the United States might receive petroleum from a Middle Eastern country.

All parts of the world have different natural resources and thus access to some goods but not others. In some parts of the world and even in some desert regions in the United States, it is impossible to grow food, making these areas dependent on others for their very survival. This makes trade relationships and **cooperation** crucial to meet the most basic needs of a community.

As cultures come into contact with each other, they may adopt some components of other cultures. Such changes may be incited by advances in communications or transportation that allow for a culture that was once fairly isolated to become part of a broader community. Economic development may also drive cultural change. In a primarily agrarian society, people may live spread out on farms; however, once industrialization occurs, a larger workforce is needed in a more finite location, and urbanization may result.

As one part of a society shifts, other facets may also transition. For example, new science or technology, such as the ability to communicate via the internet, may require new laws that govern the use of the internet, new businesses that sell goods and services online, and new social interactions that take place in a digital context.

Change can drive **conflict** within a culture as certain groups may want to keep things the way they were. Conflict can also occur between cultures based on different beliefs, religions, political or economic systems, or disagreements over borders or natural resource use.

Cultures may also experience both **unity** and **diversity** simultaneously. For example, in the United States, people are unified under a common system of government and laws. However, there exists great diversity in ethnicity, religion, and language. One common idea is that of unity *in* diversity. That is, certain cultural groups are unified under some common purposes but have a diverse body. Some say that this is the case in the United States.

Some cultures are more heterogeneous, like many parts of the United States and cities in Texas, where people of diverse cultural backgrounds can be found. Others are more homogenous and have a single and very dominant culture.

Globalization, the process by which businesses and organizations operate on an international scale, is rapidly increasing. This increase has led to a **global culture**, in which certain norms and values are shared across a global scale. The development of a global culture has both negative and positive impacts, as shared understandings lead to more interconnectedness. But sometimes more dominant cultural constructs, such as American consumerism, may spread to the detriment of local culture. While the opening of American fast-food restaurants throughout the world may unite people in their love of French fries or a certain brand of coffee, it might do so at the expense of small local restaurants that preserve traditional cooking methods and foods.

Practice Question

30. How might a first-grade teacher introduce the concept of interdependence to her class?
    - A. by discussing trade agreements such as the North American Free Trade Agreement (NAFTA)
    - B. by asking students to name the major exports of China
    - C. by asking students to list all the items in the classroom not made in America
    - D. by asking students where they got their shoes

GEOGRAPHY

Spatial Thinking

Humans have long been fascinated with geography and their place on the planet. Today, a person's geographic **location**, or exact position on the earth, is typically defined by latitude and longitude coordinates. However, even before the invention of these systems of measurement, explorers and cartographers made attempts to track location. Early **maps** and **globes** featured known land alongside *terra incognita*, or unknown land, which sparked interest in future maritime exploration. Today's maps and globes, both digital and physical, are far more complex and can help travelers navigate to very exact locations.

This precision is made possible by the geographical reference system of latitude and longitude. **Latitude** refers to the coordinates that specify the north-south position of a given point on the surface of the earth. These horizontal lines are usually marked and labeled on globes and include the **equator**—the line representing an angle of 0°—and four other named lines: the Arctic Circle at 66° north, the Antarctic Circle at 66°south, the Tropic of Cancer at 23°north, and the Tropic of Capricorn at 23°south. The climate of locations closer to the equator tends to be hotter because these areas receive more direct sunlight, while the climate of locations farther from it is colder because of the slant of the earth.

Longitude refers to the geographic coordinates that provides an east-west position on the earth's surface. This measurement far postdated the ability to calculate latitude, which could easily be calculated based on the position of the sun and stars. English clockmaker John Harrison invented a device in 1773 that calculated longitude, thereby ushering in a new wave of maritime navigation and exploration. Like latitude, lines of longitude have a central line at 0°, which is known as the **prime meridian**. While there was some initial controversy over where to designate the exact location of this line, it has now been firmly established at the Royal Observatory in Greenwich, United Kingdom. This is the origin of the term *Greenwich Mean Time* (GMT), or the solar time at this point.

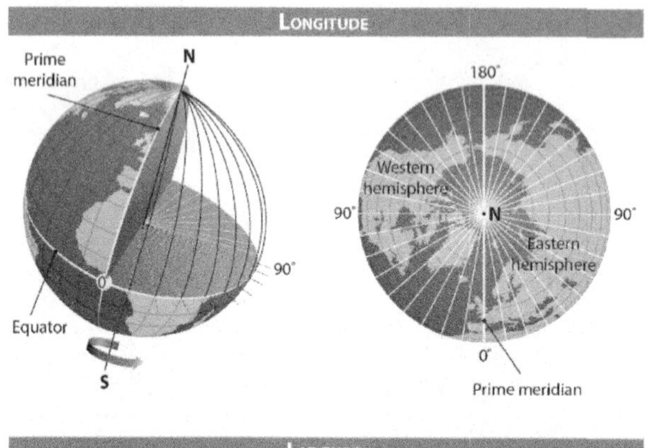

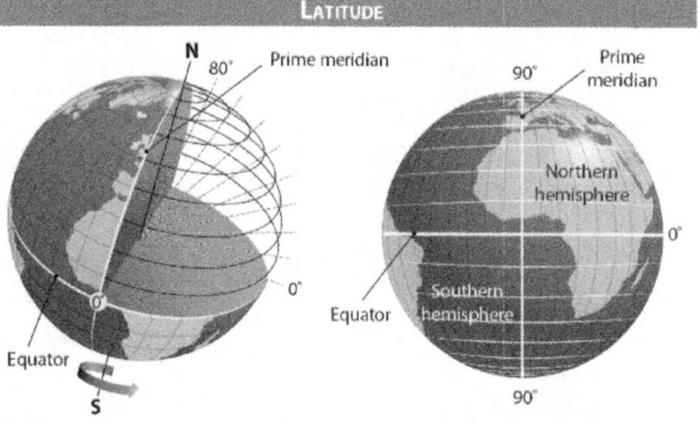

Figure 3.6. Longitude and Latitude

Globes are not practical to use when traveling, so students must be able to read and understand information on maps. Unfortunately, no completely accurate flat map exists, though there are several standard map projections that minimize the amount of distortion.

Map reading is still an essential geographical skill that helps students understand their spatial position in relationship to other locations, as well as how to interpret and understand graphics designed to convey information. Maps may be used to find an **absolute location** or a precise point, or **relative location**, or where something is in relationship with something else.

Kindergarten students should be introduced to basic **directional terms** such as *left*, *right*, *over*, and *under* and should be able to locate basic locations in familiar environments like their school. They should also begin to recognize other major **landmarks**, or easily recognizable places, in their community. By first grade, students should be able to use the cardinal directions as illustrated by the **compass rose** with some fluency to find the location of objects and places.

By second grade, students should start to use maps and globes to identify various locations, including being able to identify the map **title**, using the map's **legend** to understand what symbols or colors represent, using the **scale** to measure **distances**, and using a map's **grid** reference system to identify the coordinates of locations. Students should be afforded plenty of practice with maps and be given opportunities to use and make simple maps. This might take the form of a class-wide project to draw a map of the school in the second or third grade, or even a simple sketch of the classroom layout for kindergartners and first graders. The key is making the map-focused activities as purposeful and relevant as possible to keep student engagement high and help them recognize and practice using and creating maps with purpose.

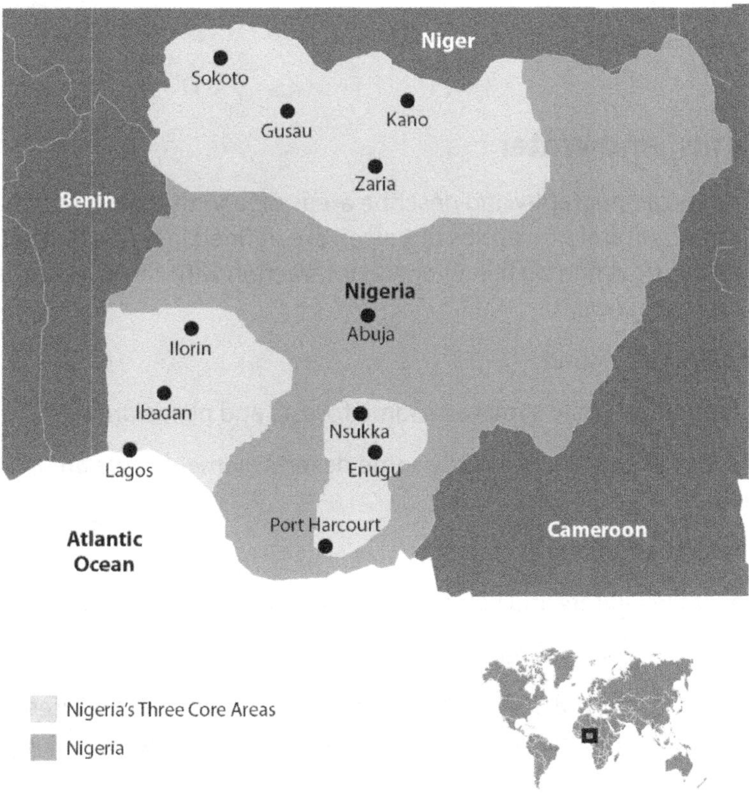

Figure 3.7. Parts of a Map

Maps are not the only type of graphic representations that students need practice with interpreting. Both **graphs** and **charts** are used in many different types of texts, and students need practice in extrapolating information from them. An appropriate chart for a kindergarten student may be a simple pictorial representation, while third-grade students will need significant practice with interpreting various bar and line graphs to meet both social studies and math objectives. The key is providing students with strategies to comprehend graphic information. Teachers can help students develop these skills by asking questions such as "What does ____mean/represent/stand for?" and "What information does ____ show?" and "What do you see in the row/column/pie?"

Check Your Understanding

What types of things might you chart in simple pictorial form in the kindergarten classroom?

Practice Questions

31. Which of the following is a landmark appropriate for a first grader to recognize?
    A. the Leaning Tower of Pisa
    B. London Bridge
    C. the Statue of Liberty
    D. the Coliseum

32. Which symbol on a map denotes north, south, east, and west?
    A. the compass rose
    B. the scale
    C. the grid
    D. the Mercator projection

Regions, Landforms, and Water

Regions are the basic units of geography and describe areas of land that have common features. Regions can be based on political or cultural similarities but often are defined in terms of climate and vegetation. These regional differences affect human behavior and interaction with the environment. The major climate regions are listed as follows:

- **polar**: cold and dry year-round
- **temperate**: cold winters, mild summers, some forests and plains/prairies
- **arid**: hot and dry year-round and include some deserts (some deserts are found in cold tundra regions as well)
- **tropical**: always hot and wet, rain forests
- **Mediterranean**: mild winters and hot, dry summers
- **tundra**: cold year-round with three subtypes:
    - Arctic tundra is found in the far Northern Hemisphere and features a very desolate landscape. The ground is frozen in these cold desert regions, making it impossible for most plants to grow.
    - Antarctic tundra is found in Antarctica and features some desolate landscape and desert. However, some areas support plant life.
    - Alpine tundra is a mountainous region also without significant plant life.

Regions of the United States are generally divided into Northeast, Southeast, Midwest, Southwest, and West. Other regional distinctions include the Central Great Plains, Great Lakes, Pacific Northwest, Rocky Mountains, mid-Atlantic, and New England. The state of Texas has seven major regions:

1. Big Bend Country in West Texas: desert mountains, plateaus; with short grasses and brush; includes the city of El Paso

2. the Gulf Coast in Southeast Texas: marshes, estuaries, prairies and grasslands; includes the cities of Houston, Galveston, and Corpus Christi

3. the Hill Country of Central Texas: hilly grasslands, springs, canyons, and the Edwards Aquifer; includes the city of Austin

4. the Panhandle in North Texas: flat grasslands and plains; deep canyons and rivers; includes the cities of Abilene, Amarillo, and Lubbock

5. the Piney Woods of East Texas: thick woodlands and swamps; includes the "Big Thicket" region of wetlands and the cities of Longview, Texarkana, and Tyler

6. the Prairies and Lakes region in North and Central Texas: rich, fertile black soil with patches of woodlands and grassland prairies; includes the city of Dallas

7. the South Texas plains: dry grasslands with some lakes, marshes, and ponds; includes the lower Rio Grande valley and the cities of Brownsville, Laredo, and San Antonio

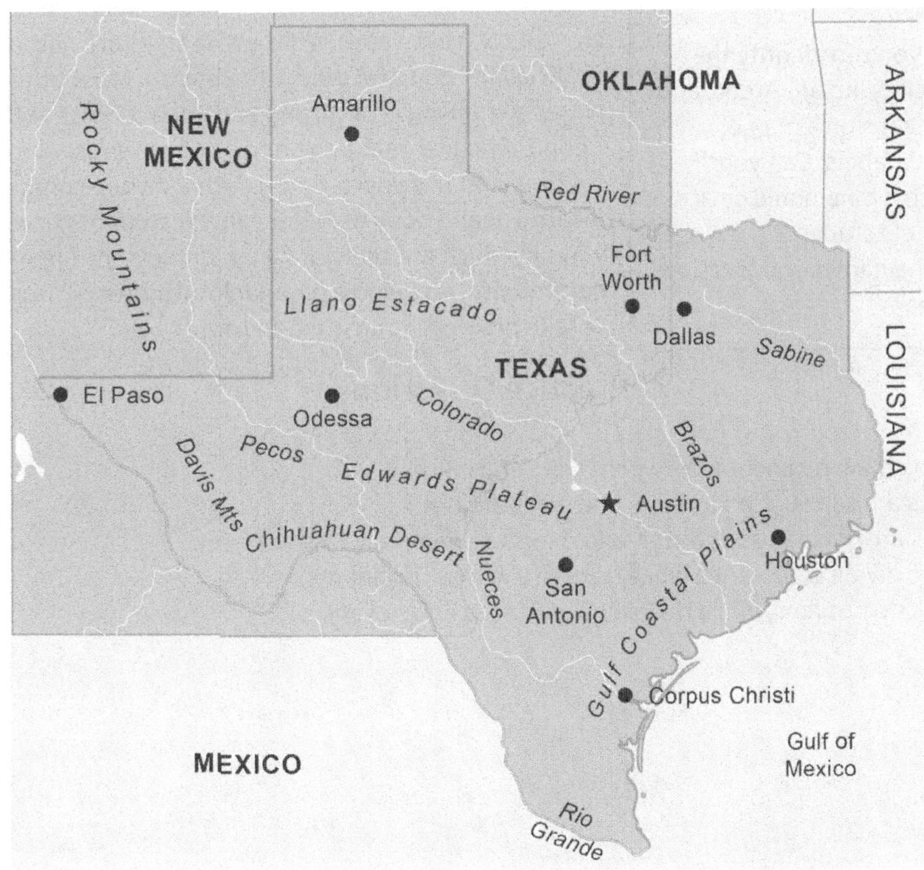

Figure 3.8. Physical Map of Texas

In addition to the six populated **continents** of North and South America, Asia, Europe, Africa, and Australia, there are two other large formations that account for the solid surface area of the planet. The North Pole is the northernmost point on the globe and is sometimes referred to as the Arctic. It is not a landform in the strictest sense because it is really a large sheet of ice that expands and contracts based on temperature. However, some definitions of "the Arctic" cover the entire region of the Arctic Ocean and inhabited areas such as parts of Canada and Greenland. The South Pole, on the other hand, is located on the continent of Antarctica and represents the southernmost point on the globe. Antarctica boasts no permanent residents, but it is, like the North Pole, an important location for research stations.

Check Your Understanding

What is the climate of your local community? How does this impact your daily life and the lives of your students?

The surface of the earth is 71 percent water, and its continents are surrounded by five **oceans**: the Atlantic, Pacific, Indian, Arctic, and Antarctic. The Antarctic Ocean is also sometimes referred to as the Southern Ocean or the Antarctic Sea. These saltwater bodies are connected by **seas**, which are generally smaller than oceans, often surrounded partly or wholly by land, saltwater, and usually connect with their larger counterparts.

Rivers and their smaller cousins, **streams**, are flowing bodies of water that empty into seas and oceans and are generally freshwater. **Lakes**, like seas, are large bodies of water that are surrounded by land; though unlike seas, they are usually freshwater. While some lakes are natural, many are artificial and constructed for recreation. Most other bodies of water are naturally occurring and impact those in their vicinity. People who live near large bodies of water use the water source for food and transportation. Teachers whose programs are located near a body of water can ask students to consider the ways in which the body of water impacts the life of the community. Is fishing a popular local industry? Does the beach or lake promote tourism to the area?

Study Tips

Ensure that you can identify the Atlantic, Pacific, Indian, Arctic, and Antarctic Oceans on a map or globe without labels. Can you come up with a mnemonic device that would help students remember the names and locations of the oceans?

Practice Questions

33. What is the main distinction between rivers and lakes?
    A. Rivers are surrounded by land, and lakes are not.
    B. Lakes are generally saltwater, and rivers are generally freshwater.
    C. Rivers divide continents, while lakes are within continents.
    D. Lakes do not flow, while rivers flow into seas and oceans.

34. Mrs. Martin, who teaches first grade in the West Texas desert, wants to help her students understand how climate affects the way humans live in a given area. Which integrated social studies and science activity would help her class understand this concept?

A. showing them a video of people shopping for a new house in another state
B. planting a few different crops in the school garden to see which ones grow
C. bringing in a guest chef to talk to the students about different flavor profiles
D. having her students design their "dream house" out of blocks

Human Geography

Human-Environment Interactions

Environmental conditions impact people in a variety of ways. People living on plains and prairies where there are few trees, for example, often have to build houses out of materials other than lumber. People living in mountain and desert regions may have to import food from other areas since the landscape makes farming difficult. People who live in particularly fragile environments, such as the rain forest, often use the intense biodiversity around them to develop innovative solutions to meet their needs, such as growing small batches of crops in the limited ground space and hunting a wide variety of animals. One challenge facing many of the world's geographic regions is the desire for economic development balanced with the preservation of natural environments. Destroying rain forests, for example, not only displaces animals but also forces their inhabitants to change their very way of life.

Science and technology can both accelerate and mitigate the way humans change the environment. For example, the development of farming instruments that require fewer people to plant and harvest may lead to more farmland being cleared and more erosion or soil nutrient depletion. However, other technology, such as smart soil monitoring systems, may help farmers mitigate environmental damage.

Nevertheless, human interactions with the natural world can permanently change ecosystems. For example, woodlands may be cleared for housing developments, or man-made lakes may change the flow of rivers. Resources in an environment, either naturally existing or created by humans, dictate how many people live there and the types of activities those people engage in.

Practice Question

35. Which is an example of the way humans have caused environmental change in Texas?

A. erosion of farmland in the panhandle during the Dust Bowl
B. movement of Native American communities from place to place
C. abandoning homes during the oil bust of the 1980s
D. tracking hurricanes in Galveston using Doppler Radar

Urban and Rural Communities

There are two primary types of human communities based on population density in an environment; each has different environmental interactions. **Rural** communities such as farms and villages contain a smaller population of people, and they often participate in an agrarian, or **farming**, lifestyle. *Farming* is a somewhat general term often used to describe the use of land or water for the production or obtainment of food. This includes **ranching**, which uses land to produce livestock, and **fishing**, which extracts food from bodies of water or raises fish in tanks. **Urban** communities are cities and towns where human activity is driven by business and the **trade**, or exchange, of goods and services.

While both urban and rural areas may be important to the overall economy, or wealth of resources, of a country or region, urban areas tend to be centers of commerce and production. Cities originally developed around markets later grew around factories as industry developed. While cities might have fewer **physical resources** such as farmland, they generally have a larger supply of **human resources**—the human population available for work.

Factories are large buildings where products are made, originally by humans and increasingly by machines controlled by humans. Some cities are known for a particular type of factory, such as the automotive production factories in Detroit, Michigan. Additionally, most cities have elaborate transportation networks that move people and goods from one place to another. People living in cities often have many public transportation options such as trains, subways, and buses. These options are more limited in rural communities because of remoteness and lack of population density.

Rural areas, however, produce many raw materials and crops that must be transported to manufacturing centers and cities for production and sale to consumers. Since those who rely on ranching and fishing require land to produce or procure their foodstuffs, they, too, tend to be located in areas remote from urban centers. A railroad system that uses **trains** to ship important commodities, and a **highway** system that uses **trucks** to transport goods are very important to the **transportation** network of rural and remote communities. Without such networks, interdependent relationships between communities would not be possible. This interdependence is often marked by raw goods and commodities such as cotton and soybeans being produced in rural areas and then shipped to urban areas for transformation into processed foods and clothing. These finished goods are then shipped and sold both to urban and rural communities.

Though transporting goods over water does not require the same type of transportation network as transporting goods over land, this method does rely on the construction of ports and canals, which might be highly relevant to the economy of a given community. Although generally more expensive, **airplanes** can be used to transport people and goods. In some very remote areas, such as rural Alaska, airplane travel is the only method of transportation available because road and rail networks do not exist. Even in urban areas, the reliance on **shipping** direct to the consumer has become very popular as more and more people rely on the internet to buy consumer goods.

Practice Question

36. A third-grade student is very interested in trains. The teacher wants to make sure Hector's research project interests him and pertains to the assignment's topic of the American economy. Which topical suggestion might the teacher make to Hector?

A. trains throughout American history
B. the role of trains in cattle ranching
C. the invention of the steam engine
D. the decline of the American railroad

Changes in Human Populations

One trend in the United States has been increasing urbanization, or the shift in population from rural to urban areas. Recent data from the US Census Bureau revealed that over 80 percent of Americans live in urban areas. In some very fast-growing cities, the pace of construction of new homes, schools, and roads is often unable to accommodate population growth. This creates many urban problems like traffic, school overcrowding, and lack of affordable housing.

The desire of people to move from a rural area to an urban one (or from any area to a new area) is generally the result of both push and pull factors. **Push factors** are situations that push people from their community. These could include drought, lack of educational or economic opportunity, or the loss of a job or livelihood. **Pull factors** are situations that pull people toward a new community. These factors could be the promise of a new job or the possibility of more educational or social opportunities. Some students may have experienced these factors in their own family's immigration to the United States. An existing network of extended family in the United States might have been a pull factor, for example.

Migration and **immigration** have been key to the development of Texas. The first American immigrants who came to Spanish and Mexican Texas were only the first wave of migrants. European immigrants founded many Texas towns and cities. Today's state is heavily influenced by immigration from Latin America. These immigrants contribute an estimated $119 billion annually to the Texas economy and are a key part of many industries such as agriculture, construction, and the service industry.

Practice Question

37. Which of the following is a pull factor that might encourage immigration to Texas?
    A. few employment opportunities in Guatemala
    B. little available housing in Guatemala
    C. family members living in Texas
    D. a high unemployment rate in Texas

ECONOMICS

Economics Foundations

The study of economics is the study of the production and consumption of products as well as how people produce and obtain these goods. It explains how people interact with the market; studying economics usually explains the behavior of people or the government.

Basic Economic Concepts

In some parts of the world where there is little industrial or scientific development, societies function in what is called a **traditional economic system**. Most of the economy rests upon small-scale agriculture. A surplus of goods beyond what the immediate community needs is rare in a traditional economic system.

The American economy is best described as a **free enterprise,** or capitalist system. In this system, market forces and consumer behaviors regulate the economy. In contrast, in a **planned** or **command economy,** a central governmental authority controls economic production. A **mixed economy** is a combination of a capitalist system and a command system. In a mixed economy, government does regulate some parts of private businesses, but some elements of free enterprise are also present. India and France are good examples of a true mixed economy.

Different economic systems have different advantages and disadvantages. The advantages of the American free enterprise system are usually cited as the efficient use of resources due to **competition**, an incentive for people and businesses to work hard to make profits, and an incentive for entrepreneurship. **Entrepreneurship** involves taking a risk to start a new business. Entrepreneurs offer tangible goods or services as **producers**, which are then sold to customers, or **consumers**. These goods or services may meet basic needs or human wants. Entrepreneurs often try to meet a need that is currently unmet or under-met in the current market.

In a free enterprise system with limited government regulation, businesses must take it upon themselves to act with ethics and morals. What a business must pay workers is only legislated to a degree (per federal and state minimum wages), so businesses themselves must make decisions about pay raises for performance or cost-of-living increases. Furthermore, while employees' health and safety is monitored by the government, these are only minimum standards. Businesses must make their own decisions about how to treat their employees.

One of the most important concepts in American and Texan economics is **supply and demand**. Supply refers to how much the market can actually offer, and demand is how much desire there is for a product or service. The demand is the relationship between price and quantity, which is how much people are willing to pay for the product. The supply simply means how much product producers are willing to supply at a certain price. This relationship between price and how much product is offered to the market is known as the supply relationship.

Price is used to show the relationship between supply and demand. When the demand is high for a product, the price generally goes up. When the demand is low, price falls. However, if the price is considered too high by the public, there may be excess supply because people will purchase less. Causes of excess supply include other price changes, including the price of alternative goods, and public preferences. Likewise, there might be excess demand if the price is set too low and many people want the product, but there may not be enough supply. This might happen if there is a government ban on the product, the government imposes a price ceiling, or suppliers decide to not raise prices.

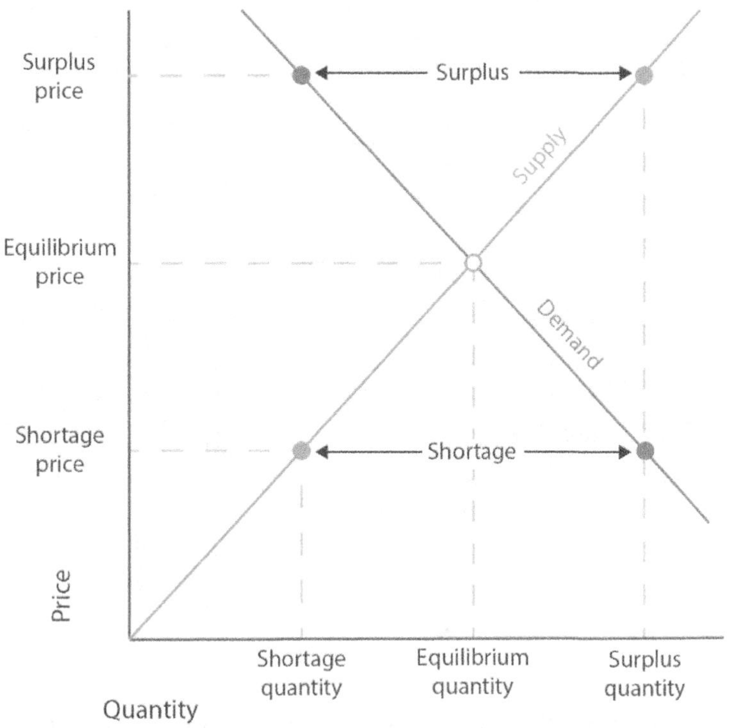

Figure 3.9. Equilibrium Price

When supply and demand are equal, the economy is at equilibrium. However, that is not always the case. When there is insufficient supply to meet demand, the result is **scarcity**. People need to choose which want to satisfy. For example, if there is a low supply of chocolate, chocolate prices will be high. Consequently, a consumer must decide whether to spend more money than usual on chocolate or not to buy any at all.

Every choice has a value. **Opportunity cost** is when a consumer makes a choice at the cost of another choice or the value of an opportunity. For example, imagine that someone must choose between eating chocolate cake or apple pie. If that person chose the chocolate cake, he or she gave up the opportunity to eat the apple pie. The opportunity cost is the apple pie. Decisions made by an individual or the government based on opportunity cost are driven by needs, wants, income, and time.

> **Check Your Understanding**
>
> What types of games or activities could be used with elementary-aged students to illustrate the concept of opportunity cost?

In the American and Texan economies, there is a **division of labor** into separate tasks, or **specializations**. For example, not everyone owns a farm or can grow a variety of produce, so consumers depend on farmers around the world to grow various agricultural products in order to obtain them. Likewise, not everyone can fix a computer; instead, consumers bring their computers to experts to be repaired.

Technological innovation is also driven by the economy (and vice versa). For example, more efficient transportation has increased trade and the exchange of wealth. Railroads enabled US businesses to transport raw materials to their production facilities, thereby increasing the production of goods. These areas then needed more people to provide labor, helping companies and individuals generate more wealth and providing jobs and salaries to workers, who themselves were thus able to generate more wealth in cash.

One economic model examines the way in which money moves through a society. Known as the **circular flow model of economic exchanges,** this model maintains that money flows from producers or firms to workers or households as wages and then back to producers as workers purchase products with their wages.

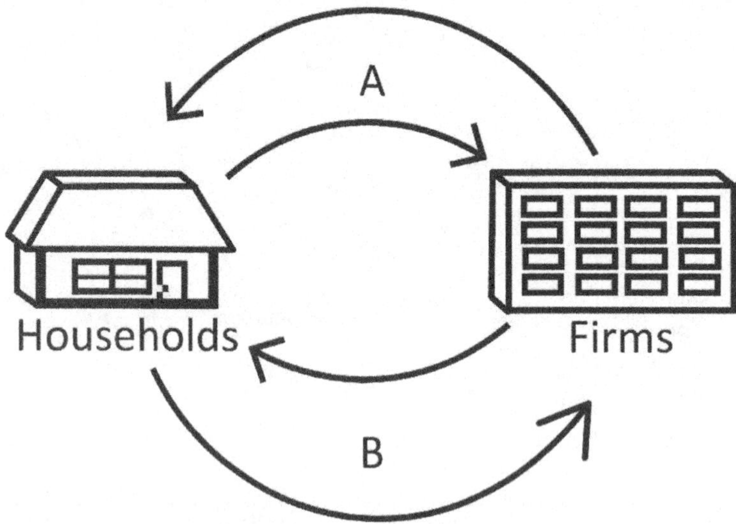

Figure 3.10. Circular Flow Model

Economic activity is also subject to the **business cycle**—the ups and downs of the economy in terms of output, employment, income, and sales. The business cycle involves both the expansion of the economy (**growth**), and the contraction of the economy (**recession**).

Practice Question

38. Due to a new labor-saving manufacturing process, most global microchip manufacturers have increased output by 30 percent. What will most likely happen as a result?
   A. Microchip demand will increase.
   B. Microchip cost will decrease.
   C. An economic recession will occur.
   D. The circular flow will be disrupted.

Economic Regulation

The federal government helps to regulate the economy. **Government regulation** falls into either economic regulation or social regulation. **Economic regulation** controls prices directly or indirectly. The government works to prevent monopolies—the control of a market for a good or service by one company or group. For example, the government may prohibit utility companies from raising their prices beyond a certain point. Antitrust law is another type of economic regulation. It strengthens market forces to protect consumers from businesses and to eliminate or minimize the need for direct regulation. These laws are intended to ensure fair competition in the US economy.

The government also sets monetary and fiscal policies. **Monetary policy** dictates the actions of central banks to regulate the economy in terms of employment and price stability. **Fiscal policy** determines how and how much the government will tax and spend tax dollars. Government policies also govern **international trade**. Protective tariffs or taxes, quotas on imports, and laws that prohibit (embargo) or restrict trade with other nations are part of the regulatory practices of the government.

Finally, the government collects **taxes** not only to cover its expenses but also to help fuel the economy. Federal taxes pay for costs like federal employees' salaries and retirement programs, government programs, and the military. Other government programs that are financed through taxes include veterans' benefits and NASA. Payroll taxes help **finance** the Medicare and Social Security programs which provide assistance for the elderly and those with low incomes. Government spending helps to increase the wealth of businesses and individuals. For example, if the government spends money to build bridges and highways, construction businesses generate more income. If an individual is retired or cannot work for health reasons, Social Security will provide assistance.

In spite of regulations, **economic globalization**, or the **interdependence** of global economies on each other, remains a central part of our world. That means that if one economy suffers, its biggest trade partners will also be impacted. This may occur on a global, national, or local scale. For example, because Texas is the largest oil producer in the United States, downturns in this industry have far-reaching impacts throughout the nation and the world.

The degree of government regulation of the economy is subject for debate. As a very conservative state, many Texans believe that government regulation is bad for consumers, businesses, and the overall economy. They see such regulation as encroachment on the free enterprise system that is self-regulating based on the ebb and flow of market forces. Others believe that the economy should be more highly regulated and that some businesses and industries (such as Amazon or the pharmaceutical industry) have gained too much power.

Practice Question

39. Which TWO areas does the federal government regulate?
    - A. locations of new retail developments
    - B. minimum wage for workers
    - C. the price of raw materials
    - D. taxes on imported goods
    - E. requirements for a driver's license

Economics Past and Present

American Economics

The United States has its origins in European exploration and colonization. While European powers had political and religious reasons for exploration and colonization, they also had strong economic motivations. The first European explorers were seeking new sea trade routes to Asia.

The new lands "discovered" in the Americas became important sources of wealth. At first, gold and silver were extracted, but then other raw materials, such as tobacco, rice, and cotton began to be shipped from the colonies to the mother country. The colonies, without their own sources of manufactures, then became markets for finished products from the mother country in a system known as **mercantilism**.

The emergence of capitalism, advancements in agriculture, and the raw materials from colonies all fueled the **Industrial Revolution**. Early American industrialization happened first in the garment industry in the New England states, but it continued in full force throughout the nineteenth century as the United States had the natural resources and the new technology (like steam engines and electricity) to produce more.

Industrialization shifted many American agrarian workers into industrial workers as they relocated from rural areas to new urban areas to meet the labor needs of factories and businesses. Many of these industrial centers, however, were concentrated in the northern states, creating an economic divide between North and South (see "American History" section for details on sectionalism).

Today, the United States has a more diversified economy, and there is much less distinction between the economic activities of the north and south. The United States is the largest economy in the world as measured by **gross domestic product (GDP)**. GDP refers to the total dollar value of goods and services produced within a country during a certain time.

The United States was not always an economic leader, and much of its growth can be attributed to waves of immigration throughout its history, which have fueled population growth. Today, **immigrants** continue to contribute to the American and Texan economy in many ways. While some argue that immigrants take jobs from people born in the United States, most research suggests that immigrants may actually help create jobs via productivity and new demands for goods and services.

The United States has long promoted the idea that there is **equal economic opportunity** for all and that **progress** occurs when people participate successfully in the economy. This idea is based on individualism—the idea that the individual is the key determiner of his destiny.

Part of individual action in the American or Texan economy rests on spending, saving, and budgeting money appropriately. The TEKS emphasize financial literacy and responsibility with the goal of helping students become individual actors in the economy (see Chapter 2).

Practice Question

40. Which statement best describes how gross domestic product (GDP) is calculated?
    A. totaling the value of goods and services produced in a nation
    B. subtracting the value of a country's imports from the value of its exports
    C. tracking changes in foreign direct investment in a nation over time
    D. multiplying cost of goods sold by the nation's population

Texas Economics

Cattle

Following the Civil War, the Texas economy began to grow—thanks in great part to cattle. A wartime halt to trade had allowed a surplus of Texas cattle to develop. **Joseph G. McCoy** built the first "cow town"—Abilene, Kansas—to receive cattle and ship them east to markets via train. This marked the beginning of the cattle trade: cattle were driven north to receiving areas, for railroads had not yet been built farther south or east than Missouri and parts of Kansas.

Cattle drives became an industry dominated and organized by contractors who led organized teams ensuring the security and progress of the animals. The ideal of the frontier cowboy took root in American folklore, but cattle-driving as an industry was short lived.

Helpful Hint

Some enterprising ranchers also raised goats to make mohair, another important Texas product, which is generated in West Texas. Made from the fleece of the Angora goat, mohair was sold for high prices. Today, the region still boasts more Angora goats than anywhere else in the United States.

Cattle originated in southern Texas, but major ranches, or "spreads," appeared throughout the state, some of which still exist. The **King Ranch**, founded in 1853 by Richard King and Mifflin Kennedy, is one of the largest. Still in use today for hunting and tourism, it encompasses more land than the state of Rhode Island. The **Matador Ranch,** based in the Texas Panhandle, historically included parcels of land throughout the Great Plains as far north as the Canadian border, and its remnants exist today as part of a larger corporation.

Ranching continued (and continues) to be a major part of the Texas economy; however, cattle drives only lasted until the end of the nineteenth century. Cattle drives were no longer necessary as meatpacking facilities opened in Texas's growing cities and as railroads extended farther west and into Texas itself. Still, the development of railroads would only add to Texas's own economic growth.

Railroads

Initially, most railroads centered on Houston and Galveston; the **Houston, East & West Texas Railroad (HE&WT)** connected Houston and Shreveport, Louisiana. Meanwhile, the first major east-west and north-south railroad crossing was built in Dallas. Eventually lines like the Kansas City Southern, Missouri Pacific, Santa Fe Regional, Texas & New Orleans, and Cotton Belt crossed the state. Existing lines like the Kansas City Southern and Union Pacific continue to do so. Crossings and construction sites gave rise to towns like Lufkin.

The construction of transcontinental railroads throughout the United States included development in Texas. Texas's geography made the state key to railroad development, and Grenville Dodge began construction of the **Texas and Pacific Railroad** in 1869 in Marshall, Texas. Jay Gould—a New York City "robber baron"—took over the T&P in Dallas in 1874, completing construction across the state to El Paso. There, the T&P connected with the **Southern Pacific**, which originated in San Diego. The Southern Pacific was able to use track to cross Texas to reach New Orleans. As a result, Texas became integral to continental rail transportation and trade.

Agriculture

Railroads were also key in promoting another important agricultural product. The terrain around Houston and Galveston close to the Gulf Coast was suitable for **rice**, and the Houston Chamber of Commerce, in conjunction with the Southern Pacific railroad, promoted rice growth in the area. Louisiana settlers had already been growing rice in the region, but the Houston Chamber of Commerce invited a Japanese scholar studying in the United States to teach Texas farmers more rice-growing techniques. Japanese immigrants in turn came to the region to take advantage of agricultural opportunities. The region produced 99 percent of the US rice by the twentieth century, and the Southern Pacific profited from transporting the product.

Rice was only one of many profitable agricultural products in Texas. Until the late nineteenth century, **cotton seeds** had been discarded in the cotton harvest. Indeed, the cotton gin had been one of the most important inventions of the Industrial Revolution, for it quickly separated the seeds from the fiber, substantially speeding up the process. However, valuable uses for cotton seeds were discovered, including its high levels of nitrogen. The pulp from crushed cotton seeds supplemented animal feed—especially feed for cattle, one of Texas's most valuable products—and was also a powerful fertilizer. Furthermore, oil for industrial lubrication could be extracted from cotton seeds. Cotton was a cash crop in Central Texas; the sharecropper system in the region was effectively an extension of slavery, allowing maximum exploitation of labor to harvest cotton seeds.

Farther north and west, **wheat** became an important agricultural product. Migrants to Texas—including recent European immigrants—began settling the area after the Civil War, and by the beginning of the twentieth century over 300,000 family farms were established in the plains regions of the state. Irrigation, crop diversification, and farming methods that allowed for maximum absorption of water enabled farmers to coax crops from the rough terrain. Eventually, better farming technology improved agriculture in the region; the discovery of the Ogallala Aquifer improved irrigation. However, the drought and Dust Bowl phenomenon of the 1930s harmed farmers throughout the Great Plains, and Texans were no exception.

Later in the early twentieth century, **citrus** products would become important in South Texas. While the Rio Grande Valley region seemed unsuitable for agriculture, in 1912 a pharmacist from Iowa, **John Harry Shary** acquired land, irrigated it, and planted citrus trees, successfully growing **grapefruit**. Meanwhile, migrant workers moved in the region with their families, finding work in the fields.

Oil and Gas

Texas's most famous product, and arguably its lifeblood, is petroleum. In 1901, Pattillo Higgins posited that there was oil under a salt hill called **Spindletop** near Beaumont, despite some ongoing production farther north in **Corsicana** since the late nineteenth century. Hiring the Czech engineer Anthony Lucas to drill, Higgins struck oil on January 10. The **Lucas Gusher** would prove to be the largest oil source in the world at that time.

Figure 3.11. Lucas Gusher

Beaumont would become home to the nascent Texas oil industry. New companies like the Guffey Oil Company (later to become Gulf Oil, and then **Chevron**) and the Texas Oil Company (**Texaco**) opened offices in Beaumont and refineries in Port Neches and Port Arthur. Oil, which demanded specialized equipment like pipelines and drills, developed a new economy of its own; it also energized existing industries, such as the timber industry.

Drilling continued at Spindletop, and in 1926 even more oil was discovered. Investors explored possibilities throughout Texas, and the oil industry developed as wells popped up in Humble, Sour Lake, Batson, and Goose Creek. Eventually exploration in the **Permian Basin**, located on public land in West Texas, yielded considerable revenue, much of which went to support education (including a substantial endowment for the University of Texas). Oil continues to be the number one Texas industry.

Because so many Texans rely on oil and gas for their livelihood, **booms**, or periods where the economy is growing and oil prices per barrel are high, and **busts**, where oil prices suddenly drop, have been a big part of Texas history. These boom and bust cycles, such as those of the 1980s, impact other parts of the economy, particularly real estate. For example, in boom times, people buy homes that they suddenly cannot afford after busts.

Technology

With many tech companies like Dell, IBM, and Oracle headquartered in Texas, this industry is another major player in the Texan economy. Some sources rank Texas as the top state for tech worker migration. Austin and Dallas are the top cities for many Texan technology companies.

Moreover, Houston is home to NASA's Johnson Space Center, the center of human spaceflight. Additionally, Boca Chica, Texas, near Brownsville, is the headquarters of SpaceX facilities. At this facility, which has been colloquially renamed Starbase by its owner Elon Musk, engineers are busy working on technology to help get humans back on the Moon.

Practice Question

41. Which event would likely have the greatest impact on the economy of Texas?
    A. New markets for cotton open up in Asia.
    B. A weevil destroys many rice fields.
    C. Consumers stop buying gas-powered cars.
    D. A tanker becomes stuck in the Suez Canal.

Government and Citizenship

Civics Foundations

Civics involves the rights and duties of citizenship in the United States and Texas. Students typically learn about basic principles upon which our government rests.

As a social studies construct, **justice** generally refers to the justice system, in which people are held accountable for the consequences of their actions within society. This typically involves the role of the courts to ascribe particular penalties for certain illicit actions. Teachers can help students understand the basic tenets of the justice system at many grade levels. Preschool and kindergarten teachers might help students identify the role of community helpers like police officers, lawyers, and judges. First-grade teachers may ask students to declare whether they believe a character in a story is guilty or innocent of a given charge. Second- and third-grade teachers may explore the justice process even more deeply and hold simple mock trials or have students participate in mock criminal investigations. It is also important to point out, as is age appropriate, that in the United States, it is the **rule of law**—the idea that it is the law itself that governs—rather than government officials. In this way, the law empowers its agents in government to enforce it. It grants them no powers outside of it.

Equality is another important civics ideology that should be discussed in the classroom and in society. It is not always easy to achieve equality in a classroom with varying student needs and limited resources or in a society with many different people with varying needs and similarly limited resources. While there are differing opinions about whether all Americans truly enjoy equality in terms of the legal system, the justice system is founded upon the principle of equality before the law in which all people should be treated equally both in the creation and implementation of the law.

Teachers should also promote **tolerance**, or the acceptance of beliefs or behaviors that one does not necessarily agree with, as appropriate in the classroom and help students understand the need for tolerance in pluralistic American society. Freedom of religion is a core tenet of the United States, and many classrooms will have students with different belief systems. Helping students to be understanding and tolerant of the beliefs of others starts with accepting differences. While some students might not understand why certain dietary or dress restrictions are observed by their peers, part of promoting tolerance includes helping students understand that there are many different ways of doing things.

Practice Question

42. Mr. Haskell is always reminding his class that it is the classroom rules that govern the classroom, not the teacher. Upon which concept is he basing this statement?
   A. justice
   B. tolerance
   C. rule of law
   D. equity

Civic Participation

Civic participation, or participating in issues of public concern, is important, but it is not practiced in many communities. Low turnouts, particularly at local elections, are evidence of this trend. However, this trend can be reversed by educating young people about how individuals in a society can help in the decision-making that affects their communities.

To participate in civic life, individuals must first be informed of the **issues**. Teachers can help their students keep up with current events on a local, national, and global scale through lessons on contemporary issues. Teachers can point out that there are often different **points of view** on any given issue and that different groups bring different backgrounds and desires to any issue. A teacher may illustrate this by proposing an increase in social studies time and a decrease in math time. The teacher might then ask the class to weigh in on the issue: Is everyone in favor? Why are some groups against this? Students are likely to have different points of view based on their ease with or interest in either subject. Often in civic matters, one must **compromise**, or meet those with a different point of view in the middle on an issue. This give-and-take is part of what makes democracy work.

In a representative democracy, such as that of the United States, power and authority in decision-making rest with elected officials who have been designated by the people. The process of electing officials and raising issues of public concern to these officials brings many different viewpoints, as illustrated by the example of students weighing in on the issue of more social studies and less math time. In this example, students approach the issue from an individual perspective: those who like social studies and dislike math would be in favor of more social studies time, while those who like math more may not be in favor. This perspective represents the individual needs of students; however, students must consider many perspectives on the issue. Would a decrease in math time leave students ill-prepared for state tests? Would students who need more math practice be at a disadvantage? These considerations might then lead to making a decision based on the overall needs of the group, which must be balanced with individual needs and preferences. This is a key part of the democratic process.

Students should understand their roles as members of many different communities. They must be involved in their local community to ensure their schools, hospitals, roads, and local services are operating smoothly and efficiently. They should also appreciate their role in the larger city, state, and nation regarding their future ability to vote, organize, and have their voices heard.

> **Did You Know?**
>
> Only around 55 percent of eligible Americans voted in the 2016 national election.

Students should also understand their role as global citizens who must protect the natural resources and biodiversity of the planet. The topic of global **citizenship,** or actions taken to promote social, political, or environmental issues on a global scale, is easily integrated with science topics such as recycling, conservation, and environmental advocacy. Environmental protection is necessary for keeping the plant and animal life on Earth diverse. It is also vital since all living things, their environment, and the economy are interdependent. A teacher might discuss this concept broadly with younger students by explaining that we must protect the earth in order to continue using its resources, such as food and water.

Older students might delve more deeply into this issue and examine the cause-and-effect relationship between lack of environmental resource protection and the local economy. For example, a community reliant on the shrimping industry might be severely impacted by pollution in the Gulf of Mexico. This action by humans on the environment impacts the shrimp in the Gulf, whose populations may die out or dwindle. This, in turn, impacts the local economy, as shrimping may no longer be possible. This can have all sorts of further consequences, as shrimpers may leave the community, forcing the businesses that served the shrimpers (e.g., grocery and clothing stores, restaurants) to also go out of business. In this way, the environment and the economy are interdependent, and an action on one will impact the other.

Practice Question

43. Ms. Sturgis happens upon two of her first-grade students in a heated argument about what game to play at recess. Which strategy might help her students learn to compromise?
   A. picking the game herself and telling the students which game to play
   B. designating one student to decide which game to play
   C. proposing that they join the kickball game already in progress
   D. suggesting that each game be played for five minutes

United States and Texas Government

The US system of government is a republican **democracy**. This is distinct from a **monarchy** (ruled by a king of queen) or a **totalitarian** government (ruled by a dictator). In a democracy, the will of the people is enacted in government. The origins of democracy lie in ancient Greece, where all male citizens made up the government assembly in a system known as **direct democracy**. The Roman civilization subsequently developed a **representative democracy**, where certain elected male citizens represented the will of all male citizens. The United States is a representative democracy.

Our nation can also be described as a **limited government** because even lawmakers must obey the law. In **unlimited governments,** supreme rulers can do whatever they wish and are not bound by law.

Understanding the basics of government will help children to grow up to be responsible citizens who select leaders fit for their office. The United States government is composed of three branches: the executive, legislative, and judicial. A system of **checks and balances** keeps each branch from having too much power.

The **executive branch** of government is made up of the **president**, **vice president**, and fifteen executive departments, including the Departments of Defense, Commerce, State, Justice, and Labor. The executive branch enforces the laws. The president and vice president are elected members of the executive branch, but officials in other executive branch departments and agencies are appointed.

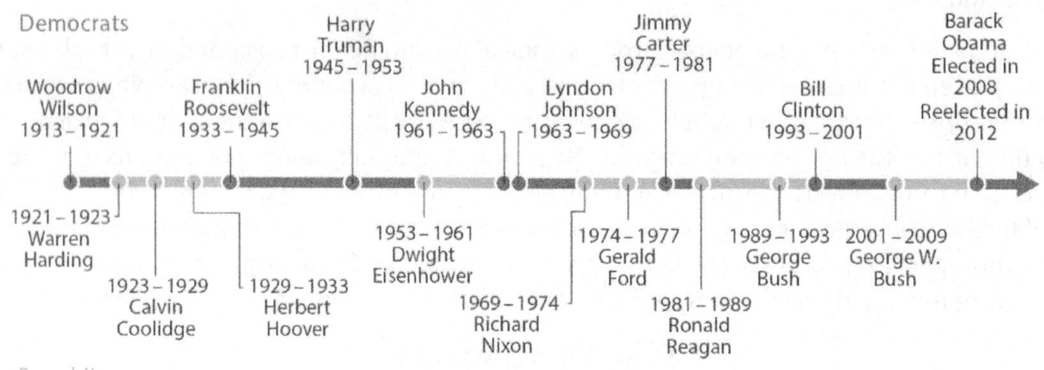

Figure 3.12. Presidential Timeline

> **Study Tips**
>
> The names of the different branches of government tell what they do. The executive branch is like the executive of a company—it ensures the "execution" of the company's objectives (like laws). The legislative branch "legislates," or deals in making laws. The judicial branch "judges," or interprets the laws.

The legislative branch includes both houses of **Congress**: the Senate and the House of Representatives. The legislative branch makes the laws. Members of both the House and the Senate are elected, with each state electing two senators per state, and the number of representatives totaling 435 but varying in number based on state population. California and Texas have the most representatives at fifty-three and thirty-six, respectively, while some less-populous states have only one representative.

The judicial branch comprises the federal court system, including the **Supreme Court**. The Supreme Court is made up of nine justices who are nominated by the president and approved by the Senate. The judicial branch interprets the meaning of the laws. The Supreme Court has decided many important cases, including those described in Table 3.3.

Table 3.3. Notable Supreme Court Cases and Decisions

Case	Year	Decision/Consequence
Marbury v. Madison	1803	established judicial review
McCulloch v. Maryland	1819	established that the federal government has certain implied powers
Plessy v. Ferguson	1896	established the doctrine of separate but equal
Brown v. Board of Education	1954	outlawed segregated schools
Engel v. Vitale	1962	prayer in public schools is violation of First Amendment
Miranda v. Arizona	1966	made it mandatory for police to inform suspects of rights (Miranda warning)
Roe v. Wade	1973	federal protection for abortion
Obergefell v. Hodges	2015	federal protection of same-sex marriage
Dobbs v. Jackson Women's Health Organization	2022	overturned *Roe v. Wade*

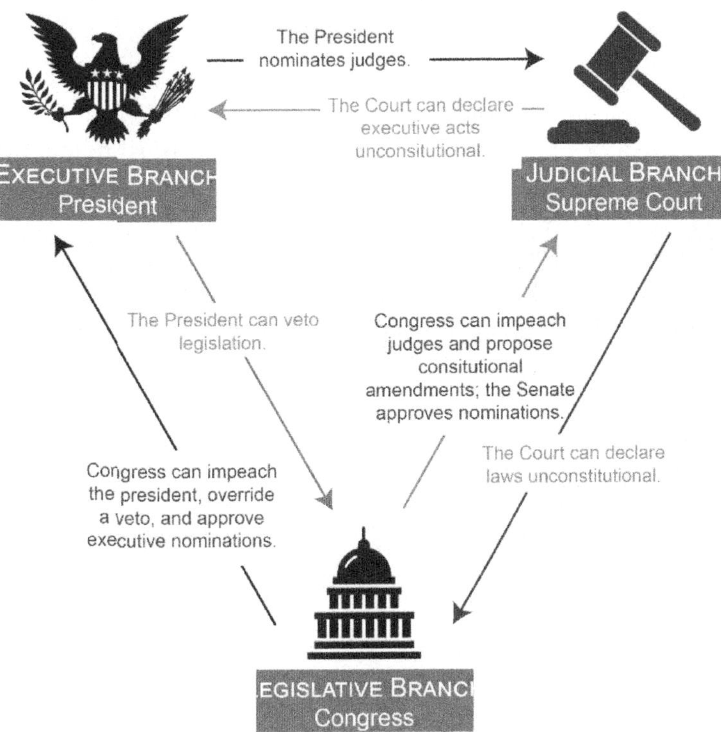
The President nominates judges.
The Court can declare executive acts unconsitutional.
EXECUTIVE BRANCH
President
JUDICIAL BRANCH
Supreme Court
The President can veto legislation.
Congress can impeach judges and propose consitutional amendments; the Senate approves nominations.
The Court can declare laws unconstitutional.
Congress can impeach the president, override a veto, and approve executive nominations.
LEGISLATIVE BRANCH
Congress

Figure 3.13. Checks and Balances

The federal government was formed by and operates based on the outline set out in the **Constitution**. (see the "Government of the Early Republic" section for more information on the Constitution). In its interpretation of the laws made by Congress, the Supreme Court frequently examines whether legislation is in line with this document. Amendments to the Constitution can be proposed by a two-thirds majority of both the House of Representatives and Senate or if two-thirds of the states propose an amendment. To take effect, three-fourths of state legislatures must ratify it or three-fourths of special state conventions must be called for this purpose.

Just as the Constitution outlines the way the federal government is organized, the Texas Constitution, adopted in 1876 and the second longest constitution of any state, explains how the state will operate. Like the US Constitution, it also includes a bill of rights. To amend the Texas Constitution, two-thirds of the Texas House and Senate must agree with the amendment. The proposed amendment is then brought before all eligible state voters in a general election.

Similarly, in Texas, the governor is the head of the executive branch. The Texas House and Senate are the legislative branch. The state has a court system, including a state supreme court.

While the basic governmental framework has been laid out in the American and Texas constitutions, the political actors are selected by citizens who **vote** in **elections**. Voting is an important American duty that contributes to the American identity. This identity might be reinforced through symbols like the bald eagle, the American flag, the Statue of Liberty, or Mount Rushmore. Holidays and celebrations such as Presidents' Day, Martin Luther King Day, Independence Day, and Juneteenth are also part of shared American identity.

Texans may also feel a sense of unity and identity. Symbols such as the Texas flag, the bluebonnet, or the longhorn may resonate with many Texans. Similarly, landmarks like the Alamo, Big Bend National Park, Palo Duro Canyon, or NASA's Johnson Space Center are also important markers of Texas identity and pride.

Practice Questions

44. Mr. Harrison wants to teach his third-grade class about how a written document, such as the Constitution, can outline the procedures an organization or country must follow. Which activity meets this goal?

A. having students research the history of the Constitution
B. directing students to draft a "classroom compact"
C. asking students to compare their rules at home with the school rules
D. organizing a school-wide recycling program

45) Which of the following is an appointed position?

A. US senator
B. US representative
C. vice president
D. secretary of state

Answer Key

1. B: All of these are examples of primary resources or those that come from firsthand sources.

2. C: In vertical alignment, the same general topics are presented with increasing complexity in each grade level.

3. D: The Karankawa tribe lived primarily in the Gulf Coast region of Texas.

4. D: Though Texas was not rich in gold and silver like Mexico, it was a frontier region which might be intruded upon if not settled.

5. A: The Law of 1830 closed further American immigration to Texas as part of an effort to increase the Mexican presence in the region.

6. B: Gonzalez is generally regarded as the first battle of the revolution and is where the phrase "Come and Take It" originates.

7. A: Many voters were only recent immigrants to Texas from the United States and were familiar with Houston's service there.

8. B: With so much territory in question, the issue of slavery remained, which led to the Compromise of 1850.

9. B: Sam Houston also a senator and representative in the Texas legislature, and a congressman and Governor of Tennessee.

10. A: The election of anti-slavery Republican Abraham Lincoln precipitated secession.

11. B, D: The Union blockade impacted Texas's cotton exportation and led to shortages and economic shifts. Some 60-70,000 Texans fought for the Confederacy.

12. A: Many Texas sharecroppers worked on the lands of those who had previously enslaved them; this reality led to a cycle of debt and dependency as formerly enslaved Texans had no way to own their land.

13. A: The Texas Populist movement lasted only a few years before becoming part of the Texas Democratic Party.

14. C: Some 200,000 American from the Great Plains moved to California during the Dust Bowl.

15. B: The *Sweatt v. Painter* case desegregated the University of Texas and set an important precedent for *Brown v. Board of Education*.

16. A, D: Ma Ferguson was the first female governor of Texas, and Ann Richards was the most recent; they are the only two women to ever serve in this office in Texas.

17. A: Houston is home to the Texas Medical Center, often regarded as the nation's premier location for medical research and treatment.

18. B, C: Native Americans were geographically displaced by colonists as well as killed by European-brought diseases to which they often had no immunity.

19. C: Colonists relied on Native American communities for crucial knowledge and supplies, and Native Americans wanted to form alliances they believed would be helpful. However, conflict over encroachment by colonists also occurred.

20. C: The colonial military did have strong leaders, and an intimate knowledge of the terrain, many having been born there.

21. D: This is the Third Amendment.

22. C: The Kansas-Nebraska Act allowed slavery north of the thirty-sixth parallel throughout the plains and the Western territories which the Missouri Compromise had previously forbidden.

23. C: The Confederacy had excellent military leaders, and much of the population strongly believed in the right of states to make decisions without federal interference.

24. D: The Emancipation Proclamation freed the slaves in the Confederacy.

25. A, B, D: All of these things occurred as part of Reconstruction. Though Americans of African descent could legally vote, Southern states worked vigorously to ensure that most could not vote in practice via restrictive laws, intimidation, and violence.

26. B: Nonviolence was a defining characteristic of the mainstream civil rights movement.

27. B: Japan's attack on Pearl Harbor occurred on December 7, 1941, and led the United States to join WWII.

28. A: Images of a New York apartment building and an igloo would be most useful for a teacher to show students in order to help them understand that housing is different in different environments.

29. C: Mr. Wyatt could use this activity as a springboard for a unit about Native Americans and various parts of this cultural heritage.

30. D: This question will help students see that they are dependent on others, since they cannot make their own shoes.

31. C: The Statue of Liberty is one of the most widely recognized American landmarks, and it would be appropriate for a first grader to recognize this symbol.

32. A: The compass rose indicates the cardinal directions.

33. D: Rivers flow into seas and oceans, but lakes do not.

34. B: Because the school is in the desert, some crops will survive and others will not (or all will die), prompting a discussion about how people living in the desert grow only certain crops or must import food.

35. A: Humans used unsustainable farming practices, which led to erosion.

36. B: This topic is pertinent to the role of trains in a subset of the American economy: cattle ranching.

37. C: Having family already living in Texas would be a factor pulling a person toward immigration to Texas.

38. B: The microchip cost will decrease because as supply increases, typically there is decrease in price.

39. B, D: The federal government sets the minimum wage and determines tariffs or taxes on imports.

40. A: The gross domestic product (GDP) refers to the total value of goods and services produced in a nation during a set time. It is usually calculated annually.

41. C: Oil is the largest industry in Texas; if consumers were to stop buying gas-powered vehicles, it would have a tremendous impact on the state's economy.

42. C: Mr. Haskell is likening his classroom rules to laws that apply to everyone, even the teacher.

43. D: This suggestion is a compromise in which both students give and take something.

44. B: This activity will help his students make the connection between the Constitution that outlines the rules our government must follow and a "classroom compact" that will outline the rules within which the classroom must operate.

45. D: The secretary of state is appointed by the president.

4 Science

Science Instruction and Assessment

Scientific Inquiry

Students should see science as interrelated to various parts of life. What scientists study, and the decisions they make, are often based on societal needs. For example, pharmacological researchers typically focus on treatments for conditions that affect many people seriously. They may also consider economic needs, such as whether there will be a market for a drug.

Most scientific study, both by professionals and students, is based on the process of investigation or inquiry. Inquiry-based science is guided by the scientific method, which provides a framework for observing, measuring, and drawing conclusions about the world.

The first step in the scientific method is **observation, often of a problem or an unknown or unexplained situation**. From observations, scientists develop questions and research the currently available information about a particular topic. This research helps them formulate a reasonable and testable explanation for their observations, a statement known as a **hypothesis**. Scientists then design and conduct an **experiment** in which they collect data that will demonstrate whether their hypothesis is false or not. It is important to note that a hypothesis can never be proven true—it can be confirmed as false, or enough data can be collected to *infer* that it is true. In order for data to support a hypothesis, it must be consistent and reproducible.

> **Helpful Hint**
>
> The phrase Queen Rachel Hopes Every Coward Gains Courage can help students remember the scientific method: question, research, hypothesis, experiment, collect data, graph/analyze data, conclusion.

While scientific inquiry varies based on the research questions at hand, some basic frameworks guide scientific thinking.

One foundation of scientific thinking is the notion of **systems**, defined as two or more parts that make a whole. There are many interconnected systems in our world such as eco*systems*, the solar *system*, and even the human digestive *system*. Within systems are **subsystems**, or self-contained systems within the broader system. For example, if we consider Earth a system, it can be divided into four main subsystems:

- lithosphere (land)
- atmosphere (air)
- hydrosphere (water)
- biosphere (life)

Scientists may focus their inquiries on one or more of these subsystems. For example, climate scientists might study the impacts of changes in atmosphere on the hydrosphere and biosphere.

Table 4.1. Characteristics of a System	
Characteristic	**Example (Respiratory System)**
All systems have a structure.	The respiratory system is highly organized.
All systems perform an action.	The respiratory system allows animals to breathe.
All systems have interacting parts.	The respiratory system is made up of many interacting parts, including the lungs, blood vessels, and bronchial tubes.
All systems have boundaries.	We can separate structures that are part of the respiratory system from those that are not.
Systems may receive input and produce output.	The respiratory system brings oxygen into the body and gets rid of carbon dioxide.
The processes in a system may be controlled by feedback.	The action of breathing is controlled in part by how much oxygen and carbon dioxide are in the body.

Systems go through cycles of stability (no observable change), cycles of change (predictable patterns, such as day and night resulting from Earth's rotation), and less predictable patterns (e.g., ecosystem destruction after a tornado or earthquake). Stable systems are often still changing but at **dynamic equilibrium**, where physical movements or chemical reactions balance each other out. For example, a community that experiences out-migration of seventy people but in-migration of seventy people is stable due to dynamic equilibrium.

Within any system or subsystem are smaller components, such as animals, cells, or atoms. These components are guided by the concept of form and function. **Form** refers to the shape or structure of a type of matter or an entire organism and how this relates to its action, behavior, or **function**. For example, a fish with sharp teeth has a body part or form related to the function of chewing its prey.

Another basic scientific principle is the **movement of energy and matter** throughout systems. Energy and matter may move through space or time, but they are not destroyed. For example, energy moves through the food chain from producers to consumers to predators. Though it changes form and even involves the death of certain organisms, it is not destroyed—only transferred.

Scientific understanding is largely linear, though certainly there have been instances where previously-held beliefs have been disproven. Major historical developments in science include the following:

- 1543 the Copernican system
- 1664 Isaac Newton and gravity
- 1686 Isaac Newton and the three laws of motion
- 1821 Michael Faraday and electricity
- 1839 Theodor Schwann and cell theory
- 1859 Charles Darwin and evolution
- 1860s Louis Pasteur and germ theory
- 1905 Albert Einstein's theory of relativity
- 1915 Alfred Wegener and continental drift/plate tectonics
- 1927 Georges Lemaître and the big bang theory

- 1928 Alexander Fleming and penicillin
- 1953 James Watson and Francis Crick and DNA

When scientists have repeatedly tested a hypothesis, and that hypothesis has become widely accepted, it becomes known as a **theory**. Theories provide a widely accepted explanation for a natural phenomenon. The theory of evolution, for example, states that natural selection is the mechanism that led to the current diversity of species found on Earth. A scientific **law** is a description of a natural phenomenon. However, unlike a theory, it does not explain how something happens. For example, Newton's law of universal gravitation states that the gravitational force between two objects depends on their distance and mass.

Science, while grounded in observation and data, is not perfect, and scientific knowledge is always growing and changing. Scientists must be able to react to new observations and adjust their hypotheses as needed to address new evidence. By constantly observing, asking questions, and rigorously testing hypotheses, scientists are able to slowly build on the collective pool of scientific knowledge.

Practice Question

1. Evolution is an example of which of the following?
   A. theory
   B. law
   C. hypothesis
   D. fact

Experimental Design

Scientists use a rigorous set of rules to design experiments. The protocols of **experimental design** are meant to ensure that scientists are actually testing what they set out to test. A well-designed experiment will measure the impact of a single factor on a system, thus allowing the experimenter to draw conclusions about that factor.

Helpful Hint

DRY MIX may help students understand how the dependent and independent variables are graphed. DRY stands for dependent or responding variable on the y-axis. MIX stands for the manipulated or independent variable on the x-axis.

Every experiment includes variables, which are the factors or treatments that may affect the outcome of the experiment. **Independent variables** are controlled by the experimenter. They are usually the factors that the experimenter has hypothesized will have an effect on the system. Often, a design will include a treatment group and a **control group,** which does not receive the treatment. The **dependent variables** are factors that are influenced by the independent variable.

For example, in an experiment investigating which type of fertilizer has the greatest effect on plant growth, the independent variable is the type of fertilizer used. The scientist is controlling, or manipulating, the type of fertilizer. The dependent variable is plant growth because the amount of plant growth depends on the type of fertilizer. The type of plant, the amount of water, and the amount of sunlight the plants receive are controls because those variables of the experiment are kept the same for each plant.

Scientists sometimes use **models** in their research. These models are a simplified representation of a system. For example, a mathematical equation that describes fluctuations in a population might be used to test how a certain variable is likely to affect that population. Or scientists might use a greenhouse to model a particular ecosystem so they can more closely control the variables in the environment.

When designing an experiment, scientists must identify possible sources of **experimental error**. These can be **confounding variables**, which are factors that act much like the independent variable and thus can make it appear that the independent variable has a greater effect than it actually does. The design may also include unknown variables that are not controlled by the scientists. Finally, scientists must be aware of human error, particularly in collecting data and making observations, and of possible equipment errors.

In order to bolster accuracy, proper use of **scientific tools** is paramount. Many of these tools provide scientists with numerical data, but this data must be gathered and read accurately. For example, thermometers that are not properly calibrated will not record accurate temperatures. Similarly, inaccurate scales will not accurately measure weight.

While careful measurement of quantitative data is important, extraneous or confounding variables and human error also contribute to the overall **reliability** of results. Reliability refers to how close the results or measurements are to known values. So, if an experiment seeks to determine at what temperature water freezes into ice and determines the temperature is 40 degrees Celsius, the experiment would lack accuracy or reliability. Similar to reliability is **replicability**, which refers to the ability of other researchers to get similar results under the same conditions. Quality scientific research is both reliable and replicable. One way to increase reliability and replicability is to repeat experiments multiple times under various conditions, especially if the results are unexpected.

During an experiment, scientists collect data, which must then be analyzed. As data is analyzed, scientists ask the following types of questions:

- Do the results seem logical? For example, if the experiment studies a new type of fertilizer and all the plants grow to double their size in only a week, scientists might want to recheck measurements as the results seem outside of common logic.
- Do the results match or refute predictions? It is not unusual for the hypothesis to be incorrect or for no change at all to have been observed during an experiment.
- Is there verifiable evidence? Scientists do not use phrases such as, "It appears like..." or "The substance kind of changed...." Instead, scientists work with empirical data.

During and after the data analysis process, scientists must protect the data by safe storage. This includes, but is not limited to, removing all personal identifiers from specimens or samples; keeping data in a secure, locked location; and keeping digital data files protected from unauthorized users.

After the data is analyzed, it must be presented appropriately. This can mean running a statistical analysis on the data (for example, finding the mean) or putting the data in graph form. An analysis allows scientists to see trends in the data and determine if those trends are statistically significant. From the data and its analysis, scientists can draw a **conclusion** about the experiment.

Scientists must describe their data in a way that others can understand but must also be cognizant of various factors that may impact results and color the data. **Scale** is one important factor to consider. For example, if the researcher uses only two different fertilizers in the plant experiment, the results may not be **generalizable**, or applicable to a broader population (such as all fertilizers). Similarly, the **proportion**, or ratio, of fertilizer to water may change results.

Further, scientists cannot always establish a **cause-and-effect** relationship as the result of a study or experiment. Often, results are reported as **correlations** versus causations, meaning that if there is a strong positive correlation between two variables (for example, one type of fertilizer is correlated with more plant growth), then *maybe* the variable (fertilizer type) was the cause—or maybe not. Other factors (e.g., confounding variables, such as soil type and individual plant health) may be responsible for the difference in plant growth. Sometimes, correlations are most appropriate when the relationship between variables is unclear. For example, though scientists know that low vitamin D levels are linked with depression, it is not known if less vitamin D causes depression or if depression decreases vitamin D levels.

Check Your Understanding

How could the differences between causation and correlation be demonstrated to young students?

Scientists often present research results using charts and graphs. Like other phases of the process of scientific inquiry, care should be taken in how data is represented in charts and graphs. The scale of the axes, the type of graphic chosen, and even the units used can all have a tremendous impact on data presentation and can make data displays effective or misleading.

Results of professional scientific research are often published to contribute to the broader base of human knowledge. Typically, such publications are most reputable when they are **peer reviewed**. Peer review involves others in the field scrutinizing the study for quality. Top peer-reviewed scientific journals include *The New England Journal of Medicine* and *Nature*.

Practice Question

2. Which of the following is the variable in a scientific investigation that is manipulated by the researcher in order to test the hypothesis?
   A. control
   B. experimental
   C. dependent
   D. hypothetical

Equipment and Safety Procedures

When choosing and setting up a lab, teachers need to remember that they are responsible for any accidents or hazardous incidents that occur under their supervision. For most classrooms, **standard laboratory equipment** includes flat top tables with stools so students can view experiments from several angles. Safety gear, microscopes, beakers, **measurement tools**, test tubes, eyedroppers, weights, magnets, and timers should be some of the available equipment. Measurement tools for length include metric rulers and tape measures. Beakers and graduated cylinders are used to measure volume. Balance scales measure mass.

Standard safety equipment like goggles, aprons, protective gloves, and a fire extinguisher must be available. In addition to using standard safety equipment, students should be instructed on appropriate **apparel**. For example, long hair should be tied back and loose clothing and jewelry should be secured. Closed-toe shoes should be worn.

If students are working with chemicals, they should be instructed in the proper handling, use, and disposal of these substances. If students are working with specimens, they should also be instructed in how to handle these specimens appropriately. This is particularly important when working with animal specimens. As living things, such specimens should not be handled in a disrespectful or joking manner.

All scientists, even amateur student scientists, should follow basic **ethical guidelines**. These principles are as follows:

- accountability
- confidentiality
- social responsibility
- animal care

- human subject protection
- transparency
- integrity
- objectivity
- honesty

Student **behavior** and ethical guidelines are important, but they take on even more significance when students are working in potentially dangerous situations. Adults should model safety practices, such as wearing goggles. Parents and students should be required to sign a document that outlines safety procedures. Students should be warned about potential dangers as they arise in each experiment. Students must be diligently supervised, and those who do not comply with safety or ethical standards should be removed from the lab.

Emergency procedures should include proactively monitoring students and equipment and wearing safety gear. Plans for emergency first aid for electric shock, poisoning, burns, fire, evacuations, spills, and animal bites should be established.

Practice Question

3. Which tool measures the volume of an object?
   A. thermometer
   B. graduated cylinder
   C. balance
   D. barometer

Assessment in Science

The TEKS require students to participate in many hands-on science activities. These activities should not only be lab-based activities but should also include activities to encourage students' higher-level thinking skills. Students should be asked to analyze, synthesize, evaluate, and problem-solve. Such higher-order thinking should involve students building upon prior knowledge. For example, if students learn about the hydrosphere, they might then gather samples of water from various sources to examine under a microscope to differentiate between different water sources.

Assessment in science will involve various strategies, both formal and informal (see "English Language Arts" chapter for more information on assessment types). Informal assessments might include the following:

- observation
- class discussions
- end-of-class exit tickets
- use of clickers or real-time polls or quizzes with apps like Kahoot!
- informal lab journals that describe challenges or observations

More formal assessments might include the following:

- written or digital lab reports
- posters or multimedia presentations
- portfolios

- student profiles or mastery checklists (for younger students)
- written assessments, both constructed-response and selected-response

Both informal and formal assessments and formative and summative assessments should be used to assess individual student strengths and needs and to modify instruction. Assessment data might reveal knowledge or skill gaps that need remediation or reteaching. It might also reveal students who could benefit from extension or enrichment activities.

Practice Question

4. After a lab where student groups use simple machines, a teacher wants to assess student understanding to determine how effective the lab was in helping students see the advantages of these devices. Which assessment is most appropriate?
   A. having students construct their own simple machine
   B. asking students to list the main types of simple machines
   C. having students list two tasks that could be done with each type of simple machine
   D. asking students to turn to a peer and describe challenges they encountered when using the simple machines in the lab

Forces and Motion

Motion refers to change in an object's position as measured by time and distance.

Speed is a measure that describes how quickly something moves using the following equation:

speed = distance/time

Velocity describes both the speed and direction of a moving object.

An object that travels a certain distance and then returns to its starting point has a velocity of zero because its final position did not change. Its speed, however, can be found by dividing the total distance it traveled by the time it took to make the trip.

Acceleration describes how quickly an object changes velocity. It is found using the following equation:

acceleration = change in velocity/time

One easy way to show an object's motion is via a graph. Two helpful types of graphs are position versus time graphs and velocity versus time graphs. In a **position versus time graph,** the distance is plotted on the *y*-axis, and the time is plotted on the *x*-axis. A horizontal line indicates that the object is at rest; the steeper the slope of the line, the faster the object is moving.

In a **velocity versus time graph,** the velocity is plotted on the *y*-axis, and the time is plotted on the *x*-axis. In this graph, a horizontal line means that the object is at a constant speed; a line sloping downward means that the object is slowing; and the steeper the slope of the line, the greater the acceleration.

Helpful Hint

Nature is sometimes said to have four fundamental forces:

1. gravitational force (attraction between objects with mass)

2. electromagnetic force (force acting on things with electric charges)

3. strong nuclear force (affects subatomic particle behavior)

4. weak nuclear force (affects subatomic particle behavior)

A push or pull on an object is called a **force**. Forces can arise from a number of different sources. Forces may be balanced or unbalanced. **Balanced forces** are equal in size but opposite in direction; the result is that the object does not move. For example, in a game of tug-of-war, when the force on the rope from both sides is equal, the rope will not move. In **unbalanced forces**, force in one direction exceeds force in another direction; this results in the object changing direction or speed. If one side in tug-of-war pulls harder, then there is an unbalanced force, and the rope will move.

The greater the net force on an object, the greater the acceleration; however, the object's mass is a key component: the larger the object, the more force it will require. This is why, for example, a stroller or shopping cart is easier to move than a parked car or tractor.

Elementary instruction starts the study of forces with gravity, which is the attraction of one mass to another mass. For example, the earth's gravitational field pulls objects toward it, and the sun's gravitational field keeps planets in motion around it. Electrically charged objects create a field that cause other charged objects in that field to move. Other forces include **tension**, which is found in ropes pulling or holding up an object; **friction**, which is created by two objects moving against each other; and the **normal force**, which occurs when an object is resting on another object. Friction sometimes serves to balance another force, preventing an object from moving.

An object that is at rest or moving with a constant speed has a net force of zero, meaning all the forces acting on it cancel each other out. Such an object is said to be at **equilibrium**. Isaac Newton proposed three **laws of motion** that govern forces:

- **Newton's first law**: An object at rest stays at rest and an object in motion stays in motion unless acted on by a force.
- **Newton's second law**: Force is equal to the mass of an object multiplied by its acceleration ($F = ma$).
- **Newton's third law**: For every action there is an equal and opposite reaction.

Helpful Hint

The normal force balances out gravity in resting objects. When a book rests on a table, gravity pulls down on it and the normal force pushes up, canceling each other out and holding the book still.

The laws of motion have made it possible to build **simple machines**, which take advantage of those laws to make work easier to perform. Simple machines include the inclined plane, wheel and axle, pulley, screw, wedge, and lever.

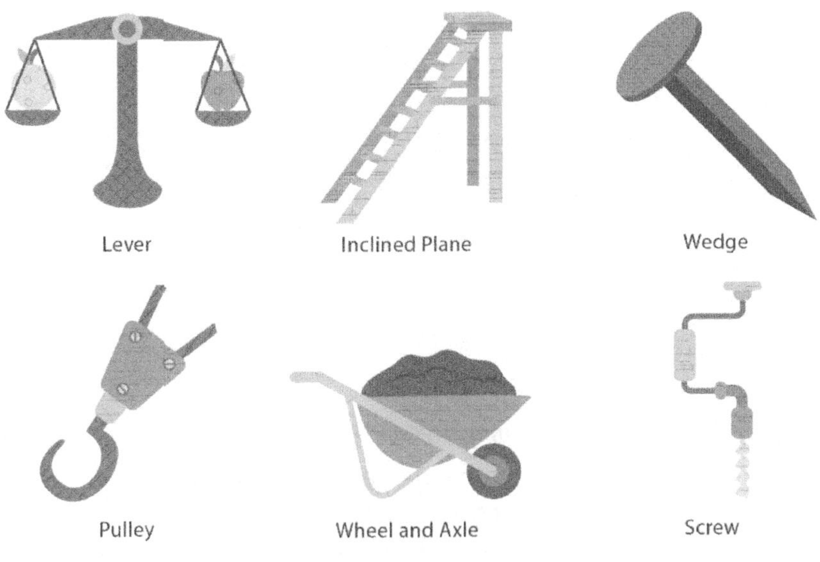

Figure 4.1. Simple Machines

Practice Question

5. The rate at which velocity changes is
   A. power.
   B. force.
   C. displacement.
   D. acceleration.

Matter

Matter takes up space and has weight. The basic unit of all **matter** is the **atom**. Atoms are composed of three subatomic particles: protons, electrons, and neutrons. **Protons** have a positive charge and are found in the nucleus, or center, of the atom. **Neutrons**, which have no charge, are also located in the nucleus. Negatively charged **electrons** orbit the nucleus. If an atom has the same number of protons and electrons, it will have no net charge. Charged atoms are called ions. Atoms that have more protons than electrons are positively charged and are called cations. Negatively charged atoms have more electrons than protons and are called anions.

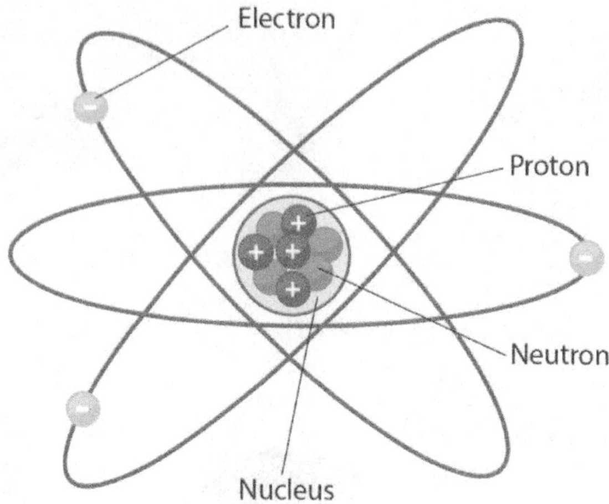

Figure 4.2. Atomic Structure

> **Helpful Hint**
>
> The parts of an atom can be remembered using PEN: protons, electrons, neutrons.

The mass of an atom is determined by adding the number of protons, neutrons, and electrons. However, electrons have very little mass, so the **atomic mass** is determined by adding just the mass of protons and neutrons.

Elements, such as hydrogen and oxygen, are substances in their simplest form that retain their unique characteristics. Each element has a distinct **atomic number** based on the number of protons in the nucleus. For example, hydrogen has one proton, and oxygen has six. An element is defined by the number of protons it has, but variations of an element that have different numbers of neutrons are called **isotopes**. Some isotopes are unstable and emit radiation as they decay. These are called radioactive isotopes or radioisotopes. Others do not decay over time and are called stable isotopes. A table of chemical elements arranged by atomic number is called **the periodic table**.

1	2	3	4	5	6	7	8	9	10	11	12	13	14	15	16	17	18
1 **H** Hydrogen 1.008																	2 **He** Helium 4.0026
3 **Li** Lithium 6.941	4 **Be** Beryllium 9.0122											5 **B** Boron 10.81	6 **C** Carbon 12.011	7 **N** Nitrogen 14.007	8 **O** Oxygen 15.999	9 **F** Fluorine 18.998	10 **Ne** Neon 20.180
11 **Na** Sodium 22.990	12 **Mg** Magnesium 24.305											13 **Al** Aluminum 26.982	14 **Si** Silicon 28.085	15 **P** Phosphorus 30.974	16 **S** Sulfur 32.06	17 **Cl** Chlorine 35.45	18 **Ar** Argon 39.948
19 **K** Potassium 39.098	20 **Ca** Calcium 40.078	21 **Sc** Scandium 44.956	22 **Ti** Titanium 47.867	23 **V** Vanadium 50.942	24 **Cr** Chromium 51.996	25 **Mn** Maganese 54.938	26 **Fe** Iron 55.845	27 **Co** Cobalt 58.933	28 **Ni** Nickel 58.963	29 **Cu** Copper 63.546	30 **Zn** Zinc 65.38	31 **Ga** Gallium 69.723	32 **Ge** Germanium 72.64	33 **As** Arsenic 74.922	34 **Se** Selenium 78.971	35 **Br** Bromine 79.904	36 **Kr** Krypton 83.798
37 **Rb** Rubidium 85.468	38 **Sr** Strontium 87.62	39 **Y** Yttrium 88.906	40 **Zr** Zirconium 91.224	41 **Nb** Niobium 92.906	42 **Mo** Molybdenum 254	43 **Tc** Technetium 98	44 **Ru** Ruthenium 101.07	45 **Rh** Rhodium 102.91	46 **Pd** Palladium 106.42	47 **Ag** Silver 107.87	48 **Cd** Cadmium 112.41	49 **In** Indium 114.82	50 **Sn** Tin 118.71	51 **Sb** Antimony 121.76	52 **Te** Tellurium 127.60	53 **I** Iodine 126.90	54 **Xe** Xenon 121.29
55 **Cs** Caesium 132.91	56 **Ba** Barium 137.33	57-71	72 **Hf** Hafnium 178.49	73 **Ta** Tantalum 183.84	74 **W** Tungsten 183.84	75 **Re** Rhenium 186.21	76 **Os** Osmium 190.23	77 **Ir** Iridium 192.22	78 **Pt** Platinum 195.08	79 **Au** Gold 196.97	80 **Hg** Mercury 200.59	81 **Tl** Thallium 204.38	82 **Pb** Lead 207.2	83 **Bi** Bismuth 208.98	84 **Po** Polonium 209	85 **At** Astatine 210	86 **Rn** Radon 222
87 **Fr** Francium 223.020	88 **Ra** Radium 226	89-103	104 **Rf** Rutherfordium 267	105 **Db** Dubnium 268	106 **Sg** Seaborgium 271	107 **Bh** Bohrium 272	108 **Hs** Hassium 277	109 **Mt** Meitnerium 276	110 **Ds** Darmstadtium 281	111 **Rg** Roentgenium 280	112 **Cn** Copernicium 285	113 **Uut** Ununtrium Unknown	114 **Fl** Flerovium 254	115 **Uup** Ununpentium Unknown	116 **Lv** Livermorium 291	117 **Uus** Ununseptium Unknown	118 **Uuo** Ununoctium Unknown

Atomic Number
Symbol
Name
Atomic Mass

Lanthanide	57 **La** Lanthanium 138.905	58 **Ce** Cerium 140.12	59 **Pr** Praseodymium 140.91	60 **Nd** Neodymium 144.24	61 **Pm** Promethium 144.913	62 **Sm** Samarium 150.36	63 **Eu** Europium 151.96	64 **Gd** Gadolinium 157.25	65 **Tb** Terbium 158.93	66 **Dy** Dysprosium 152.50	67 **Ho** Holmium 154.930	68 **Er** Erbium 167.259	69 **Tm** Thulium 168.934	70 **Yb** Ytterbium 173.065	71 **Lu** Lutetium 174.967
Actinide	89 **Ac** Actinium 227.028	90 **Th** Thorium 232.038	91 **Pa** Protactinuim 231.036	92 **U** Uranium 238.029	93 **Np** Neptunium 237.048	94 **Pu** Plutonium 244.064	95 **Am** Americium 243.061	96 **Cm** Curium 247.070	97 **Bk** Berkelium 247.070	98 **Cf** Californium 251.080	99 **Es** Einsteinium 254	100 **Fm** Fermium 257.095	101 **Md** Mendelevium 258.1	102 **No** Nobelium 259.101	103 **Lr** Lawrencium 262

Alkali Metal | Alkaline Earth Metals | Transition Metal | Basic Metal | Metalloid | Nonmetal | Halogen | Noble Gas | Lanthanide | Actinide

Figure 1.6. The Periodic Table of Elements

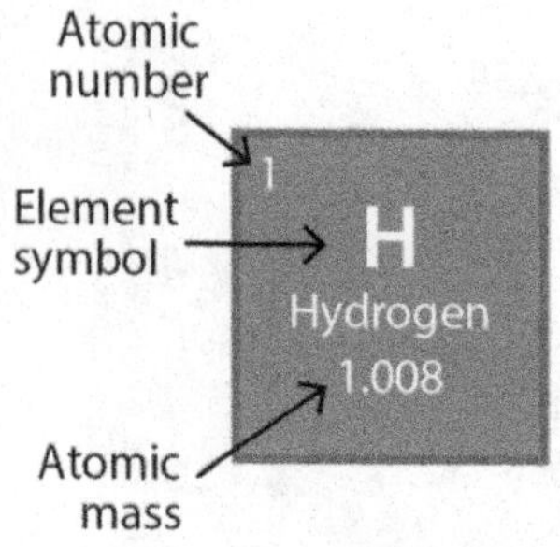

Figure 4.4. Reading the Periodic Table

When two or more atoms join together they form a **molecule**. For example, O_3 (ozone) contains three oxygen atoms bound together, and H_2O (water) contains two hydrogen atoms and one oxygen. Water is a **compound** because it is made by combining two or more different elements. Atoms can be joined together by different types of bonds by sharing or exchanging valence electrons, which are electrons that can participate in chemical reactions with other elements.

- In a **covalent bond,** the atoms share one or more valence electrons.
- In an **ionic bond,** one or more electrons are transferred from one element to another to create two ions with opposite charges that are attracted to each other and bind together.

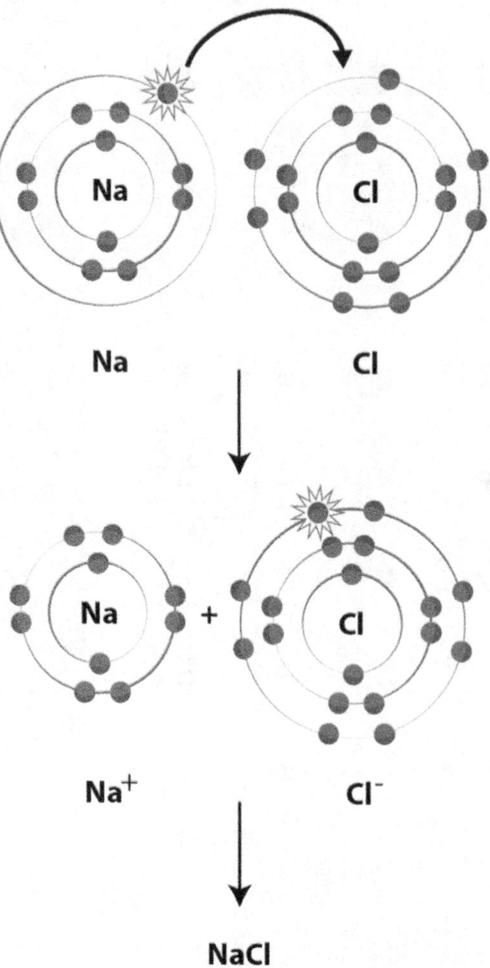

Figure 4.5. Ionic Bond in Table Salt

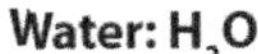

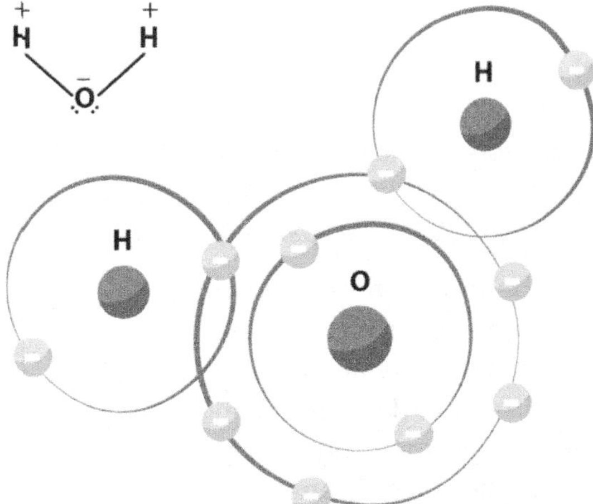

Figure 4.6. Covalent Bond in Water

All matter exists in one of four **states**: solid, liquid, gas, or plasma. **Solid** matter has densely packed molecules and does not change volume or shape. **Liquids** have more loosely packed molecules and can change shape but not volume. **Gas** molecules are widely dispersed and can change both shape and volume. **Plasma** is similar to gas but contains freely moving charged particles (although its overall charge is neutral).

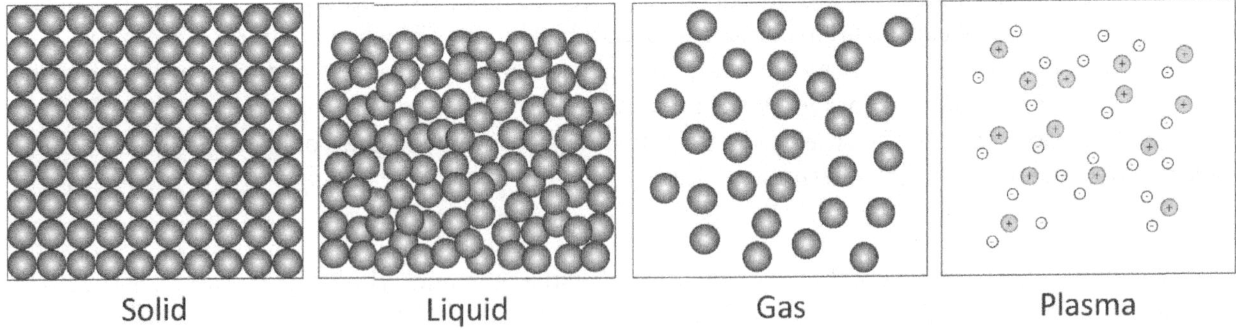

Figure 4.7. States of Matter

Changes in temperature and pressure can cause matter to change states. Generally, adding energy (in the form of heat) changes a substance to a higher-energy state (e.g., solid to liquid). Transitions from a high- to lower-energy state (e.g., liquid to solid) release energy. Each of these changes has a specific name:

- solid to liquid: melting (energy added)
- liquid to solid: freezing (energy removed)
- liquid to gas: evaporation (energy added)
- gas to liquid: condensation (energy removed)
- solid to gas: sublimation (energy added)
- gas to solid: deposition (energy removed)

When matter changes states, energy is added or removed as noted above.

Matter changing state is an example of a **physical change,** which is a change that does not alter the chemical composition of a substance. The state of matter changes, but the underlying chemical nature of the substance itself does not change. Other examples of physical changes include cutting, heating, or changing the shape of a substance.

When substances are combined without a chemical reaction to bond them, the resulting substance is called a **mixture**. In a mixture, the components can be unevenly distributed, such as in trail mix or soil. Alternatively, the components can be uniformly distributed, as in salt water. When the distribution is uniform, the mixture is called a **solution**. The substance being dissolved is the **solute,** and the substance it is being dissolved in is the **solvent**. Physical changes can be used to separate mixtures. For example, heating salt water until the water evaporates will separate a salt water solution, leaving the salt behind.

In contrast to a physical change, a **chemical change** occurs when bonds between atoms are made or broken, resulting in a new substance or substances. Chemical changes are also called **chemical reactions**. Chemical reactions are either **exothermic**, meaning that energy (heat) is released, or **endothermic**, meaning that energy (heat) is required for the reaction to take place. Photosynthesis is an endothermic reaction that converts electromagnetic energy from the sun into chemical energy. Cellular respiration is an exothermic reaction where oxygen and glucose are changed into carbon dioxide and water.

Helpful Hint

In both physical and chemical changes, matter is always conserved, meaning it can never be created or destroyed.

Chemical reactions are represented by written mathematical equations. The **reactants,** the substances that are changing in the chemical reaction, are represented on the left side of the equation. The **products,** the new substances formed during the chemical reaction, are represented on the right side of the equation. The law of conservation of mass says that the amount of each element cannot change during a chemical reaction, so the same amount of each element must be represented on each side of the equation (i.e., the reactants and products must have the same amount of each element). This is called a **balanced equation**. For example, the production of water from two molecules of hydrogen gas and one molecule of oxygen gas can be written as:

$$2H_2 + O_2 \rightarrow 2H_2O$$

The substances on the left side of the equations are called the reactants. The + sign means "reacts with," and the arrow means "produces." The substances on the right side of the equations are called the products. The number in front of the substances tells how many molecules of the substance are used, although the number is only written if it is more than one.

Common reactions include:

- **reduction/oxidation (redox)**: a chemical change in which a substance loses electrons, as when iron rusts when exposed to oxygen, forming iron oxide
- **combustion**: a chemical reaction that produces heat, carbon dioxide, and water, usually by burning a fuel
- **synthesis**: a chemical reaction in which two substances combine to form a single substance
- **decomposition**: a chemical reaction in which a single substance is broken down into two or more substances. Digestion of food is an example of a decomposition reaction.
- **neutralization**: a chemical reaction that occurs when an acid and a base react to produce a salt and water

Matter is classified by its **properties**, or characteristics. Matter has physical and chemical properties. **Physical properties** of matter refer to observed or measured characteristics that do not change the matter's identity. These include boiling and melting points, density, conductivity, solubility, malleability, color, and hardness. **Chemical properties** refer to the ability of matter to chemically react or change. Chemical properties produce something new after the change or reaction. For example, a piece of paper that burns is turned to ash.

Important physical properties covered as part of the elementary education curriculum include mass, weight, density, solubility, conductivity, and pH. **Mass** refers to the amount of matter in an object. Although the terms are often used interchangeably, mass is distinct from **weight,** which is the force of the gravitational pull on an object. Unlike weight, mass stays the same no matter where an object is located. When two objects of the same mass are on Earth and on the moon, the object on the moon will weigh less because the force of gravity on the moon is less than it is on Earth.

> **Helpful Hint**
>
> Like matter, energy is always conserved. It can be changed from one form to another, but never created or destroyed.

Density is the mass of the object divided by its volume, or the amount of space the object occupies. A denser object contains the same amount of mass in a smaller space than a less dense object. This is why a dense object, such as a bowling ball, feels heavier than a less dense object, like a soccer ball. The density of an object determines whether it will sink or float in a fluid. For example, the bowling ball will sink because it is denser than water, while the soccer ball will float.

Solubility refers to the amount of a solute that will dissolve in a solvent. **Conductivity** describes how well a material conducts heat or electricity. Silver, copper, aluminum, and iron are good conductors, while rubber, glass, and wood are poor conductors. Poor conductors are also called **insulators**.

Finally, the **pH scale** is used to describe the acidity of a substance. **Acids** are compounds that contribute a hydrogen ion (H+) when in solution, and **bases** are compounds that contribute a hydroxide ion (OH−) in solution. The pH scale goes from 1 to 14, with 7 considered neutral. Acids (such as lemon juice) have a pH lower than 7; bases (such as soap) have a pH greater than 7. Water is neutral with a pH of 7.

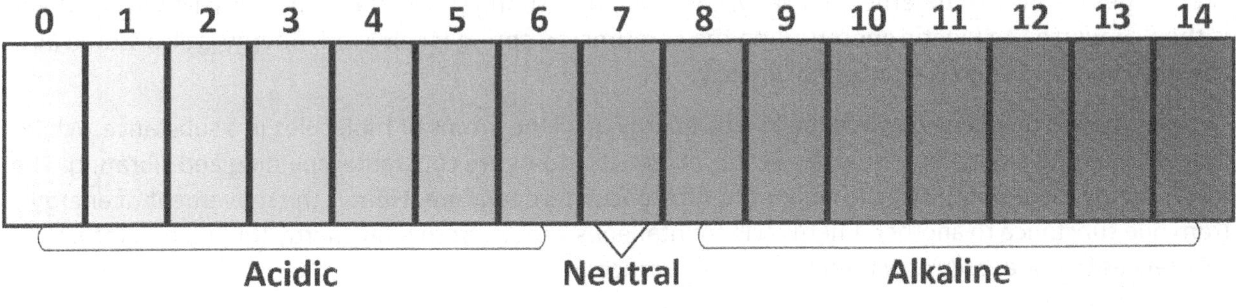

Figure 4.8. The pH Scale

Practice Questions

6. Which type of chemical reaction takes place when kerosene reacts with oxygen to light a lamp?
   A. oxidation
   B. neutralization
   C. combustion
   D. convection

7). The state of matter at which particles are most loosely packed is

A. liquid.
B. gas.
C. solid.
D. plasma.

Energy and Interactions

Energy Basics

Energy is the capacity of an object to do work, or, in other words, to cause some sort of movement or change. There are two kinds of energy: kinetic and potential. Objects in motion have **kinetic energy,** and objects that have the potential to be in motion due to their position have **potential energy**. Potential energy is defined in relation to a specific point. For example, a book held ten feet off the ground has more potential energy than a book held five feet off the ground, because it has the potential to fall farther (i.e., to do more work).

Kinetic energy can be turned into potential energy and vice versa. In the example above, dropping one of the books turns its potential energy into kinetic energy. Conversely, picking up a book and placing it on a table turns kinetic energy into potential energy. In another example, a pendulum—an object with mass hanging from a fixed point—is able to swing indefinitely after an initial input of **mechanical energy** to start the motion by repeatedly converting potential energy to kinetic energy and back again.

There are several types of potential energy. The energy stored in a book placed on a table is **gravitational potential energy**; it is derived from the pull of the earth's gravity on the book. **Electric potential energy** is derived from the interaction between positive and negative charges. Because opposite charges attract each other, and like charges repel, energy can be stored when opposite charges are moved apart or when like charges are pushed together. Similarly, compressing a spring stores **elastic potential energy, which is then converted to kinetic energy when the compressed spring is released.** Energy is also stored in chemical bonds as **chemical potential energy**.

Temperature is the name given to the kinetic energy of all the atoms or molecules in a substance. While it might look like a substance is perfectly still, in fact, its atoms are constantly spinning and vibrating. The more energy the atoms have, the higher the substance's temperature. **Heat** is the movement of energy from one substance to another. Energy will spontaneously move from high energy (high temperature) substances to low energy (low temperature) substances.

This energy can be transferred by radiation, conduction, or convection. **Radiation** does not need a medium; the sun radiates energy to Earth through the vacuum of space. **Conduction** occurs when two substances are in contact with each other. When a pan is placed on a hot stove, the heat energy is conducted from the stove to the pan and then to the food in the pan. **Convection** transfers energy through circular movement of air or liquids. For example, a convection oven transfers heat through the circular movement caused by hot air rising and cold air sinking.

Practice Questions

8. Which type of potential energy is stored in a compressed spring?

A. chemical potential energy
B. electric potential energy
C. gravitational potential energy
D. elastic potential energy

9. Which process allows the transfer of heat to occur from the contact between two substances?
   A. conduction
   B. convection
   C. radiation
   D. sublimation

Sound and Light

Energy can also be transferred through **waves,** which are repeating pulses of energy. Waves that travel through a medium, like ripples on a pond or compressions in a Slinky, are called **mechanical waves**. Mechanical waves travel faster through denser mediums; for example, sound waves move faster through water than air. Waves that vibrate up and down (like the ripples on the pond) are **transverse waves,** and those that travel through compression (like the Slinky) are **longitudinal waves**.

Energy waves are described by properties such as amplitude, wavelength, frequency, period, speed, and phase. **Amplitude** is a measure of the wave's displacement from its rest position. **Wavelength** is the distance between two points on back-to-back wave cycles. **Frequency** describes the number of times per second the wave cycles. The time between wave crests is the **period** and the speed is how fast the wave is moving. The **phase** of a wave is the position on a wave cycle at a given point in time.

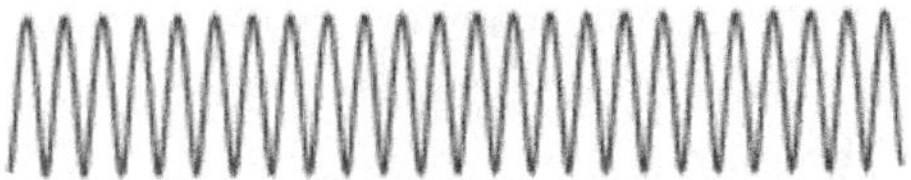

Figure 4.9. Types of Waves

Sound is a special type of longitudinal wave created by vibrations. Ears are able to interpret these waves as particular sounds. The frequency, or rate, of the vibration determines the sound's **pitch**. **Loudness** depends on the amplitude, or height, of a sound wave.

The **Doppler effect** is the difference in perceived pitch caused by the motion of the object creating the wave. For example, as an ambulance approaches, the siren's pitch appears to increase to the observer and then to decrease as the ambulance moves away. This occurs because sound waves are compressed as the ambulance approaches an observer and spread out as the ambulance moves away from the observer.

Electromagnetic waves are composed of oscillating electric and magnetic fields and thus do not require a medium to travel through. The electromagnetic spectrum classifies the types of electromagnetic waves based on their frequency. These include radio waves, microwaves, X-rays, and visible light.

The study of light is called **optics**. Because visible light is a wave, it displays properties similar to other waves. It will **reflect**, or bounce off surfaces, which can be observed by shining a flashlight on a mirror. Light will also **refract**, or bend, when it travels between substances.

Consider This

What are some other ways to demonstrate refraction?

This effect can be seen by holding a pencil upright in water and observing the apparent bend in the pencil.

Curved pieces of glass called **lenses** can be used to bend light in a way that affects how an image is perceived. Some microscopes, for example, use specific types of lenses to make objects appear larger . Eyeglasses also use lenses to correct poor vision.

The frequency of a wave in the visible light spectrum is responsible for its **color**, with red/orange colors having a lower frequency than blue/violet colors. White light is a blend of all the frequencies of visible light. Passing white light through a prism will bend each frequency at a slightly different angle, separating the colors and creating a **rainbow**. Sunlight passing through raindrops can undergo this effect, creating rainbows in the sky.

Practice Question

10. Which measurement describes the distance between crests in a wave?
    A. amplitude
    B. wavelength
    C. frequency
    D. period

Electricity and Magnetism

Electric charge is created by a difference in the balance of protons and electrons, which causes an object to have a positive or negative charge. Charged objects create an electric field that spreads outward from the object. Other charged objects in that field will experience a force: objects that have opposite charges will be **attracted** to each other, and objects with the same charge will be **repelled**, or pushed away, from each other.

Because protons cannot leave the nucleus, charge is created by the movement of electrons. Static electricity, or **electrostatic** charge, occurs when a surface has a buildup of charges. For example, when people rub a balloon on their head, the friction causes electrons to move from their hair to the balloon. This creates a negative charge on the balloon and positive charge on the hair; the resulting attraction causes the hair to move toward the balloon.

Electricity is the movement of electrons through a conductor, and an electric **circuit** is a closed loop through which electricity moves. Circuits include a **voltage** source which powers the movement of electrons, known as **current**. Sources of voltage include batteries, **generators,** and wall outlets (which are in turn powered by electric power stations). Other items, such as lights, computers, or microwaves, can then be connected to the circuit to be powered by its electricity.

Magnets are created by the alignment of spinning electrons within a substance. This alignment occurs naturally in some substances, including iron, nickel, and cobalt, all of which can be used to produce **permanent magnets**. The alignment of electrons creates a **magnetic field** which, like an electric or gravitational field, can act on other objects. Magnetic fields have north and south **poles** that have properties similar to electric charges: opposite poles attract; same poles repel each other.

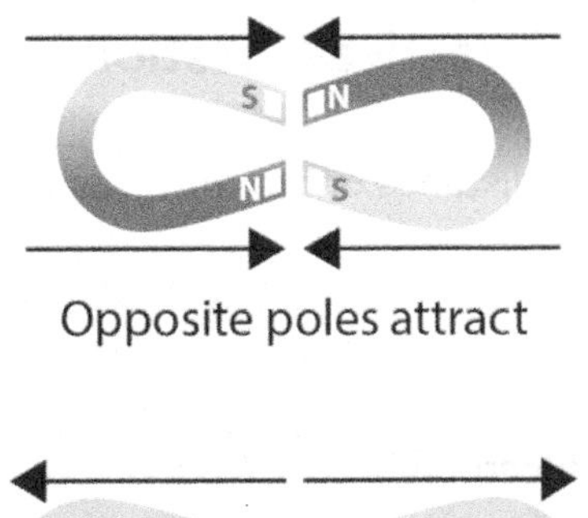

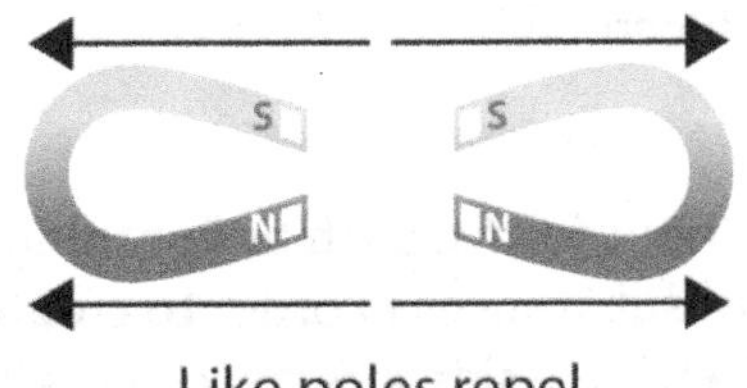

Figure 4.10. Magnets

However, unlike electric charge, which must be either positive or negative, a magnetic field always has two poles. If a magnet is cut in half, the result is two magnets that each have a north and south pole. Magnetic fields are depicted visually using **magnetic field lines**, which show the direction of the field at different points.

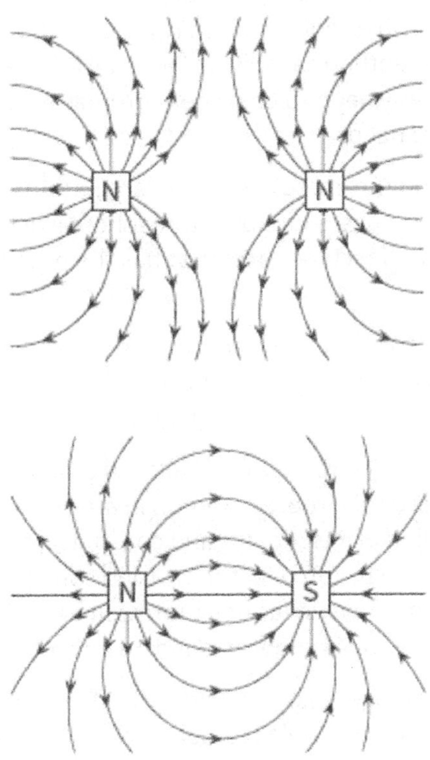

Figure 4.11. Magnetic Field Lines

Electricity and magnetism are closely related. A moving magnet creates an electric field, and a moving charged particle will create a magnetic field. A specific kind of **temporary magnet** known as an electromagnet can be made by coiling a wire around a metal object and running electricity through it. A magnetic field will be created when the wire contains a current but will disappear when the flow of electricity is stopped.

Practice Question

11. Two negative charges are held at a distance of 1 m from each other. When the charges are released, they will
    A. remain at rest.
    B. move closer together.
    C. move farther apart.
    D. move together in the same direction.

Energy Transformations

Though energy exists in nature in various forms, such as lightning as a form of electrical energy, humans frequently transform various substances in order to create energy to power their world. These transformations of energy often have side effects, especially when nonrenewable resources are used.

Fossil fuels, such as oil, natural gas, and coal, are nonrenewable resources, meaning that the earth contains a finite amount of those substances. These carbon-based fuels were produced over millions of years by the decomposition and compression of organisms that lived long ago.

As **nonrenewable resources** become depleted, scientists are making advancements in using **renewable resources** as replacements. Such possible sources of energy include nuclear energy, hydropower, **wind energy**, solar energy, **biomass**, and geothermal power. These all have less of an impact on the environment than fossil fuels, but many need to be more thoroughly researched and developed before they can supply the energy the world needs.

Nuclear power is created by releasing the energy stored in large atoms by breaking them into smaller atoms. Nuclear power does not release gases into the atmosphere like burning fossil fuels does, but nuclear power produces dangerous radioactive waste that has the potential to cause other environmental problems.

Damming rivers allows **hydropower** to convert the energy in moving water into mechanical energy, which can then be transformed into electricity. Dams do not release harmful emissions like fossil fuels do, but they can be disruptive to natural environments and waterways.

Energy from the **wind** is harnessed using turbines (also called windmills), transforming mechanical energy into electricity. Wind turbines are becoming more common in areas where windy conditions are common, including plains regions and coastlines. **Solar energy** transforms energy from the sun into electricity using solar panels. These panels can be laid out in giant arrays called solar farms in order to provide energy to a large area, but they can also be installed on individual homes or buildings.

Biofuels are biological matter that can be burned to produce heat, steam, or electricity. While biofuels such as ethanol are renewable, they can create many of the same environmental concerns as fossil fuels. Finally, **geothermal energy** converts heat from below Earth's surface into steam. This type of energy has been used since ancient times to heat water and homes and has recently been harnessed to produce electricity.

> **Consider This**
>
> What would be the pros and cons of using wind, solar, nuclear, and hydropower in your part of Texas?

Practice Question

12. Which of the following is an unrenewable resource?
    A. solar energy
    B. hydropower
    C. geothermal energy
    D. fossil fuels

Photosynthesis and Tropic Levels

Just as humans transform energy to meet their needs, so do other organisms. Some plant, algae, and bacteria cells can make their own glucose from carbon dioxide and water using energy from sunlight through **photosynthesis**. Photosynthesis involves two processes. The first is called the light reaction because it depends on light from the sun for energy. In the first part of photosynthesis, a molecule of chlorophyll absorbs a tiny packet of energy—a photon—from the sun. The photon causes the chlorophyll to donate one electron and begin a chain reaction that produces ATP and adds hydrogen to the energy-rich molecule NADPH to form $NADPH_2$.

The second part of photosynthesis is called the Calvin cycle (also referred to as the Calvin-Benson-Bassham (CBB) cycle). The Calvin cycle uses the ATP and $NADPH_2$ produced in the first step to make glucose from carbon dioxide (CO_2) in the air and water from the plant's roots. The glucose is stored, and when the plant needs energy, it is transformed into ATP by the Krebs cycle. This step is sometimes also called the dark or light-independent reaction because it can happen without light.

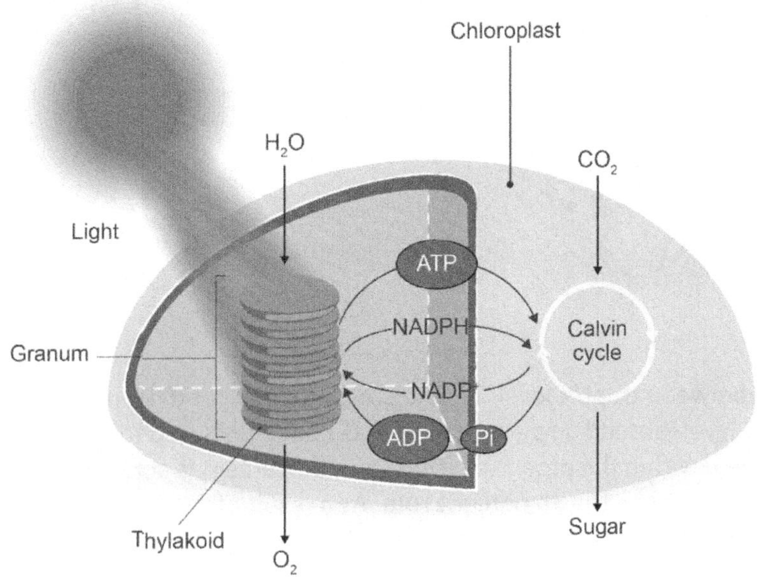

Figure 4.12. Photosynthesis

Humans and animals are also part of the transfer of energy through food webs.

In a **food web**, every species either consumes or is consumed by another (or others). An organism's place in the food web is called its trophic level.

- The lowest trophic level in the web is occupied by **producers,** which include plants and algae that produce energy directly from the sun.

- The next level are **primary consumers** (herbivores), which consume plant matter.
- The next trophic level includes **secondary consumers** (carnivores), which consume herbivores.
- A food web may also contain another level of **tertiary consumers** (carnivores that consume other carnivores). In a real community, these webs can be extremely complex, with species existing on multiple trophic levels.

> **Helpful Hint**
>
> Communities also include decomposers, which are organisms that break down dead matter.

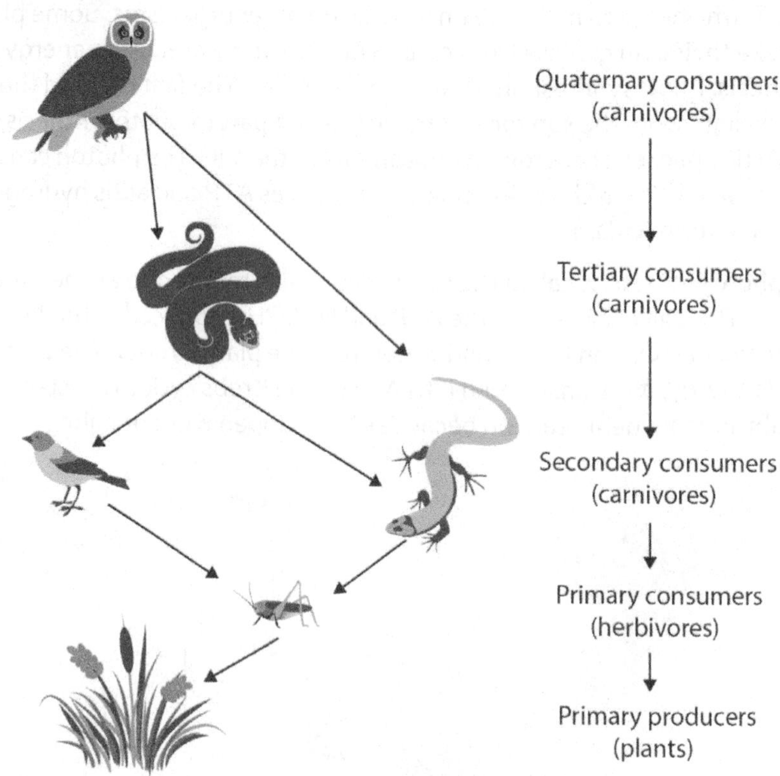

Figure 4.13. Food Web

The way energy flows between trophic levels can be presented in a food or energy pyramid. Most energy that enters any trophic level (around 90 percent) is lost as heat when used to remain alive; only 10 percent is actually kept and stored within the organism. Thus, only 10 percent is actually transferred from level to level. Some people refer to this as the **10 percent rule**. As a result of this 10 percent rule, the bottom levels of the pyramid have the most energy; the top levels have the least energy.

Practice Question

13. How do primary consumers acquire energy in a food web?
    A. decomposition of dead matter
    B. photosynthesis
    C. consuming plant matter
    D. consuming herbivores

Structure and Function of Living Things

Classification of Organisms

Scientists use the characteristics of organisms to sort them into a variety of **classifications** using a system called taxonomy. The highest level of taxonomic classification is the **kingdom**, and each kingdom is then broken down into smaller categories. The smallest level of classification is a **species**, which includes individuals with similar genetics that are capable of breeding. The entire system is given in Table 4.2.

Table 4.2. Taxonomic Classification	
▪ Kingdom ▪ Phylum ▪ Class ▪ Order	▪ Family ▪ Genus ▪ Species

Helpful Hint

The phrase King Phillip Came Over From Great Spain is a way to remember the order of taxonomic classification of organisms: kingdom, phylum, class, order, family, genus, species.

All organisms are sorted into one of five kingdoms: Monera, Protista, Fungi, Plantae, and Animalia. The kingdom **Monera** includes bacteria, which are unicellular organisms that have no nucleus. **Protists** are also unicellular organisms, but they have a nucleus. Both monera and protists reproduce **asexually** by cellular division.

Fungi are a group of unicellular and multicellular organisms that have cell walls and reproduction strategies that differ from those in the other kingdoms. This kingdom includes common organisms like mushrooms and molds. Fungi can reproduce both asexually by cellular division and **sexually** through spores. Many species of fungi are decomposers and attain energy by breaking down organic matter in the environment.

Plants are a kingdom of organisms that use the energy from sunlight to make food (the sugar glucose) through the process of photosynthesis.

The kingdom **Animalia** contains multicellular organisms that can move around and must consume other organisms for energy. The kingdom includes several notable classifications that divide organisms based on important features. These include whether the organism has a backbone or spine: **vertebrates** do, while **invertebrates** do not. Animals are also classified based on whether they are **ectotherms**, meaning their source of body heat comes from the environment, or **endotherms**, meaning their body heat is derived from metabolic processes within the body. Ectothermic animals are sometimes known as cold-blooded, and endothermic animals as warm-blooded. Animal classification also looks at animal reproduction: some animals lay eggs, while others give birth to live young.

Amphibians are ectothermic vertebrates that have gills when they hatch from eggs but develop lungs as adults. Examples of amphibians include frogs, toads, newts, and salamanders. **Reptiles**, such as snakes, lizards, crocodiles, turtles, and tortoises, are cold-blooded vertebrates that have scales and lay eggs on land. **Birds** are endothermic vertebrate animals that have wings, feathers, scaly legs, beaks, and no teeth, and bear their young in a hard-shelled egg. **Mammals** are endothermic vertebrate animals that have hair, give live birth (with a few exceptions), and produce milk for the nourishment of their young.

All organisms have a **life cycle**, or stages of life. Every organism is born, matures, reproduces, and dies. However, the stages in this life cycle vary from organism to organism. Plants, for example, often go through a cycle of seed, germination, maturing, pollination, and fruiting. In contrast, when a frog lays eggs in water, the eggs hatch to become tadpoles with gills. The tadpoles eventually grow legs and develop lungs, and the tail is absorbed into the body. At this point, a tadpole has become an adult frog.

The frog life cycle is an example of **metamorphosis**, or a change in the body of the organism during its life cycle.

Insects may have an even more complex life cycle that could involve complete metamorphosis or incomplete metamorphosis. In **complete metamorphosis**, the insect goes through four stages: egg, larva, pupa, and adult. The larva typically eats (like the caterpillar stage of the butterfly), but the pupa stage (like the cocoon stage of the butterfly) is typically totally inactive. In **incomplete metamorphosis**, there are only three stages: egg, nymph, and adult. Nymphs do not have a different body form but rather look like smaller adults.

Practice Question

14. Which of the following taxonomic ranks is the most specific, consisting of organisms that can only interbreed with one another?
    A. phylum
    B. species
    C. genus
    D. population

Cells

Organisms are living things consisting of at least one **cell**, which is the smallest unit of life that can reproduce on its own. Unicellular organisms, such as amoebas, are made up of only one cell, while multicellular organisms are composed of many cells. There are two basic types of cells: prokaryotic and eukaryotic. **Prokaryotic cells** do not have a nucleus, and some single-celled organisms like bacteria are prokaryotes. **Eukaryotic cells** contain a nucleus where the genetic material is stored and are found in multicellular organisms.

A cell consists of cytoplasm and genetic material (DNA) inside a **cell membrane**, or protective covering. Separate from the cytoplasm in eukaryotic cells is the **nucleus**, which is the membrane-bound body that holds the cell's DNA. Within the cytoplasm of eukaryotic cells are a number of **organelles** that perform specific functions. These include **mitochondria**, which produce energy; **ribosomes**, which produce proteins; and **vacuoles**, which store water and other molecules.

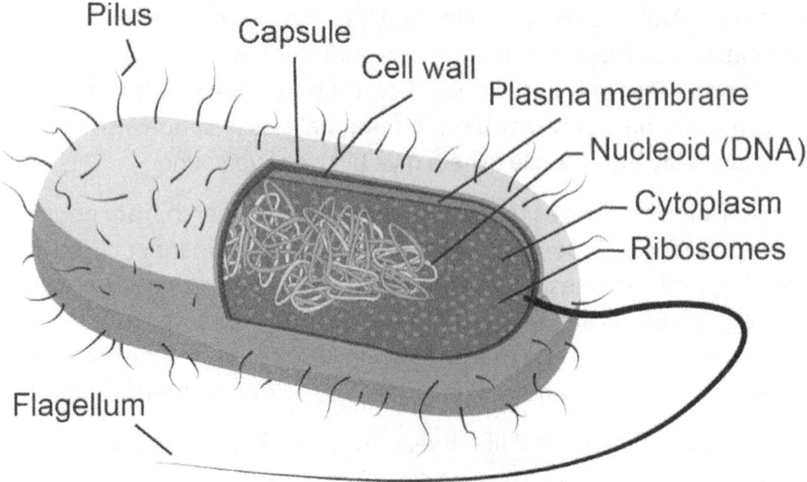

Figure 4.14. Prokaryotic Cell

Plant cells include a number of structures not found in animal cells. These include the **cell wall**, which provides the cell with a hard outer structure, and chloroplasts, where **photosynthesis** occurs. During photosynthesis, plants store energy from sunlight as sugars, which serve as the main source of energy for cell functions.

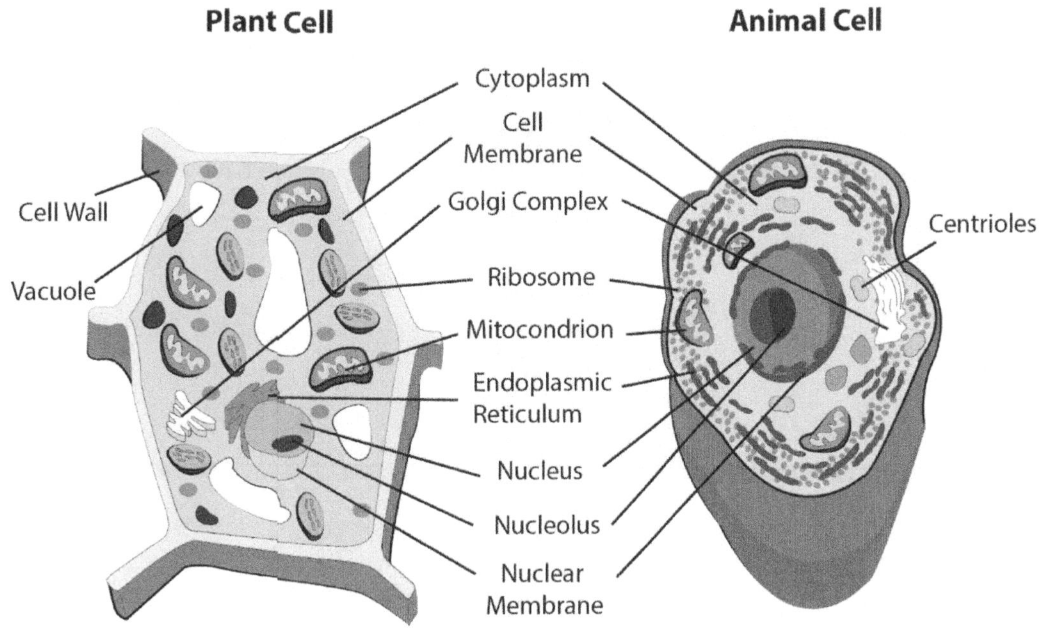

Figure 4.15. Animal Cell Versus Plant Cell

Cell division, or **mitosis**, produces two cells with the same DNA as the original cell. Mitosis has five steps: prophase, metaphase, anaphase, telophase, and interphase. Prophase is when the cell is getting ready to divide by duplicating its DNA. During metaphase, the chromosomes line up in pairs along the central axis of the cell. Anaphase is when the pairs begin to split, with one of the chromosomes moving toward one side of the cell and the other moving toward the opposite side. Once the chromosomes are at opposite sides of the cell, the cell moves into telophase: the cell membrane splits and two new cells are formed. After the division is completed, the two new cells return to a normal resting state, which is called interphase.

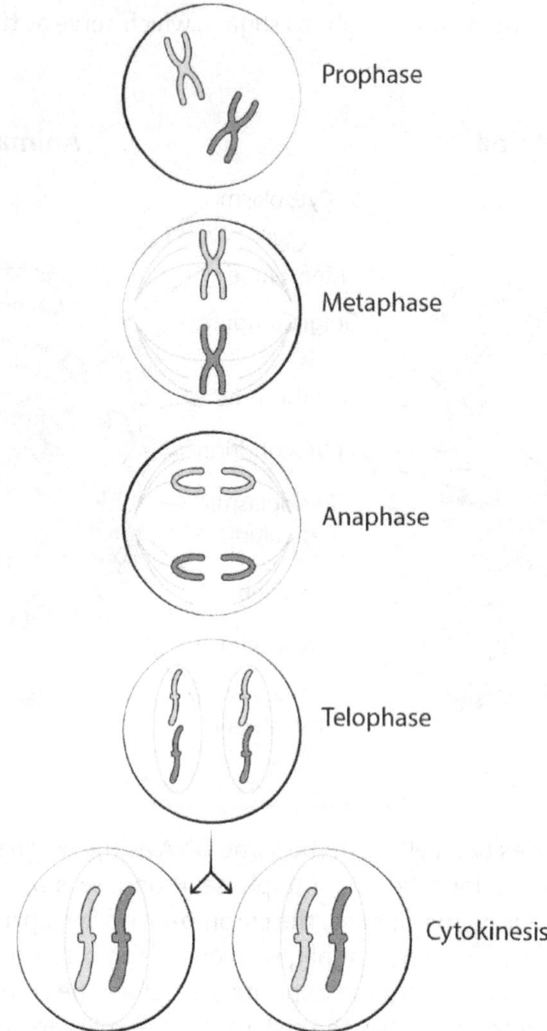

Figure 4.16. Phases of Mitosis

Meiosis is the formation of reproductive cells called gametes (eggs and sperm). Meiosis is a process that includes two cell divisions with phases similar to those of mitosis. In the first division, the chromosomes are duplicated and pairs of chromosomes align and exchange genetic material with one another during the prophase. The metaphase, anaphase, and telophase proceed much like those of mitosis. The interphase between the two division processes is very short and the DNA is not duplicated before the second division cycle. The cell divides again using the same process as described for mitosis; however, the chromosomes are not duplicated. Instead, each chromosome divides in half and each new cell receives only half of the genetic material contained in the original parent cell.

Helpful Hint

Phases of mitosis can be remembered using the phrase I Picked My Apples Today. The order is interphase, prophase, metaphase, anaphase, telophase.

When an egg is fertilized by the sperm to form a zygote, half of the new organism's chromosomes come from the egg (mother) and half come from the sperm (father). In humans, reproductive cells have twenty-three chromosomes and body cells have forty-six (one set of twenty-three from each parent).

Practice Questions

15. The chromosomes of a eukaryotic organism are found in the
    A. chloroplast.
    B. nucleus.
    C. ribosome.
    D. cytoplasm.

16. A distinct difference between a plant cell and an animal cell is the presence of
    A. ribosomes.
    B. mitochondria.
    C. a cell wall
    D. nucleus.

Human Body Systems

In a multicellular organism, cells are grouped together into **tissues**, and these tissues are grouped into **organs**, which perform specific **functions**. The heart, for example, is the organ that pumps blood throughout the body. Organs are further grouped into **organ systems**, such as the digestive or respiratory systems.

Check Your Understanding

What is a system? What is a subsystem?

Anatomy is the study of the structure of organisms, and **physiology** is the study of how these structures function. Both disciplines study the systems that allow organisms to perform a number of crucial functions, including the exchange of energy, nutrients, and waste products with the environment. This exchange allows organisms to maintain **homeostasis**, or the stabilization of internal conditions.

The human body has a number of systems that perform vital functions, including the digestive, excretory, respiratory, circulatory, skeletal, muscular, immune, nervous, endocrine, and reproductive systems.

The **digestive system** breaks food down into nutrients for use by the body's cells. Food enters through the **mouth** and moves through the **esophagus** to the **stomach**, where it is physically and chemically broken down. The food particles then move into the **small intestine**, where the majority of nutrients are absorbed. Finally, the remaining particles enter the **large intestine**, which mostly absorbs water, and waste exits through the **rectum** and **anus**. This system also includes other organs, such as the **liver**, **gallbladder**, and **pancreas**, that manufacture substances needed for digestion.

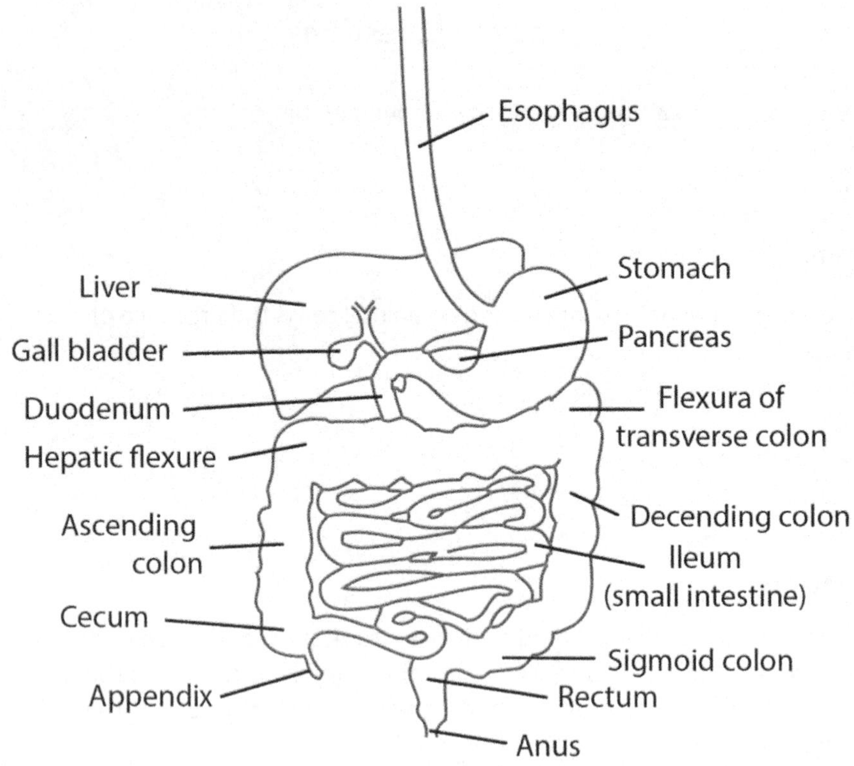

Figure 4.17. Digestive System

The **excretory system** removes waste products from the body. Its organs include the liver, which breaks down harmful substances, and the **kidneys**, which filter waste from the bloodstream. The excretory system also includes the **bladder** and **urinary tract**, which expel the waste filtered by the kidneys; the lungs, which expel the carbon dioxide created by cellular metabolism; and the skin, which secretes salt in the form of perspiration.

The **respiratory system** takes in oxygen (which is needed for cellular functioning) and expels carbon dioxide. Humans take in air primarily through the nose but also through the mouth. This air travels down the **trachea** and **bronchi** into the **lungs**, which are composed of millions of small structures called alveoli that allow for the exchange of gases between the blood and the air.

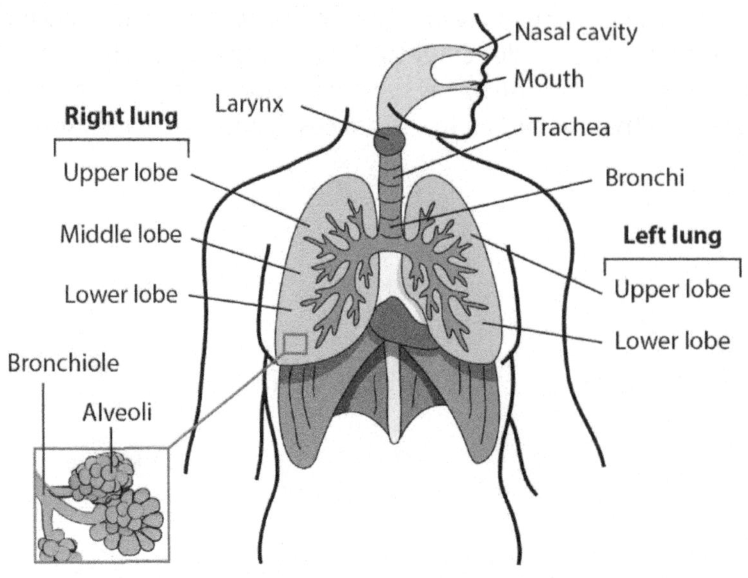

Figure 4.18. Respiratory System

The circulatory system carries oxygen, nutrients, and waste products in the blood to and from all the cells of the body. The **heart** is a four-chambered muscle that pumps blood throughout the body. The four chambers are the right atrium, right ventricle, left atrium, and left ventricle. Deoxygenated blood (blood from which all the oxygen has been extracted and used) enters the right atrium and then is sent from the right ventricle through the pulmonary artery to the lungs, where it collects oxygen. The oxygen-rich blood then returns to the left atrium of the heart and is pumped out the left ventricle to the rest of the body.

Blood travels through a system of vessels. **Arteries** branch directly off the heart and carry blood away from it. The largest artery is the aorta, which carries blood from the heart to the rest of the body. **Veins** carry blood back to the heart from other parts of the body. Most veins carry deoxygenated blood, but the pulmonary veins carry oxygenated blood from the lungs back to the heart to then be pumped to the rest of the body. Arteries and veins branch into smaller and smaller vessels until they become **capillaries,** which are the smallest vessels and the site where gas exchange occurs.

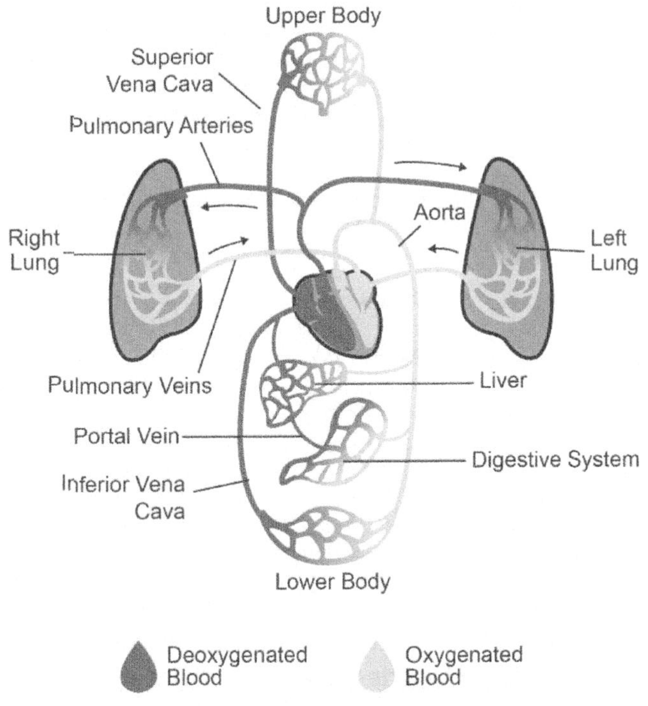

Figure 4.19. Circulatory System

The **skeletal system,** which is composed of the body's **bones** and **joints,** provides support for the body and helps with movement. Bones also store some of the body's nutrients and produce specific types of cells. Humans are born with 237 bones. However, many of these bones fuse during childhood, and adults have only 206 bones. Bones can have rough or smooth texture and come in four basic shapes: long, flat, short, and irregular.

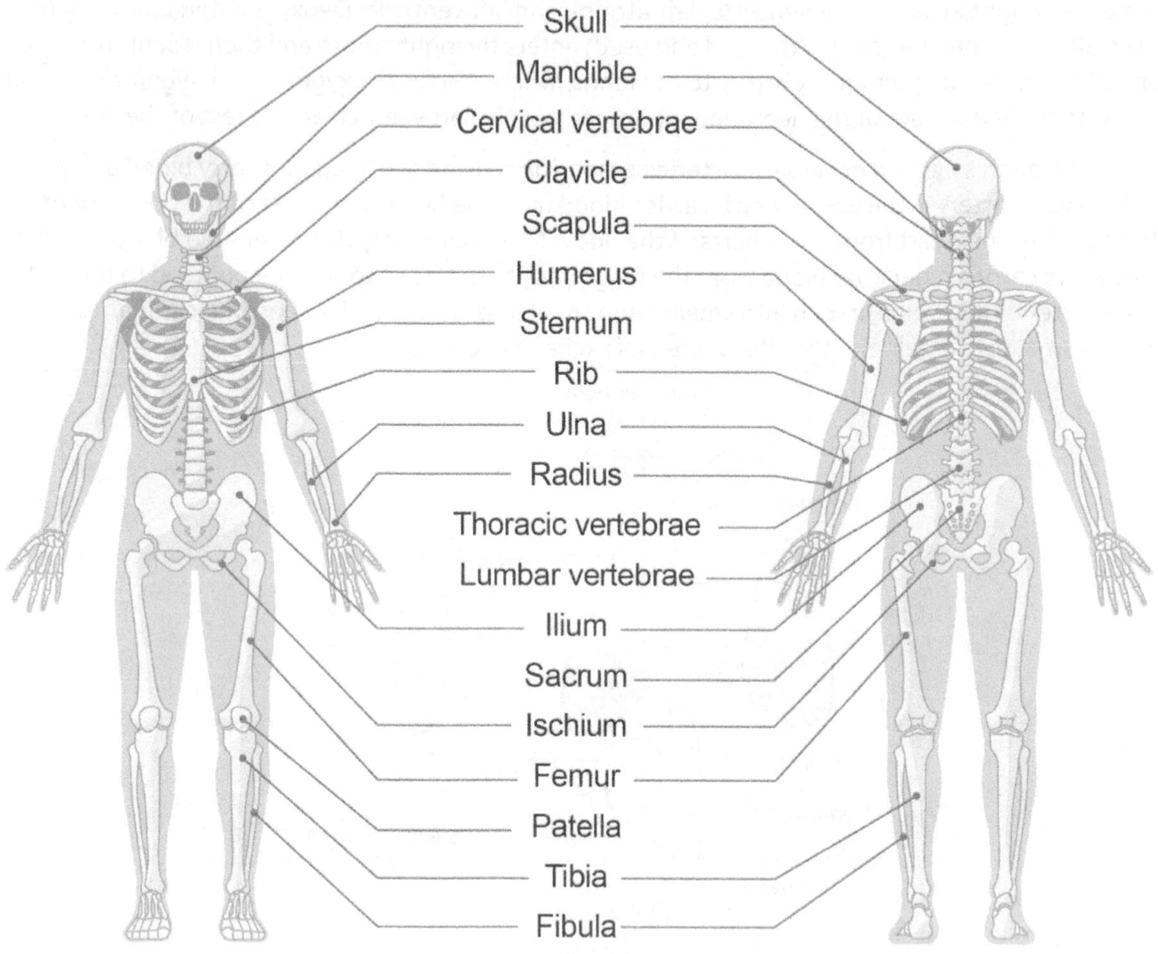

Figure 4.20. Important Bones of the Skeletal System

The **muscular system** allows the body to move and also moves blood and other substances through the body. The human body has three types of muscles. Skeletal muscles are voluntary muscles (meaning they can be controlled) that are attached to bones and move the body. Smooth muscles are involuntary muscles (meaning they cannot be controlled) that create movement in parts of the digestive tract, blood vessels, and reproduction system. Finally, cardiac muscle is the involuntary muscle that contracts the heart, pumping blood throughout the body.

The **immune system** protects the body from infection by foreign particles and organisms. It includes the **skin** and mucous membranes, which act as physical barriers, and a number of specialized cells that destroy foreign substances in the body. The human body has an adaptive immune system, meaning it can recognize and respond to foreign substances once it has been exposed to them. This is the underlying mechanism behind vaccines.

The immune system is composed of **B cells**, or B lymphocytes, that produce special proteins called **antibodies** that bind to foreign substances, called **antigens**, and neutralize them. **T cells**, or T lymphocytes, remove body cells that have been infected by foreign invaders like bacteria or viruses. **Helper T cells** coordinate production of antibodies by B cells and removal of infected cells by T cells. **Killer T cells** destroy body cells that have been infected by invaders after they are identified and removed by T cells. Finally, **memory cells** remember antigens that have been removed so the immune system can respond more quickly if they enter the body again.

The **nervous system** processes external stimuli and sends signals throughout the body. It is made up of two parts. The central nervous system (CNS) includes the brain and spinal cord and is where information is processed and stored. The brain has three parts: the cerebrum, cerebellum, and medulla. The **cerebrum** is the biggest part of the brain, the wrinkly gray part at the front and top, and controls different functions like thinking, vision, hearing, touch, and smell. The **cerebellum** is located at the back and bottom of the brain and controls motor movements. The **medulla,** or brain stem, is where the brain connects to the spinal cord and controls automatic body functions like breathing and heartbeat.

> **Think About It**
>
> What classroom activities can help students understand how human body systems work together?

The peripheral nervous system (PNS) includes small cells called **neurons** that transmit information throughout the body using electrical signals. Neurons are made up of three basic parts: the cell body, dendrites, and axons. The **cell body** is the main part of the cell where the organelles are located. **Dendrites** are long arms that extend from the main cell body and communicate with dendrites from other cells through chemical messages passed across a space called a synapse. **Axons** are extensions from the cell body and transmit messages to the muscles.

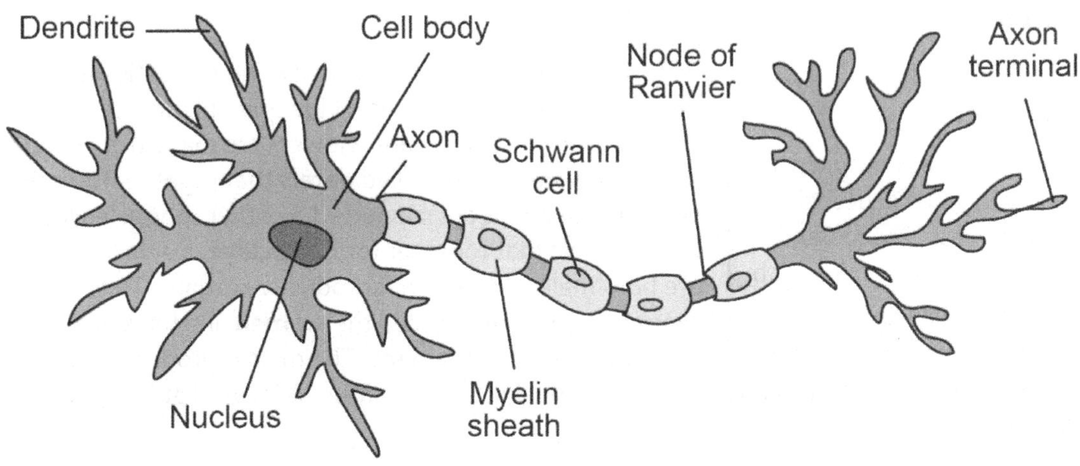

Figure 4.21. Neuron

The **endocrine system** is a collection of organs that produce **hormones,** which are chemicals that regulate bodily processes. These organs include the pituitary gland, hypothalamus, pineal gland, thyroid gland, parathyroid glands, adrenal glands, testes (in males), ovaries (in females), and the placenta (in pregnant females). Together, the hormones produced by these organs regulate a wide variety of bodily functions, including hunger, sleep, mood, reproduction, and temperature. Some organs that are part of other systems can also act as endocrine organs, including the pancreas and liver.

The reproductive system includes the organs necessary for sexual reproduction. In males, sperm is produced in the **testes (also known as testicles)** and carried through a thin tube called the **vas deferens** to the **urethra,** which carries sperm through the **penis and out of the body**. The **prostate** is a muscular gland approximately the size of a walnut that is located between the male bladder and penis and produces a fluid that nourishes and protects sperm.

In the female reproductive system, eggs are produced in the **ovaries** and released roughly once a month to move through the **fallopian tubes** to the **uterus**. If an egg is fertilized, the new embryo implants in the lining of the **uterus** and develops over the course of about nine months. At the end of **gestation,** the baby leaves the uterus through the **cervix,** and exits the body through the **vagina**. If the egg is not fertilized, the uterus will shed its lining.

Practice Questions

17. What is the primary function of the respiratory system?
    A. to create sound and speech
    B. to take oxygen into the body while removing carbon dioxide
    C. to transport nutrients to the cells and tissue of the body
    D. to act as a barrier between the body's organs and foreign pathogens

18. Which muscular organ processes food material into smaller pieces and helps mix it with saliva?
    A. pharynx
    B. tongue
    C. diaphragm
    D. stomach

Reproduction and Heredity

Plant Reproduction

Did You Know?

The term bluebonnet, referring to the Texas state flower, actually describes six species. The largest are Big Bend Bluebonnets (Lupinus havardii), which can reach three feet in height.

Vascular plants are grouped as flowering or nonflowering based on how they reproduce. Flowering plants use flowers as their reproductive organs. Flowers are made from special brightly colored leaves called **petals** that together form the **corolla**. The petals are supported by other special leaves called **sepals** that together form the **calyx**. Inside the flower are both male and female reproductive organs. The male reproductive organ is called the **stamen** and has two parts, the **anther** and the **filament**. The male reproductive cells, called **pollen**, are produced in the stamen and stored in the anther. The anther is located at the end of a stalk called the filament.

The female reproductive organ is called the **pistil**, and is usually located in the center of the flower. The pistil has two parts, the **carpel** and the **stigma**. The carpel is the ovary of the flower, where **ova** (eggs), the female reproductive cells, are produced. The stigma is where the pollen (the male reproductive cell) is received and is sometimes extended on a stalk called the **style**. Flowering plants are brightly colored to attract insects that move pollen from the anther to the stigma to fertilize the eggs.

After **fertilization** occurs, the flower forms a fruit that contains the seeds that grow from the fertilized eggs. **Seeds** are the plant embryo and come in a variety of shapes, sizes, and colors. The **fruit** provides nutrients and protects the seeds as they grow. It also attracts birds and animals that help distribute the seeds away from the plant. Seeds can also be distributed by air and water. The seeds are protected by a waxy layer called the seed coat.

Once the seed is distributed, it needs air, water, and soil to grow. When seeds begin to grow, it is called **germination**. The seed begins to form small roots and uses nutrients stored in a special organ called the **endosperm** for energy until it can form leaves and generate energy through photosynthesis. Flowering plants are also divided based on the number of embryos, or **cotyledons**, in their seeds. Plants with only one embryo in each seed, like corn or wheat, are called **monocots**. Those with two embryos in each seed, like beans, are called **dicots**. When the seed develops leaves, it is called a sprout or seedling. It continues to grow until it becomes a mature plant and can reproduce again by growing flowers.

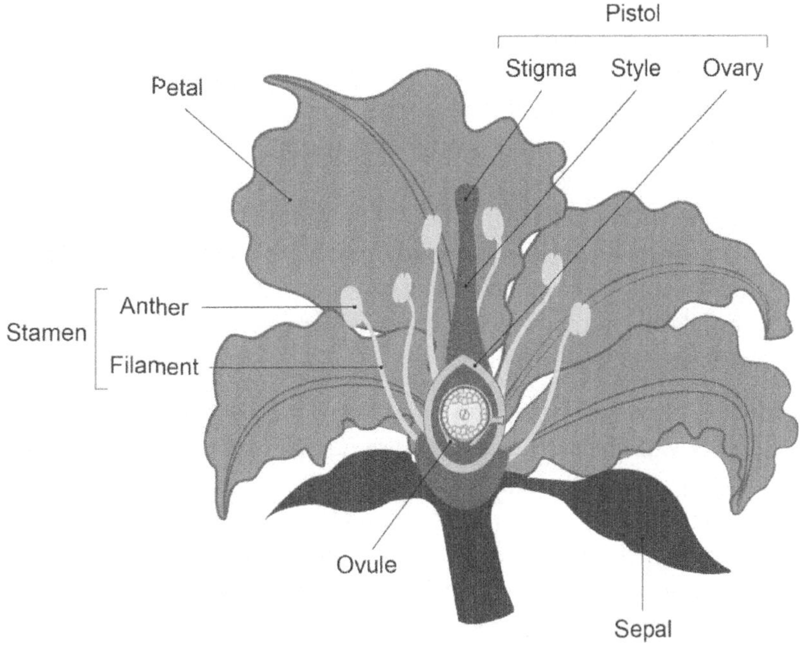

Figure 4.22. Flower with Male and Female Reproductive Structures

Nonflowering plants are divided into two groups: those that use seeds to reproduce and those that use spores to reproduce. Non-flowering plants that use seeds to reproduce are called **gymnosperms,** which literally means *naked seeds*. These plants produce seeds that do not have a covering like the fruits produced by flowering plants. **Conifers** are a major group of gymnosperm plants that use woody cones to protect their seeds. Most conifers are trees like pine, cedar, or redwood. Conifers produce male and female cones. The male cones produce pollen that is distributed by the wind, and if the pollen falls on a female cone, the female cone produces seed that are protected by the cone. The seeds produced by conifers have winged structures on them that allow them to be carried by the wind. Once they reach the ground, the seeds germinate and grow.

Practice Question

19. Why are many flowers brightly colored?
    A. to draw insects to help in reproduction
    B. to promote fruit development
    C. to emphasize the pistil
    D. to provide protection for seeds

Animal Reproduction

Animals may reproduce sexually or asexually. Asexual reproduction has the primary disadvantage of producing an organism genetically identical to the parent. Asexual reproduction may involve fission or **binary fission**, where an organisms seems to divide itself in two and regenerate lost parts. Flatworms and sea anemones are two examples of organisms that reproduce via fission. **Budding** is a form of asexual reproduction just like it sounds: the organism forms a bud that then breaks off from the "parent." Some invertebrates, like coral, reproduce via budding. **Parthenogenesis** is another type of asexual reproduction wherein an unfertilized egg grows into an adult organism. Some insects, fish, reptiles, and amphibians reproduce in this manner.

Sexual reproduction differs from asexual reproduction in that an offspring that is genetically different from its parent or parents is produced. **Hermaphroditism** is a form of sexual reproduction in which the organism has female and male sex organs in one individual. Snails and clams are examples. Most organisms reproduce with two individuals: a male that provides sperm and a female that provides the egg. This type of reproduction is often divided into organisms that use external fertilization or internal fertilization. In most **external fertilization,** females release eggs and males release sperm into water in what is known as *spawning*. Most fish and many other aquatic animals practice external fertilization. In **internal fertilization,** sperm is placed directly into the female via mating. Mating may result in the female laying a fertilized egg that develops outside the body; this is known as **oviparity** and is the practice of all birds and some other animals. Unlike oviparity, in **ovoviparity,** the fertilized egg stays in the body of the female for protection until it hatches or right before it hatches. Some fish and snakes use this type of reproduction. Many mammals like humans reproduce via **viviparity,** where offspring do not hatch from eggs but rather remain in the mother until a live birth.

When organisms reproduce, **genetic** information is passed to the next generation through deoxyribonucleic acid, or DNA. Within DNA are blocks of nucleotides called **genes,** each of which contains the code needed to produce a specific protein. Genes are responsible for **traits,** or characteristics, in organisms such as eye color, height, and flower color. During sexual **reproduction,** the child receives two copies of each gene, one each from the mother and the father. Some of these genes will be **dominant,** meaning they are expressed, and some will be **recessive,** meaning they are not expressed. Each child will have a mix of its parents' traits.

A special chart that shows all the possible genetic combinations from parents with given genotypes is called a **Punnett square**. A Punnett square is a grid with four squares, where the possible genes from one parent are written along the top and the possible genes from the other parent are written down the side. Each square is filled in with the corresponding letters from the top and side of the grid, with capital letters representing dominant genetic traits listed first, followed by lowercase letters representing recessive traits.

Helpful Hint

Many of the rules of genetics were discovered by Gregor Mendel, a nineteenth-century abbot who used pea plants to show how traits are passed down through generations.

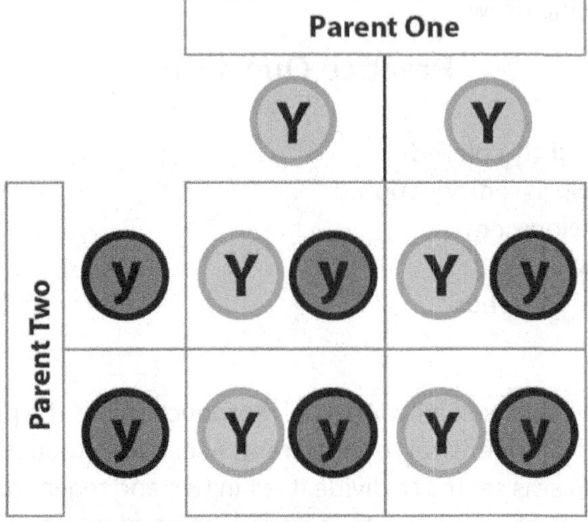

Figure 4.22. Punnett Square

When an individual's genetic code is damaged, that organism may have a **genetic disorder**. For example, cystic fibrosis, which causes difficulty with basic bodily functions such as breathing and eating, results from damage to the gene which codes for a protein called CFTR. Down syndrome, which causes developmental delays, occurs when a person has three copies of chromosome twenty-one (meaning they received two copies from one parent as a result of an error in meiosis).

Consider This

Why might a harmful mutation continue to exist in a population?

Genes are not static. Over time, **mutations** or changes in the genetic code occur that can affect an organism's ability to survive. Four common types of genetic mutations are substitution, insertion, deletion, and frameshift. Substitution mutations occur when one nucleotide is exchanged with another (such as switching the bases adenine and cytosine). Insertion mutations happen when extra nucleotide pairs are inserted into the DNA sequence. Removal of nucleotide pairs from the DNA sequence results in deletion mutations. Finally, frameshift mutations occur when the insertion or deletion of nucleotides causes the gene to be misread. Harmful mutations will appear less often in a population or be removed entirely because organisms with those mutations will be less likely to reproduce and thus will not pass on that trait.

Beneficial mutations, called **adaptations**, may help an organism thrive in a particular environment. This means the organism is more likely to reproduce, and thus that trait or adaptation will appear more often. Over time, this process, called **natural selection**, results in the **evolution** of new species. The theory of evolution was developed by naturalist Charles Darwin when he observed how finches on the Galapagos Islands had a variety of beak shapes and sizes that corresponded to different food sources, allowing the birds to coexist.

Of course, inherited traits—those that pass from parents to children, such as hair or eye color—are different from learned characteristics. **Learned characteristics** are things that organisms acquire during their lifetimes. For example, if after straying too close to a lion, a gazelle is chided by its mother, it will learn to keep its distance. Learned characteristics are distinct from **instincts**, which are inherited. For example, fish are born knowing how to swim instinctually, and human babies are born knowing how to cry.

Similar to learned characteristics are **environmental factors** that impact how traits are expressed differently. Drugs, chemicals, temperature, and light are all environmental factors that can impact gene expression. For example, a person may be genetically predisposed to large muscle mass, but this trait may only be expressed after the use of steroids. The light a caterpillar is exposed to can impact the color of the butterfly's wings. Some rabbits also develop black noses, tails, feet, and ears in response to cold temperatures.

Humans may also interfere with the reproduction of plants or animals by **selective breeding**. In selective breeding, organisms with desirable characteristics (such as watermelons with few seeds or dogs with high intelligence) are bred intentionally to produce offspring with the same characteristics.

Practice Question

20. The process of organisms with advantageous traits surviving more often and producing more offspring than organisms without these advantageous traits describes which basic mechanism of evolution?

   A. gene flow
   B. genetic drift
   C. mutation
   D. natural selection

Organisms and the Environment

Groups of organisms of the same species living in the same geographic area are called **populations**. These organisms compete with each other for resources and mates and display characteristic patterns in growth related to their interactions with the environment. For example, many populations exhibit a **carrying capacity**, which is the highest number of individuals the resources in a given environment can support. Populations that outgrow their carrying capacity are likely to experience increased death rates until the population reaches a stable level again.

Helpful Hint

The five levels of ecology, from smallest to largest (organisms, populations, communities, ecosystems, biosphere), can be remembered using the phrase, "Old People Catch Easy Breaks."

Populations of different species living together in the same geographic region are called **communities**. Within a community many different interactions among species occur. **Predators** consume **prey** for food, and some species are in **competition** for the same limited pool of resources. Two species may also have a **parasitic** relationship in which one organism benefits to the detriment of the other, such as ticks feeding off a dog. Organisms may also be involved in **symbiosis**, or a close relationship between two very different organisms. They may also engage in **mutualism**, which benefits both organisms, or **commensalism**, where only one organism benefits but leaves the other unharmed.

Consider This

What would happen if all of the decomposers disappeared from an ecosystem?

One way of looking at populations is via the lens of a **niche**, or the specific role an organism or species has in the community. The niche is often influenced by various conditions, such as the presence or absence of competitors.

The collection of biotic (living) and abiotic (nonliving) features in a geographic area is called an **ecosystem**. For example, in a forest, the ecosystem consists of all the organisms (animals, plants, fungi, bacteria, etc.) in addition to the soil, groundwater, rocks, and other abiotic features. Ecosystems are constantly developing and changing through a process called **ecological succession.** There are two types of ecological succession: primary and secondary. **Primary succession** describes the development and changes that occur during colonization of a new habitat such as newly exposed rock.

Secondary succession describes changes to previously colonized habitats that have been disrupted by events such as forest fires.

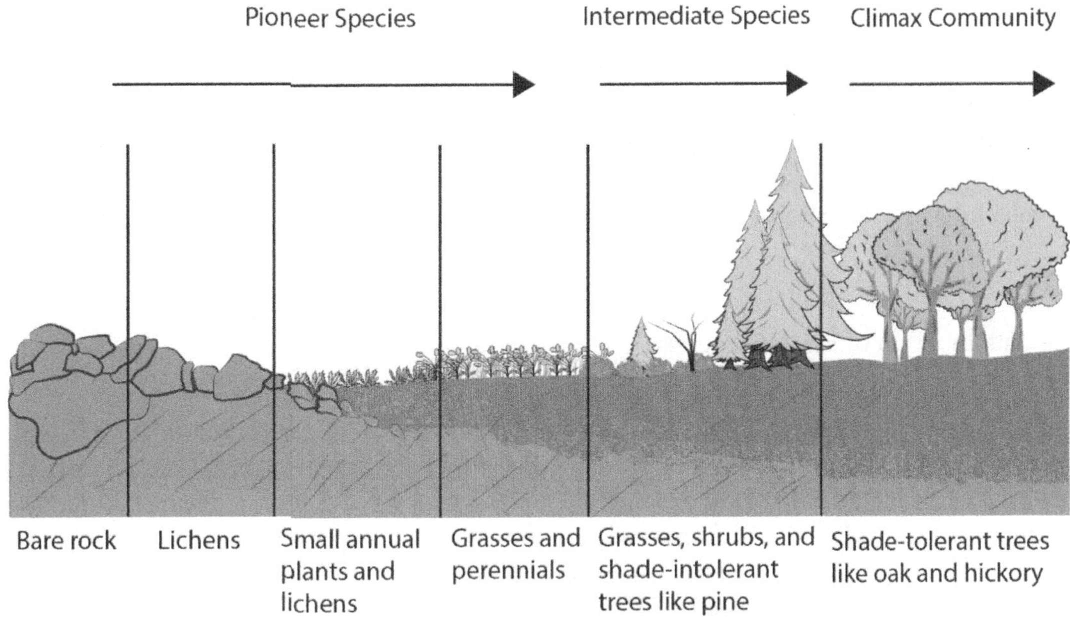

Figure 4.23. Ecological Succession

Many factors impact the size and growth of an ecosystem. Availability of basic needs like water, food, shelter, and adequate space may decrease or increase the number of organisms in an ecosystem. An increase or decrease in these resources may be the result of natural forces such as a drought or fire or human-causes such as loss of habitat due to residential development. Factors like disease or weather may also have a large impact an ecosystem. A sudden freeze might kill many plants, or an outbreak of disease may decimate an entire animal species in an ecosystem.

Living organisms must also change based on their environment. These changes may take the form of **adaptations** or **accommodations,** also known as acclimations. Adaptations are permanent changes in the chemical or physical make-up of the organism to cope with change. Acclimation or accommodations are temporary adjustments that organisms make when the environment changes. For example, a human in a cold environment may put on a coat, or a fish that is placed in an aquarium may be forced to adjust its diet.

The way organisms behave or react to their environments can be classified as an **internal stimuli** (something that causes the organism to react from within, such as hunger or thirst) or an **external stimuli** (something that causes the organism to react from the environment, such as a species taking cover under a tree in a rainstorm).

The behavior of organisms, whether from internal or external forces, may also modify the ecosystem itself. They may build structures like nests, burrows, or dams. Primary consumers without enough space may overgraze a field or prairie. Small woodland creatures may help new trees and plants grow by spreading seeds.

Sometimes, ecosystems lose their balance when new species enter and begin to dominate. These **invasive species** often get out of control because the organism that eats that species is not present in the ecosystem. In other cases, a species that is well-suited to the balance in one environment may cause destruction in another. For example, the nutria, a large rodent-like aquatic creature common in parts of East Texas, destroys wetlands and marshes.

Practice Question

21. The kudzu vine is able to grow in soil with a very low nitrogen content; as a result, it grows higher and thicker than other plants in an area, reducing the sunlight available. Which statement best describes this situation?
    A. The kudzu is reacting to external stimuli.
    B. The kudzu is involved in primary succession.
    C. The kudzu is an invasive species.
    D. The kudzu is a parasite.

Earth Systems

Structure and Function of Earth Systems

The outermost layer of Earth is called the **crust**, a very thin and broken surface layer. Beneath the crust is the **mantle**, a dense layer of rock. The mantle has an upper layer that is cooler and more rigid, and a deep mantle that is hotter and more liquid. Under the mantle is the **core**, which also includes two parts: a liquid outer core and an inner core composed of solid iron. Scientists believe the inner core spins at a rate slightly different from the rest of the planet, which creates Earth's magnetic field.

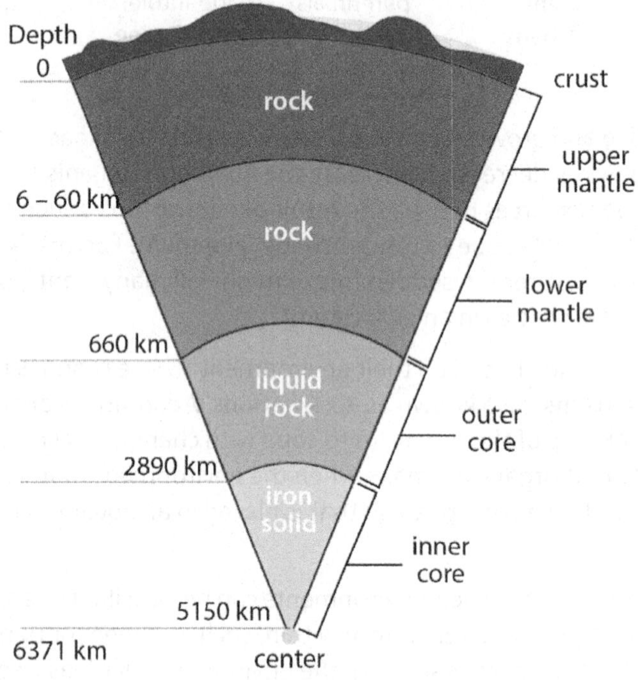

Figure 4.24. Layers of the Earth

The crust and upper layer of the mantle make up the **lithosphere**, the planet's surface layer. Under the lithosphere is a hot, semisolid part of the mantle called the **asthenosphere**. The lithosphere includes **tectonic plates**, which are the broken pieces of Earth's solid outer crust. The tectonic plates float on top of the more liquid asthenosphere that flows very slowly beneath them.

Earth's surface is divided into seven large land masses called **continents**, which are often separated by oceans. Scientists believe that over 200 million years ago the continents were joined together in one giant landmass called Pangaea. Due to **continental drift**, the slow movement of the tectonic plates, the continents gradually shifted to their current positions, and are still moving.

Earth's surface includes many bodies of water that together form the **hydrosphere; the study of water on Earth is called hydrology**. The hydrosphere is distinct but interconnected with other Earth systems. The largest bodies in the hydrosphere are salt water **oceans**. There are five oceans: the Arctic, Atlantic, Indian, Pacific, and Southern. Together, the oceans account for 71 percent of Earth's surface and 97 percent of Earth's water.

Oceans are subject to **tides,** cyclic rising and falling water levels at shorelines, which are the result of the gravitational pull of the moon and sun. **Currents** are movements of the ocean water caused by differences in salt content or temperature and winds. **Waves** carry energy through the water and are caused by wind blowing across the surface of the ocean. Tides shape coastal topography as they cause erosion, which may create new landforms like platforms or notches.

Other bodies of water include **lakes**, usually fresh water, and **seas**, mainly saltwater. Rain that falls on the land flows into **rivers** and **streams, which** are moving bodies of water that flow into lakes, seas, and oceans. The areas where rivers and streams meet saltwater are called **estuaries**. Estuaries often contain brackish water, or the mix between salt and fresh water; estuaries often boast ecosystems full of unique organisms specially adapted to this salinity.

When all the rain that falls on a given area of land flows into a single body of water, that land area is called a **watershed** or **drainage basin**. The earth also contains **groundwater**, or water that is stored underground in rock formations called **aquifers**. Groundwater is key to the exchange of water between the land and subsurface. Water from the surface moves into the subsurface and fills aquifers. The water stored in these aquifers eventually makes its way back to the surface.

Much of Earth's water is stored as ice. The North and South Poles are usually covered in large sheets of ice called **polar ice**. **Glaciers** are large masses of ice and snow that move. Over long periods of time, they scour Earth's surface, creating features such as lakes and valleys. Large chunks of ice that break off from glaciers are called **icebergs**.

Many geologic features and events are located along the boundaries where Earth's tectonic plates meet. There are three types of plate boundaries: divergent, convergent, and transform. A **divergent plate boundary** occurs when tectonic plates are moving away from one another and can form new ridges or ocean basins. A **convergent plate boundary** is where two tectonic plates collide and one plate is pushed upward on top of the other forming mountains, or one is pushed downward forming a trench. A **transform plate boundary** is formed when plates move in opposite directions along a boundary.

Plate tectonics theory explains the creation of landforms as plates move. The theory is supported by evidence such as the fact that earthquakes, volcanoes, and mountains typically occur at the boundaries of moving plates. Mid-ocean ridges caused by seafloor spreading, where magma that rises to the earth's surface in and causes tectonic plates to move away, is also commonly cited evidence for this theory.

Earthquakes happen along plate boundaries as the tectonic plates crash into each other or scrape together when they move and cause violent shaking of the ground. Volcanoes, which are vents in the earth's crust that allow molten rock to reach the surface, frequently occur along the edges of tectonic plates. However, they can also occur at hotspots located far from plate boundaries. There are three types of volcanoes: composite, shield, and cinder cone. A **composite volcano**, or stratovolcano, is cone-shaped, with steep sides, and is made of layers of solid lava, ash, and rock. A **shield volcano** is more dome-shaped, with gently sloping sides, and is made mostly of fluid lava flows. A **cinder cone volcano** is a small, steep hill formed by ash and debris surrounding a single lava vent and often has a crater at the top.

Plate tectonics influences organisms in many ways. Shifting plates can cause land to be uplifted or to sink, which can lead to rising sea levels. This can change ecosystems and organisms that rely on them. Volcanoes can release sulfates and ash into the air, causing problems for organisms in the vicinity.

Earthquakes move sediment on both land and seafloor, which can bury organisms or the plants upon which they feed.

Earthquakes can also be highly dangerous to human populations. Soil type, geology, fault location, and earthquake **magnitude** can all impact the severity of the impact on humans. The magnitude of an earthquake is measured on an instrument called a seismometer. An earthquake with a magnitude of less than 2.5 is minor and usually not even felt, while a magnitude 7.0 or greater earthquake is generally a major event.

Though most earthquakes are natural occurrences, human-induced earthquakes such as mining, wastewater disposal, or reservoir impounding have been proven to cause quakes. Thus, one way to prevent earthquakes is to limit these activities. Natural earthquakes cannot be prevented but people can prepare for them by examining fault maps, building structures to withstand most earthquakes, and creating a family or community earthquake response plan.

Practice Question

22. Where do volcanoes often form?
    A. near oceans
    B. near plate boundaries
    C. far from urban areas
    D. atop of aquifers

Cycles of Earth Systems

A **mineral** is a naturally occurring, solid, inorganic substance with a crystalline structure. There are several properties that help identify a mineral, including color, luster, hardness, and density. Examples of minerals include talc, diamonds, and topaz. Minerals form in various ways. Some form after magma or lava cools; some form in water and are what remains when the water evaporates.

Although a **rock** is also a naturally occurring solid, it can be either organic or inorganic and is composed of one or more minerals. Rocks are classified based on how they were formed. The three types of rocks are igneous, sedimentary, and metamorphic. **Igneous rocks** are the result of tectonic processes that bring **magma**, or melted rock, to the earth's surface; they can form either above or below the surface. **Sedimentary rocks** are formed when rock fragments are compacted as a result of weathering and erosion. Lastly, **metamorphic rocks** form when extreme temperature and pressure change the structure of preexisting rocks.

> **Helpful Hint**
>
> Luster describes how light reflects off the surface of a mineral. Terms to describe luster include dull, metallic, pearly, and waxy.

The rock cycle describes how rocks form and break down. Typically, the cooling and solidification of magma as it rises to the surface creates igneous rocks. These rocks are then subject to **weathering,** the mechanical and/or chemical processes by which rocks break down. During **erosion,** the resulting sediment is deposited in a new location. This **deposition** creates new sedimentary rocks. As new layers are added, rocks and minerals are forced closer to the earth's core where they are subject to heat and pressure, resulting in metamorphic rock. Eventually, they will reach their melting point and return to magma, starting the cycle over again. This process takes place over hundreds of thousands or even millions of years.

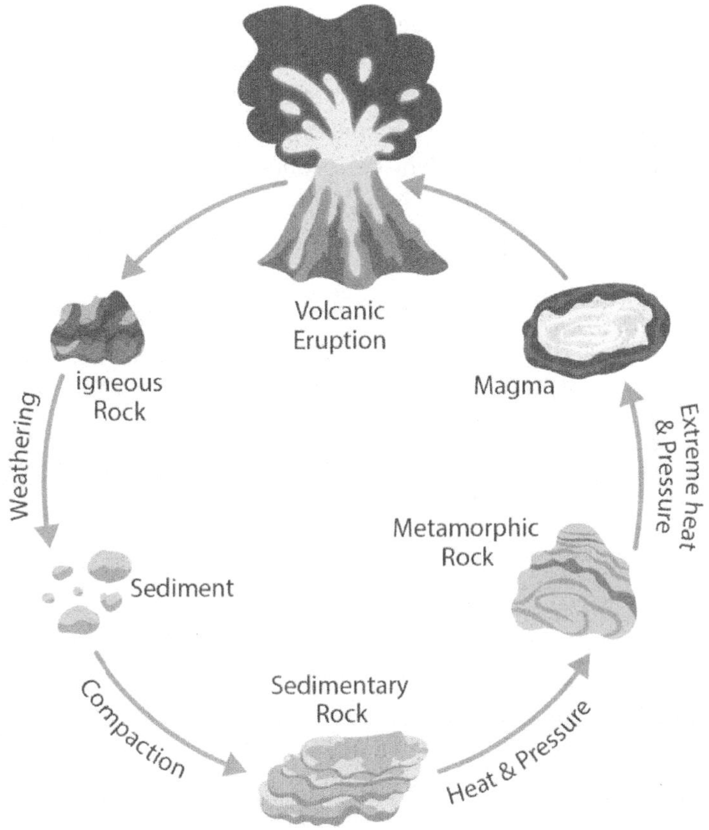

Figure 4.25. The Rock Cycle

Ecosystems contain resources that life within it relies on such as water, soil, and temperatures conducive to survival of the organisms that live there. One crucial part of any ecosystem and of all life on Earth is carbon. Plants take carbon from their environment; this carbon is found and moved between plants, the soil, the ocean, and the atmosphere in what is known as the **carbon cycle**. Carbon is often referred to as the foundation for all life because of its central role in photosynthesis and its presence in DNA.

Carbon is not the only element that is cycled; nitrogen also goes through a repeated cycle that flows through plants, animals, bacteria, soil, water, and the atmosphere. In the nitrogen cycle, nitrogen from the atmosphere is changed into ammonia in the process of **nitrogen fixation**. This may involve lightning, which breaks apart the nitrogen or bacteria. After fixation is **nitrification**, where ammonia is changed into nitrate by soil bacteria. Plants then take this nitrogen from the soil and pass it on to consumers who eat them and the other consumers who eat those organisms via **assimilation**. After animals and plants die, the nitrogen in their bodies goes back to the soil. Fungi and bacteria convert the nitrogen back into ammonia in what is known as **ammonification**. Special bacteria then turn nitrogen compounds back into nitrogen gas, which is then returned back to the atmosphere in **denitrification**.

> **Helpful Hint**
>
> Between each layer is a boundary where conditions change. This boundary takes the first part of the name of the lower layer followed by the suffix –pause. For example, the boundary between the troposphere and stratosphere is called the tropopause.

The **water cycle** is the circulation of water throughout the earth's surface, atmosphere, and hydrosphere. Water on the earth's surface **evaporates,** or changes from a liquid to a gas, and becomes water vapor. Water vapor in the air then comes together to form **clouds**. When it cools, this water vapor condenses into a liquid and falls from the sky as **precipitation,** which includes rain, sleet, snow, and hail. Precipitation replenishes groundwater and the water found in features such as lakes and rivers, starting the cycle over again.

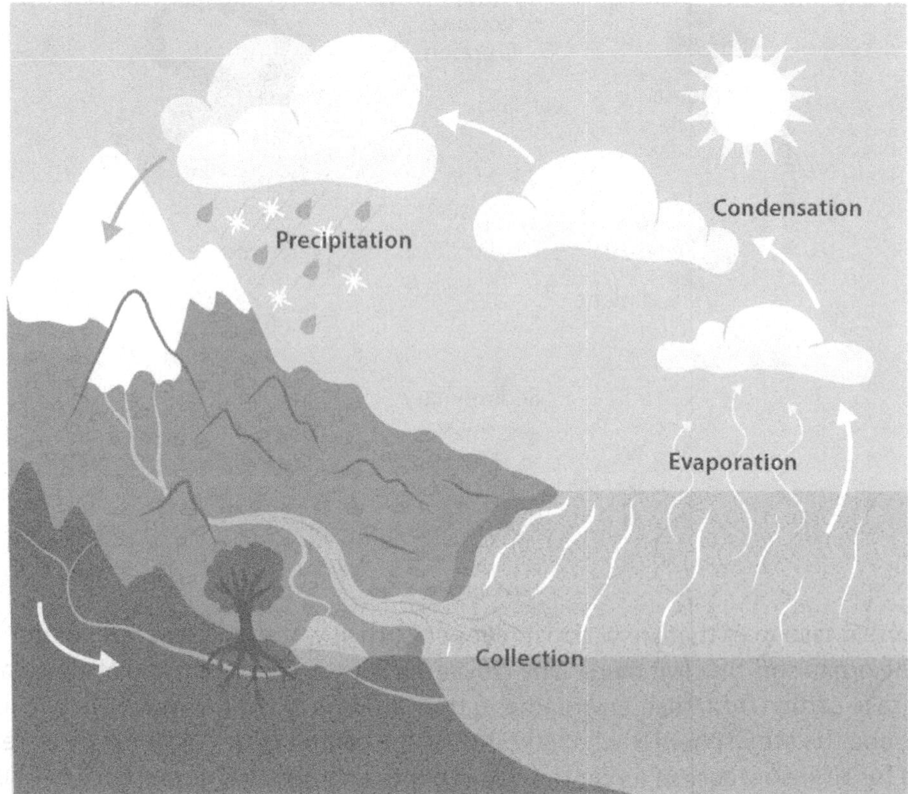

Figure 4.26. The Water Cycle

Which most of these cycles of Earth's systems are natural, human activity can alter these systems. Dams and irrigation systems built by humans can alter the water cycle. Land clearing for agriculture or other human activities can accelerate erosion and impact the rock cycle. Burning fossil fuels releases carbon dioxide into the atmosphere and impacts the carbon cycle. Human-made fertilizers increase the amount of nitrogen in the soil artificially and can impact the nitrogen cycle. It is important for humans to consider the broader impacts of their actions on Earth's systems and processes.

Practice Question

23. Which process within the rock cycle create metamorphic rock?
    A. compaction
    B. heat and pressure
    C. crystallization
    D. weathering

Weather and Climate

Above the surface of Earth is the mass of gases called the **atmosphere**. The **atmosphere** is the air or blanket of gases that surrounds Earth. It contains about 78% nitrogen, 21% oxygen, and trace amounts of other elements. The atmosphere includes the troposphere, which is closest to Earth, followed by the stratosphere, mesosphere, and thermosphere. The outermost layer of the atmosphere is the exosphere, which extends to 6,200 miles above Earth's surface. Generally, temperature in the atmosphere decreases with altitude. The **ozone layer**, which captures harmful radiation from the sun, is located in the stratosphere.

Humidity (the amount of water vapor in the air) and temperature are two major atmospheric conditions that determine the **weather** (the day-to-day changes in atmospheric conditions). Humidity is measured with a **hygrometer**, and temperature is measured with a **thermometer**. Air pressure, or **atmospheric pressure**, is another part of weather, defined as the force exerted on the earth by the air above it. A **baromete**r is used to measure air pressure. When altitude increases, atmospheric pressure drops, and the amount of oxygen in the air decreases, which is why some mountain climbers use oxygen tanks on their climbs. This pressure is also related to weather conditions. Low pressure brings rain and wind, while high pressure brings fair weather. **Wind speed** and direction are another part of weather; they are measured by an **anemometer**.

The study of weather is known as **meteorology**. A warm front occurs when warm air moves over and replaces a cold air mass, causing the air at the front to feel warmer and more humid. A cold front occurs when cold air moves under and replaces a warm air mass, causing a drop in temperature.

Sometimes, weather turns violent. Tropical cyclones, or **hurricanes**, originate over warm ocean water. Hurricanes have destructive winds of 74 miles per hour or more and create large storm surges, when sea water rises above the normal tide level, that can cause extensive damage along coastlines. Hurricanes, typhoons, and cyclones are all the same type of storm; they just have different names based on where the storm is located. Hurricanes originate in the Atlantic or Eastern Pacific Ocean, typhoons in the Western Pacific Ocean, and cyclones in the Indian Ocean. **Tornadoes** occur when unstable warm and cold air masses collide and a rotation is created by fast-moving winds.

Severe weather has many unfortunate impacts, but technological tools can help predict such events to that people can prepare. **Doppler radar**, which detects wind strength and direction and precipitation, is one such tool. Satellite imagery also helps meteorologists study and predict weather. **Weather balloons** or radiosondes, collect data from the upper stratosphere. **Automated surface-observing systems** (ASOS) also monitor and track weather on Earth's surface. Computers help analyze all this data and make predictions based on mathematical models.

Another important tool for monitoring weather is the **weather map**. Weather maps contain special symbols that show weather in an area. Typically, **low pressure**, which brings rains, clouds, and warm air, will be denoted with an *L*; **high pressure**, which brings cool air and sunshine, will be indicated with an *H*. Warm fronts are usually shown by red lines with half-moons and cold fronts by blue lines with triangles. Stationary fronts, which may lead to long-lasting rain, are the combination of warm and cold fronts. Temperatures and rain or snow may also be featured on a weather map. Temperatures are usually shown by a color code that matches a scale, and rain and snow are usually represented by dashed or dotted lines.

The long-term weather conditions in a geographic location are called **climate**. A **climate zone** is a large area that experiences similar average temperature and precipitation. The three major climate zones, based on temperature, are the polar, temperate, and tropical zones. Each climate zone is divided into sub-climates that have unique characteristics. The tropical climate zone (warm temperatures) can be divided into tropical wet, tropical wet and dry, semiarid, and arid. The temperate climate zones (moderate temperatures) include Mediterranean, humid subtropical, marine West Coast, humid continental, and subarctic. The polar climate zones (cold temperatures) include tundra, highlands, nonpermanent ice, and ice cap. Polar climates are cold and experience prolonged, dark winters due to the tilt of Earth's axis.

Because of Earth's rotation, the **Coriolis effect** impacts weather and climate. This effect means that wind is deflected to the right in the Northern Hemisphere and to the left in the Southern Hemisphere. It causes certain global wind patterns such as the westerlies, easterlies, and trade winds.

The surface of the earth (lithosphere) may also impact weather. For example, mountains may prevent the movement of air; further, the air is cooler in mountains because of its thin quality and inability to absorb heat. Changes in vegetation may also impact weather or climate. Surfaces that are covered by trees and plants absorb radiation from the sun; those with ice or snow reflect this radiation instead. Oceans also retain and store solar heat energy and add moisture to the air.

Did You Know?

Texas is a large state with a whopping eight different sub-climate zones.

The transfer of heat energy also causes weather patterns. Radiation from the sun is the primary driver of climate, but this heat is unequally distributed, causing rising and falling air that leads to wind flow across Earth's surface. Further, during the day, heat energy comes to the earth's surface, but at night, this heat energy is lost. This inflow and outflow of solar energy is sometimes referred to as **Earth's energy budget**.

Practice Question

24. In examining a weather map, a student notices an area marked *H*. What does this indicate?
    A. The area is more humid than the surrounding area.
    B. The area has higher pressure than the surrounding area and is likely to bring rain.
    C. The area has higher pressure than the surrounding area and is likely to bring sunshine.
    D. The area is hotter than the surrounding area.

Solar Systems and the Universe

Astronomy is the study of space. Earth is just one of a group of **planets** that orbit the **sun**, which is the star at the center of Earth's **solar system**. The planets in the solar system are Mercury, Venus, Earth, Mars, Jupiter, Saturn, Uranus, and Neptune. Every planet, except Mercury and Venus, has **moons**, or naturally occurring satellites that orbit a planet. The solar system also includes **asteroids** and **comets**, small rocky or icy objects that orbit the sun. Many of these are clustered in the asteroid belt, which is located between the orbits of Mars and Jupiter.

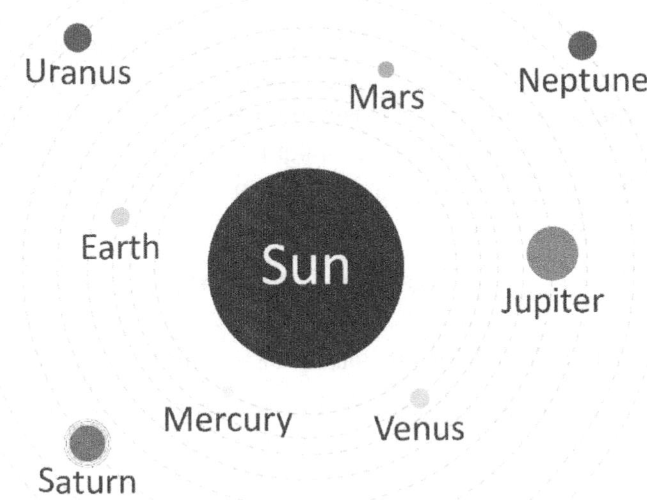

Figure 4.27. Solar System

Helpful Hint

The phrase *My Very Educated Mother Just Served Us Noodles* can help students remember the order of the planets: Mercury, Venus, Earth, Mars, Jupiter, Saturn, Uranus, Neptune.

The solar system is a small part of a bigger star system called a galaxy. (The galaxy that is home to Earth is called the Milky Way.) **Galaxies** consist of gas, dust, and hundreds of billions of **stars,** which are hot balls of plasma and gases, all held together by gravity. The universe has many types of stars, including supergiants, giants, white dwarfs, and neutron stars.

The closer and larger the star is to Earth, the brighter it will appear. Generally, stars are only apparent in the night sky when a person's portion of the earth is pointed away from the sun. This phenomenon also makes the Moon visible at night and the sun visible during the day. Additionally, because the Earth orbits the sun through the course of a year, we see different parts of the night sky during different seasons. This is why different constellations are visible at different times.

Stars form in nebulas, which are large clouds of dust and gas. When very large stars collapse, they create **black holes,** which have a gravitational force so strong that even light cannot escape.

Earth, the moon, and the sun interact in a number of ways that impact the planet. The moon reflects sunlight in what are called **lunar phases**. A **new moon** occurs when sunlight is hitting the far side of the moon that cannot be seen from Earth; sunlight reflecting off the near side we can see is called a **full moon**. During the other lunar phases (waxing crescent, first quarter, waxing gibbous, waning gibbous, third quarter, and waning crescent), people on Earth see only a portion of the moon.

When the positions of Earth, moon, and sun align, **eclipses** occur. A **lunar eclipse** occurs when Earth lines up between the moon and the sun: the moon moves into the shadow of Earth and appears dark in color. A **solar eclipse** occurs when the moon lines up between Earth and the sun: the moon covers the sun, blocking sunlight.

The cycle of day and night and the seasonal cycle are determined by Earth's motion around the sun. It takes approximately 365 days, or one year, for Earth to revolve around the sun. While Earth is revolving around the sun, it is also rotating on its axis, which takes approximately twenty-four hours, or one day. As the planet rotates, different areas alternately face toward the sun and away from the sun, creating night and day.

Earth's axis is not directly perpendicular to its orbit, meaning the planet is tilted. The seasons are caused by this tilt. When the Northern Hemisphere is tilted toward the sun, it receives more sunlight and experiences summer. At the same time that the Northern Hemisphere experiences summer, the Southern Hemisphere, which receives less direct sunlight, experiences winter. As Earth revolves, the Northern Hemisphere tilts away from the sun and moves into winter, while the Southern Hemisphere tilts toward the sun and moves into summer.

Practice Question

25. What term is used when the moon moves between Earth and the sun?
    A. aurora
    B. lunar eclipse
    C. black hole
    D. solar eclipse

Answer Key

1. A: Evolution is a scientific theory, which is a set of explanatory ideas substantiated by evidence through repeated experiments and observations.

2. B: Experimental variables, also known as independent variables, are the variables that are changed by the scientist.

3. B: A graduated cylinder measures volume.

4. C: Having students list two tasks that could be done with each type of simple machine assesses whether or not students understand the purpose of the simple machines in making tasks easier.

5. D: Acceleration describes the rate of change in velocity.

6. C: Combustion is a chemical reaction that produces carbon dioxide and water. Burning lamp oil (fuel) is combustion.

7. B: Gas is the state of matter in which atomic particles are most loosely packed, and the greatest amount of space exists among atoms.

8. D: A compressed spring is an example of elastic potential energy.

9. A: Conduction is the transfer of heat from the contact of a solid or liquid to another solid or liquid.

10. B: Wavelength is the length of each cycle of the wave, which can be found by measuring between crests.

11. C: The two charges are both negative, so they will repel each other and move apart.

12. D: Fossil fuels are a nonrenewable resource; they are depleted through use.

13. C: Primary consumers acquire energy by consuming plant matter.

14. B: *Species* is the principal taxonomic rank.

15. B: The nucleus is the organelle that carries the DNA of eukaryotic organisms.

16. C: A plant cell is enveloped by a cell wall, but animal cells do not possess cell walls.

17. B: Oxygen intake and carbon dioxide disposal are the primary functions of the respiratory system.

18. B: The tongue is the muscle that helps break apart food, mix it with saliva, and direct it toward the esophagus.

19. A: These insects help move pollen to aid in reproduction.

20. D: The mechanism of natural selection is rooted in the idea that there is variation in inherited traits among a population of organisms and that there is differential reproduction as a result.

21. C: The kudzu vine is native to Asia but has wreaked havoc as an invasive species in the United States.

22. B: Volcanoes often form near plate boundaries because they are vents in the earth.

23. B: Heat and pressure change the composition of sedimentary rock to create metamorphic rock.

24. C: *H* stands for high pressure on a weather map and is likely to result in sunshine.

25. D: When the moon moves between Earth and the sun, a solar eclipse occurs, blocking sunlight from the planet.

5 Fine Arts, Health, and Physical Education

Visual Arts

The **visual arts** include drawing, painting, sculpting, photography, and many other types of artistic expression, such as fiber art, printmaking, or art with electronic media. While the tools and techniques used in these art forms can be very different, they all rely on the same foundational elements and principles.

A good understanding of the elements and principles of art is necessary for **visual arts literacy**, defined as "the ability to create and interpret visual art." Teachers should show children that artists use these elements and principles to make decisions when creating their own art, and that students should apply this knowledge to their own works.

Elements and Principles of Art

Art is created through the use of line, shape, form, value, texture, space, and color. Together, these are known as the **elements of art**.

Line in art is called a moving dot: it can control the viewer's eye, indicate form and movement, describe edges, and point out a light source in a drawing. Artists use different line qualities and contours to suggest form. To indicate value or a light source, artists use cross-hatching lines in varying degrees.

A closed contour is what creates **shape**, which is two-dimensional. A shape can create balance and affect the composition, establishing positive and negative spaces. Different types of shapes include regular or geometric, and organic or freeform. When students understand the basics of shapes, they can create complex forms by combining simple organic and regular shapes.

Form is like shape except it is three-dimensional. Creating form requires an understanding of how light reflects upon an object, or its **value**. Teachers should help students understand where the highlight, the reflected light, the mid-tone, the core shadow, and the cast shadows are in order to create an illusion of form. Having students create a value scale and understand how it applies to objects they see is also helpful. Value also helps to create **texture**, which refers to how an object would feel if someone were to touch it. Students can develop their sense of texture through exposure to a wide variety of objects and by understanding how light reflects off rough, smooth, matte, and shiny surfaces.

> **Helpful Hint**
>
> To engage children, have them create and critique art that relates to topics that are familiar to them, such as family, friends, sports, holidays, and animals.

Creating an illusion of **space** can help students in creating an artwork on a two-dimensional surface. Students should experiment with different techniques such as overlapping shapes, shape placement, sizes of shapes, and perspective to see how objects can appear closer or farther away.

The color wheel is primarily used to teach students the theories of **color**:

- **Primary colors** (red, yellow, and blue) cannot be made using other colors.
- **Secondary colors** are made by mixing primary colors (yellow + blue = green).
- **Tertiary colors** are made by mixing one primary color with half the saturation of a second primary color (blue + 1/2 red = violet).

> **Did You Know?**
>
> Blue is the most common "favorite color" in the world.

The color wheel also shows **complementary colors**, which appear opposite each other on the wheel. When paired together, complementary colors offer a stark contrast that is pleasing to the eye.

The **principles of art** refer to the composition of the elements of art within a piece of work. These principles include

- balance,
- unity,
- contrast,
- movement,
- emphasis,
- pattern, and
- proportion.

In order to create **balance** in an artwork, colors, forms, shapes, or textures need to be combined in harmony. Harmony also helps to create **unity** in a piece of work by creating a sense of wholeness.

Artists generate **contrast** by using various elements of art, like shapes, form, colors, or lines, to capture the viewer's attention and draw it toward a certain part of the work. **Movement** guides the viewer's eye through a composition, usually to highlight areas of contrast or emphasis. Repeating occurrences of a design element, such as shapes, forms, or textures in an art piece, are called **patterns**. Finally, **proportion** describes the way the sizes of objects appear. For example, objects that are farther away appear smaller and have less detail than objects that are closer.

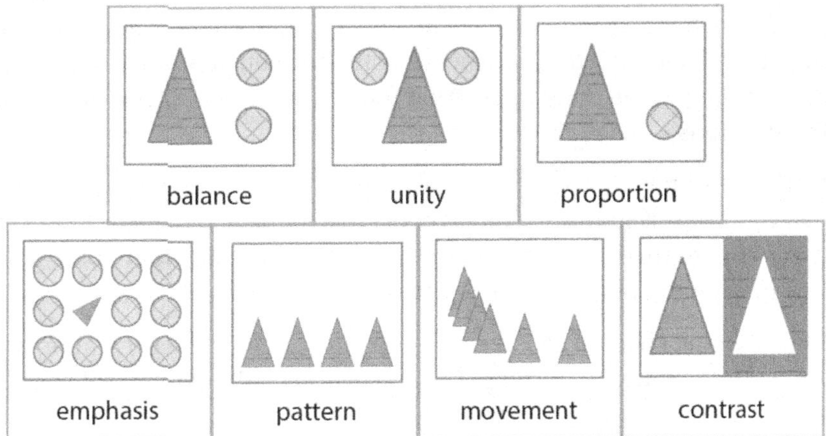

Figure 5.1. Principles of Art

Another principle of art is **rhythm**, which refers to the movement in a piece that helps the observer's eye to travel. Rhythm is often described as alternating, flowing, progressive, random, or regular depending on the way the artist creates movement. For example, Van Gogh's *Starry Night* could be said to have a flowing rhythm as the circular elements create a feeling of movement.

Classrooms will typically contain different **media** or materials used to create the piece. Common media include the following:

- drawing: pencils (graphite), charcoal, pen, colored pencil, pastels, crayons, markers
- painting: acrylic, watercolor, oil, gouache, tempera, encaustic
- printmaking: stencils, stamps, tiles, ink, carving tools
- ceramics: clay, paint, kiln
- fiber: yarn, fabric, bamboo, willow, reeds
- electronic: Adobe Illustrator, GIMP, Inkscape, Krita

Practice Questions

1. A first-grade teacher wants to show students how complementary colors can be used when painting. Which of the following colors could be used as an example. Select ALL that apply.

   A. blue and orange
   B. red and blue
   C. purple and yellow
   D. red and pink

2. A kindergarten teacher has his students paint a picture that includes animals of different sizes. What principle of art is the teacher introducing to his students?

   A. pattern
   B. movement
   C. proportion
   D. unity

Teaching Art

Art teachers should consider student capabilities and developmental appropriateness as they design activities.

Children in prekindergarten may not yet be able to use certain tools, and a kindergartner is probably not ready for an in-depth discussion of the elements of art. However, even the youngest children can mix different colors of paint or play-dough to create new colors, learning about the color wheel. Students can learn about proportion, balance, and unity by creating their own scenes—pictures of their homes, families, pets, and possessions.

While younger students are generally less self-critical than older students, students of any age might be dissatisfied with their creations. If students express concern over having made a "mistake," the teacher can help them find ways to improve their artwork to their liking. This **problem-solving** might include adding elements, covering up existing elements, or changing the focus of the piece.

Visual arts education for young children can be cross-curricular. For instance, creating animals is a great way to **integrate** science into students' learning. Children learning about different shapes, such as triangles, quadrilaterals, and circles in math can apply their skills as those shapes can transform into the ears of a cat, the eyes of an owl, or the body of a dog. Older students can likely draw shapes; younger students with less-developed motor skills can experiment with making collages from cut-out pieces of construction paper, or they can even cut the paper themselves, depending on ability. Students learning about specific animals or plants can create them in the art room or develop informational posters displaying facts they have learned.

As students learn the basics of art, they will likely begin by breaking objects down into basic shapes and adding to them, a process known as **construction**. As they progress, they will use different media and create more elaborate and complex pieces.

Students should be exposed to multiple artistic styles, including those outside of the Western tradition. Art styles from Africa (e.g., pottery or textiles) or styles from Asia (e.g., woodblock prints or screens) could easily be completed on a small, age-appropriate scale.

For any project, students should discuss the purpose and use of a piece. For example, some African art, such as masks, is created for important cultural events or ceremonies. In the classroom, some art will be made primarily for aesthetic enjoyment, but other art, like a knitted scarf or a clay mug, will be created with a use in mind.

As students examine art made by others, they should be given instruction in the process of perception. While art appreciation is first about observation, it also involves integrating what is observed with prior knowledge. Students can be prompted to do this with questions like "What have you seen like this?" or "How is this like/unlike __?" Students should also realize that art appreciation is both a cognitive and an imaginative process, though it differs from person to person. To practice thinking about art in this way, students might engage in a freewrite, a journaling exercise, or a group or pair discussion about a piece of art.

Think About It

What types of multisensory arts experiences would be good sites for a field trip?

Art may also be **multisensory**, or appealing to more than one sense. While visual art most often appeals to the sense of sight, fiber or ceramic arts may also appeal to the sense of touch. Electronic art may include sound effects to appeal to hearing.

Practice Question

3. Kimba, a third-grader, becomes frustrated when she cannot copy a drawing of a bird she sees in a book. How should the art teacher respond?

   A. encourage Kimba to consider the purpose behind the bird drawing
   B. guide Kimba in identifying and mimicking the line and proportion of the bird
   C. encourage Kimba to paint an impressionistic interpretation of the bird instead
   D. guide Kimba on how to produce the individual shapes within the bird

Music

Most music curriculum focuses on listening and responding to music others have created as well as learning the basic elements of music and participating in the creation of simple music.

> **Did You Know?**
>
> Music instruction can be incorporated into many areas of childhood education. For example, preschool children learn with music when they first begin to memorize the English alphabet. Eventually, they will figure out that the song they use for the ABCs is the same as "Twinkle, Twinkle, Little Star."

Teaching music is important to help students enhance skills that they can transfer to other subject areas. Students who are exposed to music education tend to do better in language development (such as reading tests) than students who are not. Music education helps to develop the left side of the brain, which is critical to processing language. Furthermore, research has shown links between spatial intelligence and music studies, which means that students learn to visualize different elements working together and to recognize patterns, corresponding with the problem-solving skills needed in mathematics.

It is also important for music teachers to help students make connections between music and other disciplines and the real world. To do so, teachers must vary lessons. For example, listening to music can teach students about different musical genres and expose students to musical history. Music can also be connected to literature: students may learn to conduct research for a music-related project and in the process draw upon knowledge learned in different classes. Lessons on music culture may also tie into social studies.

To make real-world connections, teachers can help students recognize the impact of music in their everyday lives. Teachers can expose students to music from popular culture, such as commercials, movies, and television shows. Teachers can also help students appreciate music in authentic performances via field trips to concerts and performances.

The goal of music education should be the development of basic **music literacy**—writing, reading, and playing music. These goals will often be simplified in elementary classrooms as developmentally appropriate.

Aspects of Music

The broadest aspect of music is **form**, or the overall structure or outline of a piece. Form may include parts like intro, chorus, verse, bridge, and outro. Form also refers to repetitions or contrasts in certain patterns.

Pitch in a musical piece can be high or low, and **scales** are created by organizing patterns of pitches with **intervals** or distances in between two notes. Having students listen to many pitches and practice the different types of scales offers them a more practical approach to learning. Usually teachers start by using a number system to help younger students learn the notes, then move onto *solfeggio* (*do, re, me, fa, so, la, ti, do*) as they progress.

The accuracy of pitch is called **intonation**. Teaching intonation usually involves students reproducing the pitch they hear, either with their voice or with an instrument. When students advance to playing musical instruments, they will learn how to **tune** or adjust the pitch of that instrument to match a reference point before they begin to play.

Rhythm governs time in music. It is a specific pattern in time—a tempo—much like a steady pulse. This pattern is organized into **meter**, which arranges these pulses into groups. These groups then can be further divided into two, three, or four smaller units. To help students develop an understanding of rhythm, teachers begin by using familiar songs or nursery rhymes and have the students clap along. The students feel and count the beats in a song, learning to distinguish when notes should start and end. Then students can understand the rhythmic patterns of the song. Students can progress to recognizing rhythm just by listening to a song, or creating one by playing a musical instrument.

Melody describes the size of the intervals of the contour (rising or falling)—the tune of a song. As such, it is the main focus of a song and a way for a composer to communicate with his or her audience. **Harmony** relies on the melody and is the use of pitches or chords simultaneously: the notes that support melodies. To develop the concept of melody, teachers should have students listen to and consider how a melody rises and falls, or have them compare melodic contours. These actions create melodic personality. Teachers can also introduce the names and sounds of notes first to help children develop a sense of melody.

The **timbre,** or **tone,** is the musical characteristic that distinguishes between different instruments. When discussing timbre, expose students to as many sounds as possible. Students can describe the sound by naming the instrument (once they have learned it) or by using different terms. Words can include *brassy, bright, raspy, shrill, dark,* or *buzzy*. As students become more advanced, they can group different timbres according to instrument type, whether it be woodwind, brass, string, or percussion. Help students understand that the timbre does not change even if the same instrument is played at different pitches and volumes.

Dynamics refers to the loud or soft parts of a piece of music. They can change gradually or suddenly (crescendo or decrescendo) or have a large dynamic range if there are very soft and incredibly loud passages in the composition.

Combining melody, rhythm, and harmony creates the **texture** in a composition, as these all determine the overall quality of the sound. Texture includes the number of layers and how these relate to one another. There are different types of musical textures. **Monophonic** is made of one voice or line with no accompaniment. **Polyphonic** includes many musical voices that imitate or counter one another, including the rhythm or melody. An example of this would be songs popular during the European Renaissance or the baroque period. **Homophonic** consists of a main melody that is accompanied by harmonic chords. An example of this would be a singer with a piano accompaniment. The texture would be considered homo-rhythmic if all parts have a similar rhythm. Teachers should introduce one texture at a time so students have a chance to listen to and develop their understanding of how to accurately identify textures. Students can also perform different songs to get a feel for how different textures work.

Students should understand that music **notation** is a method of writing down music so that anyone can play it. It helps composers create music by clearly indicating how they want it to sound; anyone who can read music will be able to play or sing the song accurately. Teachers can start helping students understand music notation by presenting it and breaking down the different elements of the modern system of notation.

The main system of notation currently used is writing musical notes on a **stave,** which is composed of a five-line **staff** with four spaces between. The music is read from left to right, and there is usually a clef in front of a staff of written music. This helps to show exactly which notes are played, such as the treble clef or the bass clef. The location of the note on the staff indicates the pitch; and sharps or flats may be in front of the note. Notes that are very high or low can be placed on ledger lines above or below the stave.

The key signature is found after the clef, which indicates which sharps or flats will be used regularly. The time signature, placed afterwards, divides the music into regular groupings of beats using bars or measures. There are usually words that show the tempo, or the speed of music. There may also be dynamic marks to indicate how loud or soft to play the music at certain points. Common dynamic marks are described in Table 5.1.

Table 5.1. Common Dynamic Marks in Music

Symbol	Meaning
pp (pianissimo)	very soft
p (piano)	soft
mp (mezzo piano)	moderately soft
mf (mezzo forte)	slightly loud
f (forte)	loud
ff (fortissimo)	very loud
fp (fortepiano)	loud then soft
sfz (sforzando)	sudden accent
cresc. or < (crescendo)	gradually louder
dim. or > (diminuendo)	gradually softer

Practice Question

4. A second-grade teacher asks her students to listen to several musical instruments and identify which instruments produce similar sounds. Which aspect of music are the students learning?

A. timbre
B. loudness
C. pitch
D. rhythm

Teaching Music

When teaching music, it is important for teachers not only to select and use manipulatives but also to choose developmentally appropriate materials in the classroom. Children in preschool and early elementary school will not have developed the fine muscle control that would allow them to play more complicated instruments. Teachers should select items such as Orff instruments and other simple percussion instruments; these are easier to play and help students practice pitch and rhythm while they develop their motor skills.

Later, recorders are usually introduced when students are able to physically play them. This simple instrument helps students develop necessary skills for more advanced instruments, such as breathing techniques. Teachers can also use the recorder to teach a wide variety of songs and ensembles using one instrument.

When choosing appropriate music for students to sing, teachers should initially select simple pieces, such as nursery rhymes. As students progress through the elementary grades, more complex pieces should be selected. These musical works should include the elements of music students need to master at that grade level, as well as a wide variety of musical styles. Choosing different contemporary and historical pieces of music helps students to compare music based on the historical context and the intent of the composer.

Teachers also must consider the different aspects of a musical piece when selecting one that is developmentally appropriate. Vocal demands should be considered to ensure that a song is not too difficult for students to master. Rather than singing scale patterns, students find it easier to sing skips, particularly descending skips. Teachers should also consider the level of rhythm patterns and the tempo. It is more difficult for younger students to sing fast songs and to move the voice quickly with difficult rhythm patterns; complex rhythm patterns are appropriate only for older classes. Furthermore, most elementary school students struggle with singing multiple notes on one syllable and repeating the same note, so this should be avoided. A song's length should also be considered. The younger the student, the shorter the song. Generally speaking, songs with four beats of four phrases are usually appropriate.

> **Helpful Hint**
>
> Call-and-response songs are popular and appropriate for early childhood choruses.

Selecting songs with lots of repetition is beneficial for younger students. Teachers should look for songs that have repeating melodies, rhythms, and words. However, younger children frequently struggle with songs that have repeating words but changing melodies. When reviewing lyrics, teachers must choose texts that are relevant to student experiences and that use appropriate vocabulary.

At the elementary level, students may learn to play simple instruments as they develop their understanding of the elements of music. At the early elementary level (up to the third grade), students may not have developed the fine muscle control that would allow them to play more complicated instruments. Teachers should select items such as Orff instruments and other simple percussion instruments; these are easier to play and help students visualize pitch and rhythm while they develop their motor skills.

Later, recorders are introduced when students are able to physically play them. This simple instrument helps students develop the skills necessary for more advanced instruments, such as breathing techniques; students also gain experience reading sheet music, which is simplified with recorders as they need only concern themselves with one tone. Teachers can also use the recorder to teach a wide variety of songs and ensembles using one instrument.

In the upper elementary grades, students should have developed the motor skills to play the types of instruments used in band programs. Since students should have learned how to read basic sheet music and utilize the breathing techniques appropriate for woodwind instruments, teachers can help students advance by applying their knowledge of other elements of music, such as harmony and timbre.

More advanced students and music classes might participate in **arrangements**, or reworking a musical piece from the original, often for voice, other instruments, or a combination. For example, a choir might sing in **canon** where different singers are at different parts of the song at once. More advanced arrangements might include some students playing instruments while others sing.

Beyond creating music, students should also learn about diverse musical styles by watching or listening to performances and evaluating and critiquing them. Older students should be encouraged to go beyond simply stating whether they did or did not like a performance and should be encouraged to consider the elements of music (e.g., pitch and rhythm) in their descriptions.

Students should also be exposed to the music and heritage of the United States and Texas. This might include songs like "America the Beautiful," "The Star-Spangled Banner," "Texas, Our Texas," (the state song), "Cotton-Eyed Joe," "Home on the Range," and Gene Autry's "Deep in the Heart of Texas." Country music (including Western swing), Tejano music, and mariachi music also have deep roots in Texas.

Exploring music-related careers should also be part of instruction. Beyond performing, students might consider working as a studio or session musician, sound or recording engineer, arranger, composer, or music teacher.

Practice Question

5. Which of the following instruments is most appropriate to use in a kindergarten classroom?
   A. recorder
   B. xylophone
   C. flute
   D. double bass

Health

Lessons on health help students learn about wellness and unhealthy behaviors. They gain the ability to explain the importance of physical activity, what contributes to disease in the body, and how nutrition, stress and substance abuse affect their growth and well-being.

> **Helpful Hint**
>
> Planting a garden is a great hands-on activity for teaching early elementary students about food and nutrition.

In the earliest grades, students might first be introduced to health concepts by study of the **five senses**: sight, smell, hearing, touch, and taste.

Teaching students about the physical systems in the body is another great introduction to the theories of health and gives them the fundamental knowledge to better understand **nutrition** and fitness. In the early elementary grades, the focus should be on the elements of a **balanced diet**. Looking at the healthy eating plate and identifying nutrients helps students learn how their choices affect their bodies.

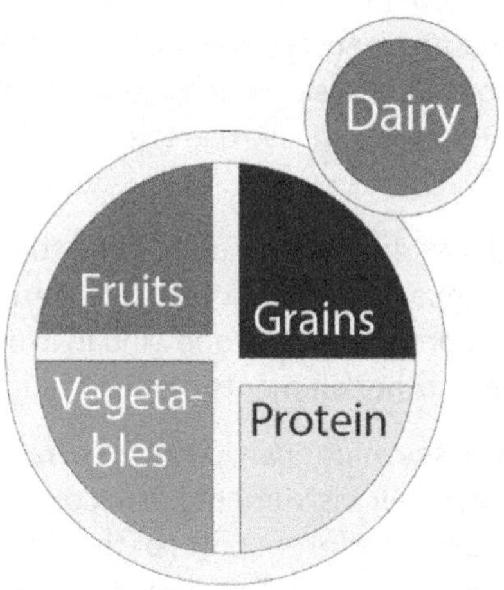

Figure 5.2. MyPlate Food Guide

Students should learn about the basic nutrients:

- water
- carbohydrates
- protein
- fat
- vitamins
- minerals

They should be able to identify foods and drinks that contain various nutrients and foods and drinks to avoid for their lack of nutrient content.

Nutrition is tied to growth and body composition, but it is not the only factor. **Body type,** which is inherited and largely unchangeable, will also impact the shape of the human body. Similarly, human **growth spurts,** or sudden increases in height and weight, are also a natural part of growing up.

> **Did You Know?**
>
> Some research suggests that the type of food we routinely eat is what we crave. This means people who are healthy eaters may actually crave healthy foods.

Disease prevention and control is another part of human health. Students should learn about practical ways to prevent disease, such as practicing **personal hygiene,** identifying symptoms of diseases and how they affect the body, and how to prevent diseases.

There are four main disease types: infectious diseases, hereditary diseases, physiological diseases, and deficiency diseases. **Infectious diseases,** which are transmitted to a person from the environment, can be limited through vaccines, handwashing, avoiding close contact with sick people, and basic practices such as not coughing or sneezing on others; however, they cannot always be avoided entirely. **Hereditary diseases** come from a genetic predisposition and cannot be prevented; they can only be treated. **Deficiency diseases** arise when an individual does not have enough of something (like a vitamin or mineral), and **physiological diseases** are those that are not from the other categories (e.g., cancer, stroke, and heart disease).

The causes of many diseases are known, while the causes of others are unknown. Nevertheless, students should understand that a healthy lifestyle, including proper nutrition and exercise, reduces the risk for many diseases. Because some degree of illness is unavoidable, students will need to know the warning signs. Among other symptoms, these include fever, nausea, rash, diarrhea, lethargy, and pain.

Most diseases can be treated by health care professionals, like doctors and nurses. Seeing a doctor annually can help prevent future diseases.

Students may also learn about injury prevention and safety. Topics would include basic safety rules, reacting to emergencies, and understanding strategies for self-protection.

Depending on students' ages and grade-levels, TEKS instruction in bodily changes during the transition from childhood to adolescence may be required. Physical changes, like development of breasts in young women and new hair growth, are natural and normal parts of growing up. Adolescence also brings emotional changes, such as mood swings or an increased awareness and sensitivity to peers.

As part of this, students also need to understand that their **mental health** contributes to social and emotional well-being. Students should learn different strategies and skills to improve their relationships with others and themselves. Topics can include

- friends and family,
- effective communication,
- appropriate emotional responses, and
- assuming responsibility for their own decisions.

Activities on goal-setting (both short- and long-term), problem-solving, and decision-making are all highly appropriate for health classrooms. As students make decisions and solve problems, tolerance, respect, empathy, and self-control should be central.

Older students will learn about stress, its effects on the body, and identifying resources and constructive ways of dealing with it. Instruction in bullying prevention will also be part of the health curriculum. Most schools have policies on bullying, which should be part of this discussion. Cyberbullying, or harassment of others online, should also be discussed, with particular emphasis on its negative effects and how one should respond if this occurs.

Learning about **substance abuse** helps older students understand the impact drugs can have on their lives. Lessons should help students understand how alcohol and other types of drugs (including some types of medications) affect the body when abused; students should learn about decision-making. More specifically, lessons can examine media, peer pressure, and other external factors (such as laws) that impact decision-making. Equally important are lessons on internal factors, such as addiction.

Substances that may be legal, like **tobacco** and **alcohol**, are also very harmful to young, growing bodies. Vaping, which has become more popular than smoking in some circles, is another health risk. While more studies of long-term effects are needed, most vapes contain highly-addictive nicotine as well as aerosol with harmful chemicals.

Herbal supplements are another newer trend and may be purchased without a prescription because they do not require Food and Drug Administration (FDA) approval. These may still be harmful if not used under a doctor's supervision, and students should be warned of the potential side effects of such products.

Overall health is also impacted by mental processes. Of particular importance is the development of a positive **self-image**, or the way a person perceives him or herself. A healthy mind and body can contribute to a positive self-image, but students must be prompted to recognize that no body is perfect.

Some people develop an **unhealthy body image**, or the belief that their bodies are not good enough. This may lead to serious impacts, such as inappropriate weight loss methods like crash diets or fasting. It may also lead to eating disorders. Common eating disorders include the following:

- anorexia—when a person severely limits food intake
- bulimia—a disease in which a person binge-eats and then purges, usually by vomiting or taking laxatives
- binge-eating—the consumption of very large amounts of food in a short period of time
- avoidant or restrictive food intake—when food intake is limited to a very small number of foods

Symptoms of eating disorders include sudden weight loss, a restrictive diet, avoiding eating with others, over-exercising, depression, and tooth enamel wear from vomiting.

In today's world, young people may feel extreme pressure to look or act a certain way. Mass media, particularly social media, often portrays unrealistic human bodies. Peers may also reinforce unrealistic expectations. For this reason, it is important for students to know where to find accurate health information. Sources like the Food and Drug Administration (FDA), Centers for Disease Control (CDC), and reputable doctors are good information sources. Blogs, social media, and YouTube are generally not good sources of health information.

Practice Question

6. Which of the following foods is highest in vitamin C?
   A. bread
   B. eggs
   C. grapefruit
   D. yogurt

Physical Education

Basic Movement Skills

Learning movement fundamentals requires movement concepts and fundamental motor skills. Teaching **movement concepts** helps children increase their understanding of body awareness and management.

The objective of **body awareness** is for students to explore the body's capabilities. In early childhood, students learn to identify and understand the locations of different body parts. They also practice the many shapes and positions they can form with their bodies. Teachers should be aware that development in children follows a **proximodistal** pattern, wherein development begins in the torso and moves outward. It also typically occurs in a **cephalocaudal** pattern, or from the top of the body downward.

Spatial awareness is understanding where the body can move. Teachers should provide ample opportunities for students to explore the spatial qualities of movement. Examples include self-space, general space, pathways, range, and the direction of movement. Students should not only recognize these examples, but also respect the space of others, travel through space in a purposeful manner, and adjust their range of movement depending on the task.

The goal in teaching the **qualities of movement** is for students to understand how balance affects movement and the qualities of static and dynamic balance. Teachers should also help students generate and modify force to accomplish assigned tasks as well as differentiate among speeds so they can move more quickly or slowly. As students progress through the elementary grades, teachers should encourage them to accomplish movements within a certain amount of time and space.

> **Helpful Hint**
>
> Developing body management skills means integrating agility, coordination, balance, and flexibility to create effective movement.

Non-locomotor skills are movements that do not require moving through space. These include bending, stretching, twisting, turning, pushing, and pulling. Object **manipulation skills,** such as volleying, dribbling, punting, or striking a ball are also part of non-locomotor skills development. As students develop their movement skills, teachers should give children ample opportunities to explore them, as well as combine them with locomotor skills so these can be applied to all physical education activities.

Locomotor skills are the numerous ways the body can move through space. They include walking, skipping, running, jumping, sliding, galloping, and leaping. Students should be given ample time to practice skills repeatedly after observing a proper demonstration. Students' **rhythmic skills** or moving to a defined beat while skipping, for example, will also develop with time given sufficient practice.

When teaching students walking skills, teachers should demonstrate that each foot alternates and that there is always one foot touching the floor. Instruct students to point toes straight head, keep their eyes forward with their heads up, and with their weight transferred from the heel to the ball of the foot. Students can also practice walking at different speeds, on their toes, or with bent legs.

Students should also be instructed in **basic movement skills** beyond walking such as how to step with the opposite foot when throwing a ball or completing the kick when using the foot to move a ball. Teachers should be aware that **mature movement patterns,** or the ability to perform a movement skill smoothly and continuously, will take time. Students must master body **control,** or the ability to stabilize and balance the body in a variety of movements.

Sliding involves students moving sideways with a leading foot. Students should focus on keeping the weight on the balls of their feet, eyes focused on the direction of travel, with hips and shoulders pointing to the front. This **locomotor pattern** is commonly used in sports such as softball, basketball, and racquet sports. In the younger grades, the focus should be on introducing the basic movements so students develop proficiency in different sports as they get older.

As students begin to refine their movement skills, teachers should introduce **biomechanics** or the science behind human movement. Biomechanics is impacted by myriad forces including gravity, which makes the human body return to the ground after jumping, friction, which causes a bowling ball to slow down as it moves toward the pins, and other laws of motion (Chapter 4).

Practice Question

7. Which TWO activities would help a student develop rhythmic skills?

A. jumping rope
B. playing tag
C. dribbling
D. catching

Exercise Physiology

Health-related fitness includes the development of flexibility, cardiorespiratory endurance, muscular strength, and endurance. **Flexibility** refers to the body's range of motion of joints and can be developed through activities like stretching, yoga, and gymnastics. **Cardiorespiratory endurance** refers to the ongoing ability of the cardiorespiratory organs to get oxygen to the muscles during activity. This type of endurance is an important part of overall health; it is best developed through running, swimming, cycling, and other aerobic exercises. Exercises that promote cardiorespiratory endurance are referred to as **conditioning**.

> **Helpful Hint**
>
> Each class and grade level's fitness goal will be different, and modifications may be needed to match a lesson plan with the students' current fitness level.

Muscular strength involves the amount of weight a muscle can move or the amount of force it can produce. Weight training and bodyweight exercises such as push-ups and planks help build muscular strength. General **endurance** refers to the body's ability to sustain a certain physical activity over time, either strength or cardio. Typically endurance improves as physical fitness increases with time.

When designing lessons to promote fitness, teachers should keep in mind the **FITT** (frequency, intensity, time, type) **principle**. This acronym describes guidelines for a fitness plan, and it can be applied to the whole class or to individual students if necessary.

Frequency refers to how often students should exercise. For example, lifestyle exercises may be scheduled more often rather than endurance ones. The **intensity** of the activity describes how hard students need to work during each class. **Time** refers to how long students should participate in the activity. Students should participate in at least thirty to sixty minutes of age-appropriate physical activity daily, ten minutes of which should be moderate to vigorous activity. The **type** of activity describes the kinds of activities students practice or play. Teachers should create different lessons incorporating a wide variety of lifestyle and recreational activities, active aerobics, flexibility, sports activities, and strength and muscular endurance exercises.

Technology can easily be integrated into physical education as appropriate. Wearable fitness technology, from basic pedometers to advanced heartrate trackers, are one tool. Virtual reality fitness programs or other fitness games are another.

Any physical activity can improve **body composition,** or the percentage of various parts of the body, such as skin, muscle, bone, fat, and water. Most measurements of body composition determine the percentage of body fat a person has. Normal ranges vary by age and sex. Broader lifestyle changes, such as healthy eating, getting enough sleep, and prioritizing mental health, can also have a positive impact on body composition.

While improved body composition and **weight control** are benefits of physical fitness, they are certainly not the only ones. Fitness improves brain function and memory and reduces negative emotions like anxiety or depression. It also promotes healthy sleep patterns and increases energy while lowering blood pressure.

Physical activity also comes with risk, the largest of which is the potential for injury. These injuries are most commonly to the muscles (such as a pulled muscle or a strain) or to the skeletal system such as a broken bone. However, people with underlying health conditions may have other risks.

Teachers must consult with a school nurse or a health professional regarding the needs of students with health conditions like asthma or diabetes; teachers should also be aware of the effects of medication students take and the symptoms of health emergencies. Lessons and physical activities may need to be modified to accommodate students' needs.

During physical education lessons, **safety** for teachers and students must be taken into consideration. Teachers should check the area before any activity or game begins to ensure there are no dangerous objects or hazards. Participants should also understand a signal from the teacher indicates the beginning and end of play. A warm-up period before starting any activity will prevent injuries. For the sake of safety, teachers should also consider omitting skills that might put students in harm's way.

While most exercise or movement might take place in a physical education class, there is a growing movement to **integrate movement** across the content areas. This might involve activities, such as a four-corners debate where students move to various corners of the room to show their opinions on certain topics, or scavenger hunts where student groups move around the room or school to locate certain items.

Teachers will need to consider the various needs of students during any physical activity. Not only will students be at various levels of fitness and have various existing body compositions, but they may also have disabilities that require special modifications or accommodations. Modifications might include adjusting the duration of activities or using sports equipment more appropriate for students' needs; for example, students with limited upper body strength could use foam balls instead of heavier baseballs or softballs.

Sometimes, whole-group activities can be adapted to be more inclusive. This is known as **adaptive physical education**. Popular adaptive physical education (PE) games often use balloons instead of balls for games like dodgeball or basketball, but many other strategies are also appropriate and may be listed on a student's individualized education plan (IEP).

Additionally, students will enter physical education programs with a wide range of past experiences, so familiarity with common American sports or games should not be assumed. Students from diverse backgrounds can also share different sports or games with the class, but the PE lessons should also aim to include sports and games from many different cultures and parts of the world.

The goal of any physical education program should be to engage all students so that they can improve their physical fitness, learn to enjoy movement and recreation, and develop appropriate social skills. To help students obtain these goals, teachers should be aware of important social aspects related to physical education which may vary based on the individual student.

Research suggests that opportunities to engage in physical activity can improve student confidence and even reduce certain delinquent behaviors. Athletic participation has been proven to foster a positive **school climate**, sense of belonging, and school pride. For maximum benefits, physical education should always be **developmentally appropriate**, or tailored to the developmental level of participants.

In planning developmentally appropriate activities, teachers should consider the physical and social-emotional development of students with a focus on inclusion. Activities that require a high degree of existing physical fitness or specific training are likely to be least appropriate for younger students and may lead to frustration. Similarly, games or activities that students have already mastered may quickly become stale.

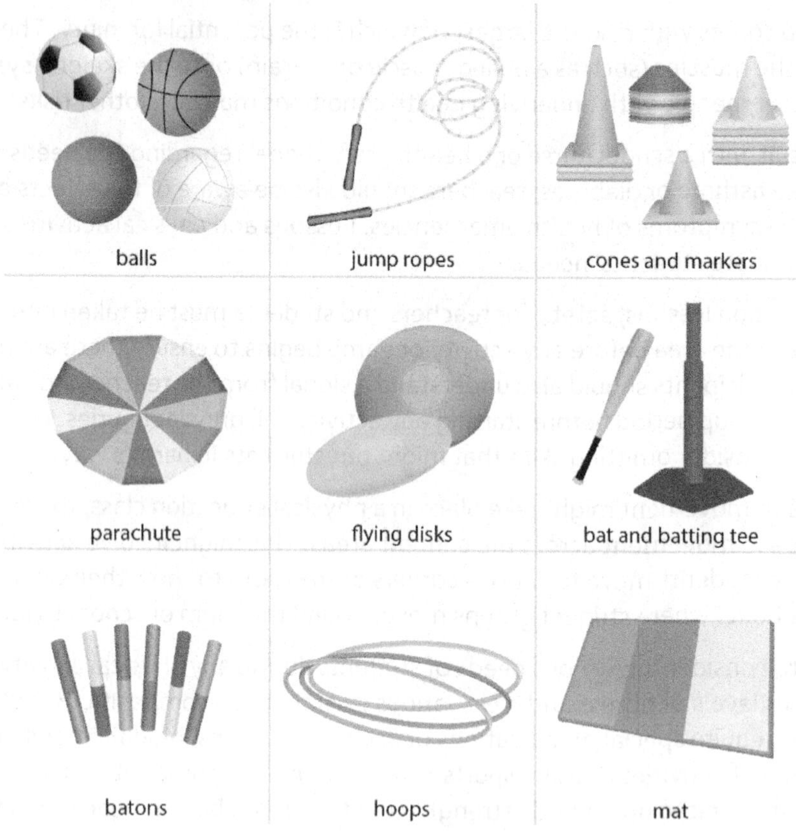

Figure 5.4. Physical Education Equipment

Activities will likely include both those that involve **competition**, such as group sports like kickball, soccer, or basketball, and those that do not, such as stretching and dance. While there is some debate about the role of competition in physical education programs, many experts believe that the most important factor is how innately competitive sports and activities are facilitated. Students must be taught **sportsmanship**, or the belief that sport is, above all, a social interaction that should be enjoyed for its own sake.

There are drawbacks to competition in sports, such as stress and possible loss of confidence. Students should be encouraged to focus on their own effort and their own improvement over time versus the outcome of a game reflected in a score. Further, **cooperation** should be emphasized over competition whenever possible. Opportunities for students to work together with each other toward a goal and improve communication and teamwork skills should be nurtured as part of group activities.

Practice Question

8. Which activity would **best** promote cardiorespiratory endurance?
   A. bowling
   B. stretching
   C. walking

D. push-ups

Theatre

Drama or **theatre** is an expression that tells a story to an audience through the actions and dialogue of characters, which are brought to life by actors who play the roles on stage. Dramatic works, called **plays,** are written in poetic or lyrical verse, or in regular prose. Along with the **dialogue** between the characters, authors rely on **stage directions** to describe the sets and to give instructions to the actors about what they are to do. Theatrical performances may be dramatic or humorous, but both involve a combination of **voice** along with **expressive movement** to aid in **characterization**, or the creation of a fictional character.

In some plays, actors perform long speeches in which the characters explain their thinking about philosophical ideas or social issues. These **monologues** can be directed toward another character. A monologue delivered as if nobody were listening is called a **soliloquy** (as in Shakespeare's famous "To be or not to be" soliloquy from *Hamlet*).

Sometimes characters have very unique attributes such as a manner of speech, dress, or a catchphrase. Such devices make characters memorable to readers and are known as **character tags**.

Dramatic interpretations may be based on **scripted dramas** or **improvised** or spontaneous scenes monologues. Younger students may participate in **guided drama experiences,** where a leader supports student actors via side-coaching and prompting without stopping the action of the play.

Students should also be given opportunities to learn about the **technical elements** of theatre, such as the integration of **lighting** and **sound** elements like music or sound effects. Props are another element and can be **representational materials**—actual objects like silk flowers or trees—or **non-representational materials**, which can be made into props via imagination, such as a beam in the cafeteria that becomes a magic tree. **Costumes** also help bring characters to life. Taken together, all the elements of theater (costumes, sound, lighting, and props) also help enhance the **mood** or overall impression of the performance as well as the **theme** or message it reflects.

Did You Know?

The Ancient Greeks were the first to put on theatrical performances, which date back to the 6th century BCE.

Materials for students to use to create their own props, scenery, puppets, and costumes should be part of the supplies of the theatre classroom. These supplies need not be elaborate and can be recycled materials like plastic bottles and cans (useful for sound effects), old boxes (useful for scenery), and scraps of fabric or discarded clothing (for costumes).

Students should also have opportunities to connect English language arts skills with theatre as they consider the plot, characterization, setting, character motivations, and dialogue in dramas they read and perform. As with music, dramatic interpretations from various cultures should be explored and analyzed for how they express important themes and ideas.

Practice Question

9. In an improvised duet scene, a student runs away from a desk in the classroom, screaming "Snake! Snake!" What does this exemplify?
   - A. guided drama experience
   - B. character tags
   - C. stage directions
   - D. non-representational materials

Answer Key

1. A, C: Blue, orange, purple, and yellow are directly opposite on the color wheel, so they are complementary colors.

2. C: Having students draw animals of different sizes introduces them to proportion, or the way the size of elements in an artwork relate to each other.

3. D: Construction, or producing individual shapes, is a fundamental skill that will help Kimba eventually draw the entire bird.

4. A: Also called tone, timbre is used to distinguish between instrumental sounds.

5. B: Orff instruments are appropriate for younger students as they develop the fine muscle control that will enable them to play more complex instruments later.

6. C: Citrus fruits like oranges and grapefruit contain vitamin C.

7. A, C: Both jumping rope and dribbling occur in a precise rhythm in order to be executed effectively.

8. C: Brisk walking for sustained periods can promote cardiorespiratory endurance and may be a good option for students with little existing cardiorespiratory endurance.

9. D: The student is using imagination to turn the desk into a snake.

Practice Test

Subtest I: English Language Arts and Reading

1. A kindergarten teacher wants to place emphasis on the onset in a word as a model to students. Which of the following words has the onset emphasized as revealed by italics?

   A. pl-*ate*
   B. *br*-oom
   C. in-*ter*-est
   D. fair-*y*

2. A teacher working with emergent readers asks, "What word am I trying to say, /p/ /i/ /n/?" and instructs students to say the word. Which strategy is the teacher using to build phoneme awareness?

   A. phoneme blending
   B. phoneme deletion
   C. phoneme segmentation
   D. phoneme substitution

3. A first-grade student is able to orally substitute the initial consonant /g/ for /b/ in the word *boat* to make the word *goat*. What concept is the student demonstrating?

   A. phonemic awareness
   B. letter-sound correspondence
   C. phonological awareness
   D. manipulation of onsets and rimes

4. Mark, a first-grade student, is sounding out the word *flat*. He sounds out the word *f-l-a-t*. Which of the following is true about Mark?

   A. He is lacking basic knowledge of the alphabetic principle.
   B. He needs more practice with affixes.
   C. He sounded out each letter individually versus the onset and rime.
   D. He has a strong knowledge of consonant blends.

5. A kindergarten teacher wants to begin phonics instruction with a letter that students will likely find easiest to master. Which of the following letters is BEST introduced first in this method of progressive phonics instruction?

   A. a
   B. g
   C. y
   D. m

6. What is the purpose of sight word instruction in an elementary classroom?

A. to help students learn letter-sound correspondences to improve accuracy
B. to help students manipulate sounds in words to improve auditory skills
C. to help students recognize words automatically to improve fluency
D. to help students use word parts to improve reading comprehension

7. A fifth-grade class is working on writing with a formal tone. What type of syntax would BEST contribute to a formal tone?

A. many simple sentences
B. many questions and answers
C. many highly complex and technical words
D. many complex and compound-complex sentences

8. A teacher plans to introduce the following new vocabulary to his third-grade class to help prepare students for an upcoming math lesson:
parallel, congruent, rhombus, trapezoid

Which of the following concepts is being developed in the students?

A. content-specific words
B. multiple-meaning words
C. different registers
D. figurative language

9. A sixth-grade teacher wants to introduce students to a citation style as part of a larger unit on research and writing. Which style would likely be easiest for students to master?

A. Chicago style
B. MLA style
C. APA style
D. Turabian style

10. A fourth-grade teacher wants to help students avoid plagiarism when using sources to help support arguments in an essay. During which phase of the research process should this be introduced?

A. locating materials
B. evaluating sources
C. note taking
D. writing

11. A teacher is working on a unit on forming the past tense of verbs with his second-grade class. Which of the following would be the most appropriate writing assignment to ensure sufficient practice with this skill?

A. writing a paragraph that compares and contrasts cars and trucks
B. writing a paragraph about what they did over the winter break
C. writing a description of their living room
D. writing a persuasive paragraph about their favorite color

12. One of a teacher's third-grade students writes the following sentences:

I gave my sister a gift. My sister asks if you know what it is.

Which of the following concepts does the teacher need to review with the student?

A. sentence fragments
B. shifts in pronoun person
C. lack of pronoun agreement
D. use of a pronoun without an antecedent

13. In a unit on morphology, a fourth-grade teacher wants to give students a list of the most common roots. Most of the English roots on the list will have originally come from which languages?

A. German or French
B. Spanish or French
C. Latin or Greek
D. Arabic or Phoenician

14. A third-grade teacher wants to model the process of metacognition during reading as a precursor to fix-up strategies. Which question would she most likely use?

A. What genre is this?
B. How are the characters developed?
C. Do I understand this paragraph?
D. Where can I learn more about this topic?

15. Mr. Hawks wants to give his first grade students a summative sight word assessment. Which of the following is the BEST way to conduct this assessment?

A. direct the students to write the sight words from memory
B. ask students to read from a sight word list while he circles the words they know
C. have students sound out each sight word as he presents it to them
D. encourage students to clap out the beat as they repeat each word after him
A. Incorrect. This activity would not aid Mr. Hawks in knowing which sight words they can read from memory, only those that they can write and spell.

16. Hannah is four and in Mr. Lawrence's prekindergarten class. Mr. Lawrence is having a conference with Hannah's mother, who has expressed concern that Hannah frequently misspells words that she uses to label pictures she draws. Which of the following is the advice Mr. Lawrence should give Hannah's mother?

A. have Hannah focus on a few target spelling words each week until she begins to label her pictures correctly
B. not to worry since Hannah is in the invented spelling phase, which is a natural part of literacy development
C. not to worry since Hannah is receiving lots of targeted phonics practice in school but to have Hannah go back and correct these pictures
D. have Hannah focus on learning new vocabulary each day as this will help with her overall spelling development

Questions 17 – 18 refer to the poem below from *A Child's Garden of Verses* by Robert Louis Stevenson.

"The Moon"

The moon has a face like the clock in the hall;

She shines on thieves on the garden wall;

On streets and fields and harbor quays,

And birdies asleep in the forks of the trees.

The squalling cat and the squeaking mouse,

The howling dog by the door of the house,

The bat that lies in bed at noon,

All love to be out by the light of the moon.

But all of the things that belong to the day

Cuddle to sleep to be out of her way;

And flowers and children close their eyes

Till up in the morning the sun shall rise.

17. This poem could be used by a fifth-grade teacher to illustrate which concepts?

A. omniscient point of view and internal rhyme
B. assonance and enjambment
C. alliteration and onomatopoeia
D. simile and rhyme scheme

18. How could the teacher help students understand that the word *quays* is pronounced using /ē/ as opposed to /ā/?

A. asking students what rhymes with *fields*
B. asking students what rhymes with *trees*
C. asking students to use roots and affixes
D. asking students to use syllable patterns

19. A fifth grade student is giving a speech on school start times. The following quote is included in his presentation:

> Elementary school should start at 9 a.m. instead of 7:30 a.m. because children do their best thinking when they get enough sleep and have time to eat a healthy breakfast.

Which of the following is the BEST paraphrase of the speaker's message?

A. Later school start times are better for learning because children get more rest and eat properly.
B. School should start at 9 a.m. instead of 7:30 a.m. because children do their best thinking when they get enough sleep and have time to eat a healthy breakfast.
C. Elementary school should start earlier than it does now.
D. Many students are too tired during the school day to concentrate on learning.

20. A second-grade teacher wants to improve students' decoding skills. Which of the following is an effective instructional strategy?

A. teaching character analysis
B. teaching word families
C. teaching active listening
D. teaching fact and opinion

21. Which of the following is true of qualitative measures of text complexity?

A. They are readability scores based on word frequency and sentence length.
B. They are analytical measurements determined by knowledge demands.
C. They are statistical measurements determined by computer algorithms.
D. They are determinations of reading level based on professional judgment.

Questions 22-24 refer to the following text excerpt from *Black Beauty* by Anna Sewell.

The name of the coachman was John Manly; he had a wife and one little child, and they lived in the coachman's cottage, very near the stables.

The next morning he took me into the yard and gave me a good grooming, and just as I was going into my box, with my coat soft and bright, the squire came in to look at me, and seemed pleased. "John," he said, "I meant to have tried the new horse this morning, but I have other business. You may as well take him around after breakfast; go by the common and the Highwood, and back by the watermill and the river; that will show his paces."

"I will, sir," said John. After breakfast he came and fitted me with a bridle. He was very particular in letting out and taking in the straps, to fit my head comfortably; then he brought a saddle, but it was not broad enough for my back; he saw it in a minute and went for another, which fitted nicely. He rode me first slowly, then a trot, then a canter, and when we were on the common he gave me a light touch with his whip, and we had a splendid gallop.

22. A sixth-grade teacher asks students to make an inference about John Manly. Which inference is BEST supported by evidence in the text?

A. John Manly does not like his job.
B. John Manly has respect for horses.
C. John Manly is a coachman with a family.
D. John Manly has bought a new horse.

23. This passage would be most appropriate for a lesson on which point of view?

A. first-person
B. second-person
C. third-person objective
D. third-person omniscient

24. The teacher wants to build students' proficiency with strategies to identify the meaning of unknown words. How can the reader BEST understand the meaning of the word *paces*?

A. The reader can find the definition of the word in the paragraph that follows.
B. The reader can figure out the word's meaning by noting its derivational morpheme.
C. The reader can use the connotation of the word to determine its meaning.
D. The reader can analyze the setting for a hint to the meaning of the word.

25. A fourth-grade student often drops the –*s* in verbs while speaking ("She go to the store.")This is consistent with the way her parents speak. How is this BEST described?

A. dialect
B. bridging
C. code switching
D. preproduction

26. A sixth-grade teacher is integrating grammar instruction with writing instruction. After a brief writing exercise, she asks students to trade papers with neighbors and underline any verbal phrases. Which group of words should be underlined in the following sentence?

Living with her Aunt Sally was something that always intrigued Marie because her aunt was such a fun and interesting lady.

A. Living with her Aunt Sally
B. that always intrigued Marie
C. because her aunt
D. such a fun and interesting lady

27. A fifth-grade teacher has the end-goal of students composing a quatrain poem. Which prewriting assignment would BEST prepare students for writing a quatrain poem?

A. an investigation of the word *quatrain*
B. listing pairs of rhyming words
C. a mini-lesson on syllabication
D. a concept map on the topic

28. Before reading a nonfiction text about sharks, a teacher's third-grade class completes a KWL chart. What is the teacher's purpose for using a KWL chart before reading?

A. to introduce students to new vocabulary
B. to prepare students to sequence text events
C. to activate student background knowledge
D. to provide an overview of the text information

29. Which assessment tool is most effective for tracking progress in oral reading fluency?

A. portfolios
B. reader's theater
C. running records
D. phonics screeners

30. A third-grade teacher wants students to practice evaluative comprehension after reading an argumentative essay on school uniforms. Which activity BEST meets this goal?

A. Students write a summary of the author's main claim and list the support the author provided.
B. Students identify and label all the facts and all the opinions in the essay.
C. Students get in pairs and discuss the strengths and weaknesses of the author's argument.
D. Students get in groups and write a list of questions they have after reading the essay.

31. A second-grade teacher is reading and responding to student writing. The teacher reads the following sentence written by a student:

> Lucy thought the first movie was better then the second one.

What feedback should the teacher give the student?

A. The verbs should be in the present tense.
B. *Then* indicates time, not comparison.
C. *One* is a dangling modifier.
D. The subject is misplaced.

32. A first-grade teacher is introducing open syllables. Which words would she use as examples? Select ALL that apply.

A. because
B. least
C. total
D. master
E. stir

33. Which types of words should students be able to spell correctly by the end of third grade?

A. most four-syllable words
B. most contractions
C. most cognates
D. most multi-meaning words

34. A fifth-grade teacher uses the Frayer Model in both reading and content-area instruction. How is this tool helpful to students?

A. by aiding in vocabulary acquisition
B. by teaching fix-up strategies
C. by annotating key details
D. by synthesizing information throughout the text

35. Before she shows a multimedia presentation to the class, a teacher tells her third-grade students about the importance of articulation. Why is articulation important?

A. to help the audience practice passive listening
B. to encourage the audience to believe the speaker
C. to enable the audience to understand the speaker
D. to encourage the audience to ask relevant questions

36. In which setting would a text at a student's frustration level be appropriate?

A. when students in need of enrichment are engaging in sustained silent reading
B. when students need ample practice to self-monitor and apply fix-up strategies
C. when students are given inferential and evaluative comprehension questions
D. when students are offered individualized scaffolding while reading

37. Which activity is most likely to promote graphomotor skills in first-grade students?

A. teaching stroke order
B. assessing letter sounds
C. freewriting exercises
D. peer feedback

38. Twice a year, all students in the first through fifth grades take a reading assessment. The results are used to identify students who might benefit from intervention. What is this process called?

A. norm-referenced assessment
B. universal screening
C. summative assessment
D. multi-tiered supports

39. Which TWO informal assessment methods BEST evaluate a student's prosody?

A. observation during written group work
B. portfolios that include oral reading recordings
C. reader's theater
D. choral reading
E. cloze exercises

40. In a unit on prereading strategies for third-grade students, which activity would most likely be included?

A. summarizing
B. setting a purpose
C. identifying point of view
D. annotating

41. A sixth-grade teacher wants to show students the difference between interrogative adverbs and interrogative pronouns. Which word pair should he use?

A. whose/who's
B. his/he's
C. then/than
D. they/their

42. As part of a unit on analyzing media messages, a fifth-grade teacher wants to include activities that allow students to identify potential bias. Which of the following activities would likely be most effective for this purpose?

A. comparing and contrasting podcasts and videos
B. making a video that includes two different logical fallacies
C. making a list of words that have negative connotations
D. identifying the nature of the organization that posted a video

43. A sixth-grade teacher assigns to each group of three students a multimedia research project to be presented orally to the class. Which of the following categories is important to include in the rubric for the assignment?

A. Multimedia elements have a purpose beyond decoration.
B. Multimedia elements are both formal and informal.
C. Multimedia elements contain at least one primary source.
D. Multimedia elements appeal to at least three of the five senses.

44. A first-grade teacher begins a unit on vowel teams with a "word of the day." Which word would be most appropriate?

A. insect
B. lost
C. pair
D. grill

45. During a conference with the parents of a second-grade student, a teacher wants to provide suggestions for practice at home to improve fluency. Which strategy should the teacher suggest?

A. timed silent reading
B. cloze exercises
C. reading aloud to a younger sibling
D. listening to an older sibling read aloud

Answer Key

1. B: The onset is the initial consonant sound, in this case the blend *br*.

2. A: The strategy of phoneme blending requires students to combine phonemes to make a word.

3. A: Phonemic awareness is an understanding of how phonemes can be orally manipulated to change the meanings of words.

4. C: He did not sound out the word into onset *fl* and rime *at*.

5. D: The letter *m* is most likely to be introduced first because it contains its sound in its name and only forms one sound in words.

6. C: Sight word instruction is designed to help students recognize high-frequency words automatically, without decoding, so they can read with fluency.

7. D: Syntax refers to the arrangement of words into sentences. The use of complex and sophisticated sentences would contribute to a formal tone.

8. A: The students need a basic knowledge of the meaning of these words before they can apply them in math class.

9. B: MLA style follows many typical conventions of capitalization and punctuation and is somewhat simpler than others.

10. C: Students need to take notes in summary or paraphrase form and not copy word for word from the text so as to avoid plagiarizing when they write the paper.

11. B: This paragraph would most logically be written in the past tense and would provide practice with forming the past tense.

12. B: The student has unnecessarily shifted to the second person, *you*, when there is no need for such a shift.

13. C: Most English roots are Greek or Latin.

14. C: Part of metacognition is assessing one's own understanding; this would be the first step before applying fix-up strategies.

15. B: This activity will help Mr. Hawks identify which students know which words and what words they need to practice more.

16. B: Her mother likely just needs the teacher's reassurance that this is a natural part of Hannah's development.

17. D: A simile is a comparison made using the words *like* or *as*, which is present in the first line of the poem. Further, the poem employs an AA/BB rhyme scheme.

18. B: The poet uses an *aabb* rhyme scheme throughout the poem, which lets the reader know that the word *quays* should be pronounced to rhyme with *trees*.

19. A: This sentence paraphrases the original sentence most accurately because it restates the speaker's main idea and reasoning in a revised and concise way.

20. B: Word family instruction is a decoding strategy that reinforces student understanding of word patterns.

21. B: Analysis of the knowledge demands required by a text is a qualitative measure of text complexity.

22. B: The way that John Manly takes care to make the horse comfortable before riding leads the reader to infer that he has respect for horses.

23. A: First-person point of view is written from the direct experience of one character—in this case, the horse—as indicated by the pronouns *I* and *my*.

24. A: The author provides a definition of the word *paces* in the next paragraph when he lists them as trot, canter, and gallop.

25. A: In some dialects, such as African American Vernacular English (AAVE), subjects and verbs do not always agree and singular subjects may take plural verbs.

26. A: "Living with her Aunt Sally" is a gerund phrase—the phrase acts as a noun and the subject of the sentence.

27. B: A quatrain poem contains one or more four-line stanzas with a rhyme scheme, so a list of rhyming words is a helpful prewriting assignment.

28. C: A KWL chart activates student background knowledge about a topic before reading.

29. C: Running records allow teachers to track oral reading progress over time.

30. C: Evaluative comprehension involves an analysis of the quality of the text and the reader's response to it.

31. B: The word *than,* which is a conjunction used to make comparisons, should be used instead of *then*, which is an adverb that means "at that time."

32. A, D: *Be-cause* has an open first syllable as does *to-tal*. Both syllables end in a vowel and make a long vowel sound.

33. B: By the end of third grade, students should be able to spell most contractions.

34. A: The Frayer Model is a four-part diagram that helps students break down a vocabulary word in terms of its definition, characteristics, examples and non-examples.

35. C: Articulation refers to the clarity of speech.

36. D: Frustration-level texts are very challenging and read at less than 90% accuracy; they are most appropriately used when individualized scaffolding while reading can be offered.

37. A: Graphomotor skills are handwriting skills, so teaching stroke order would help students develop these skills.

38. B: Universal screening is part of a multi-tiered systems of supports (MTSS)or response to intervention (RTI)framework and is the way through which students who may benefit from intervention are identified.

39. B, C: Prosody is expression while reading; assessments that include oral reading recordings and reader's theater involve students reading orally.

40. B: Setting a purpose for reading is a seminal prereading strategy.

41. A: *Whose* is an interrogative pronoun, and *who's* is an interrogative adverb.

42. D: The organization behind the media message will have a specific interest to promote, which can lead to bias.

43. A: Multimedia elements such as sound, pictures, or video must be aligned to the purpose of the presentation and not just serve as decoration.

44. C: The /ai/ in *pair* is a vowel team.

45. C: Reading aloud to a younger sibling is most likely to improve fluency and is achievable in a home environment.

Subtest II: Social Studies

1. Luther and Barbara wanted to start a business in the engineering field. They were trying to decide between hiring one staff member and using the leftover money to purchase new inventory, or hiring two staff members to increase their marketing reach. These choices would be an example of which concept?
   A. needs.
   B. scarcity.
   C. opportunity cost.
   D. supply and demand.

2. Which of the following would be the most useful for studying population patterns within the state of Texas over a period of time?
   A. a bar graph detailing population numbers over a period of 30 years
   B. a map with the number of people living in different parts of Texas in the year 2000
   C. a photograph showing how many people were at a state fair
   D. a bar graph detailing population percentages compared with other states

3. Which of the following is the responsibility of the Texas House of Representatives?
   A. approving laws
   B. making laws
   C. implementing laws
   D. enforcing laws

4. Asking citizens to be civil minded and independent and making the people as a whole sovereign is characteristic of which concept?
   A. republicanism
   B. democracy
   C. enumeration
   D. mercantilism

5. Which of the following cases established the concept of judicial review?
   A. *Plessy v. Ferguson*
   B. *Marbury v. Madison*
   C. *Engel v. Vitale*
   D. *Miranda v. Arizona*

6. Which of the following historical figures was a major architect of the US Constitution?
   A. Thomas Jefferson
   B. George Washington
   C. James Madison
   D. Patrick Henry

7. Which of the following protects against forced self-incrimination in the United States?
   A. separation of powers
   B. the First Amendment
   C. the Fifth Amendment
   D. popular sovereignty

8. Which of the following lessons helps students develop an understanding of a market economy or free enterprise system?

A. Students explore economic competition in their area and identify local business competitors.
B. Students explore making smart buying decisions by comparing prices of goods.
C. Students work together to decide what is necessary to rebuild a community.
D. Students explore how individuals generate income.

9. Students in fourth grade are studying a map of the Nile during ancient Egyptian times and answering questions related to landmarks and places. Which of the following social studies skills is being assessed in this exercise?

A. understanding spatial relationships
B. understanding historical timelines
C. using topographical maps
D. understanding physical geography

10. A worker at a strawberry farm uses some of her wages to purchase food for her family. This flow of money is part of what?

A. the circular flow model of economic exchanges
B. the business cycle
C. the monetary and fiscal policy
D. the economic growth

11. The Spanish mission frontier in Texas in the late eighteenth and early nineteenth centuries was located near which present-day city?

A. Alpine
B. San Antonio
C. Corpus Christi
D. Houston

12. Which of the following describes a relationship of economic interdependence?

A. a subsistence farmer growing all of the food his family needs
B. a desert country importing food from the US while exporting oil there
C. a local shopkeeper selling basic goods to his community
D. a family in which the members make all of their own clothing
A. Incorrect. A farmer growing his own food is independent.

13. A third-grade teacher wants to give his students an example of how they are both unified and diverse. Which example is most appropriate?

A. They all have diverse backgrounds, but they are unified in their identity as members of Mr. Fox's class.
B. They are of different races and ethnicities but share a common set of religious beliefs.
C. They are all either boys or girls, but all are US citizens.
D. They have some needs that are different, such as needing glasses or not, and some needs that are the same, such as needing extra help in math.

14. A teacher is searching online and in her curriculum resources for a map to introduce her second-grade class to the idea of a legend. Which map would be the BEST resource for her to use?

A. a political map of the United States showing each state in the same color
B. a topographical map showing different elevations
C. a map that uses corncob icons to denote the major corn-producing states in the United States
D. a map that includes latitude and longitude

15. A teacher wants to integrate math computation TEKS into a third-grade social studies lesson on charts. Which question will BEST accomplish this goal?

A. What is the difference between the populations of the city with the highest population and the city with the lowest population?
B. Why are the columns and rows on each part of the chart labeled in different colors?
C. After calculating the mean population of all the cities on the chart, is this country at risk of overpopulation?
D. What information (columns or rows) could be added to the chart to give additional information about each city?

16. A first-grade teacher wants to help her students begin to understand how to organize quantitative information in a chart. Which charting activity would be most appropriate?

A. having students classify all the books in the class library by genre and place them into a chart
B. asking each student whether he or she likes dogs, cats, horses, or fish best and then organizing this information into a pictorial chart on the board
C. asking students to conduct a school-wide survey on social media use patterns in households and having them create a digital infographic to present the results
D. showing students a variety of charts that reference various educational data such as the percentage of English language learners in the school

17. A second-grade teacher is trying to help her students learn how to use a compass rose. She gives each student a map of the United States with a compass rose. She asks students to follow a series of instructions. Which instruction might she include?

A. Point to the state that is directly above Texas.
B. Point to the capital of Florida.
C. Point to the only state that is an island.
D. Point to the state that is directly to the west of Utah.

18. A second-grade teacher asks her class the following question: "What kind of houses would people living in forests most likely build?" What is she trying to help students understand?

A. the relationship between conservation and resource depletion
B. economic interdependence
C. how people use natural resources
D. the way the global economy and the environment impact each other

19. What is one primary difference between most seas and lakes?

A. *Sea* is a European term, and *lake* is an American term.
B. Seas are surrounded by land on all sides, and lakes are not.
C. Seas are much smaller than lakes.
D. Seas are saltwater, and many lakes are freshwater.

20. The idea that the law, rather than government officials themselves, is what governs a nation is known as what?

A. justice
B. the rule of law
C. natural law
D. equality

21. How are Supreme Court justices selected?
    A. through an election
    B. nomination by the House with approval by the Senate
    C. appointment by the president
    D. nomination by the president with confirmation by the Senate

22. How could the Texas Constitution be amended?
    A. Two-thirds of the Texas Senate must vote in favor of the amendment.
    B. Two-thirds of both the Texas House and Senate must vote in favor of the amendment and then the governor must approve it.
    C. Two-thirds of both the Texas House and Senate must vote in favor of the amendment and then Texas voters must approve it by majority.
    D. Two-thirds of Texas voters must vote in favor of the amendment and then the Texas Senate must approve it with a two-thirds majority.

23. Which three content areas are part of the social studies TEKS for grades K – 8?
    A. geography, philosophy, media literacy
    B. history, historiography, graphic literacy
    C. economics, anthropology, sociology
    D. culture, social studies skills, economics

24. What drew immigrants to Mexican Texas? Select ALL that apply.
    A. desire for religious freedom
    B. no taxation for seven years
    C. wealth of natural resources like gold
    D. availability of jobs as migrant laborers
    E. land available at a low cost

25. Which battle of the Texas Revolution is celebrated with a holiday?
    A. Goliad
    B. the Alamo
    C. San Jacinto
    D. San Antonio

26. How did Texas become part of the United States?
    A. the Compromise of 1850
    B. the Treaty of Guadalupe Hidalgo
    C. annexation
    D. partition

27. Which Texas politician opposed secession from the United States?
    A. Sam Houston
    B. James Fannin
    C. Moses Austin
    D. Edward Clark

28. Which constitutional amendment recognized formerly enslaved persons as American citizens?
    A. the Thirteenth Amendment
    B. the Fourteenth Amendment
    C. the Fifteenth Amendment
    D. the Twelfth Amendment

29. Which American president was from Texas?
   A. Ronald Regan
   B. Teddy Roosevelt
   C. Lyndon Baines Johnson
   D. John F. Kennedy

30. How could a teacher BEST illustrate the concept of popular sovereignty?
   A. dividing the class into two distinct groups
   B. having the class vote on which activity to complete
   C. requiring the class to finish an activity within a set time frame
   D. asking the class to take turns using classroom materials

31. Which of the following are examples of cultural adaptation? Select ALL that apply.
   A. An American student watches cartoons made in Japan.
   B. An American student learns Spanish while living in Argentina.
   C. A European student reads books by American authors.
   D. A Japanese student studying in the United States learns to cook American food.
   E. A Guatemalan student shares traditional foods with her family

32. Which statement describes an economy at equilibrium?
   A. Supply and demand are equal.
   B. The GDP exceeds the national debt.
   C. Supply exceeds demand.
   D. The GDP and national debt are equal.

33. Which TWO industries are an important part of the Texas economy today?
   A. auto manufacturing
   B. technology
   C. coal
   D. oil
   E. gold mining

34. Which of the following is a responsibility of American citizenship?
   A. building roads
   B. paying taxes
   C. religious freedom
   D. limited government

35. What was a reasonable criticism of the Articles of Confederation?
   A. They encouraged unlimited government.
   B. They promoted mercantilism.
   C. They formed a weak federal government.
   D. They formed too many legislative bodies.

36. Which Texas industry is particularly vulnerable to boom and bust cycles?
   A. manufacturing
   B. service
   C. oil and gas
   D. agriculture and ranching

37. Which of the following is an example of the way that environment and geography affect human behavior?

A. cattle ranching in the plains and prairies of the United States
B. different religious rituals based on local custom and belief systems
C. diverse coming-of-age rituals
D. organizing territory into counties

38. A teacher has a class of four-year-old prekindergarten students. She ensures that each student throws his or her plastic lunch plate and cup away after lunch is over. What is the teacher instructing students?

A. global citizenship
B. self-regulation
C. conflict resolution
D. the norms of social behavior

39. Prior to European arrival, which Native American group lived in what is now Texas?

A. Iroquois
B. Anishinaabe
C. Navajo
D. Comanche

40. Which of the following describes an advantage of the Union during the Civil War?

A. fighting on home field territory
B. more manufacturing
C. more agriculture
D. fighting with superior leadership

Answer Key

1. C: Opportunity cost refers to the cost of the loss of one option when it is rejected for another (in this case, if Luther and Barbara choose to hire one staff member, they lose the marketing potential another employee would make possible, whereas if they choose to hire two, they lose the leftover money).

2. A: A bar graph that features the population over a number of years would help researchers analyze population patterns.

3. B: The legislative branch, including the House and Senate, make laws.

4. A: Republicanism also stresses natural rights as central values.

5. B: The *Marbury v. Madison* case established judicial review in 1803.

6. C: Madison not only advocated for the ratification of the Constitution; he had also helped to write the Federalist Papers.

7. C: This amendment allows people to abstain from giving testimony that may incriminate them.

8. A: Competition in business is an aspect of the market economy.

9. A: Introducing maps allows students to acquire an understanding of the world around them. They can use this knowledge to create their own maps.

10. A: The circular flow model of economic exchanges describes how money flows from producers (like the strawberry farmers)to workers and then back to producers.

11. B: Many of these missions near San Antonio are still standing.

12. B: Some desert countries cannot grow their own food because of the climate, so they must import food from elsewhere. Likewise, the United States does not have all the oil it needs, so it must import oil.

13. A: This example uses elements of the students' identities to clarify these two concepts.

14. C: This map will include a legend explaining that the corncobs are symbols representing areas of corn production.

15. A: Asking about the difference between the populations of each city is an appropriate math computation and social studies skill for a third-grade class.

16. B: This simple survey and quantitative organizer will help students understand how the data collected was organized into chart form.

17. D: Using a term like *west*, one of the cardinal directions, helps students use the compass rose to identify locations on a map.

18. C: The students should understand that people use what is available in their environment. In this scenario, the people would use wood from trees to build houses.

19. D: Seas are saltwater; lakes are often freshwater but may also be saltwater.

20. B: Rule of law is a key part of our system of government.

21. D: They are nominated by the president and confirmed by the Senate.

22. C: The Texas Constitution could be amended if two-thirds of both the Texas House and Senate vote in favor of the amendment and then Texas voters approve it by majority.

23. D: Culture, social studies skills, and economics are part of the social studies TEKS in grades K – 8.

24. B, E: No taxation for seven years and land available at a low cost were reasons colonists followed Stephen F. Austin to Texas and started farms or ranches.

25. C: San Jacinto Day is April 21st and celebrates the Battle of San Jacinto, which led to Texas's independence from Mexico.

26. C: Texas was annexed to the United States by President James K. Polk in 1845.

27. A: Sam Houston was replaced as governor by Lt. Governor Edward Clark because of his refusal to swear allegiance to the Confederacy.

28. B: The Fourteenth Amendment was not ratified by Texas and many other former Confederate states, which led to the state being placed under military control during Reconstruction.

29. C: Lyndon Baines Johnson and Dwight Eisenhower are the only two presidents born in Texas.

30. B: Popular sovereignty is the idea that the people are the source of power and should therefore make decisions.

31. B, D

Cultural adaptation is adjusting to a new culture or way of life and might include language, food, music, dress, and so on.

32. A: When supply and demand are equivalent, the economy is at equilibrium.

33. B, D: Many tech companies are headquartered in Texas; the oil and gas industry is still the number one industry in the state.

34. B: Unlike the rights of American citizenship, responsibilities of citizenship are things that citizens must do to keep the government running effectively, such as voting and paying taxes.

35. C: The federal government was too weak to be effective under the Articles of Confederation.

36. C: The oil bust of the 1980s proved that the oil and gas industry is particularly vulnerable to boom and bust cycles.

37. A: A wide expanse of flat land makes an ideal environment for cattle ranching.

38. D: The norms of social behavior include throwing away trash after eating.

39. D: The Comanche tribe lived in Texas prior to European arrival and was known for its horsemanship.

40. B: There were ten times as many manufacturing centers in the northern states.

Subtest III Science

1. Which pH level is classified as a base?
   A. 2
   B. 4
   C. 6
   D. 8

2. Which body system is responsible for the release of growth hormones?
   A. digestive system
   B. endocrine system
   C. nervous system
   D. circulatory system

3. Which example illustrates a physical change?
   A. Water becomes ice.
   B. Batter is baked into a cake.
   C. An iron fence rusts.
   D. A firecracker explodes.

4. Which example demonstrates refraction?
   A. rainbow
   B. echo
   C. mirror
   D. radio

5. What term describes a relationship between two organisms where one organism benefits, to the detriment of the other organism?
   A. mutualism
   B. parasitism
   C. commensalism
   D. predation

6. A researcher conducts an experiment where one plant is sprayed with a chemical every day and one plant is not. Which element of the experiment is the control group?
   A. the sprayed plant
   B. the chemical
   C. the researcher
   D. the unsprayed plant

7. Which statement is true?
   A. Earth is much closer to the sun than it is to other stars.
   B. The moon is closer to Venus than it is to Earth.
   C. At certain times of the year, Jupiter is closer to the sun than Earth is.
   D. Mercury is the closest planet to Earth.

8. Which example has the least amount of kinetic energy?
   A. a plane flying through the sky
   B. a plane sitting on the runway
   C. a ladybug flying towards a flower
   D. a meteorite falling to Earth

9. Which statement is true?
   A. Mass and weight are the same thing.
   B. Mass is affected by gravitational pull.
   C. Weight is affected by the gravitational pull.
   D. Mass is related to the surface area of an object.

10. When Earth moves between the moon and the sun, it is called a
   A. solar eclipse.
   B. lunar eclipse.
   C. black hole.
   D. supernova.

11. Which simple machine is shown in the picture?

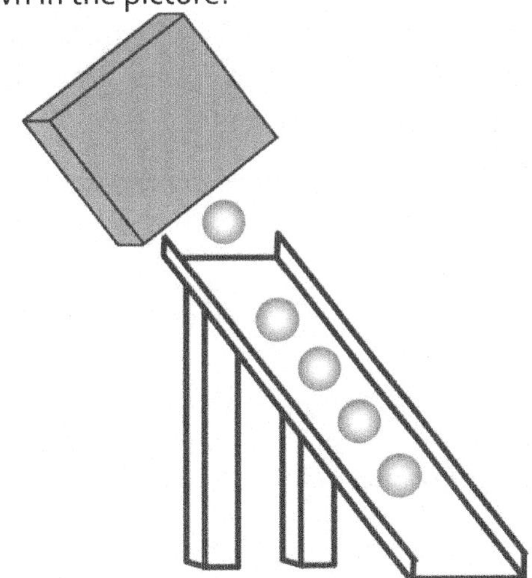

   A. inclined plane
   B. pulley
   C. screw
   D. wedge

12. Which lesson can BEST introduce a geology unit about the layers of the earth?
   A. a lesson on hydroponics
   B. a discussion on geothermal energy
   C. a lecture about solar energy
   D. a class on hydropower

13. Which activity demonstrates a chemical change?
   A. dissolving drink mix in water
   B. slicing an apple
   C. cooking an egg
   D. melting an ice cube

14. Which activity could be used to demonstrate Newton's Third Law of Motion?
   A. hitting the 8-ball with the cue ball in billiards
   B. rolling two balls of different masses down a ramp
   C. dropping a ping-pong ball
   D. swinging a pendulum

15. Which organism could be used as an example in a discussion of asexual reproduction?
   A. bacteria
   B. fish
   C. birds
   D. insects

16. A teacher wants to illustrate the way Earth's lithosphere, atmosphere, and biosphere are connected. Which illustration BEST meets this goal?
   A. the human life cycle
   B. weather and climate
   C. plate tectonics
   D. the nitrogen cycle

17. A river ecosystem experiences an extreme fluctuation in chemical composition due to pollution, and many organisms die, decreasing the total number of organisms. What can be said about this system?
   A. It is going through a life cycle change.
   B. It is NOT at dynamic equilibrium.
   C. It is NOT an open system.
   D. It is going through an accommodation.

18. If both parents are homozygous for type A blood, what will be true of their child?
   A. The child will have type AB blood.
   B. The child has a 50 percent chance of type A blood.
   C. The child will have type O blood.
   D. The child will have a 100 percent chance of type A blood.

19. Which of the following agents most directly causes the change in appearance of the earth's surface through erosion and deposition?
   A. soil
   B. fire
   C. oxygen
   D. water

20. Use the passage below to answer the question that follows:

   The largest inland desalination facility is located in El Paso, Texas. The plant helps local residents gain access to drinkable water because the groundwater in the vicinity is brackish. Brackish water from the Hueco Bolson aquifer is fed into the facility, which can produce as much as 27.5 million gallons of fresh, drinkable water each day!

Information provided in the passage would be most useful for a lesson on what?

   A. alternative energy sources
   B. mitigation of greenhouse gas emissions
   C. natural resource use
   D. the water cycle

21. Which of the following is an example of a structural adaptation in animals?
   A. A lizard has camouflaged skin.
   B. A skunk sprays a toxin to scare away prey.
   C. A spider spins a web to trap food.
   D. A bird migrates south in the winter.

22. Use the diagram below to answer the question that follows.

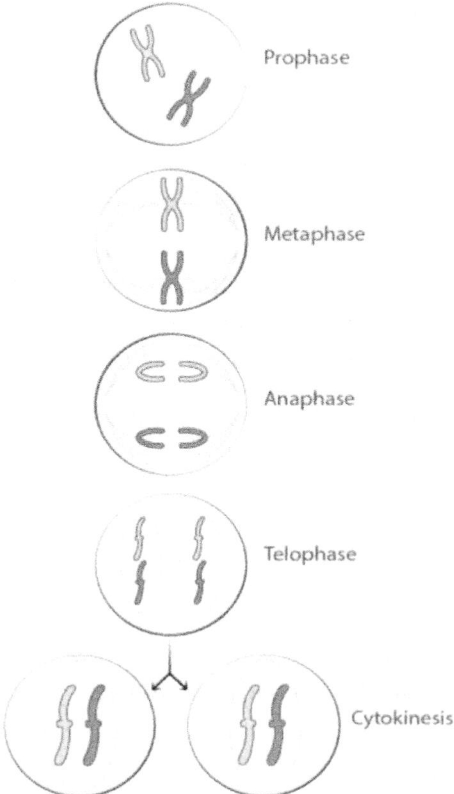

What does this diagram show?

A. gamete formation
B. cell division
C. sexual reproduction
D. cloning

23. Which of the following is an example of frictional force?

A. leaning against a wall
B. reading a book
C. sliding a book across a desk
D. bugs flying in the air

24. In an experiment designed to test whether exercise leads to weight loss in a random sample of horses at a ranch, what is the independent variable?

A. weight loss
B. exercise
C. horses at the ranch
D. the random sample

25. A first-grade teacher sets up a science center with an activity related to floating objects. The students have a bowl of salt water and a bowl of fresh water to put small objects in. Which of the following concepts is the teacher most likely trying to help students better understand through the science center?

A. states of matter
B. freshwater and saltwater habitats
C. density
D. potential energy

26. Which of the following is a characteristic of a gas?

A. The particles do not flow easily and cannot move past one another.
B. The particles are packed so tightly together that they never move
C. The particles are very far apart and constantly bouncing off one another.
D. The particles are close together, but not packed tightly.

27. Which of the following is an example of an object that uses mechanical energy?

A. microwave
B. television
C. scissors
D. solar panels

28. A first-grade teacher sets up a science center with an activity that has four candy canes and four glasses, each filled with a different liquid. The liquids are warm water, cold water, oil, and vinegar. The students are instructed to hypothesize which liquid they think will dissolve a candy cane the quickest and then test their predictions.
The teacher is likely trying to encourage student predictions on which of the following?

A. physical properties
B. physical change
C. density
D. reactions

29. Which of the following is an example of a mixture?

A. sand and water
B. salt and water
C. sugar and water
D. amalgam dental fillings

30. Which of the following agents causes the change in appearance of the earth's surface in a gradual manner by causing rocks to be broken down into smaller pieces?

A. erosion
B. weathering
C. earthquakes
D. deposition

31. Which of the following instruments measures wind speed?

A. thermometer
B. wind vane
C. anemometer
D. rain gauge

32. Which of the following is a phase of the moon?
   A. crescent
   B. waning quarter
   C. waxing quarter
   D. waxing gibbous

33. A second-grade teacher taught her students the life cycle of the butterfly and had them complete an activity where they drew and labeled a diagram of the cycle. Which student put the life cycle of a butterfly in the correct order?
   A. Cherie, who wrote *caterpillar, chrysalis, egg, butterfly*
   B. Ruthie, who wrote *chrysalis, butterfly, caterpillar, egg*
   C. Pepe, who wrote *egg, caterpillar, chrysalis, butterfly*
   D. Carla, who wrote *butterfly, chrysalis, caterpillar, egg*

34. A kindergarten teacher is teaching a unit about polar bears. Each students was given a plastic bag that was filled with vegetable shortening. They put their hand inside the bag to cover it with the fat coating and then placed the covered hand inside a bucket filled with ice. Which of the following understandings is the teacher trying to develop in students through this activity?
   A. Animals must quickly adapt to their surroundings.
   B. Structural adaptations help animals survive in extreme habitats.
   C. Structural adaptions are more important than behavioral adaptions in extreme habitats.
   D. All animals must have several layers of blubber to stay warm.

35. Which scientific development led to changes in surgery, such as use of antiseptics?
   A. cell theory
   B. germ theory
   C. awareness of mitosis
   D. awareness of miosis

36. A person who is 2 meters tall is how many centimeters tall?
   A. 200 cm
   B. 2,000 cm
   C. 20,000 cm
   D. 200,000 cm

37. Which of the following processes involve energy transfer? Select ALL that apply.
   A. photosynthesis
   B. mitosis
   C. hydrology
   D. food web
   E. doppler radar

38. A weather map shows a blue line with triangles moving into an area. What type of weather will likely follow?
   A. rain
   B. cloudy skies
   C. sunshine
   D. tornadoes

39. Which process creates sedimentary rock?
   A. volcanic eruption
   B. deposition
   C. tectonic shifts
   D. nitrification

40. What does a horizontal line on a position versus time graph indicate?
   A. The object is accelerating.
   B. The object is decelerating.
   C. The object is at a constant speed.
   D. The object is at rest.

41. Which of the following is an example of a balanced force? Select ALL that apply.
   A. a person floating in water
   B. a car accelerating
   C. a fruit dropping from a tree D. a tug of war where no one wins
   E. a penny falling out of a pocket

42. During which kind of chemical reaction is heat released?
   A. endothermic
   B. exothermic
   C. metamorphosis
   D. homeostasis

43. A teacher writes the following list on the board:
   - language
   - staying away from danger
   - following adult directions

Which biological concept is the teacher most likely illustrating?
   A. natural selection
   B. genetic mutations
   C. incomplete metamorphosis
   D. learned characteristics

44. Which of the following is an example of a redox reaction?
   A. digestion
   B. burning fossil fuels
   C. a battery
   D. rusting

Answer Key

1. D: Bases have a pH between 7 and 14.

2. B: The endocrine system releases hormones, including growth hormones.

3. A: When water changes form, it does not change the chemical composition of the substance. Once water becomes ice, the ice can easily turn back into water.

4. A: The light of the sun hits rain droplets and bends into a band of colors. The bending of waves is refraction.

5. B: Parasitism describes a relationship in which one organism benefits from another organism to the detriment of the host organism.

6. D: The control group does not receive the treatment.

7. A: The sun is the only star in our solar system. The sun is about ninety-three million miles from Earth; the next closest star is about twenty-five trillion miles away.

8. B: Something that is not moving has zero velocity; therefore it has no kinetic energy.

9. C: Weight is affected by gravitational pull.

10. B: A lunar eclipse is when Earth moves between the moon and the sun.

11. A: An inclined plane is a flat surface raised to an angle so that loads can be easily lifted.

12. B: Geothermal energy is a renewable energy source that comes from the heat within the earth. A discussion about geothermal energy would be a good setting to introduce a geology unit on the layers of the earth.

13. C: Cooking an egg is a chemical change. The heat changes the composition of the egg in an irreversible way.

14. A: Newton's Third Law of Motion states that for every action there is an equal and opposite reaction. When the cue ball hits the 8-ball, the cue ball stops, and the 8-ball moves.

15. A: Bacteria are of the Monera kingdom, and they reproduce asexually.

16. D: The nitrogen cycle involves the exchange and movement of nitrogen through the lithosphere, atmosphere, and biosphere.

17. B: When a system is at dynamic equilibrium, the physical and chemical reactions in the system balance each other out. In this case, the system is not at equilibrium because there are now fewer organisms than before.

18. D: Homozygous genes (AA or aa)mean that the child will inherit that trait. Heterozygous genes (Aa, Bb, and so on)leave a chance that the child will not inherit the trait.

19. D: Water can be found in the form of precipitation, streams, rivers, oceans, and glaciers and can cause erosion and deposition.

20. C: This passage provides information on ways that humans are using a natural resource (water) in a nuanced way.

21. A: A structural adaptation is the way an animal looks, or the body parts or physical features it has in order to survive.

22. B: This diagram shows mitosis, or cell division.

23. C: Sliding a book across a desk is an example of frictional force since the book and table have dry friction as two solid surfaces are in contact.

24. B: The exercise is what the researcher is controlling and believes will have an effect on the horses, so it is the independent variable.

25. C: Students are seeing the ability of objects to float in fresh and salt water, which can be used to explain density. Objects will float more readily in the salt water because salt water is denser than tap water.

26. C: A gas is a state of matter where the particles are very far apart and constantly bouncing off one another.

27. C: Scissors are an example of mechanical energy.

28. D: The experiment is showing students how a liquid can dissolve an object. Some liquids create a reaction that makes the candy cane dissolve more quickly than others.

29. A: Sand and water is an example of a mixture. A mixture is any time two or more different objects or materials are mixed but not combined chemically.

30. B: Weathering takes place when rocks are broken down into smaller pieces by the effects of weather.

31. C: An anemometer measures wind speed.

32. D: Waxing gibbous is a phase of the moon.

33. C: This is the correct order.

34. B: The teacher is teaching students about a structural adaption (blubber)that helps polar bears survive in cold habitats.

35. B: Introduced by Louis Pasteur in the 1860s, germ theory paved the way for antibiotics but immediately impacted surgical procedures.

36. A: One meter is 100 centimeters, so 2 meters is 200 centimeters.

37. A, D: In photosynthesis, energy from the sun is transferred to plants. In the food web, plant and animal energy is transferred among organisms.

38. A: A blue line with triangles is the symbol for a cold front, which often brings sudden rain.

39. B: Deposition is the laying down of sediment due to wind or water.

40. D: On a velocity versus time graph, a horizontal line shows that the object is moving at constant speed.

41. A, D: In both examples, the forces are equal, which leads to a state of non-movement.

42. B: In exothermic reactions, heat is released.

43. D: All of the listed characteristics of human organisms are those which have been learned.

44. C: Batteries are chemical reactions involving the exchange of electrons, or redox reactions.

Subtest IV Mathematics

1. A fifth-grade teacher wants to demonstrate the associative property of addition. Which equation could be used as an example?

A. $2 + (1 + 5) = (2 + 1) + 5$
B. $2(1 \times 5) = (2 \times 1)5$
C. $1 \times 3 = 3 \times 1$
D. $2(7 + 4) = 2 \times 7 + 2 \times 4$

2. Using the information in the table, which equation demonstrates the linear relationship between *x* and *y*?

x	y
3	3
7	15
10	24

A. $y = 6x - 6$
B. $y = 5x - 6$
C. $y = 4x - 6$
D. $y = 3x - 6$

3. Using the table, which equation demonstrates the linear relationship between *x* and *y*?

x	y
3	-18
7	-34
10	-46

A. $y = -6x - 6$
B. $y = -5x - 6$
C. $y = -4x - 6$
D. $y = -3x - 6$

4. Robbie has a bag of treats that contains 5 pieces of gum, 7 pieces of taffy, and 8 pieces of chocolate. If Robbie reaches into the bag and randomly pulls out a treat, what is the probability that Robbie will get a piece of taffy?

A. 1
B. $\frac{1}{7}$
C. $\frac{5}{8}$
D. $\frac{7}{20}$

5. Kim and Chris are writing a book together. Kim writes twice as many pages as Chris. Altogether, there are 240 pages in the book. Which equation shows how many pages Chris writes?

A. $2 + 2p = 240$
B. $p + 2p = 240$
C. $2p - p = 240$
D. $p - 2p = 240$

6. An ice chest contains 25 sodas, some regular and some diet. The ratio of diet soda to regular soda is 1:4. How many regular sodas are there in the ice chest?

A. 1
B. 4
C. 20
D. 25

7. A teacher gives the students the following images and puts them in pairs with the task of describing the relationship they see.

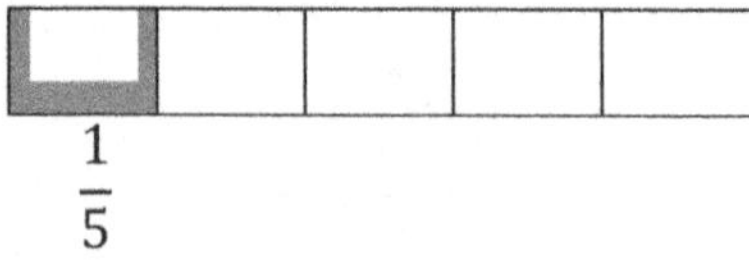

$\frac{1}{5}$

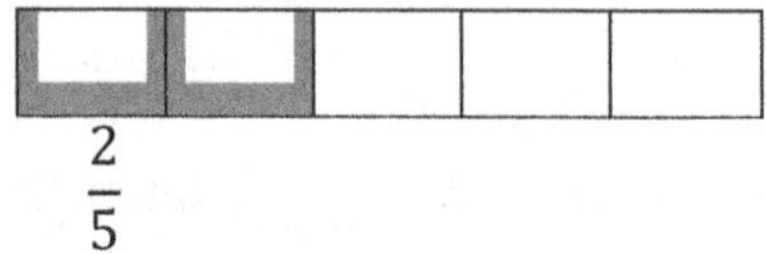

$\frac{2}{5}$

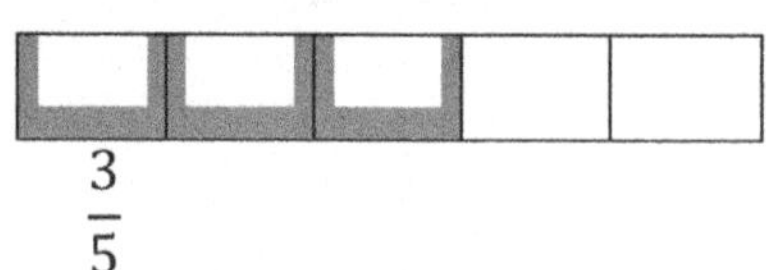

$\frac{3}{5}$

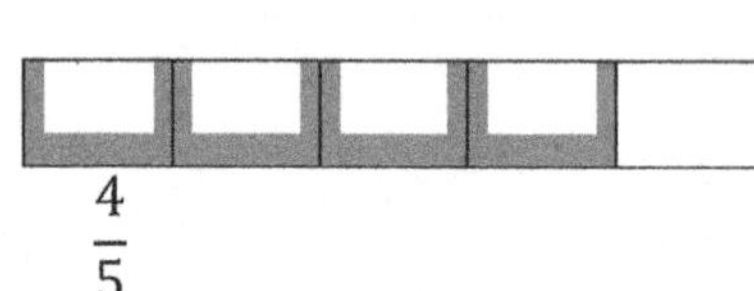

$\frac{4}{5}$

Which of the following is the relationship students are most likely meant to glean?

A. When the numerator stays the same and the denominator increases, the fraction increases.
B. When the numerator increases and the denominator stays the same, the fraction increases.
C. When the numerator and the denominator increase, the fraction decreases.
D. When the numerator stays the same and the denominator decreases, the fraction decreases.

8. Danny collects coins. The table shows how many of each type of coin Danny collects for four days. Which statement is true?

Danny's Coin Collection

	Pennies	Nickels	Dimes	Quarters
Day 1	1	4	3	0
Day 2	4	3	2	5
Day 3	5	2	2	4
Day 4	1	2	3	1

A. The mean number of nickels is greater than the mean number of quarters.
B. The mean number of quarters is greater than the mean number of pennies.
C. The range of dimes is greater than the range of quarters.
D. The median number of pennies is five.

9. A student is asked to predict the length of a classroom table. Which of the following is the most reasonable prediction?

A. 1.5 mm
B. 15 mm
C. 150 mm
D. 1,500 mm

10. How much longer is line segment MN than line segment KL?
Ruler question figure

A. 15 mm
B. 20 mm
C. 2 mm
D. 55 mm

11. A fifth-grade student is given the following problem:

How long will it take a plane to fly 4,000 miles from Chicago to London if the plane flies at a constant rate of 500 mph?

If the student determines the answer is 80 hours, what has most likely happened?

A. The student multiplied instead of divided.
B. The student divided incorrectly.
C. The student converted miles to kilometers.
D. The student forgot the formula for time and distance.

12. What is the perimeter of the shape?

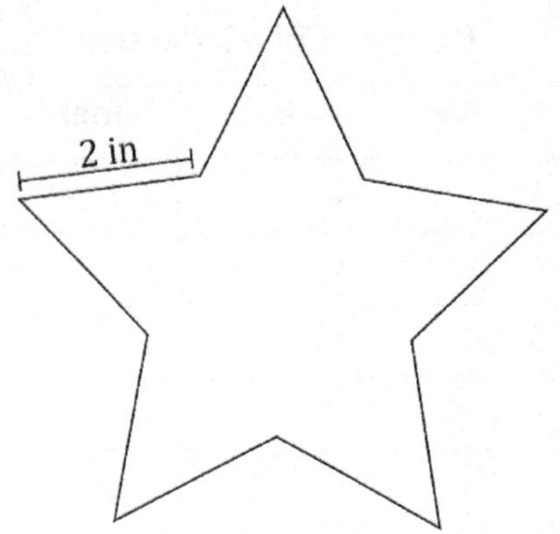

A. 2 mm
B. 4 mm
C. 10 mm
D. 20 mm

13. What is the area of the shape?

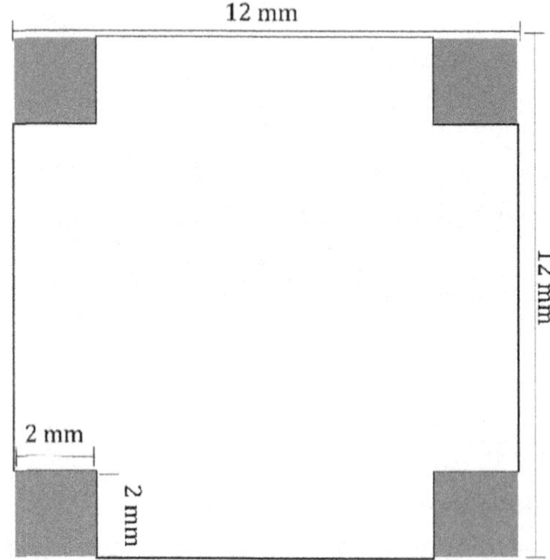

A. 64 mm^2
B. 16 mm^2
C. 128 mm^2
D. 6 mm^2

14. Which three-dimensional solid has 2 triangular faces and 3 rectangular faces?
A. pyramid
B. cube
C. rectangular prism
D. triangular prism

15. What is the equation of the following line?

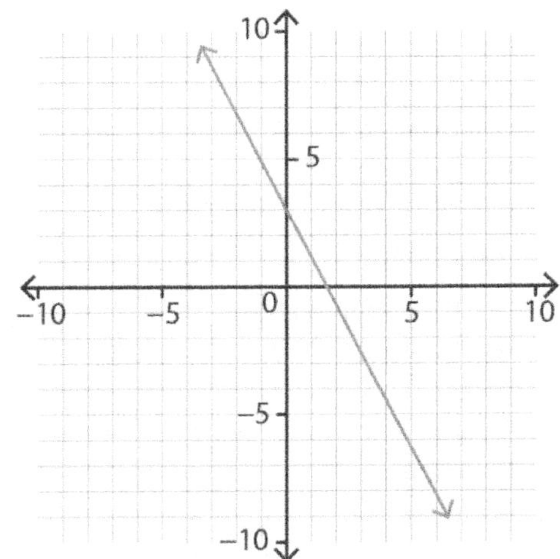

A. $y = -4x + 3$
B. $y = -2x - 3$
C. $y = 2x + 3$
D. $y = -2x + 3$

16. Which of the following expressions describes the area of the triangle below?

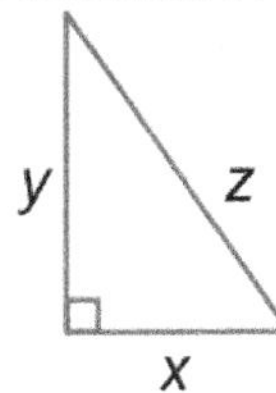

A. $x + y + z$

B. $\frac{xy}{2}$

C. xyz

D. $\frac{xyz}{2}$

17. The circle below shows a walking path through a park. If the distance from *A* to *B* is 4 km, how far will someone travel when walking along arc *AB*?
Walking circle question figure

A. 4 km
B. 2π km
C. 8 km
D. 4π km

18. Bart surveyed his classmates to determine their favorite pizza toppings. The data was as follows:

anchovy	1
pineapple	2
olives	4
pepperoni	9
bacon	2
Canadian bacon	1

Which topping is the mode?

A. anchovy
B. olives
C. pepperoni
D. pineapple

19. The figure below shows similar triangles *ABC* and *DEF*.
problem_similar_triangles

Which of the following statements is true?

A. $DF = \frac{AC}{3}$

B. $DF = AC - 16$

C. $DF = 2AC$

D. $DF = \frac{2}{3}AB$

20. One day in January, the low temperature was −7°F. During the day the temperature rose 15 degrees. What was the high temperature for that day?

A. −23°F
B. −8°F
C. 8°F
D. 23°F

21. A second-grade class is learning about the properties of two-dimensional shapes. Which of the following activities would BEST help students consider perimeter in an authentic context?

A. using play dough to make solid figures
B. working on a jigsaw puzzle
C. using toilet paper tubes to create a windsock
D. throwing a basketball through a hoop

22. A second-grade class is learning about measurements by following a recipe to make modeling clay. If the recipe calls for $2\frac{1}{4}$ cups of flour, which of the following measurement tools can students use to measure the flour?

A. $\frac{1}{4}$ cup

B. $\frac{1}{3}$ cup

C. $\frac{1}{2}$ cup

D. 1 cup

23. Jim, Abby, Megan, and Alex are third-grade students learning to count money. Their teacher passes out the following coins to each student:

Jim has 5 pennies, 2 nickels, and 3 dimes.

Abby has 8 pennies, 3 nickels, and 2 dimes.

Megan has 6 pennies, 4 nickels, and 2 dimes.

Alex has 7 pennies, 1 nickel, and 3 dimes.

Which student has the largest amount of money?

A. Jim
B. Abby
C. Megan
D. Alex

24. A class is learning to compare fractions. A student writes the following:

$\frac{5}{12}$ is greater than $\frac{5}{7}$ because 12 is greater than 7.

Which of the following is a correct assessment of the student's work?

A. The student is correct because 12 is greater than 7.

B. The student is correct because five parts out of twelve ($\frac{5}{12}$) is greater than five parts out of seven ($\frac{5}{7}$).

C. The student is incorrect because the numerators are the same, meaning the fractions are equal.

D. The student is incorrect because five parts out of twelve ($\frac{5}{12}$) is less than five parts out of seven ($\frac{5}{7}$).

25. A second-grade teacher is teaching her student to count money. Which of the following skills should students have before starting the lesson?

A. decomposing numbers
B. subitizing
C. division
D. skip counting

26. In an integrated unit on math and history, the teacher wants to explore related concepts. In a study of triangles, which civilization would be most appropriate?

A. Sumeria
B. Greece
C. Germany
D. China

27. Students were asked to find the cardinality of this set: $\{2, 4, 6, 8, 10, 12, 14\}$. Which of the following student answers is correct?

A. 56
B. 7
C. 8
D. 12

28. A teacher is introducing a unit on rounding numbers. Which of the follow activities would help introduce this concept? Select ALL that apply.

A. planning a trip to the grocery store
B. dividing a restaurant bill
C. filling out tax forms
D. telling time
E. measuring wood to build a bookshelf

29. A first-grade class is beginning a unit on basic addition. Which of the following should the teacher use to introduce the topic?

A. a calculator
B. a number line
C. manipulatives
D. written equations

30. A third-grade teacher asks students to draw a line of symmetry through a circle. How many possible lines of symmetry are there?

A. zero
B. one
C. two
D. infinite

31. After exploring the properties of cubes, a teacher asks her students to suggest a method for finding the surface area. Which of the following answers demonstrates an understanding of both the properties of cubes and the concept of surface area?

A. multiply the length by the height of one of its faces
B. find the area of one face and multiply by 6, since a cube has six square faces
C. measure the amount of space occupied inside it
D. find the area of the faces that are visible when the cube is resting on a table

32. A second-grade teacher wants to have her students collect data and create a bar graph. Which of the following would be the BEST question for her to give her students?

A. How does the temperature outside change during the day?
B. What percentage of students like different types of ice cream?
C. What is the relationship between a plant's age and height?
D. Which classroom has the largest number of students?

33. If a triangle has an interior angle that measures 55°, what must its corresponding exterior angle measure?

A. 55°
B. 305°
C. 45°
D. 125°

34. After giving explicit math instruction via modeling, which step should follow?

A. independent practice
B. summative assessment
C. guided practice
D. small-group instruction

Answer Key

1. A: The correct answer is $2 + (1 + 5) = (2 + 1) + 5$. When using the associative property, the answer will remain the same in an addition problem regardless of where the parentheses are placed.

2. D: The correct answer is $y = 3x - 6$. Solve for *y* by replacing *x* with 3.

$$y = 3(3) - 6$$

$$y = 9 - 6$$

$$y = 3$$

This is the correct answer because the table says that when $x = 3, y = 3$.

3. C: The correct answer is $y = -4x - 6$ is the correct answer. Solve for *y* by replacing *x* with 3.

$$y = -4(3)- 6$$

$$y = -12 - 6$$

$$y = -18$$

The table says that when $x = 3, y = -18$.

4. D: The correct answer is $\frac{7}{20}$. Probability is the number of favorable events divided by the number of possible events. In this case, Robbie pulls out one treat from a bag that contains 7 pieces of taffy; therefore 7 is the number of favorable events. There are 20 total treats in the bag because $5 + 7 + 8 = 20$. $7 \div 20 = \frac{7}{20}$.

5. B: The correct answer is $p + 2p = 240$ is the correct answer. If *p* is the number of pages Chris writes, the equation shows that Kim writes 2*p*, or twice as many pages as Chris writes. If the number of pages Chris writes is added to the number of pages Kim writes, the total is 240 pages.

6. C: The correct answer is 18. Use ratios to solve the problem. There is 1 diet soda for every 4 regular sodas, for a total of 5 sodas. $\text{Diet} = 1$, $\text{Regular} = 4$, and $\text{Total} = 5$.

$$\frac{4\ regular}{5\ total} = \frac{x\ regular}{25\ total}$$

Cross multiply:

$$5x = 100$$

$$x = 20$$

7. B: The images show the numerator increasing while the denominator stays the same; meanwhile, the fraction is increasing.

8. A: To calculate the mean, add all the numbers in a set and divide by how many numbers are in the set. The mean number of nickels is $4 + 3 + 2 + 2 = 11$ divided by 4 (because there are 4 numbers in the set) $= 2.75$ nickels. The mean number of quarters is $0 + 5 + 4 + 1 = 10$ divided by $4 = 2.5$ quarters. $2.75 > 2.5$.

9. D: The correct answer is 1,500 mm. 1 centimeter $= 10$ millimeters, so this table is about 150 cm long, which would be a reasonable estimate.

10. B: Line segment MN begins at 35 mm and ends at 70 mm, so $70 - 35 = 35\ mm$. Line segment MN is 35 mm. The length of line segment KL is 15 mm. To find out how much longer MN is than KL, subtract, $35\ mm - 15\ mm = 20\ mm$.

11. B: The correct answer is 8 hours. Time is distance divided by rate; $4{,}000\ mi \div 500\ mph = 8$ hours. Thus, the student most likely divided incorrectly by adding an extra zero.

12. D: 20 mm is the correct answer. There are 10 sides and each side is 2 mm in length. To find the perimeter, add the length of each side to find the total. $P = 2 + 2 + 2 + 2 + 2 + 2 + 2 + 2 + 2 + 2 = 20\ mm$.

13. C: 128 mm^2 is the correct answer. Find the area of the square as if it did not have cut-outs; each side would be 12 mm long. $12\ mm \times 12\ mm = 144\ mm^2$ Next, subtract the area of the cut-outs from the total area of the square. The area of each cut-out is $2\ mm \times 2\ mm =$

$4\ mm^2$. There are cut-outs in each of the 4 corners; therefore, multiply by 4; $4 \times 4 = 16$. Subtract the total area of the four cut-outs from the total area of the square without the cut-outs; $144 - 16 = 128\ mm^2$.

14. D: A triangle prism has 2 triangular faces and 3 rectangular faces.

15. D: The *y*-intercept can be identified on the graph as (0, 3). Thus, $b = 3$.

To find the slope, choose any two points and plug the values into the slope equation. The two points chosen here are (2, −1) and (3, −3).

$$m = \frac{(-3) - (-1)}{3 - 2} = -\frac{2}{1} = -2$$

Replace *m* with −2 and *b* with 3 in $y = mx + b$.

The equation of the line is $y = -2x + 3$.

16. B: Use the formula for the area of a triangle. In this triangle, *y* is the base and *x* is the height.

$$A = \frac{1}{2}bh = \frac{1}{2}xy = \frac{xy}{2}$$

17. B: Find the circle's radius.

$$4\ km \div 2 = 2\ km$$

Use the radius to find the circumference of the circle.

$$C = 2\pi r = 2\pi(2) = 4\pi$$

Arc *AB* is a semicircle, which means its length is half the circumference of the circle.

$$4\pi \div 2 = \mathbf{2\pi\ km}$$

18. C: The mode occurs the most often, so the mode is **pepperoni**.

19. A: Use the given lengths to find the scale ratio for the two triangles.

$$\frac{AB}{DE} = \frac{24}{8} = 3$$

The ratio of *DF* to *AC* will also be equal to 3 because they are corresponding parts of the two triangles. Set up an equation and solve for DF.

$$\frac{AC}{DF} = 3$$

$$DF = \frac{AC}{3}$$

20. C: Add 15 degrees to −7 degrees.

$$-7°F + 15°F = \mathbf{8°F}$$

21. B: The shape of the jigsaw puzzle pieces can be used to teach students about perimeter. The other options focus on three-dimensional shapes.

22. A: $2\frac{1}{4}$ is divisible by $\frac{1}{4}$, so students can use the $\frac{1}{4}$ cup to measure the flour $\left(\frac{1}{4} \times 9 = 2\frac{1}{4}\right)$.

23. C: Megan has $(6 \times 1) + (4 \times 5) + (2 \times 10) = 46$ cents.

24. D: Five parts out of twelve $\left(\frac{5}{12}\right)$ is less than five parts out of seven $\left(\frac{5}{7}\right)$.

25. D: Knowledge of skip counting will help children count the different denominations of money by their value (e.g., nickels are skip counted in fives).

26. B: Pythagoras's theorem is related to triangles, and he was Greek.

27. B: Cardinality is the measure of how many objects are in a group or set. There are seven numeric elements (objects)in this set.

28. A, B, D: Grocery store shopping involves budgeting and rounding to stay on budget. Dividing a restaurant bill involves rounding how much each person owes. Telling time usually involves rounding up to the nearest quarter.

29. C: This is a concrete representation, which is the first step in the CRA (concrete-representational-abstract) method, and therefore an appropriate first step in learning addition.

30. D: Any line that passes through the center of the circle is a line of symmetry, so there is an infinite number of possible lines of symmetry.

31. B: This gives the surface area of the entire cube.

32. D: Comparing the number of items in different categories is done on a bar graph.

33. D: The interior and exterior angles of a triangle must add up to 180°, so $180 - 55 = 125$.

34. C: After modeling, guided practice should occur, followed by independent practice.

Subtest V: Fine Arts, Health, and Physical Education

1. Which of the following is a non-locomotor skill?
   A. skipping
   B. bending
   C. throwing
   D. leaping

2. Which of the following sports or activities is not appropriate to teach in second grade?
   A. kickball
   B. football
   C. freeze tag
   D. simple obstacle courses

3. Which of the following goals is most important to develop in students participating in physical education programs?
   A. proficiencies in multiple sports and games
   B. enough cardiorespiratory endurance to run ½ mile without stopping
   C. a lifelong commitment to participation in physical activity
   D. an ability to lead a team in a physical activity

4. A third-grade teacher is showing his class pictures of the art of Michelangelo. What background knowledge about the history of this art might be important for him to tell students prior to showing them these pictures?
   A. Michelangelo was a very famous artist of the Renaissance, and his work differed from that of the baroque style that followed.
   B. Michelangelo's art reflected the religious topics that were important to his patrons.
   C. The process by which marble is fashioned into sculpture has greatly changed since Michelangelo worked in the medium.
   D. Much of Michelangelo's work has been damaged over the course of history and had to be reconstructed by art restorers.

5. What does the FIIT principle entail?
   A. flexibility, intensity, toning, and type
   B. frequency, intensity, time, and type
   C. freedom, innovation, technique, and tempo
   D. frequency, intention, time, and technique

6. How can physical education lessons BEST strive to prevent injury?
   A. following the rules of all games and sports without any accommodations or modifications
   B. offering opportunities for students to increase flexibility and range of movement
   C. giving students clear goals to accomplish during each activity
   D. providing choices of activities at various stations or centers

7. To prepare students for a gymnastics unit that will involve use of a balance beam, activities might include
   A. object manipulation
   B. locomotor skills development
   C. hopping on one foot
   D. doing push ups

8. Which physical education activity would BEST allow for an integrated unit on Newton's Laws of Motion?

A. softball
B. cross-country running
C. hurdles
D. high-intensity interval training

9. Which personal safety topic is most appropriate for a first-grade physical education class?

A. avoiding drunk driving
B. responsible social media use
C. knowing parents' phone numbers
D. use of evasive self-defense movements

10. Which food group makes up the largest part of the MyPlate recommendation?

A. protein
B. dairy
C. grains
D. vegetables

11. A first-grade art teacher wants to encourage her students to use texture in their art. Which medium/project would be BEST for this purpose?

A. a pastel drawing
B. an acrylic painting
C. a feather collage
D. a pinch pot vase

12. Which type of class structure is most likely to help students of all abilities participate in physical activity?

A. teacher-directed drills
B. student choice stations
C. circuit training
D. free play time

13. Cross-hatching is a part of which element of art?

A. line
B. shape
C. form
D. color

14. On a field trip to an art museum, a third-grade teacher stops the class in front of a canvas painted half black and half white. What principles of art might he discuss as they pertain to this painting?

A. contrast and proportion
B. movement and balance
C. pattern and emphasis
D. emphasis and movement

15. Which of the following would be an appropriate activity for first graders during a simple lesson on rhythm?

A. The teacher makes loud and soft sounds on a drum.
B. The teacher plays a pattern on the drum, and students try to repeat it.
C. Students listen to different percussion instruments.
D. The teacher plays music at different speeds and students clap to indicate the tempo.

16. Which of the following reasons BEST describes the reason a teacher would introduce the recorder to students in an elementary class?

A. It can help students learn proper breathing techniques.
B. It allows teachers to teach a wide variety of songs and ensembles effectively.
C. It is appropriate for students who may not have well-developed motor skills.
D. It helps teachers show students pitch and rhythm.

17. Which of the following types of media would be BEST to help students learn about functional art?

A. acrylic paint
B. textiles
C. collage
D. pen and ink

18. Which of the following descriptions BEST describes timbre in music?

A. Timbre refers to the different sounds of various instruments.
B. Timbre refers to the loudness of an instrument.
C. Timbre refers to the pitch of an instrument.
D. Timbre refers to combining melody, harmony, and rhythm.

19. Which of the following is a representational material for a dramatic production?

A. a pole in the gym that is labeled "tree."
B. a square on the floor that a character knows to run to
C. a memorable phrase like "see ya'" that a character utters
D. a real quilt used as a prop in a scene

20. A first-grade teacher wants to integrate an art and math lesson with the objective of having students determine which shape comes next in a sequence. Which principle of art could she apply?

A. unity
B. emphasis
C. pattern
D. contrast

21. A kindergarten teacher gives students small paintbrushes for an activity because she wants them to work on more detailed painting. One student named Mila, however, is behind the rest of the class in fine motor skills. What modification might the teacher make?

A. give Mila a different activity such as making a play-dough figure
B. give Mila a larger paintbrush or a paintbrush with a sponge on the end
C. have Mila finger paint instead of using a brush
D. encourage Mila to make her painting abstract instead of realistic

22. A kindergarten teacher gives her students egg-shaker maracas to shake while she plays the morning welcome song. Which musical concept is she encouraging students to develop?

A. timbre
B. pitch
C. rhythm
D. tone

23. A music teacher instructs her second-grade choir students to sing very loudly during one part of the song and to sing very softly during another part. What is this an example of?

A. pitch
B. tone
C. dynamics
D. harmony

24. Which method of assessment is most useful to track student progress in visual arts?

A. observational notes
B. portfolios
C. summative assessment
D. oral assessment

25. A third-grade physical education teacher notices that one of his students has lower levels of overall endurance and a harder time completing activities designed to build cardiovascular fitness. What modifications might he make for this student?

A. excusing the student from all activities outside of stretching
B. decreasing the time and intensity of the student's exercises
C. encouraging the student to develop greater body awareness
D. helping the student to develop more fundamental motor skills

26. Which of the following activities would aid in a student developing static balance?

A. walking on a balance beam
B. jumping from one marked-off spot on the floor to another
C. standing on one foot
D. skipping in a straight line

27. According to the MyPlate food guide, how much of the grains serving should be whole grains?

A. At least a quarter of the grains consumed should be whole grains.
B. At least half of the grains consumed should be whole grains.
C. At least three-quarters of the grains consumed should be whole grains.
D. All grains of the grains consumed should be whole grains.

28. Which recommendation is based on the MyPlate food guide?

A. serving more fruit juice and less whole fruit
B. focusing mostly on red and orange vegetables
C. making proteins the largest portions
D. changing to low-fat or fat-free milk

29. Which of the following activities would be appropriate for a first-grade class to participate in to work on understanding mental health?

A. filling out a questionnaire to determine their conflict resolution style
B. learning about different types of psychiatric disorders and how they are treated
C. a discussion of how to maintain healthy relationships with friends and family members
D. organizing a guest speaker to talk to the class about life in an inpatient psychiatric facility

30. A third-grade teacher shows students how to draw a house by starting with basic shapes and gradually adding to them. What process is this teacher using?

A. construction
B. proportion
C. dimensionality
D. generativity

31. An elementary school choir is struggling with intonation. Which activity would be most useful?

A. identifying the rising and falling in a song
B. adding additional voice accompaniments
C. copying the pitch of a note played on the piano
D. singing in canon instead of individually

32. Which of the following are nutrients? Select ALL that apply.

A. ribosomes
B. water
C. protein
D. fat
E. enzymes

33. Which of the following is a deficiency disease?

A. scoliosis
B. dysentery
C. heatstroke
D. scurvy

34. Which of the following describes the phenomenon when a child's development begins in the torso and radiates outward?

A. cephalocaudal
B. proximodistal
C. biolocomotion
D. biomechanics

35. Which of the following is an example of a theme a play might contain?

A. dark and mysterious
B. rhythmic and melodic
C. Money is not everything.
D. Props are not important.

36. Which of the following is a warning sign of a potential eating disorder?

A. erosion of tooth enamel
B. sore muscles
C. sudden interest in new activities
D. slower speech

37. Which health topic is particularly troubling because more research is needed to fully understand all of its negative effects?
   A. alcohol
   B. stimulants
   C. opioids
   D. vaping

38. What topic would be most likely to come up in a lesson on changes that occur in the transition to adolescence?
   A. cyberbullying
   B. binge-eating
   C. menstruation
   D. macronutrients

39. Which symbol tells a musician to play very softly?
   A. *f*
   B. *sfz*
   C. *mp*
   D. *pp*

40. Which activity is aimed at helping students develop empathy?
   A. writing about how they would feel if cyberbullied
   B. writing about the dynamics in their families
   C. discussing the diversity in the classroom
   D. discussing changes needed in the school

41. Which activity demonstrates cardiorespiratory endurance?
   A. completing twenty sit-ups in forty-five seconds
   B. lifting a twenty-pound weight
   C. running two miles without stopping
   D. finishing four full turns on the balance beam

42. Which project would promote the heritage of Texas?
   A. sketching a scene in the school lunchroom
   B. making a bluebonnet out of six-pack soda rings
   C. performing the musical *Our Town*
   D. creating costumes for a performance of *Oklahoma*

43. Which of the following is an example of multisensory art?
   A. a sculpture that is also painted
   B. a warm quilt that is brightly colored
   C. a painting that contains line and shape
   D. a drawing that is made with a digital tool

44. In one part of a play, a character gives a long speech. How is this BEST described?
   A. duet
   B. monologue
   C. improvisation
   D. representation

Answer Key

1. B: Non-locomotor skills, like bending, are usually movements that tend not to require moving through space.

2. B: Second graders may not be coordinated enough to play football; furthermore, the sport poses numerous safety hazards.

3. C: In light of information on lifelong health outcomes, this is a very important goal for any physical education program.

4. B: With this information, students will understand why a certain subject matter is emphasized in the work of Michelangelo.

5. B: The FIIT principle should guide exercise planning.

6. B: Increased flexibility and range of motion can be improved via stretching and yoga; this decreases likelihood of injuries like pulled muscles and falls as students have a better ability to move their bodies.

7. C: This will help students develop balance.

8. A: Students could observe the way force on the ball (throwing it, hitting it, etc.) leads to the motion of the ball.

9. C: Students at this age are likely not developmentally ready for the other topics.

10. D: In a balanced diet, vegetables should make up the largest portion of the plate per the United States Department of Agriculture (USDA) guidelines.

11. C: Feathers in a collage would create very unique textures, and students could explore this through touch.

12. B: Student choice stations can be set up so that there are options for students of various fitness levels and physical abilities.

13. A: Cross-hatching helps indicate a light source, which is an element of line in art.

14. A: This painting shows the contrast of black and white and has equal proportions of one half of each.

15. B: Teaching patterns is an appropriate introduction to the concept of rhythm.

16. B: Using the recorder is a great way to teach songs and ensembles without teaching a new instrument every time.

17. B: Textiles are often worn or used for practical purposes.

18. A: Also called tone, timbre is used to distinguish between instrumental sounds.

19. D: Representational materials are real or actual props; in contrast, non-representational materials are things that are deemed to have another identity (such as a paper towel role that becomes a sword.)

20. C: The teacher could integrate the art concept of patterns of shapes into an activity in which students draw or choose the shape that comes next in the sequence.

21. B: Giving Mila a different tool is a modification that will allow her to participate and feel successful.

22. C: Rhythm refers to the tempo or time pattern in music. Egg shakers can be used to help students shake the eggs in the same rhythm as the music.

23. C: Dynamics refers to the loud and soft parts of a piece of music.

24. B: Portfolios create an excellent way for teachers to track student progress over time in visual arts, as artifacts will likely reflect increasing proficiency.

25. B: Here, the FITT principle is used. It should guide each student's fitness plan.

26. C: This is static balance because the student is not moving but is balancing while still. The other options would help develop dynamic balance.

27. B: Per the MyPlate food guide, at least half of grains should be whole grains.

28. D: Consuming low-fat or fat-free milk is a recommendation based on the MyPlate food guide.

29. C: Discussing healthy relationships would be a developmentally appropriate activity for a first-grade class.

30. A: Construction in art refers to forming an object out of basic shapes.

31. C: Intonation refers to the accuracy of pitch, so this exercise will help students identify and copy a set pitch.

32. B, C, D: The basic nutrients are water, carbohydrates, protein, fat, vitamins, and minerals.

33. D: Scurvy results from a deficiency of vitamin C.

34. B: Proximodistal development is the reason why a young child can often sit up before walking or holding a small object between her fingers.

35. C: A theme is the overall message about life or the human condition that is communicated in a play.

36. A: Erosion of tooth enamel may result from vomiting, which occurs in bulimia.

37. D: While some negative impacts of vaping are known, more research is still needed. This means that the full range of potential harmful effects may not yet be known.

38. C: Menstruation is part of puberty for young women.

39. D: The symbol *pp* stands for *pianissimo* and prompts the musician to play very softly.

40. A: Empathy involves putting oneself in the place of another person.

41. C: Cardiorespiratory endurance involves sustained aerobic activity like running.

42. B: The bluebonnet is the Texas state flower.

43. B: A quilt appeals to the senses of touch and sight.

44. B: A monologue involves only one character speaking.

Online Resources

Trivium includes online resources with the purchase of this study guide to help you fully prepare for the exam.

Practice Test

In addition to the practice test included in this book, we also offer an online exam. Since many exams today are computer based, practicing your test-taking skills on the computer is a great way to prepare.

Review Questions

Need more practice? Our review questions use a variety of formats to help you memorize key terms and concepts.

Flash Cards

Trivium's flash cards allow you to review important terms easily on your computer or smartphone.

Cheat Sheets

Review the core skills you need to master the exam with easy-to-read Cheat Sheets.

From Stress to Success

Watch "From Stress to Success," a brief but insightful YouTube video that offers the tips, tricks, and secrets experts use to score higher on the exam.

Reviews

Leave a review, send us helpful feedback, or sign up for Trivium promotions—including free books!

Access these materials at: www.cirrustestprep.com/texes-core-subjects

Made in the USA
Coppell, TX
02 November 2023

GREYSCALE

BIN TRAVELER FORM

Cut By [illegible] Qty 35 Date 2/3/25

Scanned By__________ Qty__________ Date__________

Scanned Batch IDs

__________ __________ __________

Notes / Exception